3/8/99

Inside
Windows NT®
Second Edition

David A. Solomon

PUBLISHED BY
Microsoft Press
A Division of Microsoft Corporation
One Microsoft Way
Redmond, Washington 98052-6399

Copyright © 1998 by David A. Solomon. Portions copyright © 1998 by Microsoft Corporation.

Library of Congress Cataloging-in-Publication Data
Solomon, David A.
    Inside Windows NT / David A. Solomon. -- 2nd ed.
        p.   cm.
    Includes index.
    ISBN 1-57231-677-2
    1. Microsoft Windows NT.   2. Operating systems (Computers)
    I. Title.
    QA76.76.063S629   1998
    005.4'469--dc21   97-31952
                                                                   CIP

Printed and bound in the United States of America.

1 2 3 4 5 6 7 8 9   QMQM   3 2 1 0 9 8

Distributed in Canada by ITP Nelson, a division of Thomson Canada Limited.

A CIP catalogue record for this book is available from the British Library.

Microsoft Press books are available through booksellers and distributors worldwide. For further information about international editions, contact your local Microsoft Corporation office. Or contact Microsoft Press International directly at fax (425) 936-7329. Visit our Web site at mspress.microsoft.com.

Macintosh is a registered trademark of Apple Computer, Inc. Intel is a registered trademark of Intel Corporation. ActiveX, BackOffice, DirectX, Microsoft, Microsoft Press, MS-DOS, Visual C++, Win32, Windows, and Windows NT are registered trademarks and IntelliMirror, MSDN, and NetMeeting are trademarks of Microsoft Corporation. Other product and company names mentioned herein may be the trademarks of their respective owners.

Acquisitions Editor: Eric Stroo
Project Editor: Sally Stickney
Technical Editor: Jim Fuchs

*To my grandparents, Joe and Rita Solomon, who gave me
my first computer and whose lives were—and still are—a source
of inspiration and guidance for me.*

BRIEF CONTENTS

CONTENTS

CHAPTER FIVE

Memory Management   **217**

CHAPTER SIX

Security   **305**

CHAPTER SEVEN

The I/O System   **325**

CHAPTER TEN

Windows NT 5.0 and Beyond   **451**

Overview of the New Features in Windows NT 5.0 451

FOREWORD

People have constantly been asking me when the first edition of *Inside Windows NT* would be updated. After three major releases of Windows NT, it became obvious that enough things had changed that a revised edition was desperately needed. For example, the client/server model for the graphics engine was completely redone in Windows NT 4.0, moving most of the USER and GDI components into kernel mode. Completion ports, which are the cornerstone of high-performance I/O applications, didn't exist when the first edition of the book was published. Many other small enhancements have been made to the system as well, such as scatter/gather I/O, locking changes in the scheduler and the memory manager for better scalability, changes in the scheduling algorithm, and support for new APIs. Even though these changes have made Windows NT a more robust and powerful operating system (although I'd like to think that the fact that no kernel component has had to undergo major changes is a testimony to the thoroughness of the initial design), they have also meant that the material in the first edition of *Inside Windows NT,* which has become a bible for Windows NT developers, has become somewhat dated and in need of expansion.

About a year ago, David Solomon agreed to work on the second edition of *Inside Windows NT*; and like most people, he greatly underestimated the time it would take to write this book. (Even so, he did release it before Windows NT 5.0!) However, when I heard that David was slated to revise this important book, I knew it would be the success the first edition was.

I first met David while we both worked for Digital Equipment Corporation. Even then, his interest in Windows NT was apparent. David called me just after Microsoft announced the first Windows NT Professional Developers Conference (PDC) and asked me whether I thought that giving seminars to aid customers migrating people from VAX/VMS to Windows NT would be an undertaking that could succeed. Having great faith in Windows NT—and in David—I told him to go for it. At the PDC, David was already working on a book describing Windows NT in VAX/VMS terminology and had pages of questions to ask me and anyone else he could find.

David has done a fantastic job explaining how various pieces of the operating system interact, describing the policies and rules that govern the kernel and the kernel-mode architecture. Besides updating the content to reflect

Windows NT 4.0, David has gone into greater depth on some of the data structures and internal components and has showed how to use tools distributed with the system and with the Windows NT Resource Kit to examine internal system structures and see their interrelationships. He has also folded in the material on the Windows NT file system (NTFS), which was originally in a separate publication, and has added an entire chapter on the cache manager.

Oddly, Windows NT 4.0, the version that this book is based on, is actually the fourth version of Windows NT. I say "oddly" because the version number of a software release rarely corresponds to the number of times the product has been released in the retail market. The first version of Windows NT was released in July 1993 with the version number 3.1. The version number wasn't picked to make people believe they were getting a more mature product—that is, we weren't saying not to buy any version having a number smaller than 3.0. Rather, the 3.1 was chosen to maintain compatibility with existing applications. Applications are built to use certain features of an operating system. To ensure that those features exist, the application queries the operating system version number. If the version number isn't high enough, the application doesn't install. Version-number checking is itself a black art. In designing Windows NT, we tried to make it easier by providing simple APIs to check the version number. Yet with each new release, you'll find certain applications that don't install properly on the higher-version system because their version check is incorrect. (One popular application tested for equality assuming that if the version wasn't 4.0, it must be 3.51.)

Because the first version of Windows NT was compatible with Windows 3.1, "get version number" returned 3.1. Hence, we could have called the product Windows NT version 1.0 and returned a 3.1 to the applications. Application writers have enough to worry about already, however, and this wrinkle would only have added to the confusion. After much debate, we decided that it would be 3.1, the same as 16-bit Windows.

The second version of Windows NT, code-named Daytona and released in September 1994, was version 3.5. The version debate here was whether to call it 3.2 or 3.5. This version focused on size and performance optimizations.

The third version of Windows NT was released in May 1995. This version concentrated on minor improvements in the feature set, support for the Power PC, and numerous performance optimizations. Because the feature set was largely the same as that in 3.5, the version number was 3.51. The version number signified that this version was basically 3.5 with minimal feature changes and that corporations shouldn't expect significant operating issues when they upgraded.

In July 1996, the fourth version was released: Windows NT 4.0. This version, code-named SUR (for Shell Update Release), had the same look and feel as Windows 95. But the changes to Windows NT 4.0 were more than cosmetic: for example, it contained many new features, and the performance of the graphic subsystem was greatly enhanced by moving the graphic engine (USER, GDI, and the video drivers) from a user-mode process (CSRSS) into kernel mode. In the previous versions of Windows NT, the graphic engine was in a separate process and the local procedure call mechanism was used to issue requests. Moving the graphic engine into kernel mode eliminated the overhead of process context switches while retaining the ability to share data among multiple processes—the data is shared in the kernel's address space rather than in the user-mode process.

One of the changes in this edition of the book is that it doesn't include any discussion about the engineers or who did what, and why. It's been nearly ten years since a small group of people got together and designed the overall kernel architecture for Windows NT. Since that time, the number of people working on Windows NT has grown considerably, and it would be very hard to be accurate with the names and not offend someone. With that said, let me tell you who was present in November 1988 when we started designing what would become Windows NT: Dave Cutler, Darryl Havens, Gary Kimura, Mark Lucovsky, Steve Wood, and I. Since then, the Windows NT team has grown to include over 200 full-time engineers who work on the core components (kernel, graphics, drivers, file systems, network, directory services, security, setup, administration, shells, OLE, RPC, and so on). Even more people work on ancillary products (such as Internet Explorer, NetMeeting, language run-time libraries, and utilities).

I highly recommend the second edition of *Inside Windows NT* to everyone who has an interest in the inner workings of Windows NT. After reading this book, you'll have a much greater understanding of how the system is tuned, how to analyze a Windows NT system's performance and capacity, and how the pieces of Windows NT fit together. Even though I've worked on kernel-mode code since the inception of Windows NT, reading David's book was a treat. So I'm sure you'll enjoy it too!

Lou Perazzoli
Director, Windows NT Core OS
Microsoft Corporation

ACKNOWLEDGMENTS

Having an interest in and a love for operating system internals, I have felt a calling to write a book on the internals of Windows NT since I started teaching a class on the topic in 1993. I had planned on doing my own book from scratch until Frank Artale, director of Windows NT Program Management at Microsoft, approached me after my Windows NT internals talks at TechEd 96 (to which 3000 came) to ask whether I was interested in writing the second edition of *Inside Windows NT*. Having a great respect for the first edition—but with definite ideas about how to improve it—I agreed; a few months later, a contract was signed. After over a year of hard work, the book is finished. And although I didn't do everything I envisioned, there is always the next edition....

I want to thank the following people for their support and assistance for this project, people without whom this book wouldn't have seen the light of day:

- First, Helen Custer, for having written the first edition and established such high expectations for the quality of information in this book.

- Frank Artale, who first approached me about doing this book.

- Lou Perazzoli, director of the Windows NT Core OS group, for his kind support for this project and his expertise on the memory manager.

- Stacey Lemire, Lou's admin, who put up with my regular requests for temporary office space and cardkeys on my many visits to Redmond.

- Dave Cutler, Windows NT architect, who originally approved source code access so that Jamie Hanrahan and I could develop the seminar on which this book was based.

- Landy Wang, lead developer for the memory manager, for carefully reviewing chapters on short notice and for spending time explaining the intricacies of that awe-inspiring component of the system.

- David Fields, Windows NT Workstation performance lead, for scrutinizing the description of working set trimming.

- Tom Miller, cache manager guru, for reviewing the cache manager chapter before leaving for a big sailing trip.

- Brian Andrew, who reviewed the original NTFS book and then spent time with me in the cafeteria going over his comments and previewing the planned NTFS 5.0 extensions.

- Ken Hiatt, lord of the Windows NT build lab, who always responded instantly to my various requests for access to servers, special builds, and source code trees.

- Eric Stroo, acquisitions manager at Microsoft Press, who shepherded me through the ups and downs of the project, being at the same time encouraging and stern. Phone calls from Eric were the most feared.

- Sally Stickney, my editor at Microsoft Press, whose careful attention to detail amazed me throughout the whole process. Although Sally was friendly and encouraging even when progress was slow, next to Eric, phone calls from her were second on the "most feared" list.

- Jim Fuchs, my technical editor, who ironed out technical details and issues in the manuscript (and redid all my screen snapshots because I sent them in wrong!).

- Jeffrey Richter, for reviewing many chapters, letting me stay at his house during the final weeks of the book project, and in general expressing disbelief that I was able to finish.

- Jamie Hanrahan, co-author of the Windows NT internals seminar we give, for letting me use some of the figures he developed.

- Trevor Porter and Richard Mouser of Compaq Corporation, who arranged for the loan of a super speedy dual processor Pentium Pro Compaq Professional Workstation 5000 for the book project. (You can see me happily using it in Redmond in my bio in the back of this book.) I used this machine for both kernel debugging and searching through the Windows NT source code.

- My reliable and trusted office staff, Mark Stevens and Ronnie Diaz, for keep my distractions to a minimum (and for calling me during the day to ask, "What are you doing?").

- Last but not least, thanks to my wife, Shelly, and our three children, Daniel, Rebecca, and Sarah, for enduring my absences, for giving me patient encouragement to keep focused (even when I procrastinated), and for the nice party when I came back home. Thanks for the balloon. Moo.

David Solomon
March 1998

INTRODUCTION

The second edition of *Inside Windows NT* is intended for advanced computer professionals (both developers and system administrators) who want to understand how the core components of the Microsoft Windows NT operating system work internally. With an understanding of Windows NT internals, developers can better comprehend the rationale behind design choices when building applications specific to the Windows NT platform. Such knowledge can also help them in debugging complex problems. System administrators can benefit from this information as well, because understanding how the operating system works under the covers will facilitate understanding the performance behavior of the system as well as make it easier to troubleshoot system problems when things go wrong. After reading this book, you should have a better understanding of how Windows NT works and why it behaves as it does.

This book is based on Windows NT 4.0, Service Pack 3. Where Windows NT 5.0 changes are known, they are called out in the text as notes and identified by a "Windows NT 5.0" graphic in the left margin, like this:

 N O T E   This kind of note describes a change planned for Windows NT 5.0. You'll find notes like this throughout the text.

Differences in the Second Edition

This new edition of *Inside Windows NT* covers all the topics that were in the first edition plus the cache manager, the Windows NT file system (NTFS), and a preview of forthcoming changes in Windows NT 5.0. This edition is also much more detailed than the first edition. For example, I've included code flows of key system functions as well as more detailed descriptions of key internal data structures and system global variables. I obtained this information primarily from reading the Windows NT 4.0 source code and talking with key Windows NT developers and architects. (I gratefully thank Microsoft for this support!)

Another key new feature of this revision is its hands-on approach. Although I relied on the source code to gather information for this edition, you can learn or deduce much about Windows NT internals by using standard tools (such as the kernel debugger and Performance Monitor) as well as other tools in the Windows NT Resource Kit, the Win32 Software Development Kit (SDK), and the Windows NT Device Driver Kit (DDK). So when a tool can be used to expose or demonstrate some aspect of Windows NT internal behavior, the steps necessary to try the tool yourself are listed in "Experiment" boxes. These appear throughout the book, and I encourage you to try these as you're reading—seeing visible proof of how Windows NT works internally will make much more of an impression than just reading about it.

Topics Not Covered

Windows NT is a large and complex operating system. This book doesn't cover everything relevant to Windows NT internals but instead focuses on the base system components. The only topic that was in the first edition that isn't covered in this edition is networking. Windows NT networking has grown to be such a significant part of the system that it merits its own book. I would hope that someone writes such a book someday.

The other major area of the system not explored in this book is COM (Component Object Model). COM (and DCOM—Distributed COM) is the foundation of the Windows distributed object-oriented programming infrastructure. COM is covered in detail in several other Microsoft Press books, one of which is *Inside COM,* by Dale Rogerson.

Finally, because this is an internals book and not a user, programming, or system administration book, it doesn't describe how to use, program, or configure Windows NT.

Structure of the Book

With the exception of the first three chapters (Concepts and Tools, System Architecture, and System Mechanisms, respectively), which lay the foundation terms and concepts used throughout the rest of the book, you can read the remaining chapters—Processes and Threads, Memory Management, Security, The I/O System, Cache Manager, Windows NT File System (NTFS), and Windows NT 5.0 and Beyond—in any order. You'll get the most out of them, however, if you read them in sequence.

A Warning and Caveat

Because this book describes the internal architecture and operation of Windows NT, much of the information is subject to change between releases (although external interfaces, such as the Win32 API, are not subject to incompatible changes). For example, I refer to internal Windows NT system routines, data structures, and variables as well as to algorithms and values used internally to make resource-sizing and performance-related decisions. These details, by definition, can change between releases.

By "subject to change," I don't necessarily mean that details described in this book *will* change between releases—but you can't count on them not changing. Any software that makes use of these undocumented interfaces might not work on future releases of Windows NT. Even worse, software that runs in kernel mode (such as device drivers) that makes use of these undocumented interfaces might result in a system crash when upgrading to a newer release of Windows NT.

Updated Information and Errata

This book isn't perfect. No doubt it contains some inaccuracies; or possibly, I've omitted something I should have covered. If you find anything you think is incorrect or if you believe I should have included material that isn't here, please feel free to send me e-mail at *daves@solsem.com*. If any significant errors are discovered in this edition, I plan to publish them as Knowledge Base articles in the Microsoft Press support Knowledge Base. You can search this Knowledge Base by going to *http://mspress.microsoft.com/support/support.htm*.

CHAPTER ONE

Concepts and Tools

In this chapter, I'll introduce the key Microsoft Windows NT concepts and terms I'll be using throughout the book, such as the Microsoft Win32 API, processes, threads, virtual memory, kernel mode and user mode, objects, handles, security, and the registry. I'll also introduce the tools that you can use to explore Windows NT internals, such as Performance Monitor, the kernel debugger, and the various tools in the Windows NT Resource Kit and the Platform Software Development Kit (SDK). In addition, I'll explain how you can use the Windows NT Device Driver Kit (DDK) as a resource for finding further information on Windows NT internals.

Be sure that you understand everything in this chapter—the remainder of the book is written assuming that you do.

Foundation Concepts and Terms

In the course of this book, I'll be referring to some structures and concepts that might be unfamiliar to some readers. In this section, I'll define the terms I'll be using throughout the book. You should become familiar with them before proceeding to subsequent chapters.

Win32 API

The Win32 application programming interface (API) is the primary programming interface to the Microsoft Windows operating system family, including Windows NT, Microsoft Windows 9x (including both Windows 95 and Windows 98), and Microsoft Windows CE. Although this book does not describe the Win32 API, it explains the internal behavior and implementation of key Win32 API functions. For a comprehensive guide to programming the Win32 API, see Jeffrey Richter's book *Advanced Windows* (third edition, Microsoft Press, 1997).

Each operating system implements a different subset of Win32. For the most part, Windows NT is a superset of all Win32 implementations. (A few functions that exist in Windows 95 are not in Windows NT 4.0, but these will be added in Windows NT 5.0.) The specifics of which services are implemented on which platforms are included in the reference documentation for the Win32 API (available for free online at *www.microsoft.com/msdn* or on the MSDN Library CD-ROMs). This information is also detailed in the file \mssdk\lib\win32api.csv (a comma-delimited text file) installed as part of the Platform SDK that comes with MSDN Professional.

> **NOTE** MSDN stands for Microsoft Developer Network, Microsoft's support program for developers. MSDN offers four CD-ROM subscription programs: MSDN Library, Professional, Enterprise, and Universal. The content of MSDN Library is also available online at the MSDN Web site. For more information, see *www.microsoft.com/msdn*.

What used to be a separate entity called the Win32 SDK has been incorporated into the Platform SDK. The Platform SDK includes the functions that were formerly grouped separately as Win32, Microsoft BackOffice, and Microsoft ActiveX. The Platform SDK header files, libraries, and documentation are part of MSDN Professional. (The reference documentation is on MSDN Library or online as noted earlier.)

For the purposes of this book, the Win32 API refers to the core set of functions that cover areas such as processes, threads, memory management, I/O, windowing, and graphics. The internals of the other major categories in the Platform SDK, such as transactions, database, messaging, multimedia, and networking services, are not covered in this book.

> **NOTE** Although less interesting today, a small subset of Win32 (called Win32s) is available for Windows 3.1, thus allowing some 32-bit Windows applications to run unchanged on Windows 3.1. Also, as part of the cross-platform support for the Microsoft Foundation Classes (MFC), object linking and embedding (OLE), and Component Object Model (COM), a subset of Win32 has been implemented on UNIX and OpenVMS. For more information on cross-platform support, see *www.mainsoft.com* or *www.bristol.com*.

Although Windows NT was designed to support multiple programming interfaces, Win32 is the primary, or preferred, interface to the operating system. Win32 has this position because, of the three environment subsystems (Win32, POSIX, and OS/2), it provides the greatest access to the underlying Windows NT system services. As explained in Chapter 2, application programs on Windows NT don't call native Windows NT system services directly—rather, they must go through one of the provided environment subsystem libraries.

Interestingly, Win32 wasn't slated to be the original programming interface to Windows NT. Because the Windows NT project started as a replacement for OS/2 version 2, the primary programming interface was the 32-bit OS/2 Presentation Manager API. A year into the project, however, Microsoft Windows 3.0 hit the market and took off. As a result, Microsoft changed direction and made Windows NT the future replacement for the Windows family of products as opposed to the replacement for OS/2. It was at this juncture that the need to specify the Win32 API arose—prior to this point, the Windows API existed only as a 16-bit interface.

Although the Win32 API would introduce many new functions that had not been available on Windows 3.1, Microsoft decided to make the new API compatible with the 16-bit Windows API in function names, semantics, and use of data types whenever possible to ease the burden of porting existing 16-bit Windows applications to Windows NT. So those of you who are looking at the Win32 API for the first time and wondering why many function names and interfaces seem inconsistent should keep in mind that the reason for the inconsistency is to ensure that the Win32 API is compatibile with the old 16-bit Windows API.

Services, Functions, and Routines

Several terms in the Windows NT user and programming documentation have different meanings in different contexts. For example, the word *service* can refer to a callable routine in the operating system, a device driver, or a server process. The following list describes what certain terms mean in this book:

- **Win32 API functions**   Documented, callable subroutines in the Win32 API. Examples include *CreateProcess, CreateFile, GetMessage,* and so on.

- **Windows NT system services (or executive system services)** Undocumented functions callable from user mode. For example, *NtCreateProcess* is the internal system service the Win32 *CreateProcess* function calls to create a new process.

- **Windows NT internal routines**   Subroutines inside the Windows NT executive, kernel, or hardware abstraction layer (HAL) callable only from kernel mode (such as from device drivers or other Windows NT operating system components). For example, *ExAllocatePool* is the routine device drivers call to allocate memory from the Windows NT system heaps.

■ **Windows NT services**   Processes started by the Windows NT service control manager. (Although the registry defines Windows NT device drivers as "services," I don't refer to them as such in this book.) For example, the Schedule service is a user-mode process that supports the *at* command (which is equivalent to the UNIX command *cron*).

■ **DLL (dynamic-link library)**   A set of callable subroutines linked as a binary image that can be dynamically loaded by applications that use them. Examples include MSVCRT.DLL (the Microsoft Visual C++ run-time library) and KERNEL32.DLL (one of the Win32 API subsystem libraries).

Processes and Threads

Although programs and processes appear similar on the surface, they are fundamentally different. A *program* is a static sequence of instructions, whereas a *process* is a set of resources reserved for the thread(s) that execute the program. At the highest level of abstraction, a Windows NT process comprises the following:

■ An executable program, which defines initial code and data

■ A private *virtual address space,* which is a set of virtual memory addresses that the process can use

■ System resources, such as semaphores, communication ports, and files, that the operating system allocates to the process when threads open them during the program's execution

■ A unique identifier called a *process ID* (internally called a *client ID)*

■ At least one thread of execution

A thread is the entity within a process that Windows NT schedules for execution. Without it, the process's program can't run. A thread includes the following essential components:

■ The contents of a set of volatile registers representing the state of the processor

■ Two stacks, one for the thread to use while executing in kernel mode and one for executing in user mode

■ A private storage area for use by subsystems, run-time libraries, and DLLs

■ A unique identifier called a *thread ID* (also internally called a *client ID*—process IDs and thread IDs are generated out of the same namespace, so they never overlap)

The volatile registers, the stacks, and the private storage area are called the thread's *context*. Because this information is different for each machine architecture that Windows NT runs on, this structure, by necessity, is architecture-specific. In fact, the CONTEXT structure returned by the Win32 *GetThreadContext* function is the only public data structure in the Win32 API that is machine-dependent.

Although threads have their own execution context, every thread within a process shares the process's virtual address space (in addition to the rest of the resources belonging to the process), meaning that all the threads in a process can write to and read from each other's memory. Threads can't reference the address space of another process, however, unless the other process makes available part of its private address space as a *shared memory section* (called a *file mapping object* in the Win32 API).

Windows NT 5.0 ▶ **NOTE** Windows NT 5.0 introduces a job object. A job is a collection of processes that share a set of quotas, limits, and/or security restrictions. For more information on this new object, see Chapter 10.

Because in writing about multithreaded processes it's often easier to state "a process executes" rather than "a thread within a process executes," in this text I'll occasionally refer to a process as requesting memory or generating an exception. You should understand, however, that in Windows NT, the actual agent of execution is always a thread within the process.

In addition to a private address space and one or more threads, each process has a security identification and a list of open handles to objects such as files, shared memory sections, or one of the synchronization objects such as mutexes, events, or semaphores, as illustrated in Figure 1-1.

The process access token contains the security identification and credentials for the process. By default, threads don't have their own access token, but they can obtain one, thus allowing individual threads to impersonate remote clients without affecting other threads in the process. (See Chapter 6 for more details on process and thread security.)

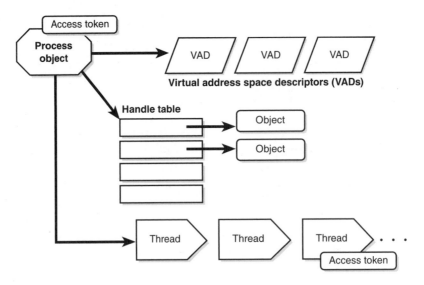

Figure 1-1
A process and its resources

The virtual address space descriptors (VADs) keep track of the virtual addresses the process is using. The process can't read or alter these structures directly; the virtual memory manager creates and modifies them indirectly as the program allocates memory. These data structures are described in more depth in Chapter 5.

You'll find out much more about the internal structure of processes and threads, the mechanics of process and thread creation, and the thread scheduling algorithms in Chapter 4, which is devoted to these topics.

Virtual Memory

Windows NT implements a virtual memory system based on a flat (linear) 32-bit address space. Thirty-two bits of address space translates into 4 GB of virtual memory. On most systems, Windows NT gives half of this address space (2 GB) to processes for their unique private storage and uses the other half for its own protected operating system memory utilization. However, Windows NT Server, Enterprise Edition, has a boot-time option on *x*86 systems (the /3GB qualifier in boot.ini) that gives processes a 3-GB private address space (leaving 1 GB for the operating system). This option (the base support was added in Windows NT 4.0 Service Pack 3) allows applications such as database servers to keep larger portions of a database in the process address space, thus reducing the need to map subset views of the database. Figure 1-2 shows the two virtual address space layouts supported by Windows NT.

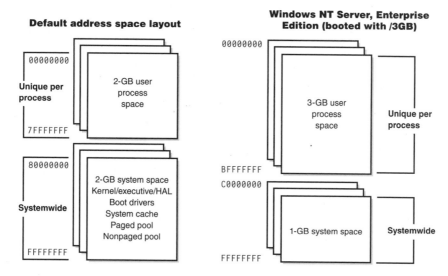

Figure 1-2
Address space layouts supported by Windows NT

Recall that a process's virtual address space is the set of addresses available for the process's threads to use. Virtual memory provides a logical view of memory that might not correspond to its physical layout. At run time, the memory manager, with assistance from hardware, translates, or *maps,* the virtual addresses into physical addresses, where the data is actually stored. By controlling the protection and mapping, the operating system can ensure that individual processes don't bump into one another or overwrite operating system data. Figure 1-3 on the following page illustrates three virtually contiguous pages mapped to three discontiguous pages in physical memory.

Because most systems have much less physical memory than the total virtual memory provided to the running processes (2 GB or 3 GB for each process), when physical memory becomes full, the memory manager transfers, or *pages,* some of the memory contents to disk. Paging data to disk frees physical memory so that it can be used for other processes or for the operating system itself. When a thread accesses a virtual address that has been paged to disk, the virtual memory manager loads the information back into memory from disk.

Details of the implementation of the memory manager, including how address translation works and how Windows NT manages physical memory, are described in detail in Chapter 5.

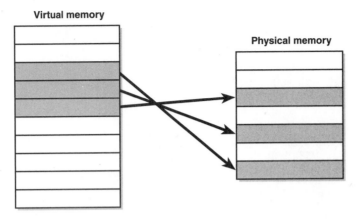

Figure 1-3
Mapping virtual memory to physical memory

Kernel Mode vs. User Mode

To protect user applications from accessing and/or modifying critical operating system data, Windows NT uses two *processor access modes* (even if the processor on which Windows NT is running supports more than two): *user mode* and *kernel mode*. User application code runs in user mode, whereas operating system code (such as system services and device drivers) runs in kernel mode. Kernel mode refers to a mode of execution in a processor that grants access to all system memory and all CPU instructions. By providing the operating system software with a higher privilege level than application software has, the processor provides a necessary foundation for operating system designers to ensure that a misbehaving application can't disrupt the stability of the system as a whole.

> **NOTE** The architecture of the *x86* processor defines four privilege levels, or *rings*, to protect system code and data from being overwritten either inadvertently or maliciously by code of lesser privilege. Windows NT uses privilege level 0 (or ring 0) for kernel mode and privilege level 3 (or ring 3) for user mode. The reason Windows NT uses only two levels is to maintain source code portability across the RISC-based architectures supported by Windows NT, since all mainstream RISC-based processors have only two privilege levels.

For example, although each Win32 process has its own private memory space, the operating system shares a single virtual address space. Each page in virtual memory is tagged as to what access mode the processor must be in to read and/or write the page. Pages in system space (the upper half of the 4-GB virtual address space, from x80000000 through xFFFFFFFF) can be accessed only from kernel mode, whereas all pages in the user address space (the lower half, addresses x00000000 through x7FFFFFFF) are accessible from user mode. Read-only pages (such as those that contain executable code) are not writable from any mode.

Windows NT doesn't provide any protection for components running in kernel mode. In other words, once in kernel mode, system code has complete access to system space memory and can bypass Windows NT security to access objects. Because the bulk of the Windows NT operating system code runs in kernel mode, it is vital that it be carefully designed and tested to ensure that it doesn't violate system security. This lack of protection also emphasizes the need to take care when loading a third-party device driver since once in kernel mode, the software has complete access to all operating system data.

As you'll see in Chapter 2, user applications switch from user mode to kernel mode when they make a system service call. For example, a Win32 *ReadFile* function eventually needs to call the internal Windows NT executive routine that actually handles reading data from a file. That routine, because it accesses internal system data structures, must run in kernel mode. The transition from user mode to kernel mode is accomplished by the use of a special instruction that causes the processor to change into kernel mode. The operating system traps this instruction, notices that a system service is being requested, validates the arguments the thread passed to the system function, and then executes the service. Before returning control to the user thread, the processor mode is switched back to user mode. In this way, the operating system protects itself and its data from perusal and modification by user processes.

NOTE A transition from user mode to kernel mode (and back) does *not* affect thread scheduling in itself—a mode transition is *not* a context switch. Further details on system service dispatching are included in Chapter 3.

Thus, it's normal that a user thread spends part of its time executing in user mode and part in kernel mode. In fact, because the bulk of the graphics and windowing system also runs in kernel mode, graphics-intensive applications will spend more of their time in kernel mode than in user mode. An easy way to test this is to run a graphics-intensive application such as Microsoft Paint or Microsoft Pinball and watch the time split between user mode and kernel mode using one of the performance counters listed in Table 1-1 on the next page.

Table 1-1   **Mode-Related Performance Counters**

Object: Counter	Function
System: % Total Privileged Time	Percentage of time that the entire system has run in kernel mode during a specified interval
System: % Total User Time	Percentage of time that the entire system has run in user mode during a specified interval
Processor: % Privileged Time	Percentage of time that an individual CPU has run in kernel mode during a specified interval
Processor: % User Time	Percentage of time that an individual CPU has run in user mode during a specified interval
Process: % Privileged Time	Percentage of time that the threads in a process have run in kernel mode during a specified interval
Process: % User Time	Percentage of time that the threads in a process have run in user mode during a specified interval
Thread: % Privileged Time	Percentage of time that a thread has run in kernel mode during a specified interval
Thread: % User Time	Percentage of time that a thread has run in user mode during a specified interval

EXPERIMENT: Kernel Mode vs. User Mode

You can use Performance Monitor to see how much time your system spends executing in kernel mode versus in user mode. Add the system counters % Total User Time and % Total Privileged Time to a new chart, and then move the mouse rapidly back and forth. You should notice the % Total Privileged Time line spiking, reflecting both the mouse interrupts and the graphics updating required by PerfMon itself. (See Figure 1-4.)

To see how Performance Monitor uses kernel time and user time, rerun the experiment with the addition of the process counters % User Time and % Privileged Time for every process in the system:

1. Select the Process object.

2. Select all processes in the Instance box (except the _Total process).

3. Click Add, and then click Done.

4. Move the mouse rapidly back and forth.

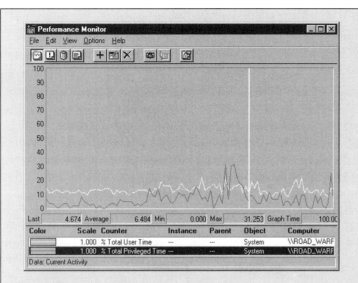

Figure 1-4
Performance Monitor showing time split between kernel mode and user mode

5. Type *Ctrl-H* to turn on highlighting mode. This highlights the currently selected counter in white.

6. Scroll through the counters to identify the processes that were running when you moved the mouse, and note whether they were running in user mode or kernel mode.

You should see Performance Monitor's kernel-mode *and* user-mode time go up when you move the mouse, since it is executing application code in user mode and calling Win32 functions that run in kernel mode. You'll also notice a process named System running in kernel mode. This process is the home for kernel-mode system threads—parts of the operating system or device drivers that are running as independent threads. (See Chapter 3 for more information about these threads.) What you're seeing is the Win32 subsystem's Raw Input Thread handling the mouse input. Finally, the process named Idle that you see spending nearly 100 percent of its time in kernel mode is not really a process—it's a fake process to account for idle CPU cycles. As you can observe from the mode in which the Idle process runs, when Windows NT has nothing to do, it does it in kernel mode.

Objects and Handles

In the Windows NT executive, an *object* is a single, run-time instance of a statically defined object type. An *object type* (sometimes called an *object class*) comprises a system-defined data type, services that operate on instances of the data type, and a set of object attributes. If you write Win32 applications, you encounter process, thread, file, and event objects, to name just a few examples. These objects are based on lower-level objects that are created and managed by the Windows NT executive. In Windows NT, a process is an instance of the process object type, a file is an instance of the file object type, and so on.

An *object attribute* is a field of data in an object that partially defines the object's state. An object of type *stack*, for example, would have a stack pointer as one of its most important attributes. *Object services,* the means for manipulating objects, usually read or change the object attributes. For example, the push service for a stack object would change the value of the stack pointer.

NOTE   Although there is a parameter named *ObjectAttributes* that a caller supplies when creating an object using either the Win32 API or native object services, that parameter should not be confused with the more general meaning of the term as used in this book.

The most fundamental difference between an object and an ordinary data structure is that the internal structure of an object is hidden from view. You must call an object service to get data out of an object or to put data into it. You can't directly read or change data inside an object. This difference separates the underlying implementation of the object from code that merely uses it, a technique that allows object implementations to be changed easily over time.

Objects provide a centralized means for accomplishing three important operating system tasks:

- Providing human-readable names for system resources
- Sharing resources and data among processes
- Protecting resources from unauthorized access

Not all data structures in the Windows NT executive are objects. Only data that needs to be shared, protected, named, or made visible to user-mode programs (via system services) is placed in objects. Structures used by only one component of the executive to implement internal functions, for example, are not objects. Objects and handles (references to an open instance of an object) are discussed in more detail in Chapter 3.

Security

Windows NT supports C2-level security as defined by the U.S. Department of Defense Trusted Computer System Evaluation Criteria (DoD 5200.28–STD, December 1985). This standard includes discretionary (need-to-know) protection for all shareable system objects (such as files, directories, processes, threads, and so forth), security auditing (for accountability of subjects and the actions they initiate), password authentication at logon, and the prevention of one user from accessing uninitialized resources that were deallocated by another user (such as free memory or disk space).

Windows NT 3.51 was formally evaluated at the C2 level and is on the U.S. government Evaluated Products List. (Windows NT 4.0 is still in the evaluation process.) Also, Windows NT has met the European organization ITSEC (IT Security Evaluation Criteria) at the FC2/E3 (functional level C2 and assurance level E3, something normally associated only with B-level systems) security level. Achieving a government-approved security rating allows an operating system to compete in that arena. Of course, many of these required capabilities are advantageous features for any multiuser system.

Windows NT has two forms of access control over objects. The first form—discretionary access control—is the protection mechanism that most people think of when they think of protection under Windows NT. It's the method by which owners of objects (such as files or printers) grant or deny access to others.

Privileged access control is necessary for those times when discretionary control isn't enough. It's a method of ensuring that someone can get to protected objects if the owner isn't available. For example, if the owner of an important file grants read-only access to a select group of people on Friday and then ends up in the hospital from a car crash on Saturday, on Monday you're going to need access to that protected object, just in case you need to change the access privileges. In that case, under Windows NT, you (as an administrator) can take ownership of the file so that you can manage its rights as necessary.

Security pervades the interface of the Win32 API. Its security features are user-mode extensions to the security capabilities originally designed into the Windows NT executive's object architecture. The Win32 subsystem implements object-based security in the same way the Windows NT executive does; the Win32 subsystem protects shared Windows objects from unauthorized access by placing Windows NT security descriptors on them. As in the Windows NT executive, the first time an application tries to access a shared object, the Win32 subsystem verifies the application's right to do so. If the security check succeeds, the Win32 subsystem allows the application to proceed.

EXPERIMENT: C2 Compliance

C2CONFIG, a tool in the Windows NT Resource Kit, can help you determine how secure your system is and what elements are lacking for full security. Keep in mind that some security measures reduce the usefulness of Windows NT. For example, while I can live without the POSIX subsystem (whose existence is a security violation, since only the Win32 subsystem is permitted), removing networking capability seems a little harsh for a network operating system. Figure 1-5 shows the C2CONFIG utility in action.

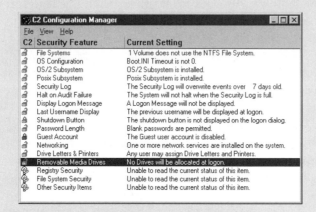

Figure 1-5
The C2CONFIG utility from the Windows NT Resource Kit

Closed red padlocks indicate that the security feature is C2-compliant. As you can see in Figure 1-5, the system on which this snapshot was taken fails miserably. But also notice that not all security measures on this list are required for compliance.

The Win32 subsystem implements object security on a number of shared objects, some of which were built on top of native Windows NT objects. The Win32 objects include desktop objects, window objects, menu objects, and—as in the Windows NT executive—files, processes, threads, and several synchronization objects. Security internals will be discussed in more detail in Chapter 6.

Registry

If you've worked at all with Windows 95 or Windows NT, you've probably heard about or looked at the registry. You can't talk much about Windows NT internals without referring to the registry, because it contains the information required to boot and configure the system, systemwide software settings that control the operation of Windows NT, the security database, and per-user profile settings.

In addition, the registry is a window into in-memory volatile data, such as the current hardware state of the system (what devices are loaded, the resources they are using, and so on) as well as the Windows NT performance counters. The performance counters, which aren't actually "in the registry," are accessed through the registry functions. (See the Win32 API documentation for more information about accessing performance counter information.)

Although many Windows NT users and administrators will never need to look directly into the registry (since you can view or change most of the configuration settings with standard administrative utilities), it is still a useful source of Windows NT internals information because it contains the bulk of the information needed to boot, configure, and operate the system. You'll find references to individual registry keys throughout this book as they pertain to the component being described. Since most registry keys referred to in this book are under HKEY_LOCAL_MACHINE, the abbreviations shown in Table 1-2 are used throughout the book.

Table 1-2 **Registry Abbreviations**

Registry Path	Abbreviation
HKEY_LOCAL_MACHINE\System\CurrentControlSet\Control	\System\...\Control
HKEY_LOCAL_MACHINE\System\CurrentControlSet\Services	\System\...\Services
HKEY_LOCAL_MACHINE\Software	\Software

For further information on the registry and its structure, see the *Windows NT Server Concepts and Planning* manual as well as the *Windows NT Workstation Resource Guide*. Also, the Windows NT Resource Kit has a help file named regentry.hlp that describes most of the individual registry keys and values. This file is the best place to go if you find a registry key and aren't sure what it is.

Networking

The increasing availability of personal computers in the 1980s irrevocably altered the nature of computing. Whereas once a single, large mainframe computer might serve an entire company, smaller and cheaper microcomputers proliferated and are now standard issue for rank-and-file employees. Enhanced networking capabilities allow the smaller computers to communicate with one another, often sharing hardware resources such as disk space or processing power (in the form of file servers, print servers, or application servers). To accommodate this change, the Windows NT system has networking capabilities built directly into the operating system and provides the means for applications to distribute their work across multiple computer systems.

Windows NT also interoperates well with other operating systems, even non-Microsoft ones. Thus, Windows NT is capable of communicating with Macintosh, UNIX, OpenVMS, NetWare, OS/2, and OS/400 as well as Windows 95, Windows 3.1, and MS-DOS. It supports the following network transport protocols. (The first three protocols come with both Windows NT Workstation and Windows NT Server—the latter two only with Windows NT Server.)

- NetBEUI (local Microsoft networks, not routable unless tunneled in TCP/IP)

- TCP/IP (fully routable, used on the Internet)

- IPX/SPX (NetWare, or high-speed routing)

- DLC (mainframes and printers connected directly to the network)

- AppleTalk (Macintosh networks)

 NOTE Windows NT 5.0 will contain significant networking enhancements, most notably a distributed global directory service named the Active Directory. Besides storing objects such as computers, users, groups, and printers, the Active Directory is programmatically extensible. For a brief description of this and other extensions to Windows NT networking, see Chapter 10.

As mentioned in the Introduction to this book, networking isn't covered in this edition of *Inside Windows NT*. This topic should be treated some day in detail in a separate Windows NT networking internals book.

Unicode

Windows NT differs from most other operating systems in that most internal text strings are stored and processed as 16-bit-wide Unicode strings. Unicode is an international character set standard that defines unique 16-bit values for most of the world's known character sets. (For more information about Unicode, see *www.unicode.org* as well as the programming documentation in the MSDN Library.)

Because most existing applications deal with 8-bit (single-byte) strings, Win32 functions that accept string parameters have two entry points: a Unicode (wide) and an ANSI (narrow) version. If you call the narrow version, input string parameters are converted to Unicode before being processed by the system and output parameters are converted from Unicode to ANSI before being returned to the application. Thus, if you have an older service or piece of code that you need to run on Windows NT but this code is written in 8-bit text strings, Windows NT will convert the 8-bit strings into Unicode for its own use. However, Windows NT never converts the *data* inside files—it's up to the application to decide whether to store data as Unicode or as ANSI.

Windows NT 5.0 ▶ **NOTE** Windows NT 5.0 reaps the fruits of years of groundwork laid by basing all text processing on Unicode. This version will have a single worldwide binary for the operating system (instead of the separate language versions that currently exist) that allows for the separation of the language of the user, application, and input method. Applications can also take advantage of new Win32 functions that allow single worldwide application binaries that can support multiple languages. For more information on the use of Unicode under Windows NT 5.0, see Chapter 10.

Tools for Digging into Windows NT Internals

Although much of the information in this book is based on the Windows NT source code, you don't have to take *everything* on faith. Many details about the internals of Windows NT can be learned, exposed, and demonstrated using existing tools that come with Windows NT, the Windows NT Resource Kit, the Platform SDK, and the Windows NT DDK. These packages are briefly described later in this section.

Throughout the book are "Experiment" sidebars that describe steps you can take to examine a particular aspect of Windows NT internal behavior. I encourage you to try out these experiments so that you can see in action many of the internals topics described in this book.

Table 1-3 shows a complete list of all the tools used in this book and where they come from. Although the capabilities of many of these tools overlap quite a bit in terms of the information that they can display, each of them shows at least one unique piece of information not available in any other utility.

In addition, you'll find several utilities at *www.ntinternals.com* that are also useful for displaying (and even changing) internal Windows NT system information. Because many of these tools rely on undocumented interfaces, however, you run them at your own risk: neither I nor Microsoft Corporation endorse or guarantee these utilities. Also, since many of these utilities involve the installation and execution of kernel-mode device drivers (which require administrator access), you're adding trusted code to the system that can bypass system security, crash the system, or render the system unbootable. That said, many of these utilities are useful for digging into the internals of Windows NT.

Table 1-3   Tools for Viewing Windows NT Internals

Tool	Image Name	Origin
Performance Monitor	PERFMON	Windows NT
Task Manager	TASKMAN	Windows NT
Kernel debugger	I386KD and ALPHAKD	Windows NT CD-ROM \support\debug directory
Windows debugger (another kernel debugger)	WINDBG	Platform SDK
Dependency Walker	DEPENDS	Resource Kit, Platform SDK
API Monitor	APIMON	Windows NT CD-ROM \support\debug directory or Resource Kit
Quick Slice	QSLICE	Resource Kit
Process Viewer	PVIEWER (in the Resource Kit) or PVIEW (in the Platform SDK)	Resource Kit or Platform SDK
Process Explode	PVIEW	Resource Kit
Process Statistics	PSTAT	Resource Kit or Platform SDK
Task List	TLIST	Resource Kit
Object Viewer	WINOBJ	Platform SDK
Global Flags	GFLAGS	Resource Kit*
Open Handles	OH	Resource Kit*
Process Walker	PWALK	Platform SDK
Page Fault Monitor	PFMON	Resource Kit or Platform SDK

* Supplement 2 or later.

Windows NT Resource Kits

The Windows NT Resource Kits are essential packages for power users, administrators, and even developers. Besides including many tools useful for displaying internal system state, they contain a significant amount of "internals" documentation in the *Windows NT Workstation Resource Guide.* This guide covers such topics as system architecture, registry structure, file system structure, performance monitoring, crash dumps, and how to use the Windows NT kernel debugger. (The title of this guide is not representative of its contents, since most of the material found in the book also applies to Windows NT Server—think of the *Windows NT Workstation Resource Guide* simply as more advanced Windows NT technical documentation that isn't included in the base product documentation set.)

> **NOTE** Only a small subset of the Windows NT Resource Kit tools have shortcuts in the Start menu folder, because many are command-line-based. To see a complete list of the tools, open the Windows NT Resource Kit Tools help file (rktools.hlp).

There are two editions of the Resource Kits: the Windows NT Workstation Resource Kit and the Windows NT Server Resource Kit. The latter kit is a superset of the former and can be installed on a Windows NT Workstation system. In fact, only the Windows NT Server Resource Kit is shipped to MSDN and TechNet subscribers. (For information on MSDN, go to *www.microsoft.com/msdn*. For TechNet information, see *www.microsoft.com/technet*.)

The license for the Windows NT Resource Kit tools permits multiple installations at a single site. Updates to the kits' tools are available on *ftp.microsoft.com/bussys/winnt/winnt-public/reskit/nt40*.

Platform SDK and Windows NT DDK

The Platform SDK and Windows NT DDK are part of the MSDN Development Platform. They are available through MSDN Professional, a quarterly CD-ROM subscription.

Items of interest in the Platform SDK from an internals perspective include the Win32 API header files (\mssdk\include) as well as several utilities (pviewer.exe, pwalk.exe, pfmon.exe, winobj.exe). Some of the Platform SDK tools are also shipped as example source code in both the Platform SDK and the MSDN Library.

The Windows NT DDK is an abundant source of internals information. It documents many of the internal system routines and data structures used by device drivers. Besides the design and reference documentation, the actual DDK kit itself contains header files that define key internal data structures and constants as well as interfaces to many internal system routines. (See the \ddk\inc directory—in particular, ntddk.h.) Also, the file \ddk\hlp\lsaauth.hlp describes interfaces related to the security authentication system.

Key Windows NT Base Tools

Two tools that come with Windows NT bear special mention, since they provide access to the majority of the accessible internal Windows NT system information: Performance Monitor and the kernel debugger.

Performance Monitor

I'll refer to Performance Monitor, in the Administrative Tools folder, throughout this book—it can provide more information about how your system is operating than can any other single utility. It includes hundreds of counters for various objects. For each major topic described in this book, a table of the relevant Windows NT performance counters is included.

Performance Monitor contains a brief description for each counter. To see the descriptions, click the Explain button while selecting a counter. For information on how to interpret these counters to perform bottleneck detection or capacity planning, see the several chapters on performance monitoring in the *Windows NT Workstation Resource Guide*, which, as mentioned earlier in the chapter, is part of the Windows NT Resource Kit. These chapters are "must reading" for anyone seriously interested in understanding Windows NT performance.

> **NOTE** All the Windows NT performance counters are accessible programmatically—see the documentation on the Win32 performance counter APIs in the MSDN Library. Also, the complete source code for the Windows NT Performance Monitor utility as well as the sources for other tools that use performance counters (such as PVIEWER) are included as sample code with the Platform SDK and MSDN Library.

Kernel Debuggers

Microsoft provides two kinds of kernel debuggers: the command-line versions (I386KD.EXE for *x*86 systems and ALPHAKD for Alpha systems) that ship with Windows NT and a GUI version (WINDBG.EXE) that ships with the Platform SDK. You can use either kernel debugger, although some commands work better in the command-line version (and vice versa). To debug a live system, the Microsoft kernel debuggers require two computers: one to run the kernel debugger and one to be the debugging target. There is also a kernel debugger named SoftICE for Windows NT that doesn't require two machines for live kernel debugging. It is available for purchase from NuMega Corporation. (See *www.numega.com* for details.) SoftICE runs only on *x*86 systems.

Although the main purpose of a kernel debugger is for crash dump analysis or device driver debugging, it is also a useful tool for investigating Windows NT internals because it can display internal Windows NT system information not visible through any standard utility. For example, it can dump internal data structures such as thread blocks, process blocks, page tables, I/O, and pool structures. Throughout the book, the relevant kernel debugger commands and output are included as they apply to each topic under discussion.

The command-line kernel debuggers are documented in the *Windows NT Workstation Resource Guide* in the chapter "Windows NT Debugger." Additional details aimed at device driver writers are included in the Windows NT DDK (which is also where the GUI version is described). Also, there are several useful Knowledge Base articles on the kernel debugger. Search for "debugref" in the Windows NT Knowledge Base on *www.microsoft.com* (or look on the TechNet CD-ROM, if you receive it). However, there is no complete list of the full set of kernel debugger extension commands that dump internal Windows NT structures. To get a brief list, type *!?* from the kernel debugger prompt.

The kernel debugger has two modes of operation:

■ Open a crash dump file created as a result of a Windows NT system crash. For additional information, see the Knowlege Base article Q148658, "How to Load Windows NT MEMORY.DMP File Using I386KD.EXE." (Knowledge Base articles are available online at *www.microsoft.com/support*, as well as through TechNet and MSDN.)

■ Connect to a live system and examine the system state (or set breakpoints, if you're debugging system code). This operation requires two computers—a target and a host. The target system can be either local (connecting the computer being debugged to a host running the debugger via a null modem cable) or remote (connecting the target via a modem). The target system must be booted with the /DEBUG qualifier (in the boot selection entry in c:\boot.ini or in firmware settings for RISC systems).

The kernel debuggers and related files are *not* installed when you install Windows NT. They reside underneath the \support\debug directory of the Windows NT Workstation or Server distribution CD-ROM. As for the main directory tree that contains the Windows NT binaries, there is a subdirectory for each hardware architecture. For example, the \support\debug\i386 directory contains the kernel debugger and tools for the Intel platform. Also, in each directory is a kernel debugger for each hardware architecture so that you can, for example, open an Intel crash dump from an Alpha AXP system or vice versa.

NOTE Even though Windows NT no longer runs on the 386 chip, for historical reasons, the *x*86 directories on the Windows NT distribution media are still called i386. Thus, the *x*86 kernel debugger is called i386kd.exe.

In addition to the kernel debugger and related tools, the Windows NT CD-ROM includes the debug symbol table files for all the Windows NT executable images, libraries, and drivers. These are in the \support\debug\<platform>\ symbols tree. The file of most interest for this book is ntoskrnl.dbg (or ntkrnlmp.dbg for multiprocessor systems), the symbol table file for the base operating system image (NTOSKRNL.EXE) and the appropriate HAL .dbg file. Later in the book, you'll see how you can use these symbol table files to display the names of internal Windows NT system routines and global variables.

> **NOTE** Symbol table files must match the version of the image they were taken from. For example, if you install a Windows NT service pack, you must obtain the matching, updated DBG files for any of the images that have changed, or you will get a checksum error when trying to load them with the kernel debugger. These updated DBG files are *not* included or installed when you download and install a Service Pack from *www.microsoft.com*—they must be downloaded separately. (If you receive MSDN Professional or TechNet, they're included on the Service Pack CD-ROMs in the \support directory.) Then they must be installed on top of a copy of the base DBG files off the Windows NT CD-ROM. For more information, see Knowledge Base article Q148659, "How to Set Up Windows NT Debug Symbols."

The experiment on pages 24–25 will show you how to generate a crash dump you can use with the kernel debugger.

Free Builds and Checked Builds

There are two versions of Windows NT: the *free build* and the *checked build*. The free build is the normal version of the system that you can purchase as a retail product. It is built with full compiler optimizations turned on and has internal symbol table information stripped out from the images. (These symbol table files, or .DBG files, are shipped separately on the Windows NT CD-ROM in the \support\debug\xxx\symbols subdirectory.)

The checked build is a special debug version of Windows NT Workstation (no checked build is available for Windows NT Server) that is available only as part of the MSDN Professional (or higher) subscription. The checked build is created by compiling the Windows NT sources with the compile-time flag DEBUG set to TRUE. Much of the additional code in the checked-build binaries is a result of using the ASSERT macro defined in the DDK header file NTDDK.H. This macro tests some condition (such as the validity of a data structure or parameter), and if the expression evaluates to FALSE, sends a message to the kernel debugger and causes a breakpoint. (If the system was not booted with the kernel debugger, failure of an ASSERT test will crash the system.)

EXPERIMENT: Generating a Crash Dump to Use with the Kernel Debugger

For the purposes of experimentation, the easiest thing to do is to look at a static crash dump file, since that doesn't require two systems. How can you reliably generate a Windows NT crash dump? Just kill the Win32 subsystem process (csrss.exe) or the Windows NT logon process (winlogon.exe) with the Windows NT Resource Kit tool kill.exe. (You must have administrator privileges to do this.) But first be sure that you've enabled your Windows NT system to take a crash dump. To do this, open the System applet in the Control Panel, click the Startup-/Shutdown tab, and ensure that you've checked Write Debugging Information To. The default name of the debugging file is MEMORY.DMP, and it will be located in the system root directory. If you didn't have crash dumps enabled, you'll be instructed to reboot the system. When you've got the settings done properly, the dialog box should look like the one in Figure 1-6.

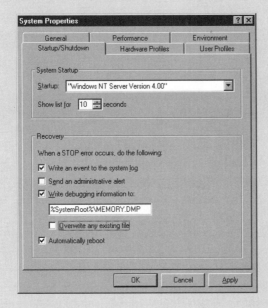

Figure 1-6
Settings for creating a dump file

(continued)

EXPERIMENT: Generating a Crash Dump to Use with the Kernel Debugger *continued*

To create a memory dump file, you'll need a paging file that's at least the size of the physical memory on your system plus free space on your system partition to store the dump file. (Dump files are written first to the paging file and then copied out after the system boots.) For example, if your system has 64 MB of RAM, you'll need at least a 64-MB page file and an additional 64 MB of free space to copy the crash dump to. If you want to create a smaller dump file, reboot your system after adding the /MEMUSAGE qualifier in boot.ini to tell Windows NT to use less physical memory than is actually present in the machine.

When you're ready to crash the system, make sure to save anything you're working on, open a command prompt, and type *kill csrss.exe*. (This operation requires the Windows NT Resource Kit to be installed.) This will terminate the Win32 subsystem process, which then results in the session manager (smss.exe) waking up and crashing the system. The process security descriptor for this process doesn't allow administrators to kill it. (Try killing it with Task Manager—you'll get an "access denied" error.) The Kill utility in the Windows NT Resource Kit, however, enables a user right that allows bypassing object security.

After the system reboots, open the crash dump file, following these steps:

1. Open a command prompt window.

2. Type *set _NT_SYMBOL_PATH=d:\support\debug\i386\symbols* (or the address where your copy of the DBG files resides—as noted earlier, you need to make sure you have the updated versions if you have a Windows NT service pack installed).

3. Type *i386kd -z c:\winnt\memory.dmp* (or whatever the file specification of your crash dump file is).

Once you're in the kernel debugger, try the ? and !? commands to see the online help. For example, type *!process 0 8* for a list of the processes that were running at the time of the crash. Note that you can log your kernel debugger session to a file using the .logopen and .logclose commands. Specific experiments with the kernel debugger are spread throughout the remainder of this book, so keep this crash dump around for later use.

The checked build is useful for device driver developers because stricter argument validation is performed by key kernel-mode system support routines. For example, if a driver (or some other piece of kernel-mode code) makes an invalid call to a system function that is checking parameters with ASSERT statements (such as acquiring a spinlock and the wrong interrupt level), the system will stop execution when the problem is detected rather than allowing some data structure to be corrupted and the system to crash at a later time. There are more than 15,000 ASSERT tests just in the core operating system components of Windows NT!

Examining Internal Data Structures and Variables

This book describes the key internal Windows NT data structures through diagrams that show the connection between structures as well as through tables that list the important elements of these structures. Although the general layout and content of these structures is shown, detailed field-level descriptions (such as size and data types) are not. However, a number of these data structures (such as object dispatcher headers, wait blocks, events, mutants, semaphores, and so on) are defined in the Windows NT DDK C header files (see \ddk\inc*.h) and described in the DDK documentation.

This book also describes a number of internal system global variables. These variables can contain, for example, numeric values of interest that might not be accessible through any of the Windows NT performance counters (such as the system maximum working set size, which is computed each time the system boots). Or they can contain addresses or list heads of key system data structures (such as the process or thread list).

Most of these internal structures and variables exist in the system address space as static global data or are allocated from one of the Windows NT system heaps (paged and nonpaged pool, which are examined in more detail in Chapter 5). Since data in the system address space can be accessed only while in kernel mode, if you want to access this data yourself, you must either write your own device driver or use one of the system kernel-mode debuggers described earlier. Of course, the location and content of these variables can change from release to release, since they are not documented or supported for user access.

Conclusion

In this chapter, you've been introduced to the key Windows NT technical concepts and terms that will be used throughout the book. You've also gotten a glimpse of the many useful tools available for digging into Windows NT internals. Now we're ready to begin our exploration of the internal design of the system, beginning with an overall view of the system architecture and its key components.

CHAPTER TWO

System Architecture

Now that we've covered the terms, concepts, and tools you need to be familiar with, we're ready to start our exploration of the internal design goals and structure of Microsoft Windows NT. This chapter explains the overall architecture of the system—the key components, how they interact with each other, and the context in which they run. To provide a framework for understanding the internals of Windows NT, let's first review the requirements and goals that shaped the original design and specification of the system.

Requirements and Design Goals

The following requirements drove the specification of Windows NT back in 1989:

- Provide a true 32-bit, preemptive, reentrant, virtual memory operating system
- Run on multiple hardware architectures and platforms
- Run and scale well on symmetric multiprocessing systems
- Be a great distributed computing platform, both as a network client and a server
- Run most existing 16-bit MS-DOS and Microsoft Windows 3.1 applications
- Meet government requirements for POSIX 1003.1 compliance
- Meet government and industry requirements for operating system security
- Be easily adaptable to the global market by supporting Unicode

To guide the thousands of decisions that had to be made to create a system that met these requirements, the Windows NT design team adopted the following design goals at the beginning of the project:

- **Extensibility** The code must be written to comfortably grow and change as market requirements change.

- **Portability** The system must be able to run on multiple hardware architectures and must be able to move with relative ease to new ones as market demands dictate.

- **Reliability and robustness** The system should protect itself from both internal malfunction and external tampering. Applications should not be able to harm the operating system or other running applications.

- **Compatibility** Although Windows NT should extend existing technology, its user interface and application programming interfaces (APIs) should be compatible with older versions of Windows as well as older operating systems such as MS-DOS. It should also interoperate well with other systems such as UNIX, OS/2, and NetWare.

- **Performance** Within the constraints of the other design goals, the system should be as fast and responsive as possible on each hardware platform.

As we explore the details of the internal structure and operation of Windows NT, you'll see how these design goals and market requirements were woven successfully into the construction of the system. But before we start that exploration, let's examine the overall design model for Windows NT and compare it to other modern operating systems.

Operating System Models

In most operating systems, applications are separated from the operating system itself—the operating system code runs in a privileged processor mode (referred to as *kernel mode* in this book), with access to system data and to the hardware; applications run in a nonprivileged processor mode (called *user mode*), with a limited set of interfaces available and with limited access to system data. When a user-mode program calls a system service, the processor traps the call and then switches the calling thread to kernel mode. When the system service completes, the operating system switches the thread context back to user mode and allows the caller to continue.

The design of the internal structure of the kernel-mode portion of such systems varies widely. For example, traditional operating systems were monolithic in nature, as illustrated in Figure 2-1. The system was constructed as a single, large software system with many dependencies among internal components. This interdependency meant that extensions to the system might require many changes across the entire code base. Also, in a monolithic operating system, the bulk of the operating system code runs in the same memory space, which means that any operating system component could corrupt data being used by other components.

A different structuring approach divides the operating system into modules and layers them one on top of the other. Each module provides a set of functions that other modules can call. Code in any particular layer calls code only

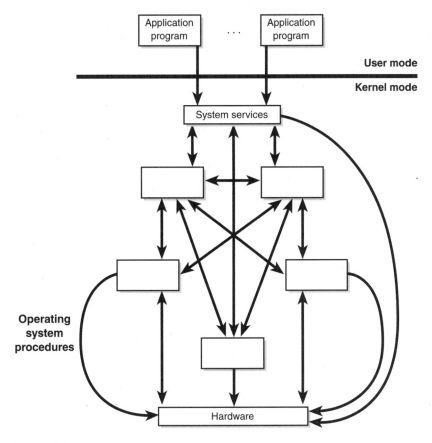

Figure 2-1

Monolithic operating system

in lower layers. On some systems, such as the Digital Equipment Corporation (DEC) OpenVMS or the old Multics operating system, hardware even enforces the layering (using multiple, hierarchical processor modes). One advantage of a layered operating system structure is that because each layer of code is given access to only the lower-level interfaces (and data structures) it requires, the amount of code that wields unlimited power is limited. This structure also allows the operating system to be debugged starting at the lowest layer, adding one layer at a time until the whole system works correctly. Layering also makes it easier to enhance the operating system because individual layers can be modified or replaced without affecting other parts of the system.

Another approach to structuring an operating system is the client/server microkernel model. The architecture in this approach divides the operating system into several server processes, each of which implements a single set of services—for example, memory management services, process creation services, or processor scheduling services. Each *server* runs in user mode, waiting for a client request for one of its services. The *client*, which can be either another operating system component or an application program, requests a service by sending a message to the server. An operating system microkernel running in kernel mode delivers the message to the server; the server performs the operation; and the kernel returns the results to the client in another message, as illustrated in Figure 2-2.

> **NOTE** The client/server model of networking is distinctly different from the client/server model of processing. In client/server networking, a server provides resources (such as files, printer, and storage space) to the clients. Client/server processing is a method of distributing the processing load required by an application to best suit the capabilities of network, server, and client so that one part of an application is processed on a server machine while another is processed on the client.

In reality, client/server systems fall within a spectrum, some doing very little work in kernel mode and others doing more. For example, the Carnegie Mellon University Mach operating system, a contemporary example of the client/server microkernel architecture, implements a minimal kernel that comprises thread scheduling, message passing, virtual memory, and device drivers. Everything else, including various APIs, file systems, and networking, runs in user mode. However, commercial implementations of the Mach microkernel operating system typically run at least all file system, networking, and memory management code in kernel mode. The reason is simple: the pure microkernel design is commercially impractical because it is too computationally expensive—that is, it's too slow.

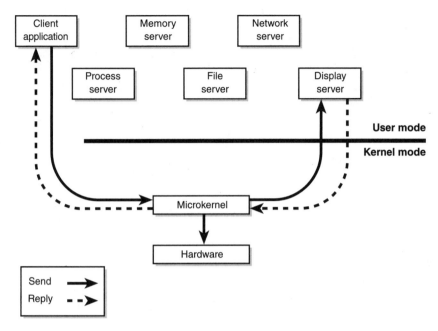

Figure 2-2
Client/server operating system

So what model does Windows NT embody? It merges the attributes of a layered operating system with those of a client/server or microkernel operating system. Performance-sensitive operating system components run in kernel mode, where they can interact with the hardware and with each other without incurring the overhead of context switches and mode transitions. For example, the memory manager, cache manager, object and security managers, network protocols, file systems (including network servers and redirectors), and all thread and process management run in kernel mode.

Of course, all of these components are fully protected from errant applications, because applications don't have direct access to the code and data of the privileged part of the operating system (though they can quickly call other kernel services). This protection is one of the reasons that Windows NT has the reputation for being both robust and stable as an application server and a workstation platform yet fast and nimble from the perspective of core operating system services, such as virtual memory management, file I/O, networking, and file and print sharing.

Does the fact that so much of Windows NT runs in kernel mode mean it is more susceptible to crashes than a true microkernel operating system? Not really. Consider the following scenario: suppose the file system code of an operating system has a bug that causes it to crash from time to time. In a traditional operating system or a modified microkernel operating system, a bug in kernel-mode code such as the memory manager or the file system would likely crash the entire operating system. In a pure microkernel operating system, such components run in user mode, so theoretically a bug would simply mean that the component's process exits. But in practical terms, the failure of such a critical process would result in a system crash, since recovery from the failure of such a component would likely be impossible.

The kernel-mode components of Windows NT also embody basic object-oriented design principles. For example, they don't reach into one another's data structures to access information maintained by individual components. Instead, they use formal interfaces to pass parameters and access and/or modify data structures.

Despite its pervasive use of objects to represent shared system resources, however, Windows NT is not an object-oriented system in the strict sense. Most of the operating system code is written in C for portability and because development tools are widely available. C does not directly support object-oriented constructs, such as dynamic binding of data types, polymorphic functions, or class inheritance. Therefore, the C-based implementation of objects in Windows NT borrows from, but does not depend on, esoteric features of particular object-oriented languages.

Architecture Overview

Now that you understand the basic model of Windows NT, let's take a look at the key system components that comprise its architecture. A simplified version of this architecture is shown in Figure 2-3. Keep in mind that this diagram is basic—it doesn't show everything. The various components of Windows NT are covered in detail later in the chapter.

In Figure 2-3, first notice the line dividing the user-mode and kernel-mode parts of the Windows NT operating system. The boxes above the line represent user-mode processes, and the components below the line are kernel-mode operating system services. As mentioned in Chapter 1, user-mode threads execute in a protected process address space (although while they are executing in kernel mode, they have access to system space). Thus, system processes, server processes (services), the environment subsystems, and user applications each have their own private process address space.

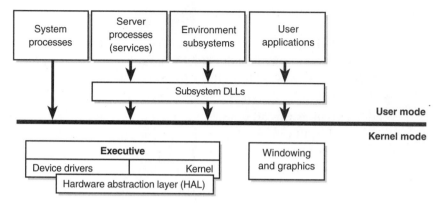

Figure 2-3
Simplified Windows NT architecture

The four basic types of user processes are described in the following list:

- Special *system support processes,* such as the logon process and the session manager, that are not Windows NT services (that is, not started by the service controller).

- *Server processes* that are Windows NT services, such as the Event Log and Schedule services. Many add-on server applications, such as Microsoft SQL Server and Microsoft Exchange Server, also include components that run as Windows NT services.

- *Environment subsystems,* which expose the native operating system services to user applications, thus providing an operating system *environment,* or personality. Windows NT ships with three environment subsystems: Win32, POSIX, and OS/2 1.2.

- *User applications,* which can be one of five types: Win32, Windows 3.1, MS-DOS, POSIX, or OS/2 1.2.

In Figure 2-3, notice the "Subsystem DLLs" box below the "User applications" one. Under Windows NT, user applications do not call the native Windows NT operating system services directly; rather, they go through one or more *subsystem dynamic-link libraries (DLLs).* The role of the subsystem DLLs is to translate a documented function into the appropriate undocumented Windows NT system service calls. This translation might or might not involve sending a message to the environment subsystem process that is serving the user application.

The kernel mode of the operating system includes these components:

- The Windows NT *executive* contains the base operating system services, such as memory management, process and thread management, security, I/O, and interprocess communication.

- The Windows NT *kernel* performs low-level operating system functions, such as thread scheduling, interrupt and exception dispatching, and multiprocessor synchronization. It also provides a set of routines and basic objects that the rest of the executive uses to implement higher-level constructs.

- The *hardware abstraction layer* (*HAL*) is a layer of code that isolates the kernel, device drivers, and the rest of the Windows NT executive from platform-specific hardware differences.

- *Device drivers* include both file system and hardware device drivers that translate user I/O function calls into specific hardware device I/O requests.

- The *windowing and graphics system* implements the graphical user interface (GUI) functions (better known as the Win32 USER and GDI functions), such as dealing with windows, controls, and drawing.

Each of these components is covered in greater detail both later in this chapter and in the chapters that follow.

Before we dig into the details of these system components, though, let's review two key attributes of the Windows NT architecture—portability and multiprocessing—and also examine the differences between Windows NT Workstation and Windows NT Server.

Portability

Windows NT was designed to run on a variety of hardware architectures, including Intel-based CISC systems as well as RISC systems. The initial release of Windows NT supported the *x*86 and MIPS architecture. Support for the DEC Alpha AXP was added shortly thereafter. Support for a fourth processor architecture, the Motorola PowerPC, was added in Windows NT 3.51. Because of changing market demands, however, support for both the MIPS and PowerPC was dropped after the release of Windows NT 4.0. Windows NT 5.0 will run only on *x*86 and Alpha machines. Eventually, Windows NT will also run on the Merced chip, the first implementation of the new 64-bit architecture family being jointly developed by Intel and Hewlett-Packard, called IA64 (for Intel Architecture 64). As Microsoft has stated publicly, Windows NT will be enhanced to support a true 64-bit programming interface on both IA64 and Alpha systems.

Windows NT achieves portability across hardware architectures and plat-forms in two primary ways:

- Windows NT has a layered design, with low-level portions of the sys-tem that are processor-architecture-specific or platform-specific iso-lated into separate modules so that upper layers of the system can be shielded from the differences among hardware platforms. The two key components that provide operating system portability are the HAL and the kernel. Functions that are architecture-specific (such as thread context switching) are implemented in the kernel. Functions that can differ from machine to machine within the same architecture are implemented in the HAL.

- The majority of Windows NT is written in a portable language—the operating system executive, utilities, and device drivers are written in C, and portions of the graphics subsystem and user interface are written in C++. Assembly language is used only for those parts of the operating system that must communicate directly with system hardware (such as the interrupt trap handler) or that are extremely performance-sensitive (such as context switching). Assembly lan-guage code exists not only in the kernel and the HAL but also in a few places within the executive (such as the executive routines that implement interlocked instructions as well as one module in the local procedure call facility), in the kernel-mode part of the Win32 subsystem, and even in some user-mode libraries, such as the pro-cess startup code in NTDLL.DLL (explained later in this chapter).

Symmetric Multiprocessing

Multitasking is the operating system technique for sharing a single processor among multiple threads of execution. When a computer has more than one processor, however, it can execute two threads simultaneously. Thus, whereas a multitasking operating system only appears to execute multiple threads at the same time, a multiprocessing operating system actually does it, executing one thread on each of its processors.

As mentioned at the beginning of the chapter, a key Windows NT design goal from the start of the project was to run well on multiprocessor computer systems. Windows NT supports *symmetric multiprocessing* (*SMP*). There is no master processor—the operating system as well as user threads can be scheduled to run on any processor. Also, all the processors share just one memory space. This model contrasts with *asymmetric multiprocessing (ASMP)*, in which the operating system typically selects one processor to execute operating system code while other processors run only user code. The differences in the two multiprocessing models are illustrated in Figure 2-4.

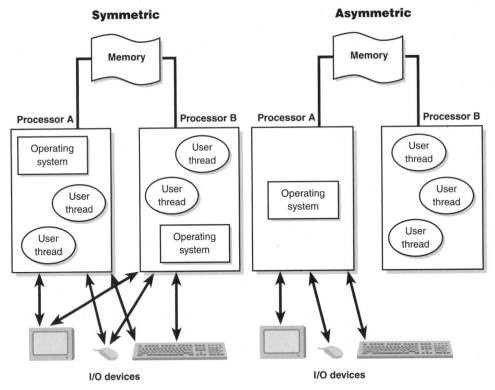

Figure 2-4
Symmetric vs. asymmetric multiprocessing

Windows NT was architecturally designed to run on up to 32 processors. The number of licensed processors is stored in the registry at HKLM\System\CurrentControlSet\Control\Session Manager\LicensedProcessors. (Tampering with that data is a violation of the software license; and besides, modifying Windows NT to use more processors is more complicated than just changing this value.) The default value depends on the edition of Windows NT, as you can see in Table 2-1.

Table 2-1 Number of Licensed Processors for Various Editions of Windows NT

Edition	Number of Licensed Processors
Windows NT Server, Enterprise Edition	8
Windows NT Server	4
Windows NT Workstation	2

System manufacturers that sell Windows NT Server systems that support more than eight processors must ship their own remastered Windows NT CD-ROM with a registry set to enable a higher number of processors. They might also need to provide their own HAL.

One of the key issues with multiprocessor systems is scalability. To run correctly on an SMP system, operating system code must adhere to strict guidelines and rules to ensure correct operation. Resource contention and other performance issues are more complicated in multiprocessing systems than in ordinary operating systems and must be accounted for in the system's design. Windows NT incorporates several features that are crucial to its success as a multiprocessing operating system:

- The ability to run operating system code on any available processor and on multiple processors at the same time. With the exception of its kernel component, which handles thread scheduling and interrupts, all operating system code can be preempted (forced to give up a processor) when a higher-priority thread needs attention.

- Multiple threads of execution within a single process, each of which can potentially execute simultaneously on different processors.

- Fine-grained synchronization within the kernel as well as within device drivers and server processes allow more components to run concurrently on multiple processors.

- Server processes that use multiple threads to process requests from more than one client simultaneously.

- Convenient mechanisms for sharing objects among processes and flexible interprocess communication capabilities, including shared memory and an optimized message-passing facility.

Chapter 4 describes how threads are scheduled in a multiprocessor system.

Are there two versions of Windows NT—one for uniprocessor systems and one for multiprocessor ones? Not really. Besides the HAL, which by its very nature is different for a uniprocessor system than for a multiprocessor system, of the more than 2000 files on the Windows NT CD-ROM, only *one file* is shipped in different uniprocessor and multiprocessor versions: the core operating system image that contains the executive and kernel, NTOSKRNL.EXE. The rest of the binary files that comprise Windows NT (including all utilities, libraries, and device drivers) are built to run properly on both uniprocessor and multiprocessor systems. For example, they handle multiprocessor synchronization issues correctly. You should use this approach on any software you build, whether it be a Win32 application or a device driver—build your code assuming it might run on a multiprocessor system so that if it does, it won't break.

The Windows NT CD-ROM includes two versions of NTOSKRNL:

- NTOSKRNL.EXE is the executive and kernel for uniprocessor systems.

- NTKRNLMP.EXE is the executive and kernel for multiprocessor systems.

These two images are built from the same source files. They are built using compile-time conditional code so that multiprocessor-specific support is not included in the uniprocessor version of NTOSKRNL and vice versa. Because of this, single processor systems don't have to pay for the overhead of multiprocessor synchronization at the operating system level.

At installation time, the appropriate file is selected and copied to the local \winnt\system32 directory. In either case, however, the file is named NTOSKRNL.EXE on the local hard drive.

You'll notice that on the checked build CD-ROM (the special debug version of Windows NT, which is explained on page 22 in Chapter 1), both NTOSKRNL.EXE and NTKRNLMP.EXE are identical—they are both built for multiprocessor systems. In other words, there is no uniprocessor version of the checked build version of NTOSKRNL.

EXPERIMENT: Checking Which Version of NTOSKRNL You're Running

You can tell which version of NTOSKRNL you're running by running WINMSD.EXE. (From the Start menu, choose Programs, and then select Administrative Tools, Windows NT Diagnostics.) If you click the Version tab, you'll see something like the following:

As you can see, the system is running the multiprocessor free build for *x86* systems. (This screen shot was taken from the dual processor Pentium Pro workstation that Compaq so graciously loaned me for this book project.)

Windows NT Workstation vs. Windows NT Server

Many people wonder what exactly the differences are between Windows NT Workstation, Windows NT Server, and Windows NT Server, Enterprise Edition. First, Windows NT Server behaves differently than Windows NT Workstation does—Windows NT Server is optimized to be a high-performance network server platform, whereas Windows NT Workstation, although it has server capabilities, is optimized for interactive desktop use.

Second, Windows NT Server, Enterprise Edition, is a superset of Windows NT Server, which in turn is a superset of Windows NT Workstation. For example, the following optionally installable networking and server components come with Windows NT Server but are not available for Windows NT Workstation:

- Enterprise network management and directory services through the formation of domains (groups of Windows NT systems treated as a single security perimeter)

- Disk fault-tolerance features (striping with parity and mirroring)

- Services for Macintosh: file and printer sharing, user administration

- Gateway Service for NetWare, which permits a number of Windows NT clients to access a NetWare server using the Windows NT Server as a gateway

- TCP/IP server addressing management, such as a complete Domain Name System (DNS) and Dynamic Host Configuration Protocol (DHCP)

- Remote boot server for diskless MS-DOS, Windows 3.1, and Windows 95 PCs

Windows NT Server, Enterprise Edition, contains additional components and features beyond those in Windows NT Server, such as Microsoft Cluster Server, Microsoft Message Queue Server, and Microsoft Transaction Server. (The Windows NT 4.0 Option Pack, which installs on both Windows NT Server and Windows NT Server, Enterprise Edition, includes the latter two components in addition to Microsoft Internet Information Server 4.0 and Internet Connection Services for Microsoft RAS.) Also, on $x86$ systems, Windows NT Server, Enterprise Edition, can allow certain applications to have a 3-GB user address space (as opposed to 2 GB on the other editions). This capability is explained in further detail in Chapter 5.

There are also licensing differences between Windows NT Workstation and Windows NT Server:

- The Windows NT Workstation license permits only 10 unique IP connections in a 10-minute period (though the code doesn't enforce this connection limit). Windows NT Server has no such restriction.

- Windows NT Server supports an unlimited number of clients (assuming that you have licenses for all of them) accessing the built-in file and print-sharing services, whereas Windows NT Workstation permits only up to 10 simultaneous inbound connections to shared files or printers.

■ Windows NT Server, Enterprise Edition, supports eight processors, Windows NT Server four, and Windows NT Workstation only two.

Although Windows NT Server and Windows NT Server, Enterprise Edition, contain significant added functionality over Windows NT Workstation, the majority of the files in all three products are identical, including such core components as the executive, kernel, device drivers, utilities, and libraries. However, a number of these components operate differently depending on which edition is running.

How does Windows NT know which product is running? At boot time, the registry is queried and the result is stored in the system global variable *MmProductType*. One element of this information is in the registry key HKLM\System\CurrentControlSet\Control\ProductOptions. Changing this information is a violation of the software license. Table 2-2 shows the values for this key as they correspond to the different editions of Windows NT.

Table 2-2 **Product Type Registry Values**

Edition of Windows NT	Value of ProductOptions*
Windows NT Workstation	WinNT
Windows NT Server (domain controller)	LanmanNT
Windows NT Server (server only)	ServerNT

* A different key, ProductSuite, distinguishes Windows NT Server, Enterprise Edition.

If user programs need to determine which Windows NT product is running, they can query for this information. (For sample code to do this, see the article Q124305 "Which Windows NT (Server or Workstation) Is Running?" in the MSDN Knowledge Base.) Device drivers running in kernel mode can call the internal executive routine used by Windows NT itself, *MmIsThisAn-NtasSystem*, documented in the Windows NT Device Driver Kit (DDK).

Based on the product type, several resource allocation decisions are made differently at system boot time, such as the size and number of operating system heaps (or pools), the number of internal system worker threads, and the size of the system data cache. Also, run-time policy decisions, such as the way the memory manager trades off system and process memory demands, differ

Windows NT vs. Windows 95 and Windows 98

Windows NT and Windows 95 (and its follow-on release, Windows 98) are part of the "Windows family of operating systems," sharing a common subset API (Win32 and COM), device driver model (WDM), and in some cases shared operating system code. Although Windows NT 4.0 doesn't have some of the features that Windows 95 has today, Microsoft has always made it clear that Windows NT was to be the strategic operating system platform for the future—not just for servers and business desktops but eventually for consumers as well. Following are some of the architectural differences and advantages that Windows NT has over Windows 95. (These comparisons also apply to Windows 98.)

- Windows NT supports multiprocessor systems—Windows 95 doesn't.

- Windows NT runs on a variety of machine architectures—Windows 95 is limited to *x*86 systems.

- Windows 95 doesn't have a file system that supports security (such as discretionary access control).

- Windows NT is a fully 32-bit operating system—it contains no 16-bit code. Windows 95 contains a large amount of old 16-bit code from its predecessors, Windows 3.1 and MS-DOS.

- Windows NT is fully reentrant—significant parts of Windows 95 are nonreentrant (mainly the older 16-bit code taken from Windows 3.1). This nonreentrant code includes the majority of the graphics and window management functions (USER and GDI). When a 32-bit application on Windows 95 attempts to call a system service implemented in nonreentrant 16-bit code, it must first obtain a systemwide lock (or mutex) to block other threads from entering the nonreentrant code base. And even worse, a 16-bit application holds this lock *while running.* Thus, although the core of Windows 95 contains a preemptive 32-bit multithreaded scheduler, because so much of the system is still implemented in nonreentrant code, applications many times run single threaded.

- Windows NT provides an option to run 16-bit Windows applications in their own address space—Windows 95 always runs 16-bit Windows applications in a shared address space, in which they can corrupt (and hang) each other.

- Shared memory on Windows NT is visible only to the processes that have the same shared memory section (called *file mapping objects* in the Win32 API) open. On Windows 95, all shared memory is visible and writable from all processes. Thus, any process can write to any file mapping object.

- Windows 95 has some critical operating system pages that are writable from user mode, thus allowing a user application to crash the system.

What does Windows 95 have that Windows NT 4.0 doesn't? Full Plug and Play, power management, infrared support, and support for the FAT32 file system. However, all of these features will be a part of Windows NT 5.0, making it the first release of Windows NT to be a true superset of the Windows platform.

The one thing both Windows 95 and Windows 98 can do that Windows NT will never do is run *all* older MS-DOS and Windows 3.1 applications (notably ones that require direct hardware access) as well as 16-bit MS-DOS device drivers. Whereas 100 percent compatibility with MS-DOS and Windows 3.1 was a mandatory goal for Windows 95, the goal for Windows NT was to run *most* existing 16-bit applications.

between Windows NT Server and Windows NT Workstation. Even some thread-scheduling details are handled differently in the two editions. Where there are significant operational differences in the two products, these are highlighted in the pertinent chapters throughout the rest of the book. Thus, unless otherwise noted, everything in this book applies to both Windows NT Server and Windows NT Workstation.

Key System Components

Now that we've looked at the high-level architecture of Windows NT, let's delve deeper into the internal structure and the role each of the key operating system components plays. Figure 2-5 is a more detailed and complete diagram of the Windows NT system architecture and components than was shown earlier in the chapter (in Figure 2-3).

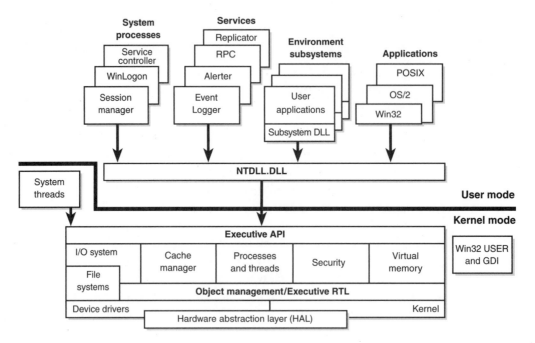

Figure 2-5

Windows NT architecture

The following sections elaborate on each major element of this diagram. Chapter 3 explains the primary control mechanisms used by the system (such as the object manager, interrupts, and so forth). Then the remaining chapters of this book explore in even more detail the internal structure and operation of key areas such as processes and threads, memory management, security, the I/O system, the cache manager, and the Windows NT file system (NTFS).

Table 2-3 lists the filenames of the key components shown in Figure 2-5. (You'll need to know these filenames because I'll be referring to some system files by name.)

Table 2-3 **Key Windows NT System Files**

Filename	Component(s)
SERVICES.EXE	Service controller process
WINLOGON.EXE	Logon process
SMSS.EXE	Session manager process
PSXSS.EXE	POSIX subsystem process
OS2SS.EXE	OS/2 subsystem process
CSRSS.EXE*	Win32 subsystem process
NTDLL.DLL	Internal support functions and system service dispatch stubs to executive functions
KERNEL32.DLL, USER32.DLL, GDI32.DLL.	Win32 subsystem DLLs
PSXDLL.DLL	POSIX subsystem DLL
NTOSKRNL.EXE**	Executive and kernel
HAL.DLL	Hardware abstraction layer
WIN32K.SYS	Win32 USER and GDI kernel-mode components

* CSRSS stands for "client/server run-time subsystem"—but all the subsystems are client/ server run-time subsystems.

** Remember that there are two versions of NTOSKRNL on the Windows NT CD-ROM: one for uniprocessors and one for multiprocessor systems. The correct one is copied to the local system at installation time. Also, the filename NTOSKRNL is a bit misleading because the kernel is only a small percentage of the total code in this file. (The majority of the code comprises the executive.)

Environment Subsystems and Subsystem DLLs

As shown in Figure 2-5, Windows NT has three environment subsystems: POSIX, OS/2, and Win32. (OS/2 is available only for *x*86 systems.) As I'll explain shortly, of the three, the Win32 subsystem is special in that Windows NT can't run without it. In fact, the other two subsystems are configured to start on demand, whereas the Win32 subsystem must always be running.

The subsystem startup information is stored under the registry key HKLM\ System\CurrentControlSet\Control\Session Manager\Subsystems. The screen shot from the Registry Editor in Figure 2-6 on the next page shows the values under this key.

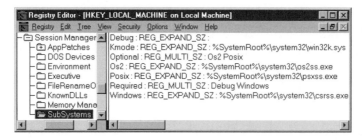

Figure 2-6
Registry Editor showing Windows NT startup information

The Required value lists the subsystems that load when the system boots. The value has two strings: Windows and Debug. The Windows value contains the file specification of the Win32 subsystem: CSRSS.EXE. Debug is blank (it's used for internal testing) and therefore does nothing. The Optional value indicates that the OS/2 and POSIX subsystems will be started on demand. The registry value Kmode contains the filename of the kernel-mode portion of the Win32 subsystem, WIN32K.SYS (explained later in this chapter).

The role of an environment subsystem is to expose some subset of the base Windows NT executive system services to application programs. Each subsystem can provide access to different subsets of the native services in Windows NT. That means that some things can be done from an application built on one subsystem that can't be done by an application built on another subsystem. For example, a Win32 application can't use the POSIX fork function.

Each executable image (.EXE) is bound to one and only one subsystem. When an image is run, the process creation code examines the subsystem type code in the image header so that it can notify the proper subsystem of the new process. This type code is specified with the /SUBSYSTEM qualifier of the *link* command and can be viewed with the built-in quick viewer in Windows NT Explorer, the *link /DUMP* command, or the Exetype tool in the Windows NT Resource Kit.

Function calls can't be mixed between subsystems. In other words, a POSIX application can call only services exported by the POSIX subsystem, and a Win32 application can call only services exported by the Win32 subsystem. As I'll explain later, this restriction is the reason that the POSIX subsystem, which implements a very limited set of functions (only POSIX 1003.1), is not a useful environment for porting UNIX applications.

As mentioned earlier, user applications don't call Windows NT system services directly. Instead, they go through one or more subsystem DLLs. These libraries export the documented interface that the programs linked to that

EXPERIMENT: Viewing the Image Subsystem Type

You can see the image subsystem type by using either the Exetype tool in the Windows NT Resource Kit or by dumping the image header with the built-in quick viewer for images in Windows NT Explorer. For example, notice the image types for two different Win32 images, NOTEPAD.EXE (the simple text editor) and CMD.EXE (the Windows NT command prompt):

```
C:\>exetype \winnt\system32\notepad.exe
File "\winnt\system32\notepad.exe" is of the following type:
    Windows NT
    32 bit machine
    Built for the Intel 80386 processor
    Runs under the Windows GUI subsystem

C:\>exetype \winnt\system32\cmd.exe
File "\winnt\system32\cmd.exe" is of the following type:
    Windows NT
    32 bit machine
    Built for the Intel 80386 processor
    Runs under the Windows character-based subsystem
```

In reality, there is just one Windows subsystem, not separate ones for graphical images and for character-based, or console, images. Also, Windows NT is not supported on the Intel 386 processor—the text output by the Exetype program hasn't been updated.

You can glean the same information from the output of the quick viewer for images. The following example of a POSIX image was generated by running Windows NT Explorer, selecting the file \NTRESKIT\ POSIX\LS.EXE (one of the POSIX utilities in the Windows NT Resource Kit), doing a right mouse click, and selecting Quick View. Note that the subsystem type is POSIX.

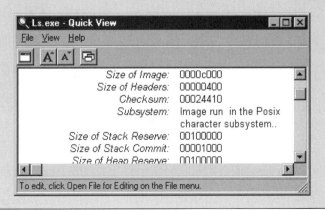

subsystem can call. For example, the Win32 subsystem DLLs (such as KERNEL32.DLL, USER32.DLL, and GDI32.DLL) implement the Win32 API functions. The POSIX subsystem DLL implements the POSIX 1003.1 API.

When an application calls a function in a subsystem DLL, one of three things can occur:

- The function is entirely implemented in user mode inside the subsystem DLL. In other words, no message is sent to the environment subsystem process, and no Windows NT executive system services are called. The function is performed in user mode, and the results are returned to the caller. Examples of such functions include *PtInRect* and *IsRectEmpty*.

- The function requires one or more calls to the Windows NT executive. For example, the Win32 *ReadFile* and *WriteFile* functions involve calling the underlying internal (and undocumented) Windows NT I/O system services *NtReadFile* and *NtWriteFile*, respectively.

- The function requires some work to be done in the environment subsystem process. (The environment subsystem processes, running in user mode, are responsible for maintaining the state of the client applications running under their control.) In this case, a client/server request is made to the environment subsystem in that a message is sent to the subsystem to perform some operation, perhaps using the Windows NT executive's *local procedure call* (*LPC*) facility (described in more detail on page 60). The subsystem DLL then waits for a reply before returning to the caller.

Some functions can be a combination of the second and third items above, such as the Win32 *CreateProcess* and *CreateThread* functions.

Although Windows NT was designed to support multiple, independent environment subsystems, from a practical perspective, having each subsystem implement all the code to handle windowing and display I/O would result in a large amount of duplication of system functions that, ultimately, would have negatively affected both system size and performance. Because Win32 was the primary subsystem, the Windows NT designers decided to locate these basic functions there and have the other subsystems call on the Win32 subsystem to perform display I/O. Thus, the POSIX and OS/2 subsystems will call services in the Win32 subsystem to perform display I/O (specifically, console or character cell I/O).

Let's take a closer look at each of the environment subsystems.

Win32 Subsystem

The Win32 subsystem consists of the following major components:

- The environment subsystem process (CSRSS.EXE), which contains support for:

  - Console (text) windows

  - Creating and deleting processes and threads

  - Portions of the support for 16-bit virtual DOS machine (VDM) processes

  - Other miscellaneous functions, such as *GetTempFile, DefineDos-Device, ExitWindowsEx,* and several natural language support functions

- The kernel-mode device driver (WIN32K.SYS), which contains the following:

  - The window manager controls window displays; manages screen output; collects input from keyboard, mouse, and other devices; and passes user messages to applications.

  - The Graphical Device Interface (GDI) is a library of functions for graphics output devices. It includes functions for line, text, and figure drawing and for graphics manipulation.

- Subsystem DLLs (such as USER32.DLL, ADVAPI32.DLL, GDI32.DLL, and KERNEL32.DLL), which translate documented Win32 API functions into the appropriate undocumented kernel-mode system service calls to NTOSKRNL.EXE and WIN32K.SYS.

- Graphics device drivers, which are hardware-dependent graphics display drivers, printer drivers, and video miniport drivers.

Applications call the standard USER functions to create windows and buttons on the display. The window manager communicates these requests to the GDI, which passes them to the graphics device drivers, where they are formatted for the display device. A display driver is paired with a video miniport driver to complete video display support. Each video miniport driver provides hardware-level support for its associated display driver.

The GDI provides a set of standard functions that let applications communicate with graphics devices, including displays and printers, without knowing anything about the devices. GDI functions mediate between applications and graphics devices such as display drivers and printer drivers. The GDI interprets application requests for graphic output and sends them to graphics display drivers. It also provides a standard interface for applications to use varying graphics output devices. This interface enables application code to be independent of the hardware devices and their drivers. The GDI tailors its messages to the capabilities of the device, often dividing the request into manageable parts. For example, some devices can understand directions to draw an ellipse; others require the GDI to interpret the command as a series of pixels placed at certain coordinates. For more information about the graphics and video driver architecture, see the book *Graphics Drivers Design Guide* in the Windows NT DDK.

Prior to Windows NT 4.0, the window manager and graphics services were part of the user-mode Win32 subsystem process. In Windows NT 4.0, the bulk of the windowing and graphics code was moved from running in the context of the Win32 subsystem process to a set of callable services running in kernel mode (in the file WIN32K.SYS). The primary reason for this shift was to improve overall system performance. Having a separate server process that contains the Win32 graphics subsystem required multiple thread and process context switches, which consumed considerable CPU cycles and memory resources even though the original design was highly optimized.

For example, for each thread on the client side there was a dedicated, paired server thread in the Win32 subsystem process waiting on the client thread for requests. A special interprocess communication facility called *fast LPC* was used to send messages between these threads. Unlike normal thread context switches, transitions between paired threads via fast LPC don't cause a rescheduling event in the kernel, thereby enabling the server thread to run for the remaining time slice of the client thread before having to take its turn in the kernel's preemptive thread scheduler. Moreover, shared memory buffers were used to allow fast passing of large data structures, such as bitmaps, and clients had direct but read-only access to key server data structures to minimize the need for thread/process transitions between clients and the Win32 server. Also, GDI operations were (and still are) batched. *Batching* means that a series of graphics calls by a Win32 application aren't "pushed" over to the server and drawn on the output device until a GDI batching queue is filled. You can set the size of the queue by using the Win32 *GdiSetBatchLimit* function, and you can flush the queue at any time with *GdiFlush*. Conversely, read-only properties and data structures of GDI, once they were obtained from the Win32 subsystem process, were cached on the client side for fast subsequent access.

Despite these optimizations, however, the overall system performance was still not adequate for graphics-intensive applications. The obvious solution was to eliminate the need for the additional threads and resulting context switches by moving the window and graphics system into kernel mode. Also, once applications have called into the window manager and the GDI, those subsystems can access other Windows NT executive components directly without the cost of user-mode or kernel-mode transitions. This direct access is especially important in the case of the GDI calling through video drivers, a process that involves interaction with video hardware at high frequencies and high bandwidths.

Is Windows NT Less Stable with Win32 USER and GDI in Kernel Mode?

Some developers wondered whether moving this much code into kernel mode would substantially affect system stability. The answer is that it hasn't. The reason the impact on system stability has been minimal is that prior to Windows NT 4.0 (and this is still true today), a bug (such as an access violation) in the user-mode Win32 subsystem process (CSRSS) resulted in a system crash. This crash occurs because the parent process of CSRSS (the session manager, SMSS, which is described on page 75) does a wait operation on the process handle to CSRSS, and if the wait ever returns, SMSS crashes the system—because the Win32 subsystem process was (and still is) a vital process to the running of the system. Because it was the process that contained the data structures that described the windows on the display, the death of that process would kill the user interface. However, even a Windows NT system operating as a server, with no interactive processes, couldn't run without this process, since server processes might be making use of window messaging to drive the internal state of the application. With Windows NT 4.0, an access violation in the same code now running in kernel mode simply crashes the system more quickly, since exceptions in kernel mode result in a system crash.

There is, however, one additional theoretical danger that didn't exist prior to moving the windowing and graphics system into kernel mode. Because this body of code is now running in kernel mode, a bug (such as the use of a bad pointer) could result in corrupting kernel-mode protected data structures. Prior to Windows NT 4.0, such references would have caused an access violation, since kernel-mode pages are not writable from user mode. But a system crash would have then resulted, as described earlier. With the code now running in kernel mode, a bad pointer reference that caused a write operation to some

(continued)

Is Windows NT Less Stable with Win32 USER and GDI in Kernel Mode? *continued*

kernel-mode page might not immediately cause a system crash, but if it corrupted some data structure, a crash would likely result soon after. There is a small chance, however, that such a reference could corrupt a memory buffer (rather than a data structure), possibly resulting in returning corrupt data to a user program or writing bad data to the disk.

Another area of possible impact can come from the move of the graphics drivers into kernel mode. Previously, some portions of a graphics driver ran within CSRSS, and others ran in kernel mode. Now, the entire driver runs in kernel mode. Although Microsoft doesn't develop all the graphics device drivers supported in Windows NT, it does work directly with hardware manufacturers to help ensure that they are able to produce reliable and efficient drivers. All drivers shipped with the system are submitted to the same rigorous testing as other executive components.

Finally, it's important to understand that this design (running the windowing and graphics subsystem in kernel mode) is not fundamentally risky. It is identical to the approaches many other device drivers use (for example, network card drivers and hard disk drivers). All of these drivers have been operating in kernel mode since the inception of Windows NT with a high degree of reliability.

Some people have speculated that the move of the window manager and the GDI into kernel mode will hurt the preemptive multitasking capability of Windows NT. The theory is that with all the additional Win32 processing time spent in kernel mode, other threads will have less opportunity to be run preemptively. This view is based on a misunderstanding of the Windows NT architecture. It is true that in many other nominally preemptive operating systems, executing in kernel mode is never preempted by the operating system scheduler—or is preempted only at a certain limited number of predefined points of kernel reentrancy. In Windows NT, however, threads running anywhere in the executive are preempted and scheduled alongside threads running in user mode, and all code within the executive is fully reentrant. Among other reasons, this capability is necessary to achieve a high degree of system scalability on SMP hardware.

Another line of speculation is that SMP scaling will be hurt by this change. This theory goes like this: previously, an interaction between an application and the window manager or the GDI involved two threads, one in the application and one in CSRSS.EXE. Therefore, on an SMP system, the two threads could run in parallel, thus improving throughput. This analysis shows a misunderstanding of how Windows NT worked prior to version 4.0. In most cases, calls from a client application to the Win32 subsystem process run synchronously; that is, the client thread entirely blocks waiting on the server thread and begins to run again only when the server thread has completed the call. Therefore, no parallelism on SMP hardware can ever be achieved. This phenomenon is easily observable with a busy graphics application using Performance Monitor on an SMP system. The observer will discover that on a two-processor system each processor is approximately 50 percent loaded, and it's relatively easy to find the single CSRSS thread that is paired off with the busy application thread. Indeed, because the two threads are fairly intimate with each other and sharing state, the processors' caches must be flushed constantly to maintain coherency. This constant flushing is the reason that with Windows NT 3.51 a single-threaded graphics application typically runs slightly slower on an SMP machine than on a single processor system.

As a result, the changes in Windows NT 4.0 have increased SMP throughput of applications that make heavy use of the window manager and the GDI, especially when more than one application thread is busy. When two application threads are busy on a two-processor Windows NT 3.51–based machine, a total of four threads (two in the application plus two in CSRSS) are battling for time on the two processors. Although only two are typically ready to run at any given time, the lack of a consistent pattern in which threads run results in a loss of locality of reference and cache coherency. This loss occurs because the busy threads are likely to get shuffled from one processor to another. In the Windows NT 4.0 design, each of the two application threads essentially has its own processor, and the automatic thread affinity of Windows NT tends to run the same thread on the same processor indefinitely, thus maximizing locality of reference and minimizing the need to synchronize the private per-processor memory caches.

As you can see, moving the window manager and the GDI from user mode to kernel mode has provided improved performance without decreasing system stability.

So, what remains in the user-mode process part of the Win32 subsystem? All the drawing and updating for console or text windows are handled by it, since console applications have no notion of repainting a window. It's easy to see this activity—simply open a command prompt and drag another window over it, and you'll see the Win32 subsystem process running like crazy as it repaints the console window. But other than console window support, only a few Win32 functions result in sending a message to the Win32 subsystem process anymore: process and thread creation and termination, network drive letter mapping, and creation of temporary files. In general, a running Win32 application won't be causing many, if any, context switches to the Win32 subsystem process.

POSIX Subsystem

POSIX, an acronym loosely defined as "a portable operating system interface based on UNIX," refers to a collection of international standards for UNIX-style operating system interfaces. The POSIX standards encourage vendors implementing UNIX-style interfaces to make them compatible so that programmers can move their applications easily from one system to another.

Windows NT implements only one of the many POSIX standards, POSIX.1, formally known as ISO/IEC 9945-1:1990 or IEEE POSIX standard 1003.1-1990. This standard was included primarily to meet U.S. government procurement requirements set in the mid-to-late 1980s that mandated POSIX.1 compliance as specified in Federal Information Processing Standard (FIPS) 151-2, developed by the National Institute of Standards and Technology. Windows NT 3.5, 3.51, and 4.0 have been formally tested and certified according to FIPS 151-2. The required POSIX Conformance Document is shipped in the \HELP directory in the Platform SDK.

Because POSIX.1 compliance was a mandatory goal for Windows NT, the operating system was designed to ensure that the required base system support was present to allow for the implementation of a POSIX.1 subsystem (such as the fork service, which is implemented in the Windows NT executive, and the support for hard file links in the Windows NT file system). However, because POSIX.1 defines a limited set of services (such as process control, interprocess communication, simple character cell I/O, and so on), the POSIX subsystem alone is not a complete programming environment. And because applications can't mix calls between subsystems on Windows NT, POSIX applications are limited to the strict set of services defined in POSIX.1. This restriction means that a POSIX executable on Windows NT can't create a thread or a window or use remote procedure calls (RPCs) or sockets. You can, however, do all these

EXPERIMENT: Watching the POSIX Subsystem Start

The Windows NT Resource Kit includes an optional set of POSIX utilities that are installed in a \POSIX subdirectory underneath your Resource Kit directory. If you have this directory installed, follow these steps:

1. Start a command prompt.

2. Type *tlist /t*, and check that the POSIX subsystem isn't already running (that is, that there's no PSXSS.EXE process underneath SMSS.EXE).

3. Run one of the POSIX utilities in the Windows NT Resource Kit (such as \NTRESKIT\POSIX\LS.EXE).

4. You'll notice a slight pause while the POSIX subsystem starts and the LS command displays the directory contents.

5. Run *tlist /t* again. This time, notice the existence of PSXSS.EXE as a child of SMSS.EXE.

6. Rerun LS.EXE a second time; you'll notice a quicker response (now that the POSIX subsystem is already started).

7. Rerun LS.EXE, but pause the output by pressing Ctrl-S; issue a *tlist /t* from another command prompt, and notice that the POSIX support image (POSIX.EXE) was the process created from the first command prompt and that it in turn created the LS.EXE process. You should see something similar to the following annotated output:

```
System (2)
    smss.exe (23) ───────────────── Session manager
      csrss.exe (31) ─────────────── Win32 subsystem
      .

      .

      .

      psxss.exe (187) ───────────── POSIX subsystem
explorer.exe (69) Program Manager
    CMD.EXE (93) Command Prompt - ls
        posix.exe (178) ─────────── POSIX support process
          ls.exe (97) ───────────── POSIX application
                                     being run
```

things in a Win32 application, the preferred subsystem environment for Windows NT, which is why several companies—such as DataFocus (*www.datafocus.com*) and ConsenSys (*www.consensys.com*) provide third-party UNIX-to-Win32 porting libraries. With this approach, a UNIX application can be recompiled and relinked as a Win32 executable and can slowly start to integrate calls to native Win32 functions. For companies that want to port UNIX applications to Windows NT with as few changes as necessary, the product OpenNT from OpenWay (*www.openway.com*) includes a replacement (enhanced) POSIX subsystem with a complete UNIX system service and utilities environment.

To compile and link a POSIX application on Windows NT requires the POSIX headers and libraries from the Platform SDK. POSIX executables are linked against the POSIX subsystem library, PSXDLL.DLL. Because by default Windows NT is configured to start the POSIX subsystem on demand, the first time you run a POSIX application, the POSIX subsystem process (PSXSS.EXE) must be started. It remains running until the system reboots. (If you kill the POSIX subsystem process, you won't be able to run more POSIX applications until you reboot.) The POSIX image itself is not run directly—instead, a special support image called POSIX.EXE is launched, which in turn creates a child process to run the POSIX application.

For more information on the POSIX subsystem, see Chapter 29 in the *Windows NT Workstation Resource Guide.* For more information on porting UNIX applications to Windows NT, see the articles in MSDN Library. (Do a search for POSIX.)

OS/2 Subsystem

The OS/2 environment subsystem, like the POSIX subsystem, is fairly limited in usefulness:

- It supports only OS/2 1.2 16-bit character-based or video I/O (VIO) applications.

- It is supported only on *x*86 systems.

Microsoft does sell an add-on OS/2 1.2 Presentation Manager subsystem for Windows NT, but even with this addition, you can't run OS/2 2.*x* (or later) applications.

Also, because Windows NT doesn't allow direct hardware access by user applications, OS/2 programs that contain I/O privilege segments that attempt to perform IN/OUT instructions (to access some hardware device) as well as advanced video I/O (AVIO) aren't supported. Applications that use the

CLI/STI instructions are supported—but all the other OS/2 applications in the system and all the other threads in the OS/2 process issuing the CLI instructions are suspended until an STI instruction is executed. Also worth noting is the special support for calling 32-bit DLLs from OS/2 16-bit applications on Windows NT, which can be useful in porting programs. (See the section "Win32 Thunking Mechanism" in Chapter 28 of the *Windows NT Workstation Resource Guide.*)

The 16-MB memory limitation on native OS/2 1.2 doesn't apply to Windows NT—the OS/2 subsystem uses the 32-bit virtual address space of Windows NT to provide up to 512 MB of memory to OS/2 1.2 applications, as illustrated in Figure 2-7.

The tiled area is 512 MB of virtual address space that is reserved up front and then committed or decommitted when 16-bit applications need segments. The OS/2 subsystem maintains a local descriptor table (LDT) for each process, with shared memory segments at the same LDT slot for all OS/2 processes.

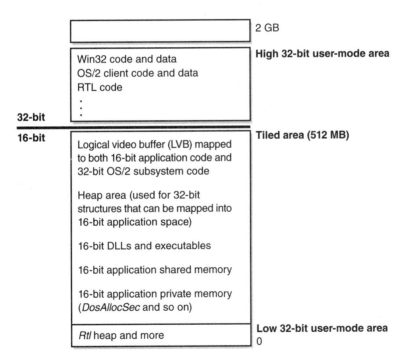

Figure 2-7
OS/2 subsystem virtual memory layout

As we'll discuss in detail in Chapter 4, threads are the element of a program that execute, and as such they must be scheduled for processor time. Although Windows NT priority levels range from 0 through 31, the 64 OS/2 priority levels (0 through 63) are mapped to Windows NT dynamic priorities 1 through 15. OS/2 threads never receive Windows NT real-time priorities 16 through 31.

As with the POSIX subsystem, the OS/2 subsystem starts automatically the first time you activate a compatible OS/2 image. It remains running until the system is rebooted.

For more information on how Windows NT handles running POSIX and OS/2 applications, see the section "Flow of *CreateProcess*" on page 156 in Chapter 4 of this book. For further information about the OS/2 subsystem on Windows NT, see Chapter 28 in the *Windows NT Workstation Resource Guide*. For a list of the OS/2 APIs supported, unsupported, and partially supported under Windows NT, refer to the file OS2API.TXT in the Windows NT Resource Kit.

NTDLL.DLL

NTDLL.DLL is a special system support library primarily for the use of subsystem DLLs. It contains two types of functions:

- System service dispatch stubs to Windows NT executive system services

- Internal support functions used by subsystems, subsystem DLLs, and other native images

The first group of functions provides the interface to the Windows NT executive system services that can be called from user mode. There are more than 200 such functions, such as *NtCreateFile, NtSetEvent,* and so on. As noted earlier, most of the capabilities of these functions are accessible through the Win32 API. (A number are not, however, and are for Microsoft internal use only.)

For each of these functions, NTDLL contains an entry point with the same name. The code inside the function contains the architecture-specific instruction that causes a transition into kernel mode to invoke the system service dispatcher (explained in more detail later in the chapter), which after making some verifications, calls the actual kernel-mode system service that contains the real code inside NTOSKRNL.EXE.

NTDLL also contains many support functions, such as the image loader (functions that start with *Ldr*), the heap manager, and Win32 subsystem process communication functions (functions that start with *Csr*), as well as general run-time library routines (functions that start with *Rtl*). It also contains the user-mode asynchronous procedure call (APC) dispatcher and exception dispatcher. (APCs and exceptions are explained in Chapter 3.)

Executive

The Windows NT executive is the upper layer of NTOSKRNL.EXE. (The kernel is the lower layer.) The executive includes five types of functions:

- Functions that are exported and callable from user mode. (The interface to these functions exists in NTDLL.DLL, and the functions are accessible through the Win32 API or some other environment subsystem.)

- Functions that are exported and callable from user mode but are not currently available through any documented subsystem function. (Examples include LPCs and various query functions such as *NtQueryInformationxxx*, specialized functions such as *NtCreatePagingFile*, and so on.)

- Functions that can be called only from kernel mode that are exported and documented in the Windows NT DDK.

- Functions that are meant to be called between kernel-mode components but that are not documented (for example, internal support routines used within the executive).

- Functions that are internal to a component.

The executive contains the following major components, each of which is covered in detail in a subsequent chapter of this book:

- The *process and thread manager* (explained in Chapter 4) creates and terminates processes and threads. The underlying support for processes and threads is implemented in the Windows NT kernel; the executive adds additional semantics and functions to these lower-level objects.

- The *virtual memory manager* (explained in Chapter 5) implements *virtual memory*, a memory management scheme that provides a large, private address space for each process and protects each process's address space from other processes. The memory manager also provides the underlying support for the cache manager.

■ The *security reference monitor* (described in Chapter 6) enforces security policies on the local computer. It guards operating system resources, performing run-time object protection and auditing.

■ The *I/O system* (explained in Chapter 7) implements device-independent input/output and is responsible for dispatching to the appropriate device drivers for further processing.

■ The *cache manager* (explained in Chapter 8) improves the performance of file-based I/O by causing recently referenced disk data to reside in main memory for quick access (and by deferring disk writes by holding the updates in memory for a short time before sending them to the disk). As you'll see, it does this using the memory manager's support for mapped files.

In addition, the executive contains four main groups of support functions that are used by the executive components just listed. About a third of these support functions are documented in the DDK, since they are also used by device drivers. The four categories of support functions include:

■ The *object manager,* which creates, manages, and deletes Windows NT executive objects and abstract data types that are used to represent operating system resources such as processes, threads, and the various synchronization objects. The object manager is explained later in this chapter.

■ The *LPC facility* passes messages between a client process and a server process on the same computer. LPC is a flexible, optimized version of *remote procedure call (RPC),* an industry-standard communication facility for client and server processes across a network.

■ A broad set of common *run-time library* functions, such as string processing, arithmetic operations, data type conversion, and security structure processing.

■ *Executive support routines,* such as system memory allocation (paged and nonpaged pool), interlocked memory access, as well as two special types of synchronization objects: resources and fast mutexes.

Kernel

The kernel performs the most fundamental operations in Windows NT, determining how the operating system uses the processor or processors and ensuring that they are used prudently. It is the lowest layer in NTOSKRNL.EXE.

These are the primary functions the kernel provides:

- Thread scheduling and dispatching
- Trap handling and exception dispatching
- Interrupt handling and dispatching
- Multiprocessor synchronization
- Providing the base kernel objects that are used (and in some cases exported to user mode) by the executive

The kernel is different from the rest of the executive in several ways. Unlike other parts of the executive, the bulk of the kernel is never paged out of memory. Similarly, although the kernel can be interrupted to execute an interrupt service routine (see Chapter 3), its execution is never preempted by another running thread. The kernel always runs in kernel mode and is designed to be small, compact, and as portable as performance and differences in processor architectures allow. For example, it does not probe accessibility of parameters, since it assumes that its callers know what they are doing. The kernel code is written primarily in C, with assembly code reserved for those tasks that require the fastest possible code or that rely heavily on the capabilities of the processor.

Like the various executive support functions mentioned in the preceding section, a number of functions in the kernel are documented in the DDK (search for functions beginning with *Ke*), since they are needed to implement device drivers.

Kernel Objects

One goal for the kernel was to provide a low-level base of well-defined, predictable operating system primitives and mechanisms that would allow higher-level components of the executive to do what they need to do. The kernel separates itself from the rest of the executive by implementing operating system mechanisms and avoiding policy making. It leaves nearly all policy decisions to the executive, with the exception of thread scheduling and dispatching, which the kernel implements.

Outside the kernel, the executive represents threads and other shareable resources as objects. These objects require some policy overhead, such as object handles to manipulate them, security checks to protect them, and resource quotas to be deducted when they are created. This overhead is eliminated in the kernel, which implements a set of simpler objects, called *kernel objects,* that help the kernel control central processing and support the creation of executive objects. Most executive-level objects encapsulate one or more kernel objects, incorporating their kernel-defined attributes.

One set of kernel objects, called *control objects,* establishes semantics for controlling various operating system functions. This set includes the kernel process object, the APC object, the *deferred procedure call* (*DPC*) object, and several objects used by the I/O system, such as the interrupt object.

Another set of kernel objects, known as *dispatcher objects,* incorporates synchronization capabilities and alters or affects thread scheduling. The dispatcher objects include the kernel thread, mutex (called *mutant* internally), event, kernel event pair, semaphore, timer, and waitable timer. The executive uses kernel functions to create instances of kernel objects, to manipulate them, and to construct the more complex objects it provides to user mode. Objects are explained in more detail later in this chapter, and process and thread objects are described in Chapter 4.

Hardware Support

The other major job of the kernel is to abstract or isolate the executive and device drivers from variations between the hardware architectures supported by Windows NT. This job includes handling variations in functions such as interrupt handling, exception dispatching, and multiprocessor synchronization.

Even for these hardware-related functions, the design of the kernel attempts to maximize the amount of common code. The kernel supports a set of interfaces that are portable across architectures and that are semantically identical across architectures. Most of the code that implements this portable interface is also identical across architectures.

Some of these interfaces are implemented differently on different architectures, however, or some of the interfaces are partially implemented with architecture-specific code. These architecturally independent interfaces can be called on any machine, and the semantics of the interface will be the same whether or not the code varies by architecture. Some kernel interfaces (such as spinlock routines, which are described in Chapter 3) are actually implemented in the HAL (described in the next section) because their implementation can vary for systems within the same architecture family.

The kernel also contains a small amount of code with *x*86-specific interfaces needed to support old MS-DOS programs. These *x*86 interfaces are not portable in the sense that they can't be called on a machine based on any other architecture; they won't be present. This *x*86-specific code, for example, supports calls to manipulate global descriptor tables (GDTs) and LDTs, hardware features of the *x*86.

Other examples of architecture-specific code in the kernel include the interface to provide translation buffer and CPU cache support. This support requires different code for the different architectures because of the way caches are implemented.

Another example is context switching. Although at a high level the same algorithm is used for thread selection and context switching (the context of the previous thread is saved, the context of the new thread is loaded, and the new thread is started), there are architectural differences among the implementations on different processors. Because the context is described by the processor state (registers and so on), what is saved and loaded varies depending on the architecture.

Hardware Abstraction Layer (HAL)

As mentioned at the beginning of the chapter, one of the crucial elements of the Windows NT design was its portability across a variety of hardware platforms. The HAL is a key part of making this portability possible. The HAL is a loadable kernel-mode module (HAL.DLL) that provides the low-level interface to the hardware platform on which Windows NT is running. It hides hardware-dependent details such as I/O interfaces, interrupt controllers, and multiprocessor communication mechanisms—any functions that are architecture-specific and machine-dependent.

So rather than access hardware directly, Windows NT internal components as well as user-written device drivers maintain portability by calling the HAL routines when they need platform-dependent information. For this reason, the HAL routines are documented in the Windows NT DDK. To find out more about the HAL and its use by device drivers, refer to the DDK.

Although there are many HALs on the Windows NT distribution media (look for HAL*.DLL), only one is chosen at installation time and copied to the system disk with the filename HAL.DLL. (Other operating systems, such as VMS, select the equivalent of the HAL at system boot time.) For HALs needed to support newer platforms that were not included on the Windows NT CD-ROM, the manufacturer can supply the HAL with the system.

EXPERIMENT: List the HALs on Your Windows NT CD-ROM

To see the list of HALs and their corresponding machine type, run the Uniprocessor to Multiprocessor Upgrade utility in the Windows NT Resource Kit (UPTOMP.EXE). This utility will copy the multiprocessor version of the operating system image (NTKRNLMP.EXE) to the \winnt\system32 directory, replacing the uniprocessor version (NTOSKRNL.EXE). (Note that the file is still called NTOSKRNL.EXE on the system disk.) It will also copy the appropriate HAL for the hardware platform.

To run the utility, set your default directory to the Resource Kit and type *cputomp*. The utility looks for the Windows NT Workstation or Windows NT Server CD-ROM in the location you installed from (in this case, a local CD-ROM). If your distribution media is accessible, you should see a dialog box like this:

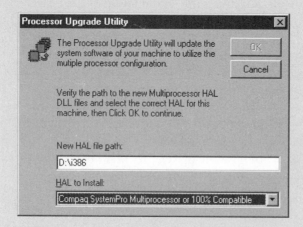

To see the list of HALs, click the HAL To Install drop-down list box.

Device Drivers

Although device drivers are explained in detail in Chapter 6, this section provides a brief overview of the types of drivers and explains how to list the drivers installed and loaded on your system.

Device drivers are loadable kernel-mode modules (typically ending in .SYS) that interface between the I/O system and the relevant hardware. As stated in the preceding section, device drivers on Windows NT don't manipulate hardware directly, but rather they call parts of the HAL to interface with the hardware. Drivers are typically written in C (sometimes C++) and therefore, with proper use of HAL routines, can be source code portable across the CPU architectures supported by Windows NT and binary portable within an architecture family.

There are several types of device drivers:

- *Hardware device drivers* manipulate hardware (using the HAL) to write output to or retrieve input from a physical device or network.

- *File system drivers* are Windows NT drivers that accept file-oriented I/O requests and translate them into I/O requests bound for a particular device.

- *Filter drivers,* such as those that perform disk mirroring and encryption, intercept I/Os and perform some added-value processing before passing the I/O to the next layer.

- *Network redirectors* and *servers* are file system drivers that transmit remote I/O requests to a machine on the network and receive such requests, respectively.

Because installing a device driver is the only way to add user-written kernel-mode code to the system, some programmers have written device drivers simply as a way to access internal operating system functions or data structures that are not accessible from user mode. For example, many of the utilities on *www.ntinternals.com* combine a Win32 GUI image and a device driver that is used to gather internal system state not accessible from the Win32 API.

You can list the installed drivers by going to Control Panel and clicking the Devices icon. This displays the list of device drivers defined in the registry. Device drivers and Win32 service processes are both defined in the same place: HKLM\System\CurrentControlSet\Services. However, they are distinguished by a type code—type 1 is a kernel-mode device driver, and type 2 is a file system driver. For further details on the information stored in the registry for device drivers, see the Registry Entries help file (REGENTRY.HLP) in the Windows NT Resource Kit under the main chapter heading "CurrentControl-Set\Services Subkeys."

You can also list the currently loaded device drivers with the Drivers utility (DRIVERS.EXE in the Windows NT Resource Kit) or the Pstat utility (shipped in the Windows NT Resource Kit as well as in the \support\debug directory on a Windows NT CD-ROM). The output at the top of the next page comes from the Drivers utility.

```
C:\>drivers
ModuleName    Code    Data    Bss   Paged    Init        LinkDate
-------------------------------------------------------------------------
ntoskrnl.exe  282816  42112     0  435392   84352  Sun May 11 00:11:27 1997
    hal.dll    24992   4224     0    9920   21120  Mon Mar 10 16:40:06 1997
  atapi.sys    20736   1088     0       0     768  Thu Apr 10 15:06:59 1997
SCSIPORT.SYS    9824     32     0   15552    2208  Mon Mar 10 16:42:27 1997
cpq32fs2.sys   62080    288     0       0     640  Tue Aug 13 02:19:00 1996
   Disk.sys    3328       0     0    7072    1600  Thu Apr 24 22:27:46 1997
 CLASS2.SYS    7040       0     0    1632    1152  Thu Apr 24 22:23:43 1997
   Ntfs.sys   68160    5408     0  269632    8704  Thu Apr 17 22:02:31 1997
 Floppy.SYS    1088     672     0    7968    6112  Wed Jul 17 00:31:09 1996
  Cdrom.SYS   12608      32     0    3072    3104  Wed Jul 17 00:31:29 1996
   Null.SYS       0       0     0     288     416  Wed Jul 17 00:31:21 1996
  KSecDD.SYS    1280     224     0    3456    1024  Wed Jul 17 20:34:19 1996
   Beep.SYS    1184       0     0       0     704  Wed Apr 23 15:19:43 1997
auddrive.SYS   15296     320     0   17632   11008  Wed Sep 04 17:09:02 1996
  :
  :
-------------------------------------------------------------------------
     Total 2540928  219552     0 1689184  320736
```

Each loaded kernel-mode component (NTOSKRNL, the HAL, as well as device drivers) is shown, along with the sizes of the sections in each image. (The meaning of these sizes is explained in Chapter 5 in the experiment "Accounting for Physical Memory" on page 288.)

The Pstat utility also shows the loaded driver list, but only after it first displays the process list and the threads in each process. Pstat includes one important piece of information that the Drivers utility doesn't: the load address of the module in system space. As I'll explain later, this address is crucial to mapping running system threads to the device driver in which they exist.

Device drivers run in one of three contexts:

- In the context of the user thread that initiated an I/O function

- In the context of a kernel-mode system thread

- As a result of an interrupt (called arbitrary thread context)

Interrupt processing is explained in Chapter 3. Further details about the I/O system, including the flow of control of an I/O request, are included in Chapter 7.

Peering into Undocumented Interfaces

Just examining the names of the exported or global symbols in key system images (such as NTOSKRNL.EXE, HAL.DLL, or NTDLL.DLL) can be very enlightening—you can get an idea of the kinds of things Windows NT can do versus what happens to be documented and supported today. Of course, just because you know the names of these functions doesn't mean that you can or should call them—the interfaces are undocumented and are subject to change. I suggest that you look at these functions purely to gain more insight into the kinds of internal functions Windows NT performs, not to bypass supported interfaces.

For example, looking at the list of functions in NTDLL.DLL gives you the list of all the system services that Windows NT provides to user-mode subsystem DLLs vs. the subset that each subsystem exposes. Although many of these functions map clearly to documented and supported Win32 functions, several are not exposed via the Win32 API. Conversely, it's also interesting to examine the imports of Win32 subsystem DLLs (such as KERNEL32.DLL or ADVAPI32.DLL) and which functions they call in NTDLL. Table 2-4 lists most of the commonly used function name prefixes in alphabetical order.

Table 2-4 **Commonly Used Prefixes**

Prefix	Component
Cc	Cache manager
Ex	Executive support routines
FsRtl	File system driver run-time library
Hal	Hardware abstraction layer
Io	I/O system
Ke	Kernel
Lsa	Local security authentication
Mm	Memory manager
Nt	Windows NT system services (most of which are exported as Win32 functions)
Ob	Object manager
Ps	Process support
Rtl	Run-time library
Se	Security
Zw	Mirror entry point for functions beginning with *Nt* that assume the previous caller was in kernel mode

Another interesting image to dump is NTOSKRNL.EXE—although many of the exported routines used by kernel-mode device drivers are documented in the Windows NT DDK, quite a few are not. You might also find it interesting

EXPERIMENT: Listing Undocumented Functions

You can dump the export and import tables of an image in several ways. The easiest way is to use the built-in quick viewer for images in Windows NT Explorer. Just select the image, right mouse click, and select Quick View from the pop-up menu.

The following output is an excerpt from doing a quick view on the Windows NT 4.0 Service Pack 3 version of NTOSKRNL.EXE. As indicated here, there are 0x3F6 (1014) exported functions:

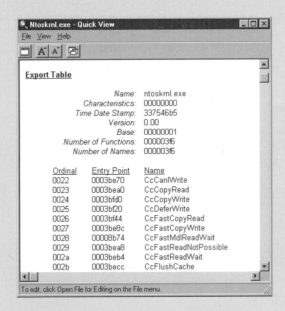

Another tool to examine the exports and imports of images is the Dependency Walker (DEPENDS.EXE), which is contained in the Windows NT Server Resource Kit (Supplement 2 or later) and the Platform SDK. To use the Dependency Walker to examine an image, select the file in Windows NT Explorer, right mouse click, and select View Dependencies in the pop-up menu. Or you can run it directly by running DEPENDS.EXE in the Windows NT Resource Kit directory; or if you have the Platform SDK installed, from the Start menu, choose Programs and then select Platform SDK, Tools, Depends.

Here is a sample of output you can see by viewing the dependencies of NTOSKRNL using this tool:

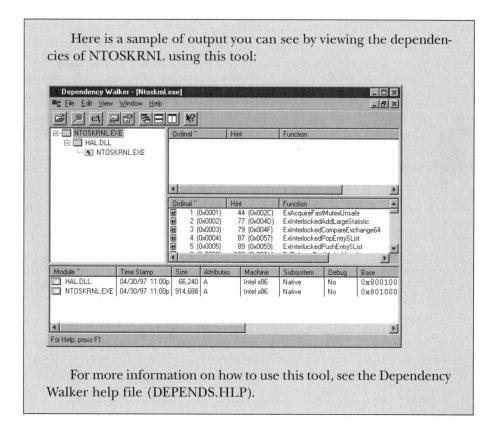

For more information on how to use this tool, see the Dependency Walker help file (DEPENDS.HLP).

to take a look at the import table for NTOSKRNL and the HAL; this table shows the list of functions in the HAL that NTOSKRNL uses and vice versa.

You can decipher the names of these exported functions more easily if you understand the naming convention for Windows NT system routines. The general format is:

<Prefix><Operation><Object>

In this format, *Prefix* is the internal component that exports the routine, *Operation* tells what is being done to the object or resource, and *Object* identifies what is being operated on.

For example, *ExAllocatePoolWithTag* is the executive support routine to allocate from paged or nonpaged pool. *KeInitializeThread* is the routine that allocates and sets up a kernel thread object.

System Processes

The following system processes appear on every Windows NT system. (Two of these—Idle and System—don't have a user-mode address space.)

- Idle process (contains one thread per CPU to account for idle CPU time)
- System process (contains the kernel-mode system threads)
- Session manager (SMSS.EXE)
- Win32 subsystem (CSRSS.EXE)
- Logon process (WINLOGIN.EXE)
- Local security authentication server (LSASS.EXE)
- Service controller (SERVICES.EXE) and its associated service processes

To help you understand the relationship of these processes, use the Windows NT Resource Kit *tlist /t* command to display the process "tree," that is, the parent/child relationship between processes. Here is some annotated output from *tlist /t*:

```
C:\>tlist /t
System Process (0)————————————— Idle process
System (2)————————————————————— Home for kernel-mode system threads
  smss.exe (20)———————————————— Session manager
   csrss.exe (30)—————————————— Win32 subsystem
   WINLOGON.EXE (34)—————————— Logon process
      SERVICES.EXE (40) ———————— Service controller
       SPOOLSS.EXE (65)————————— Spooler service
        RPCSS.EXE (80)—————————— RPC services
         NETDDE.EXE (194)———————— Network DDE service
      LSASS.EXE (43)—————————————— Local security authentication server
EXPLORER.EXE (87)————————————————— Shell (parent of user process tree)
  CMD.EXE (156)———————————————————— Process from which tlist was launched
    TLIST.EXE (174)—————————————————— Process running tlist producing this output
```

The next sections explain the key system processes shown in this output.

Idle Process

Despite the name shown, the first process listed in the preceding sample *tlist /t* output (process ID 0) is actually the System Idle process. As explained in Chapter 4, processes are identified by their image name. However, this process (as well as process ID 2, named System) is not running real user-mode images. Hence, the names shown by the various system display utilities are hard-coded text values that differ from utility to utility. Although most utilities call process ID 2 System, not all do. Table 2-5 lists several of the names given to the Idle process. (The Idle process is explained in detail in Chapter 4.)

Table 2-5   Names for Process ID 0 in Various Utilities

Utility	Name for Process ID 0
Task Manager	System Idle process
Process Viewer (PVIEWER.EXE)	Idle process
Process Status (PSTAT.EXE)	Idle process
Process Exploder (PVIEW.EXE)	System process
Task List (TLIST.EXE)	System process
Quick Slice (QSLICE.EXE)	System process

Now let's look at system threads and the purpose of each of the system processes that are running real images.

System Process and System Threads

The System process (always process ID 2) is the home for a special kind of thread that runs only in kernel mode: a *system thread.* System threads have all the attributes and contexts of regular user-mode threads (such as a hardware context, priority, and so on) but are different in that they run only in kernel-mode executing code loaded in system space, whether that be in NTOS-KRNL.EXE or in any other loaded device driver. In addition, system threads don't have a user process address space and hence must allocate any dynamic storage from operating system memory heaps, such as paged or nonpaged pool.

System threads are created by the *PsCreateSystemThread* function (documented in the DDK), which can be called only from kernel mode. Windows NT as well as various device drivers create system threads during system initialization to perform operations that require thread context, such as issuing and waiting for I/Os or other objects or polling a device.

EXPERIMENT: Examining the System Process

You can see that the threads inside the System process must be kernel-mode system threads because the start address for each thread is greater than the start address of system space (which on most Windows NT systems begins at 0x80000000). Also, if you look at the CPU time for these threads, you'll see that those that have any CPU time have run only in kernel mode.

For example, the memory manager uses system threads to implement such functions as writing dirty pages to the page file or mapped files, swapping processes in and out of memory, and so forth. The kernel creates a system thread called the *balance set manager* that wakes up once per second to check and possibly initiate various scheduling and memory management–related events. The cache manager also uses system threads to implement both read-ahead and write-behind I/Os. The file server device driver (SRV.SYS) uses system threads to respond to network I/O requests for file data. Even the floppy driver has a system thread to poll the floppy device. Further information on specific system threads is included in the chapters in which the component is described.

When you're troubleshooting or going through a system analysis, it's useful to be able to map the execution of individual system threads back to the driver or even to the subroutine that contains the code. For example, on a heavily loaded file server, the System process will likely be consuming considerable CPU time. But the knowledge that when the System process is running "some system thread" is running isn't enough to determine which device driver or operating system component is running.

So if the System process is running, look at the execution of the threads within that process (for example, with Performance Monitor). Once you find the thread (or threads) that is running, get the start address of the thread (for example, with Process Viewer, Pstat, or Tlist utility). Then, using the system memory map displayed at the end of the output from the Pstat utility, you can determine which system component contains the system thread that is running. The detailed steps in the following experiment describe exactly how you can map a system thread to a device driver.

EXPERIMENT: Mapping a
System Thread to a Device Driver

In this experiment, we'll find the Raw Mouse Input thread, a system thread in the Win32 subsystem that determines which threads should be notified of mouse movements and events. To cause this system thread to run, simply move the mouse back and forth rapidly while monitoring process CPU time (using Task Manager, Performance Monitor, or the Windows NT Resource Kit Qslice utility), and notice that the System process runs for a short period. As mentioned earlier, however, this indicates that some system thread is running but not the specific driver that the system thread resides in. The following steps show how to go down to the thread granularity to find out which driver contains the thread that is running.

1. Run Performance Monitor, click Add Counter (or type *Ctrl-I*), select the thread object, and then select the % Processor Time counter (or % Privileged Time—the value would be identical).

2. Go to the Instance box, and select all the threads in the System process. Do this by scrolling down in the Instance box to the process named System, selecting the first thread (thread 0), and while holding the mouse down, scroll down until the process name changes. You should see something like this:

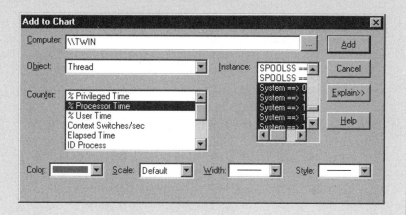

(continued)

EXPERIMENT: Mapping a System Thread to a Device Driver *continued*

3. Click Add, and then move the mouse rapidly back and forth until you see one or two of the system threads running in Performance Monitor's display.

4. Type *Ctrl-H* to turn on highlighting mode. (This highlights the currently selected counter in white.)

5. Scroll through the counters to identify a thread that was running when you moved the mouse.

6. Notice the relative thread number in the instance column on the bottom of Performance Monitor's graph window.

7. Now run Process Viewer (PVIEWER.EXE in the Windows NT Resource Kit or PVIEW.EXE in the Platform SDK or in Visual C++), and select the System process (process ID 2).

8. Scroll through the list of threads until you find the thread with the same relative thread number you obtained in step 5. Select this thread by clicking on it with the mouse, as shown here:

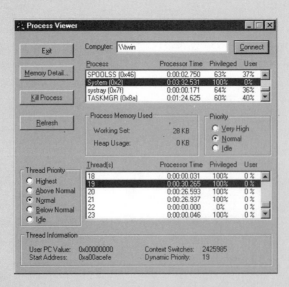

9. Notice that the start address for thread 19 is 0xa00acefe.

10. Run Pstat, and find the driver that has the start and end address containing the start address of the thread in question. In the following partial output, notice that WIN32K.SYS starts at 0xa0000000 and continues for 1,162,624 bytes (0x11bd80).

```
ModuleName    Load Addr   Code    Data   Paged          LinkDate
--------------------------------------------------------------------
ntoskrnl.exe 80100000   282816   42112  435392 Sat May 10 21:11:27 1997
hal.dll       80001000    24992    4224    9920 Mon Mar 10 13:40:06 1997
atapi.sys     80012000    20736    1088       0 Thu Apr 10 12:06:59 1997
 .
 .
 .
win32k.sys   a0000000  1162624   40064       0 Fri Apr 25 18:17:32 1997
```

Therefore, the ending address would be 0xa011bd80, and the thread in question clearly falls within this range.

If the address falls within NTOSKRNL.EXE, you can determine the name of the specific subroutine by looking it up in the list of global symbols contained in the associated symbol table file NTOSKRNL.DBG. The easiest way to generate the list of global symbols in NTOSKRNL is to start the kernel debugger (either by connecting to a live system or by opening a crash dump file) and typing the *x ** command in the kernel debugger with just NTOSKRNL.DBG loaded. Before typing *x **, use the *!logopen* command to create a log file of your kernel-debugging session. That way, you can save the output in a file and then search for the addresses in question. You can also use the Visual C++ Dumpbin utility (type *dumpbin /symbols ntoskrnl.dbg*), but you then have to search for the address minus the base address of NTOSKRNL, since only the offsets are listed.

Session Manager (SMSS)

The session manager (SMSS.EXE) is the first user-mode process created in the system. A kernel-mode system thread running the routine *ExInitializeSystem* creates the actual SMSS process. Besides performing a number of key system initialization steps, the session manager acts as a switch and monitor between applications and debuggers.

Much of the configuration information in the registry that drives the initialization steps of SMSS can be found under \System…\Control\Session Manager. You'll find it interesting to examine the kinds of data stored there. (For a description of the keys and values, see the Registry Entries help file, REGENTRY.HLP, in the Windows NT Resource Kit.)

The following is a list of the initialization steps performed by the main thread of SMSS:

1. Creates an LPC port object (*\SmApiPort*) and two threads to wait for client requests (such as to load a new subsystem or create a session).

2. Creates system environment variables.

3. Defines the symbolic links for MS-DOS device names (such as COM1 and LPT1).

4. Creates additional paging files.

5. Opens known DLLs (so that the pages can be reused even if no user processes are active).

6. Loads the kernel-mode part of the Win32 subsystem (WIN32K.SYS).

7. Starts the subsystem processes. (As noted earlier, the POSIX and OS/2 subsystems are defined to start on demand.)

8. Starts the logon process (WINLOGON).

9. Creates LPC ports for debug event messages (*DbgSsApiPort* and *DbgUiApiPort*) and threads to listen on those ports.

After performing these initialization steps, the main thread in SMSS waits forever on the process handles to CSRSS and WINLOGON. If either of these processes terminates unexpectedly, SMSS crashes the system, since Windows NT relies on their existence.

Of course, the other threads inside SMSS are responding to messages sent to the LPC ports listed above, such as requests to load subsystems, new subsystems starting up, and debug events.

Logon (WINLOGON)

The Windows NT logon process, WINLOGON, handles interactive user logons and logoffs. WINLOGON is notified of a user logon request when the *secure attention sequence* (*SAS*) keystroke combination is entered. The default SAS on Windows NT is the combination Ctrl-Alt-Delete. The reason for the SAS is to protect users from password-capture programs that simulate the logon process. Once the username and password have been captured, they are sent to the local security authentication server process (described in the next section) to be validated. If they match, a process named USERINIT.EXE is created. This process then looks in the registry and creates the system-defined shell (by default, EXPLORER.EXE). Then USERINIT exits. This is the reason

EXPLORER is shown with no parent—its parent has died, and as explained earlier, Tlist left-justifies processes whose parent is not running. (In reality, EXPLORER is the grandchild of WINLOGON.)

The identification and authentication aspects of the logon process are implemented in a replaceable DLL named *GINA* (Graphical Identification and Authentication). The standard Windows NT GINA DLL, MSGINA.DLL, implements the default Windows NT logon interface. However, developers can provide their own GINA DLL to implement other identification and authentication mechanisms in place of the standard Windows NT username/password method. In addition, WINLOGON can load additional network provider DLLs that need to perform secondary authentication. This capability allows multiple network providers to gather identification and authentication information all at one time during normal logon.

WINLOGON is active not only during user logon and logoff but also whenever it intercepts the SAS from the keyboard. For example, when you press Ctrl-Alt-Delete while logged in, the Windows NT Security dialog box comes up, providing the options to log off, start the Task Manager, lock the workstation, shut down the system, and so forth. WINLOGON is the process that handles this interaction.

Local Security Authentication Server (LSASS)

The local security authentication server process receives authentication requests from WINLOGON and calls the appropriate authentication package (implemented as a DLL) to perform the actual verification, such as checking whether a password matches what is stored in the SAM (the part of the registry that contains the definition of the users and groups).

Upon a successful authentication, LSASS generates an access token object that contains the user's security profile. WINLOGON then uses this access token to create the initial shell process. Processes launched from the shell then by default inherit this access token.

For more details about security authentication and authentication packages, check out the DDK help file LSAAUTH.HLP.

Service Controller (SERVICES)

Recall from earlier in the chapter that "services" on Windows NT can refer either to a server process or to a device driver. This section deals with services that are user-mode processes. Services are like UNIX "daemon processes" or VMS "detached processes" in that they can be configured to start automatically at system boot time without requiring an interactive logon. They can also be started manually (such as by the Control Panel Services applet or by calling the Win32 *StartService* function).

Service programs are really just Win32 images that call special Win32 functions to interact with the service controller, such as registering their successful startup, responding to status requests, or pausing or shutting down the service. For information on building services, see the technical articles as well as the sample code in MSDN Library.

A number of Windows NT components are implemented as services, such as the spooler, event log, support for RPCs, and various other networking components. You can list the installed services by running Control Panel and clicking the Services icon or by using the Windows NT Resource Kit Netsvc utility. Services are defined in the registry under HKLM\System\CurrentControlSet \Services. The Resource Kit registry Entries help file (REGENTRY.HLP) documents the subkeys and values for services.

Services are started and stopped by the service controller, a special system process running the image SERVICES.EXE that is responsible for starting, stopping, and interacting with service processes. As mentioned earlier, using the *tlist /t* command makes it easy to see which of the processes are service processes. As shown in the following code, the processes underneath SERVICES.EXE are service processes:

```
WINLOGON.EXE (34) ─────────── Logon process
    SERVICES.EXE (40) ─────── Service controller
     SPOOLSS.EXE (65) ─────── Spooler service
      RPCSS.EXE (80) ─────── RPC services
      NETDDE.EXE (194)─────── Network DDE service
```

Keep in mind that services have three names: the process name you see running on the system, the internal name in the registry, and the display name shown in Control Panel and in other utilities. (Not all services have a display name—if a service doesn't have a display name, the internal name is shown.) So, to map a service process you see running back to the actual service that is started, search the registry for the image name and you'll find the service that is defined to run that image.

There isn't always one-to-one mapping between service process and running services, however, because some services share a process with other services. In the registry, the type code indicates whether the service runs in its own process or shares a process with other services in the image. But at least you can get some idea of the services that might be running inside that process.

Conclusion

In this chapter, we've taken a broad look at the overall system architecture of Windows NT. We've examined the key components of Windows NT and seen how they interrelate. In the next chapter, we'll look in more detail at the core system mechanisms that these components are built on, such as the object manager and various synchronization objects.

CHAPTER THREE

System Mechanisms

Microsoft Windows NT provides several base mechanisms that kernel-mode components such as the executive, the kernel, and device drivers use. This chapter explains the following system mechanisms and describes how they are used:

- Trap dispatching, including interrupts, deferred procedure calls (DPCs), asynchronous procedure calls (APCs), exception dispatching, and system service dispatching

- The executive object manager (briefly introduced in Chapter 1)

- Synchronization, including spinlocks, kernel dispatcher objects, and how waits are implemented

- Miscellaneous mechanisms such as Windows NT global flags

- Local procedure calls (LPCs)

Trap Dispatching

Interrupts and exceptions are operating system conditions that divert the processor to code outside the normal flow of control. Either hardware or software can detect them. The term *trap* refers to a processor's mechanism for capturing an executing thread when an exception or an interrupt occurs, switching it from user mode into kernel mode, and transferring control to a fixed location in the operating system. In Windows NT, the processor transfers control to the kernel's *trap handler,* a module that acts as a switchboard, fielding exceptions and interrupts detected by the processor and transferring control to code that handles the condition. Figure 3-1 on the following page illustrates some of the conditions that activate the trap handler and the modules the trap handler calls to service them.

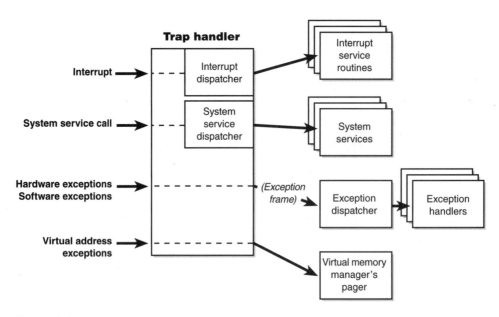

Figure 3-1

Trap dispatching

The kernel distinguishes between interrupts and exceptions in the following way. An *interrupt* is an asynchronous event (one that can occur at any time) that is unrelated to what the processor is executing. Interrupts are generated primarily by I/O devices, processor clocks, or timers, and they can be enabled (turned on) or disabled (turned off). An *exception,* in contrast, is a synchronous condition that results from the execution of a particular instruction. Running the same program with the same data under the same conditions can reproduce exceptions. Examples of exceptions include memory access violations, certain debugger instructions, and divide-by-zero errors. The kernel also regards system service calls as exceptions (although technically they're system traps).

Either hardware or software can generate exceptions and interrupts. For example, a bus error exception is caused by a hardware problem, whereas a divide-by-zero exception is the result of a software bug. Likewise, an I/O device can generate an interrupt, or the kernel itself can issue a software interrupt (such as an APC or DPC, described later in this section).

When invoked, the trap handler disables interrupts briefly while it records the machine state (information that would be wiped out if another interrupt or exception occurred). It creates a *trap frame* in which it stores the execution state of the interrupted thread. This information allows the kernel to resume execution of the thread after handling the interrupt or the exception. The trap frame is usually a subset of a thread's complete context. (Thread context is described in Chapter 4.)

The trap handler resolves some problems (such as some virtual address exceptions) itself, but in most cases, it determines the condition that occurred and transfers control to other kernel or executive modules. For example, if the condition was a device interrupt, the kernel transfers control to the *interrupt service routine* (*ISR*) that the device driver provided for the interrupting device. If the condition was caused by a call to a system service, the trap handler transfers control to the system service code in the executive. The remaining exceptions are fielded by the kernel's own exception dispatcher. The following sections describe interrupt, exception, and system service dispatching in greater detail.

Interrupt Dispatching

Hardware-generated interrupts typically originate from I/O devices that must notify the processor when they need service. Interrupt-driven devices allow the operating system to get the maximum use out of the processor by overlapping central processing with I/O operations. The processor starts an I/O transfer to or from a device and then executes other threads while the device completes the transfer. When the device is finished, it interrupts the processor for service. Pointing devices, printers, keyboards, disk drives, and network cards are generally interrupt driven.

System software can also generate interrupts. For example, the kernel can issue a software interrupt to initiate thread dispatching and to asynchronously break into the execution of a thread. The kernel can also disable interrupts so that the processor isn't interrupted, but it does so only infrequently—at critical moments while it's processing an interrupt or dispatching an exception, for example.

A submodule of the kernel's trap handler, called the *interrupt dispatcher,* responds to interrupts. It determines the source of an interrupt and transfers control either to an external routine (the ISR) that handles the interrupt or to an internal kernel routine that responds to the interrupt. Device drivers supply ISRs to service device interrupts, and the kernel provides interrupt handling routines for other types of interrupts.

In the following subsections, you'll find out about the types of interrupts the kernel supports, the way device drivers interact with the kernel (as a part of interrupt processing), and the software interrupts the kernel recognizes (plus the kernel objects that are used to implement them).

Interrupt Types and Priorities

Different processors are capable of recognizing different numbers and types of interrupts. The interrupt dispatcher maps hardware-interrupt levels onto a standard set of *interrupt request levels* (*IRQLs*) recognized by the operating system.

IRQL priority levels have a completely different meaning than thread-scheduling priorities (which are described in Chapter 4). A scheduling priority is an attribute of a thread, whereas an IRQL is an attribute of an interrupt source, such as a keyboard or a mouse. In addition, each processor has an IRQL setting that changes as operating system code executes.

The kernel defines a set of portable IRQLs, which it can augment if a processor has special interrupt-related features (a second clock, for example). These IRQL levels are not the same as interrupt requests (IRQs) on an *x86* system—the *x86* architecture doesn't implement the concept of IRQLs in hardware (Alpha does). IRQLs rank interrupts by priority. Interrupts are serviced in priority order, and a higher-priority interrupt preempts the servicing of a lower-priority interrupt. Figure 3-2 shows the mapping of the portable IRQLs to the Alpha and *x86* architectures.

The IRQLs from high level down through device level are reserved for hardware interrupts. Dispatch/DPC-level and APC-level interrupts are software interrupts that the kernel and device drivers generate. (DPCs and APCs

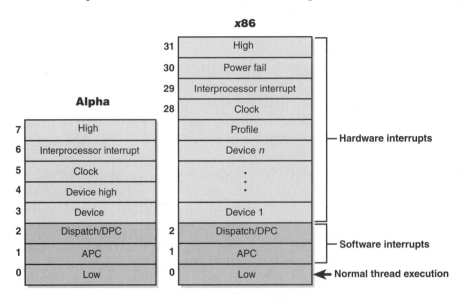

Figure 3-2
Interrupt request levels (IRQLs)

are explained in more detail later in the chapter.) The low IRQL (also called passive level) isn't really an interrupt level at all; it's the setting at which normal thread execution takes place and all interrupts are allowed to occur.

Each processor's IRQL setting determines which interrupts that processor can receive. IRQLs are also used to synchronize access to kernel-mode data structures. (You'll find out more about synchronization later in the chapter.) As a kernel-mode thread runs, it raises or lowers the processor's IRQL. As Figure 3-3 illustrates, interrupts from a source with an IRQL above the current setting interrupt the processor, whereas interrupts from sources with IRQLs equal to or below the current level are blocked, or *masked*, until an executing thread lowers the IRQL.

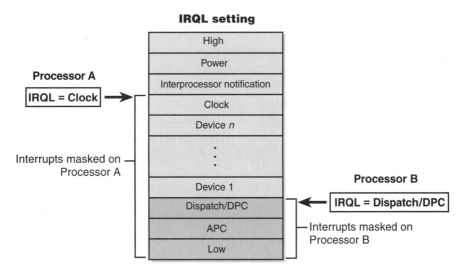

Figure 3-3
Masking interrupts

A kernel-mode thread raises and lowers the IRQL of the processor on which it is running, depending on what it's trying to do. For example, when an interrupt occurs, the trap handler (or perhaps the processor) raises the processor's IRQL to the assigned IRQL of the interrupt source. This elevation blocks all interrupts at and below that IRQL (on that processor only), which ensures that the processor servicing the interrupt is not waylaid by an interrupt at the same or a lower level. The masked interrupts are either handled by another processor or held back until the IRQL drops. Because changing a processor's IRQL has such a significant effect on system operation, the change can be made only in kernel mode—user-mode threads can't change the processor's IRQL.

Each interrupt level has a specific purpose. For example, the kernel issues an interprocessor interrupt in order to request that another processor perform an action, such as dispatching a particular thread for execution or updating its translation look-aside buffer cache. The system clock generates an interrupt at regular intervals, and the kernel responds by updating the clock and measuring thread execution time. If a hardware platform supports two clocks, the kernel adds another clock interrupt level to measure performance. The HAL provides a number of interrupt levels for use by interrupt-driven devices; the exact number varies with the processor and system configuration. The kernel uses software interrupts (described later in this chapter) to initiate thread scheduling and to asynchronously break into a thread's execution.

Interrupt Processing

When an interrupt occurs, the trap handler saves the machine's state and then calls the interrupt dispatcher with interrupts disabled. The interrupt dispatcher immediately raises the processor's IRQL to the level of the interrupt source to mask interrupts at and below that level while interrupt servicing is in progress. It then reenables interrupts so that higher-priority interrupts can still be serviced.

Windows NT uses an *interrupt dispatch table* (*IDT*) to locate the routine that will handle a particular interrupt. The IRQL of the interrupting source serves as a table index, and table entries point to the interrupt-handling routines, as shown in Figure 3-4.

On *x*86 systems, the IDT is a hardware structure pointed to by the processor control region (PCR), whereas on Alpha systems, the IDT is a software structure filled in at system initialization. The PCR and its extension the processor control block (PRCB) contain information about the state of each processor in the system. The kernel and the hardware abstraction layer (HAL) use this information to perform architecture-specific and machine-specific actions. The structures include such information as the currently running thread, the next thread selected to run, the interrupt level of the processor, and so forth. On Alpha systems, the PCR includes information on the version of the PAL-code ("Privileged Architecture Library"—the Alpha operating system–specific support code that is similar to BIOS libraries), the sizes of the various processor caches, the address of the machine check handler, and so forth. The PCR and PRCB structures are defined publicly in the Windows NT Device Driver Kit (DDK) header file ntddk.h, so you can examine that file for a complete definition of these structures.

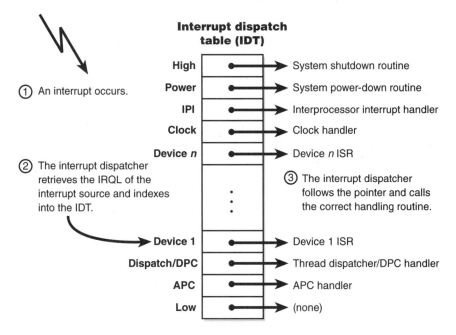

Figure 3-4
Servicing an interrupt

On *x*86 systems, external I/O interrupts actually come into one of the lines on an interrupt controller. The controller in turn interrupts the processor on a single line. Once the processor is interrupted, it queries the controller to get the interrupt vector. The processor uses this vector to index into the hardware IDT and to transfer control to the appropriate interrupt dispatch routine. Although the *x*86 architecture can support up to 256 interrupt lines, the number of lines a particular machine can support is determined by the design of the interrupt controller the machine uses. Most *x*86 PCs have interrupt controllers that use 16 interrupt lines.

On Alpha systems, when an interrupt occurs, PALcode determines the vector at which the interrupt occurred. The PALcode makes this determination in a processor-specific manner using system-specific information from the HAL. The PALcode also disables interrupts appropriately so that it can pass control to the kernel. Once the PALcode has determined the vector at which the interrupt occurred and disabled further interrupts, it calls the kernel, passing the vector. The kernel uses this vector to index into the IDT and jump to the appropriate interrupt dispatch routine.

EXPERIMENT: Viewing the Processor Control Region

You can view the contents of the PCR with the kernel debugger using the *!pcr* command. The following example is from an *x*86 system. (You won't be able to view the PRCB on an *x*86 system because the kernel debugger doesn't have a *!pcrb* command; you can, however, view the PRCB on an Alpha system.)

```
> !pcr
PCR Processor 0 @ffdff000
       NtTib.ExceptionList: 8014896c
         NtTib.StackBase: 80148c50
        NtTib.StackLimit: 80145cc0
      NtTib.SubSystemTib: 00000000
            NtTib.Version: 00000000
        NtTib.UserPointer: 00000000
           NtTib.SelfTib: 00000000

                  SelfPcr: ffdff000
                     Prcb: ffdff120
                     Irql: 0000001c
                      IRR: 00000004
                      IDR: ffff28d0
            InterruptMode: 00000000
                      IDT: 80036400
                      GDT: 80036000
                      TSS: 80264000

            CurrentThread: 80145a80
               NextThread: 00000000
               IdleThread: 80145a80
```

After the service routine executes, the interrupt dispatcher lowers the processor's IRQL to where it was before the interrupt occurred and then loads the saved machine state. The interrupted thread resumes executing where it left off. When the kernel lowers the IRQL, lower-priority interrupts that were blocked might materialize. If this happens, the kernel repeats the process to handle the new interrupt.

Each processor has a separate IDT so that different processors can run different ISRs, if appropriate. For example, in a multiprocessor system, each processor receives the clock interrupt, but only one processor updates the system clock in response to this interrupt. All the processors, however, use the interrupt to measure thread quantum and to initiate rescheduling when a thread's quantum ends. Similarly, some system configurations might require that a particular processor handle certain device interrupts.

Most of the routines that handle interrupts reside in the kernel. The kernel updates the clock time, for example, and shuts down the system when a power-level interrupt occurs. External devices such as keyboards, pointing devices, and disk drives, however, also generate many interrupts. Therefore, device drivers need a way to tell the kernel which routine to call when a device interrupt occurs.

The kernel provides a portable mechanism—a kernel control object called an *interrupt object*—that allows device drivers to register ISRs for their devices. An interrupt object contains all the information the kernel needs to associate a device ISR with a particular level of interrupt, including the address of the ISR, the IRQL at which the device interrupts, and the entry in the kernel's IDT with which the ISR should be associated. When an interrupt object is initialized, a few instructions of assembly language code, called the *dispatch code,* are stored in the object. When an interrupt occurs, this code is executed. This interrupt-object resident code calls the real interrupt dispatcher, passing it a pointer to the interrupt object. The interrupt object contains information this second dispatcher routine needs in order to locate and properly call the ISR the device driver provides. This two-step process is required because there is no way to pass a pointer to the interrupt object (or any other argument for that matter) on the initial dispatch since the initial dispatch is done by hardware.

Associating an ISR with a particular level of interrupt is called *connecting an interrupt object,* and dissociating an ISR from an IDT entry is called *disconnecting an interrupt object.* These operations, accomplished by calling a kernel function, allow a device driver to "turn on" an ISR when the driver is loaded into the system and to "turn off" the ISR if the driver is unloaded.

Using the interrupt object to register an ISR prevents device drivers from fiddling directly with interrupt hardware (which differs among processor architectures) and from needing to know any details about the IDT. This kernel feature aids in creating portable device drivers because it eliminates the need to code in assembly language or to reflect processor differences in device drivers.

Interrupt objects provide other benefits as well. By using the interrupt object, the kernel can synchronize the execution of the ISR with other parts of a device driver that might share data with the ISR. (See Chapter 7 for more information about how device drivers respond to interrupts.) Furthermore, interrupt objects allow the kernel to easily call more than one ISR for any interrupt level. If multiple device drivers create interrupt objects and connect them to the same IDT entry, the interrupt dispatcher calls each routine when an interrupt occurs at the specified interrupt line. This capability allows the kernel to easily support "daisy-chain" configurations, in which several devices interrupt on the same interrupt line.

Software Interrupts

Although hardware generates most interrupts, the Windows NT kernel also generates software interrupts for a variety of tasks, including these:

- Initiating thread dispatching

- Handling timer expiration

- Asynchronously executing a procedure in the context of a particular thread

- Supporting asynchronous I/O operations

These tasks are described in the following subsections.

Dispatch or deferred procedure call (DPC) interrupts   When a thread can no longer continue executing, perhaps because it has terminated or because it voluntarily enters a wait state, the kernel calls the dispatcher directly to effect an immediate context switch. Sometimes, however, the kernel detects that rescheduling should occur when it is deep within many layers of code. In this situation, the ideal solution is to request dispatching but defer its occurrence until the kernel completes its current activity. Using a DPC software interrupt is a convenient way to achieve this delay.

The kernel always raises the processor's IRQL to dispatch/DPC level or above when it needs to synchronize access to shared kernel structures. This disables additional software interrupts and thread dispatching. When the kernel detects that dispatching should occur, it requests a dispatch/DPC-level interrupt; but because the IRQL is at or above that level, the processor holds the interrupt in check. When the kernel completes its current activity, it lowers the IRQL below dispatch/DPC level, and the dispatch interrupt surfaces.

Activating the thread dispatcher by using a software interrupt is a way to defer dispatching until conditions are right. However, Windows NT uses software interrupts to defer other types of processing as well.

In addition to thread dispatching, the kernel also processes deferred procedure calls (DPCs) at this IRQL. A DPC is a function that performs a system task—a task that is less important than the current one. The functions are called *deferred* because they might not execute immediately.

DPCs provide the operating system with the capability to generate an interrupt and execute a system function in kernel mode. The kernel uses DPCs to process timer expiration (and release threads waiting on the timers) and to reschedule the processor after a thread's quantum expires. Device drivers use DPCs to complete I/O requests. (See Chapter 7 for more information on DPCs and the I/O system.)

A DPC is represented by a *DPC object,* a kernel control object that is not visible to user-mode programs but is visible to device drivers and other system code. The most important piece of information the DPC object contains is the address of the system function that the kernel will call when it processes the DPC interrupt. DPC routines that are waiting to execute are stored in a kernel-managed queue called the *DPC queue.* To request a DPC, system code calls the kernel to initialize a DPC object and then places it in the DPC queue.

Placing a DPC in the DPC queue prompts the kernel to request a software interrupt at dispatch/DPC level. Because DPCs are generally queued by software running at a higher IRQL, the requested interrupt doesn't surface until the kernel lowers the IRQL to APC level or low level. DPC processing is depicted in Figure 3-5.

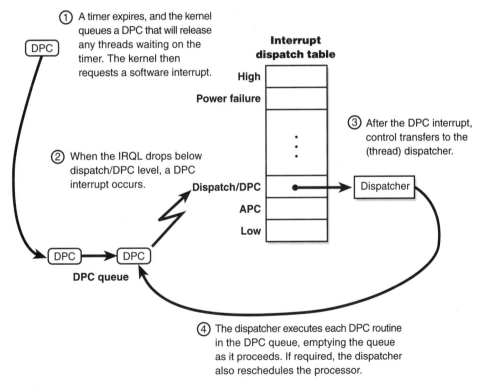

Figure 3-5
Delivering a DPC

Because user-mode threads execute at low IRQL, the chances are good that a DPC will interrupt the execution of an ordinary user's thread. DPC routines execute without regard to what thread is running, meaning that when a DPC routine runs, it can't assume what process address space is currently mapped. DPC routines can call kernel functions, but they can't call system services, generate page faults, or create or wait on objects. They can, however, access nonpaged system memory addresses, since system address space is always mapped regardless of what the current process is.

DPCs are provided primarily for device drivers, but the kernel uses them too. The kernel most frequently uses a DPC to handle quantum expiration. At every tick of the system clock, an interrupt occurs at clock IRQL. The clock interrupt handler (running at clock IRQL) updates the system time and then decrements a counter that tracks how long the current thread has run. When the counter reaches zero, the thread's time quantum has expired and the kernel might need to reschedule the processor, a lower-priority task that should be done at dispatch/DPC IRQL. The clock interrupt handler queues a DPC to initiate thread dispatching and then finishes its work and lowers the processor's IRQL. Because the DPC interrupt has a lower priority than do device interrupts, any pending device interrupts that surface are handled before the DPC interrupt occurs.

Asynchronous procedure call (APC) interrupts   Asynchronous procedure calls (APCs) provide a way for user programs and/or system code to execute code in the context of a particular user thread (and hence a particular process

EXPERIMENT: Monitoring Interrupt and DPC Activity

Using Performance Monitor, you can watch the percentage of time your system spends on handling interrupts and DPCs. The processor object and the system object both have % Interrupt Time and % DPC Time counters, which means you can monitor the activity on a per-CPU or a systemwide basis. These objects also have counters to measure the number of interrupts and DPCs per second.

One situation in which you might want to look at these counters is if your system is spending an inordinate amount of time in kernel mode and you can't attribute all the kernel-mode CPU time to processes. If total kernel-mode time is greater than the total kernel time of all processes, the remaining time has to be interrupts or DPCs, because time spent at interrupt level and DPC level is not charged to any thread or process.

address space). Because APCs are queued to execute in the context of a particular thread and run at an IRQL less than 2, they don't operate under the same restrictions as a DPC. An APC routine can acquire resources (objects), wait on object handles, incur page faults, and call system services.

Like DPCs, APCs are described by a kernel control object, called an *APC object*. APCs waiting to execute reside in a kernel-managed *APC queue*. Unlike the DPC queue, which is systemwide, the APC queue is thread-specific—each thread has its own APC queue. When asked to queue an APC, the kernel inserts it into the queue belonging to the thread that will execute the APC routine. The kernel, in turn, requests a software interrupt at APC level, and when the thread eventually begins running, it executes the APC.

There are two kinds of APCs: user mode and kernel mode. Kernel-mode APCs don't require "permission" from a target thread to run in that thread's context, as user-mode APCs do. Kernel-mode APCs interrupt a thread and execute a procedure without the thread's intervention or consent.

The executive uses kernel-mode APCs to perform operating system work that must be completed within the address space (in the context) of a particular thread. It can use kernel-mode APCs to direct a thread to stop executing an interruptible system service, for example, or to record the results of an asynchronous I/O operation in a thread's address space. Environment subsystems use kernel-mode APCs to make a thread suspend or terminate itself or to get or set its user-mode execution context. The POSIX subsystem uses kernel-mode APCs to emulate the delivery of POSIX signals to POSIX processes.

Device drivers also use kernel-mode APCs. For example, if an I/O operation is initiated and a thread goes into a wait state, another thread in another process can be scheduled to run. When the device finishes transferring data, the I/O system must somehow get back into the context of the thread that initiated the I/O so that it can copy the results of the I/O operation to the buffer in the address space of the process containing that thread. The I/O system uses a kernel-mode APC to perform this action. (The use of APCs in the I/O system is discussed in more detail in Chapter 7.)

Several Win32 APIs, such as *ReadFileEx*, *WriteFileEx*, and *QueueUserAPC*, use user-mode APCs. For example, the *ReadFileEx* and *WriteFileEx* functions allow the caller to specify a completion routine to be called when the I/O operation finishes. The I/O completion is implemented by queueing an APC to the thread that issued the I/O. However, the callback to the completion routine doesn't necessarily take place when the APC is queued, because user-mode APCs are delivered to a thread only when it's in an *alertable wait state*. A thread can enter a wait state either by waiting on an object handle and specifying that its wait is alertable (with the Win32 *WaitForMultipleObjectsEx* function) or by testing directly whether it has a pending APC (using *SleepEx*). In both cases, if a user-mode APC is pending, the kernel interrupts (alerts) the thread, transfers control to the APC routine, and resumes the thread's execution when the APC routine completes.

APC delivery can reorder the wait queues—the lists of which threads are waiting on what, and in what order they are waiting. (Wait resolution is described later in this chapter.) If the thread was in a wait state when an APC is delivered, after the APC routine completes, the wait is reissued or reexecuted. If the wait is still not resolved, the thread returns to the wait state, but now it will be at the end of the list of objects it is waiting on. For example, because APCs are used to suspend a thread from execution, if the thread was waiting on any objects, its wait will be removed until the thread is resumed, after which it will be at the end of the list for the objects it was waiting on. For further details on the queue wait order, see the Win32 Software Development Kit (SDK) Knowledge Base article Q125657 "Mutex Wait Is FIFO But Can Be Interrupted" (which you can find at *http://support.microsoft.com/support/* or on the MSDN Library CD-ROMs).

Exception Dispatching

In contrast to interrupts, which can occur at any time, exceptions are conditions that result directly from the execution of the program that is running. Win32 introduced a facility known as *structured exception handling*, which allows applications to gain control when exceptions occur. The application can then either fix the condition and return to the place the exception occurred, unwind the stack (thus terminating execution of the subroutine that raised the exception), or declare back to the system that the exception isn't recognized, and to continue searching for an exception handler that might process the exception. This section assumes you're familiar with the basic concepts behind Win32 structured exception handling—if you're not, you should read the overview in the Win32 API reference documentation on the Platform SDK or Chapter 16 in Jeffrey Richter's book *Advanced Windows* (third edition, Microsoft Press, 1997) before proceeding. Keep in mind that although exception handling is made accessible through language extensions (for example, the __try construct in Microsoft Visual C++), it is a system mechanism and hence is not language-specific. Other examples of consumers of Windows NT exception handling include C++ and Java exceptions.

All exceptions, except those simple enough to be resolved by the trap handler, are serviced by a kernel module called the *exception dispatcher*. The exception dispatcher's job is to find an exception handler that can "dispose of" the exception. Examples of architecture-independent exceptions that the kernel defines include memory access violations, integer divide-by-zero, integer overflow, floating-point exceptions, and debugger breakpoints. For a complete list of architecture-independent exceptions, consult the Win32 API reference documentation.

The kernel traps and handles some of these exceptions transparently to user programs. For example, encountering a debugger breakpoint while executing a program being debugged generates an exception, which the kernel handles by calling the debugger. The kernel handles certain other exceptions by returning an unsuccessful status code to the caller.

A few exceptions are allowed to filter back, untouched, to user mode. For example, a memory access violation or an arithmetic overflow generates an exception that the operating system doesn't handle. An environment subsystem can establish *frame-based exception handlers* to deal with these exceptions. The term *frame-based* refers to an exception handler's association with a particular procedure activation. When a procedure is invoked, a stack frame representing that activation of the procedure is pushed onto the stack. A stack frame can have one or more exception handlers associated with it, each of which protects a particular block of code in the source program. When an exception occurs, the kernel searches for an exception handler associated with the current stack frame. If none exists, the kernel searches for an exception handler associated with the previous stack frame, and so on, until it finds a frame-based exception handler. If no exception handler is found, the kernel calls its own default exception handlers.

When an exception occurs, whether it is explicitly raised by software or implicitly raised by hardware, a chain of events begins in the kernel. The CPU hardware transfers control to the kernel trap handler, which creates a trap frame (as it does when an interrupt occurs). The trap frame will allow the system to resume where it left off if the exception is resolved. The trap handler also creates an exception record that contains the reason for the exception and other pertinent information.

If the exception occurred in kernel mode, the exception dispatcher simply calls a routine to locate a frame-based exception handler that will handle the exception. Because unhandled kernel-mode exceptions are considered fatal operating system errors, you can assume that the dispatcher always finds an exception handler.

If the exception occurred in user mode, the exception dispatcher does something more elaborate. As you'll see in Chapter 4, the Win32 subsystem has a debugger port and an exception port to receive notification of user-mode exceptions in Win32 processes. The kernel uses these in its default exception handling, as illustrated in Figure 3-6.

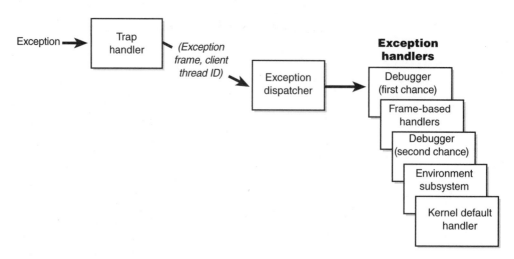

Figure 3-6
Dispatching an exception

Debugger breakpoints are common sources of exceptions. Therefore, the first action the exception dispatcher takes is to see whether the process that incurred the exception has an associated debugger process. If so, it sends the first-chance debug message (via an LPC port) to the debugger port associated with the process that incurred the exception. (The message is sent to the session manager process, which then dispatches it to the appropriate debugger process.)

If the process has no debugger process attached, or if the debugger doesn't handle the exception, the exception dispatcher switches into user mode and calls a routine to find a frame-based exception handler. If none is found, or if none handles the exception, the exception dispatcher switches back into kernel mode and calls the debugger again to allow the user to do more debugging. (This is called the second-chance notification.)

All Win32 threads have an exception handler declared at the top of the stack that processes unhandled exceptions. This exception handler is declared in the internal Win32 *start-of-process* or *start-of-thread* function. The start-of-process function runs when the first thread in a process begins execution. It calls the main entry point in the image. The start-of-thread function runs when a user creates additional threads. It calls the user-supplied thread start routine specified in the *CreateThread* call.

EXPERIMENT: Viewing the Real
User Start Address for Win32 Threads

The fact that each Win32 thread begins execution in a system-supplied function (and not the user-supplied function) explains why the start address for thread 0 is the same for every Win32 process in the system (and why the start addresses for secondary threads are also the same). The start address for thread 0 in Win32 processes is the Win32 start-of-process function; the start address for any other threads would be the Win32 start-of-thread function. To see the user-supplied function address, use the Tlist utility in the Windows NT Resource Kit. Type *Tlist process-name* or *Tlist process-id* to get the detailed process output that includes this information. For example, compare the thread start addresses for the Windows NT Explorer process as reported by Pstat and Tlist:

```
C:\> pstat
.
.
.
pid: 96 pri: 8 Hnd:   63 Pf:    7573 Ws:    1796K explorer.exe
 tid pri Ctx Swtch StrtAddr    User Time  Kernel Time  State
  95  14     21525 77f052cc  0:00:09.373  0:00:45.745  Wait:UserRequest
  56  14       988 77f052c0  0:00:00.020  0:00:00.140  Wait:UserRequest
  3e  14       108 77f052c0  0:00:00.010  0:00:00.010  Wait:LpcReceive
  b3   8      2397 77f052c0  0:00:01.992  0:00:04.496  Wait:UserRequest
.
.
.
C:\> tlist explorer
 150 explorer.exe       Program Manager
   CWD:       C:\WINNT\Profiles\Administrator\Desktop\
   CmdLine: Explorer.exe
   VirtualSize:    25348 KB   PeakVirtualSize:    31052 KB
   WorkingSetSize:  1804 KB   PeakWorkingSetSize:  3276 KB
   NumberOfThreads: 4
    149 Win32StartAddr:0x01009dbd LastErr:0x0000007e State:Waiting
     86 Win32StartAddr:0x77c5d4a5 LastErr:0x00000000 State:Waiting
     62 Win32StartAddr:0x00000977 LastErr:0x00000000 State:Waiting
    179 Win32StartAddr:0x0100d8d4 LastErr:0x00000002 State:Waiting
.
.
.
```

The start address of thread 0 reported by Pstat is the internal Win32 start-of-process function; the start addresses for threads 1 through 3 are the internal Win32 start-of-thread functions. Tlist, on the other hand, shows the user-supplied Win32 start address (the user function called by the internal Win32 start function).

The generic code for these internal start functions is shown here:

```
void Win32StartOfProcess(
    LPTHREAD_START_ROUTINE lpStartAddr,
    LPVOID lpvThreadParm){
    __try {
        DWORD dwThreadExitCode = lpStartAddr(lpvThreadParm);
        ExitThread(dwThreadExitCode);
    } __except(UnhandledExceptionFilter(
    GetExceptionInformation())) {
        ExitProcess(GetExceptionCode());
    }
}
```

Notice that the Win32 unhandled exception filter is called if the thread has an exception that it doesn't handle. This function looks in the registry in the HKLM\Software\Microsoft\Windows NT\CurrentVersion\AeDebug key to determine whether to run a debugger immediately or to ask the user first. The default "debugger" on Windows NT is DRWTSN32.EXE (Dr. Watson), which isn't really a debugger but rather a postmortem tool that captures the state of the application "crash" and records it in a log file. If you have a compiler such as Visual C++ installed, the debugger that is to be run is changed to MSDEV.EXE so you can debug programs that incur unhandled exceptions.

If the debugger isn't running and no frame-based handlers are found, the kernel sends a message to the exception port associated with the thread's process. This exception port, if one exists, was registered by the environment subsystem that controls this thread. The exception port gives the environment subsystem, which presumably is listening at the port, the opportunity to translate the exception into an environment-specific signal or exception. For example, when POSIX gets a message from the kernel that one of its threads generated an exception, the POSIX subsystem sends a POSIX-style signal to the thread that caused the exception. However, if the kernel progresses this far in processing the exception and the subsystem doesn't handle the exception, the kernel executes a default exception handler that simply terminates the process whose thread caused the exception.

EXPERIMENT: Viewing Exception Activity

You can monitor the exception-dispatching rate on your system with Performance Monitor. Enter chart view, press Ctrl-I to add a counter to the chart, select the System object, select the Exception Dispatches/Sec counter, and then click the Add button to add the counter to the chart.

System Service Dispatching

As Figure 3-1 illustrated, the kernel's trap handler dispatches interrupts, exceptions, and system service calls. In the preceding sections, you saw how interrupt and exception handling work; in this section, you'll learn about system services. A system service dispatch is triggered as a result of executing a *syscall* instruction on Alpha processors or an *int 2E* on Intel *x86* processors. Both of these instructions cause a system trap, which causes the executing thread to transition into kernel mode and enter the system service dispatcher. A numeric argument indicates the system service number being requested. As Figure 3-7 illustrates, the kernel uses this argument to locate the system service information in the *system service dispatch table*. This table is similar to the interrupt dispatch table described earlier in the chapter except that each entry contains a pointer to a system service rather than to an interrupt handling routine.

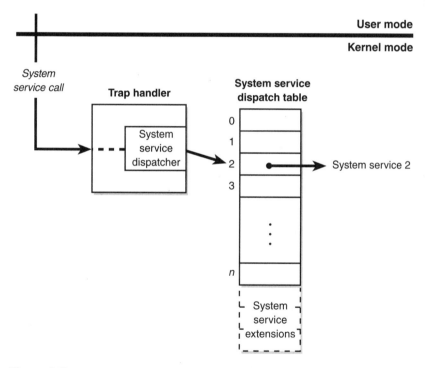

Figure 3-7
System service exceptions

The system service dispatcher verifies the correct minimum number of arguments and copies the caller's arguments from the thread's user-mode stack to its kernel-mode stack (so that the user can't change the arguments willy-nilly) and then executes the system service. If the arguments passed to a system service point to buffers in user space, these buffers must be probed for accessibility before kernel-mode code can copy data to or from them.

As you'll see in Chapter 4, each thread has a pointer to its system service table. Windows NT has two built-in system service tables (though more can be supported). The primary default table defines the core executive system services implemented in NTOSKRNL.EXE. The other table includes the Win32 USER and GDI services implemented in the kernel-mode part of the Win32 subsystem, WIN32K.SYS. The first time a Win32 thread calls a Win32 USER or GDI service, the address of the thread's system service table is changed to point to a table that includes the Win32 USER and GDI services.

The system service dispatch instructions for Windows NT executive services exist in the system library NTDLL.DLL. Subsystem DLLs call functions in NTDLL to implement their documented functions. The exception is Win32 USER and GDI functions, in which the system service dispatch instructions are implemented directly in USER32.DLL and GDI32.DLL—there is no NTDLL-.DLL in the middle. These two cases are shown in Figure 3-8.

As shown in Figure 3-8, the Win32 *WriteFile* function in KERNEL32.DLL calls the *NtWriteFile* function in NTDLL.DLL, which in turn executes the appropriate instruction to cause a system service trap, passing the system service number representing *NtWriteFile*. The system service dispatcher (function *KiSystemService* in NTOSKRNL.EXE) then calls the real *NtWriteFile* to process the I/O request. For Win32 USER and GDI functions, the system service dispatch calls functions in the loadable kernel-mode part of the Win32 subsystem, WIN32K.SYS.

EXPERIMENT: Viewing System Service Activity

You can monitor system service activity by watching the System Calls/ Sec performance counter in the System object. Run Performance Monitor, and in chart view, press Ctrl-I to add a counter to the chart; select the System object, select the System Calls/Sec counter, and then click the Add button to add the counter to the chart.

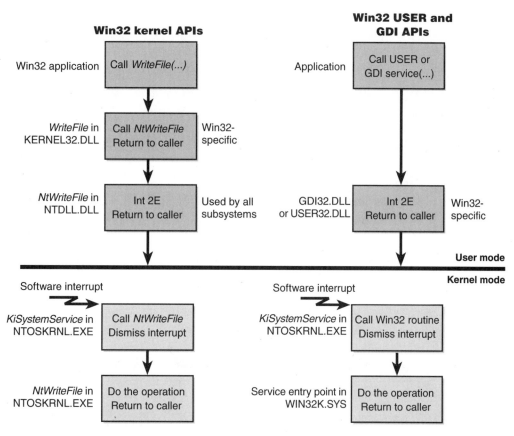

Figure 3-8
System service dispatching

Object Manager

As mentioned in Chapter 2, Windows NT implements an object model to provide consistent and secure access to the varied internal services implemented in the executive. This section describes the Windows NT *object manager,* the executive component responsible for creating, deleting, protecting, and tracking objects. The object manager centralizes resource control operations that otherwise would be scattered throughout the operating system. It was designed to meet the goals listed on page 103.

EXPERIMENT: Exploring the Object Manager

Throughout this section, you'll find experiments that show you how to peer into the object manager database. These experiments make use of the following tools, which you should become familiar with if you aren't already:

- Object viewer (Platform SDK, in \MSSDK\BIN\WINNT\ WINOBJ.EXE)

- Open handles (Windows NT Resource Kit, in \NTRESKIT\ OH.EXE) (This utility was added to the Windows NT Server Resource Kit Supplement Two. You won't find it in earlier editions of the Windows NT Server Resource Kit.)

- Kernel debugger *!handle* and *!object* commands

The object viewer provides a way to traverse the namespace that the object manager maintains. (As I'll explain later, not all objects have names.) Try running this utility and examining the layout as shown here:

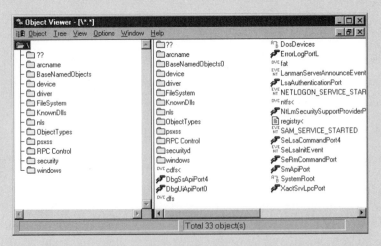

In the Windows NT Resource Kit tools help for OH, you'll find out that you must enable object tracking—an internal debugging feature in the executive—to run this utility. To enable object tracking, set one of the Windows NT global flags and reboot your system. (See page 135 for more on global flags.) If you run OH and the flag isn't on, the utility will set the flag in the registry and tell you to reboot. Because this flag uses additional memory to track object usage information, you should disable it with the Gflags utility after you've experimented with OH and then reboot your system again.

An object viewer utility named Winobj is also available; you can find it at *www.ntinternals.com.* Although not shown in the examples that follow, Winobj displays more information about objects (such as the reference count, the number of open handles, security descriptors, and so forth) than the object viewer in the Platform SDK does.

The object manager was designed to meet these goals:

- Provide a common, uniform mechanism for using system resources

- Isolate object protection to one location in the operating system so that C2 security compliance can be achieved

- Provide a mechanism to charge processes for their use of objects so that limits can be placed on the usage of system resources

- Establish an object-naming scheme that can readily incorporate existing objects, such as the devices, files, and directories of a file system, or other independent collections of objects

- Support the requirements of various operating system environments, such as the ability of a process to inherit resources from a parent process (needed by Win32 and POSIX) and the ability to create case-sensitive filenames (needed by POSIX)

- Establish uniform rules for object retention (that is, keeping an object available until all processes have finished using it)

Internally, Windows NT has two kinds of objects: *executive objects* and *kernel objects.* Executive objects are objects implemented by various components of the executive (such as the process manager, memory manager, I/O subsystem, and so on). Kernel objects are a more primitive set of objects implemented by the Windows NT kernel. These objects are not visible to user-mode code but are created and used only within the executive. Kernel objects provide fundamental capabilities, such as synchronization, on which executive objects are built. Thus, many executive objects contain (encapsulate) one or more kernel objects, as shown in Figure 3-9.

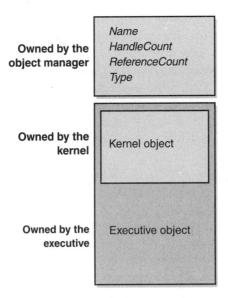

Figure 3-9
Executive objects that contain kernel objects

Details about the structure of kernel objects and how they are used to implement synchronization are given later in this chapter. In the remainder of this section, we'll focus on how the object manager works and on the structure of executive objects, handles, and handle tables. And although I'll describe only briefly here how objects are involved in implementing Windows NT security access checking, I'll cover this topic thoroughly in Chapter 6.

Executive Objects

Each Windows NT environment subsystem projects to its applications a different image of the operating system. The executive objects and object services are primitives that the environment subsystems use to construct their own versions of objects and other resources.

Executive objects are typically created either by an environment subsystem on behalf of a user application or by various components of the operating system as part of their normal operation. For example, to create a file, a Win32 application calls the Win32 *CreateFile* function, implemented in the Win32 subsystem DLL KERNEL32.DLL. After some validation and initialization, *CreateFile* in turn calls the native Windows NT service *NtCreateFile* to create an executive file object.

The set of objects an environment subsystem supplies to its applications might be larger or smaller than that the executive provides. The Win32 subsystem uses executive objects to export its own set of objects, many of which correspond directly to executive objects. For example, the Win32 mutexes and semaphores are directly based on executive objects (which are in turn based on corresponding kernel objects). In addition, the Win32 subsystem supplies named pipes and mailslots, resources that are based on executive file objects. Some subsystems, such as POSIX, don't support objects as objects at all. The POSIX subsystem uses executive objects and services as the basis for presenting POSIX-style processes, pipes, and other resources to its applications.

Table 3-1 lists the primary objects the executive provides and briefly describes what they represent. You can find further details on executive objects in the chapters that describe the related executive components (or in the case of executive objects directly exported to Win32, in the Win32 API reference documentation).

Table 3-1 **Executive Objects**

Object Type	Represents
Object directory	A container object for other objects. The object directory is used to implement the hierarchical namespace within which other object types are stored.
Symbolic link	A mechanism for referring to an object name indirectly.
Process	The virtual address space and control information necessary for the execution of a set of thread objects.
Thread	An executable entity within a process.
Section	A region of shared memory (called a file mapping object in Win32).
File	An instance of an opened file or an I/O device.
Port	A mechanism to pass messages between processes.
Access token	The security profile (security ID, user rights, and so on) of a process or a thread.
Event	An object with a persistent state (signaled or not signaled) that can be used for synchronization or notification.
Semaphore	A counter that provides a resource gate by allowing some maximum number of threads to access the resources protected by the semaphore.
Mutant*	A synchronization mechanism used to serialize access to a resource.
Timer	A mechanism to notify a thread when a fixed period of time elapses.

* Externally in the Win32 API, mutants are called *mutexes*. References to mutexes from here on refer to the kernel mutant object.

(continued)

Table 3-1 *continued*

Object Type	Represents
Queue	A method for threads to enqueue and dequeue notifications of the completion of I/O operations (called an I/O completion port in the Win32 API).
Key	A mechanism to refer to data in the registry. Although keys appear in the object manager namespace, they are managed by the registry, in a way similar to that in which file objects are managed. Zero or more key values are associated with a key object; key values contain data about the key.
Profile	A mechanism for measuring execution time for a process within an address range.

Object Structure

As shown in Figure 3-10, each object has an object header and an object body. The object manager controls the object header, and the owning executive components control the object bodies of the object types they create. In addition, each object header points to the list of processes that have the object open and a special object called the *type object* that contains information common to each instance of the object.

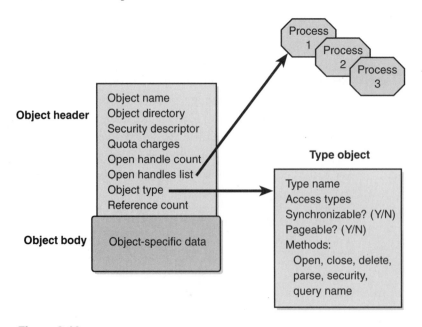

Figure 3-10
Structure of an object

Object Headers

The object manager uses the data stored in an object's header to manage objects without regard to their type. Table 3-2 briefly describes the object header attributes.

Table 3-2 **Standard Object Header Attributes**

Attribute	Purpose
Object name	Makes an object visible to other processes for sharing
Object directory	Provides a hierarchical structure in which to store object names
Security descriptor	Determines who can use the object and what they can do with it
Quota charges	Lists the resource charges levied against a process when it opens a handle to the object
Open handle count	Counts the number of times a handle has been opened to the object
Open handles list	List of the processes that have opened handles to the object
Object type	Points to a type object that contains attributes common to objects of this type
Reference count	Counts the number of times a kernel-mode component has referenced the address of the object

In addition to an object header, each object has an object body whose format and contents are unique to its object type; all objects of the same type share the same object body format. By creating an object type and supplying services for it, an executive component can control the manipulation of data in all object bodies of that type.

The object manager provides a small set of generic services that operate on the attributes stored in an object's header and can be used on objects of any type (although some generic services don't make sense for certain objects). These generic services, some of which the Win32 subsystem makes available to Win32 applications, are listed in Table 3-3 on the following page.

Although these generic object services are supported for all object types, each object has its own create, open, and query services. For example, the I/O system implements a create file service for its file objects, and the process manager implements a create process service for its process objects. Although a single create object service could have been implemented, such a routine would have been quite complicated, because the set of parameters required to initialize a file object, for example, differs markedly from that required to initialize a process object. Also, the object manager would have incurred additional processing overhead each time a thread called an object service to

Table 3-3 Generic Object Services

Service	Purpose
Close	Closes a handle to an object
Duplicate	Shares an object by duplicating a handle and giving it to another process
Query object	Gets information about an object's standard attributes
Query security	Gets an object's security descriptor
Set security	Changes the protection on an object
Wait for a single object	Synchronizes a thread's execution with one object
Wait for multiple objects	Synchronizes a thread's execution with multiple objects

determine the type of object the handle referred to and to call the appropriate version of the service. For these reasons and others, the create, open, and query services are implemented separately for each object type.

Type Objects

Object headers contain data that is common to all objects but that can take on different values for each instance of an object. For example, each object has a unique name and can have a unique security descriptor. However, objects also contain some data that remains constant for all objects of a particular type. For example, you can select from a set of access rights specific to a type of object when you open a handle to objects of a particular type. The executive supplies terminate and suspend access (among others) for thread objects and read, write, append, and delete access (among others) for file objects. Another example of an object-type-specific attribute is synchronization, the ability of a thread to wait for objects of a particular type to be set to the signaled state, described shortly.

To conserve memory, the object manager stores these static, object-type-specific attributes once when creating a new object type. It uses an object of its own, a type object, to record this data. As Figure 3-11 illustrates, a type object also links together all objects of the same type, allowing the object manager to find and enumerate them, if necessary.

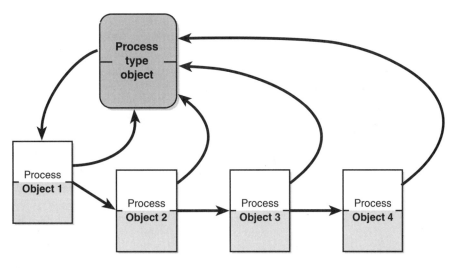

Figure 3-11
Process objects and the process type object

EXPERIMENT: Viewing the Type Objects

You can see the list of type objects declared to the object manager with the Object Viewer utility in the Platform SDK. Run \MSSDK\BIN\ WINNT\WINOBJ.EXE, and click on the \ObjectTypes directory, as shown here:

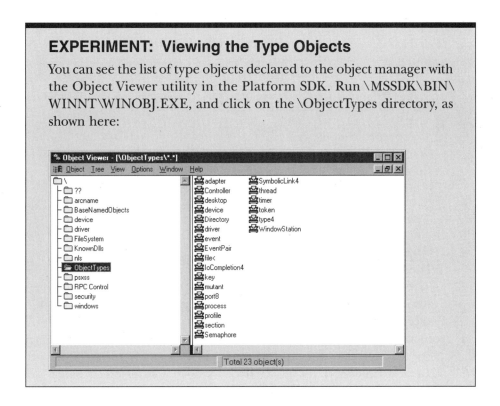

Type objects can't be manipulated from user mode because the object manager supplies no services for them. However, some of the attributes they define are visible through certain native services and through Win32 API routines. The attributes stored in the bodies of type objects are described in Table 3-4.

Table 3-4   Type Object Attributes

Attribute	Purpose
Object type name	The name for objects of this type ("process," "event," "port," and so on)
Pool type	Whether objects of this type should be allocated from paged or nonpaged memory
Default quota charges	Default paged and nonpaged pool values to charge to process quotas
Access types	The types of access a thread can request when opening a handle to an object of this type ("read," "write," "terminate," "suspend," and so on)
Generic access rights mapping	A mapping between the four generic access rights (read, write, execute, and all) to the type-specific access rights
Synchronization	Whether a thread can wait on objects of this type
Methods	One or more routines that the object manager calls automatically at certain points in an object's lifetime

Synchronization, one of the attributes visible to Win32 applications, refers to a thread's ability to synchronize its execution by waiting for an object to change from one state to another. A thread can synchronize with executive process, thread, file, event, semaphore, mutex, and timer objects. Section, port, access token, object directory, symbolic-link, profile, and key objects don't support synchronization.

Object Methods

The last attribute in Table 3-4, methods, comprises a set of internal routines that are similar to C++ constructors and destructors, that is, routines that are automatically called when an object is created or destroyed. The object manager extends this idea by calling an object method in other situations as well, such as when someone opens or closes a handle to an object or when someone attempts to change the protection on an object. Some object types specify methods, whereas others don't, depending on how the object type is to be used.

When an executive component creates a new object type, it can register one or more methods with the object manager. Thereafter, the object manager calls the methods at well-defined points in the lifetime of objects of that type, usually when an object is created, deleted, or modified in some way. The methods that the object manager supports are listed in Table 3-5.

Table 3-5 Object Methods

Method	When Method Is Called
Open	When an object handle is opened
Close	When an object handle is closed
Delete	Before the object manager deletes an object
Query name	When a thread requests the name of an object, such as a file, that exists in a secondary object domain
Parse	When the object manager is searching for an object name that exists in a secondary object domain
Security	When a process reads or changes the protection of an object, such as a file, that exists in a secondary object domain

An example of the use of a close method occurs in the I/O system. The I/O manager registers a close method for the file object type, and the object manager calls the close method each time it closes a file object handle. This close method checks whether the process that is closing the file handle owns any outstanding locks on the file and, if so, removes them. Checking for file locks is not something that the object manager itself could or should do.

The object manager calls a delete method, if one is registered, before it deletes a temporary object from memory. The memory manager, for example, registers a delete method for the section object type that frees the physical pages being used by the section. It also verifies that any internal data structures the memory manager has allocated for a section are deleted before the section object is deleted. Once again, this is work the object manager can't do because it knows nothing about the internal workings of the memory manager. Delete methods for other types of objects perform similar functions.

The parse method (and similarly, the query name method) allows the object manager to relinquish control of finding an object to a secondary object manager if it finds an object that exists outside the object manager namespace. When the object manager looks up an object name, it suspends its search when it encounters an object in the path that has an associated parse method. The object manager calls the parse method, passing to it the remainder of the object name it is looking for.

For example, when a process opens a handle to the object named \Device-\Floppy0\docs\resume.doc, the object manager traverses its name tree until it reaches the device object named Floppy0. It sees that a parse method is associated with this object, and it calls the method, passing to it the rest of the object name it was searching for—in this case, the string \docs\resume.doc. The parse method for device objects is an I/O routine. The routine takes the name string and passes it to the appropriate file system, which finds the file on the disk and opens it.

The security method, which is used by the I/O system, is similar to the parse method. It is called whenever a thread tries to change the security information protecting a file. This information is different for files than for other objects because security information is stored in the file itself rather than in memory. The I/O system, therefore, must be called in order to find the security information and change it.

Object Handles and the Process Handle Table

When a process creates or opens an object by name, it receives a *handle* that represents its access to the object. Referring to an object by its handle is faster than using its name because the object manager can skip the name lookup and find the object directly. Processes can also acquire handles to objects by inheriting handles at process creation time (if the creator specifies the inherit handle flag on the *CreateProcess* call and the handle was marked as inheritable, either at the time it was created or afterwards by using the Win32 *SetHandleInformation* function) or by receiving a duplicated handle from another process. (See the Win32 *DuplicateHandle* function.)

All user-mode processes must own a handle to an object before their threads can use the object. Using handles to manipulate system resources is not a new idea. C and Pascal (and other language) run-time libraries, for example, return handles to opened files. Handles serve as indirect pointers to system resources; this indirection keeps application programs from fiddling directly with system data structures.

NOTE Executive components and device drivers can access objects directly, since they are running in kernel mode and therefore have access to the object structures in system memory. However, they must declare their usage of the object by incrementing either the open handle count or the reference count so that the object will not be deallocated while it's still being used. (See the description of object retention later in this section.)

Object handles provide additional benefits. First, except for what they refer to, there is no difference between a file handle, an event handle, and a process handle. This similarity provides a consistent interface to reference objects, regardless of their type. Second, the object manager has the exclusive right to create handles and to locate an object that a handle refers to. This means that the object manager can scrutinize every user-mode action that affects an object to see whether the security profile of the caller allows the operation requested on the object in question.

EXPERIMENT: Viewing Open Handles with OH

As shown in the following example, the OH tool in the Windows NT Server Resource Kit (supplement 2 or later) can display the handles open by any or all processes. (Remember that OH requires enabling an internal option to track object information.)

```
C:\>oh /?
Usage: OH [-p n] [-t typeName] [-a] [name]
where: -p n -
 displays only open handles for process with ClientId of n
      -t typeName -
 displays only open object names of specified type.
         -a includes objects with no name.
         name - displays only handles that contain the specified name.


C:\>oh -a
   2 System          Process        0004
   2 System          Key            0008 \REGISTRY
   2 System          Key            000c
      \REGISTRY\Machine\Hardware\Description\System\PCMCIA PCCARDs
   2 System          File           0010 \WINNT\system32\config\system
   2 System          Port           0014 \SeRmCommandPort
   2 System          Key            0018 \REGISTRY\Machine\System\Setup
   2 System          Directory      001c \Device\Harddisk0
   2 System          Thread         0020
```

The display above shows the first eight open handles in the System process. The process ID appears first, followed by the process image name (except that the System process, as explained in Chapter 1, doesn't have an image), object type, handle value, and object name. Because we specified the -a flag, handles to objects that don't have names (handle numbers 0x4, 0x1c, and 0x20) are included.

An object handle is an index into a process-specific *handle table,* pointed to by the executive process (EPROCESS) block (described in Chapter 4). The first handle index is 4, the second 8, and so on. A process's handle table contains pointers to all the objects that the process has opened a handle to. It consists of a fixed header and a variable size portion. The variable size part is an array of handle table entries, each describing one open handle. If a process opens more handles than can fit in the variable portion, the system allocates a new, larger array and copies the old array into the new one.

 NOTE In Windows NT 5.0, the handle table is implemented as a three-level tree that can expand without requiring the recopying of the existing handle table.

As shown in Figure 3-12, each handle entry consists of a structure with two 32-bit members. The first 32-bit member contains both a pointer to the object header and three flags. (Because object headers are always 32-bit aligned, the low-order 3 bits of this field are free for use as flags.) The second member is the granted access mask for that object. (Access masks are described in Chapter 6.)

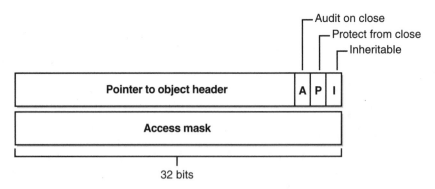

Figure 3-12
Structure of a handle table entry

The first flag is the *inheritance designation*—that is, whether processes created by this process will get a copy of the handle in their handle tables. As already noted, handle inheritance can be specified on handle creation or later with the *SetHandleInformation* function. The second flag indicates whether the caller is allowed to close this handle. (This flag can also be specified with the Win32 *SetHandleInformation* function.) The third flag indicates whether closing the object should generate an audit message. (This flag is not exposed to Win32—it is used internally by the object manager.)

EXPERIMENT: Viewing the Handle Table with the Kernel Debugger

The *!handle* command in the kernel debugger takes three arguments:

```
!handle <handle index> <flags> <processid>
```

The handle index identifies the handle entry in the handle table. (Zero means display all handles.) The first handle is index 4, the second 8, and so on. For example, typing *!handle 4* will show the first handle for the current process.

The flags you can specify are a bitmask, where bit 0 means display only the information in the handle entry, bit 1 means display free handles (not just used handles), and bit 2 means displays information about the object that the handle refers to. The following command displays full details about the handle table for process ID 0xaa:

```
> !handle 0 7 aa
processor number 0
Searching for Process with Cid == aa
PROCESS 8053f670  Cid: 00aa    Peb: 7ffdf000  ParentCid: 005b
    DirBase: 01549000  ObjectTable: 80699a88  TableSize: 30.
    Image: CMD.EXE

Handle Table at 80699a88 with 30. Entries at e1ab3410 -
 FIFO Order
0004: Object: e19be540  GrantedAccess: 000f001f
Object: e19be540  Type: (80691bc0) Section
    ObjectHeader: e19be528
        HandleCount: 1  PointerCount: 1

0008: Object: 80570310  GrantedAccess: 00100003
Object: 80570310  Type: (80694160) Event
    ObjectHeader: 805702f8
        HandleCount: 1  PointerCount: 1
```

Object Security

When you open a file, you must specify whether you intend to read or to write. If you try to write to a file that is opened for read access, you get an error. Likewise, in the executive, when a process creates an object or opens a handle to an existing object, the process must specify a set of *desired access rights*—that is, what it wants to do with the object. It can request either a set of standard access rights (such as read, write, and execute) that apply to all object types or specific access rights that vary depending on the object type. For example, the process can request delete access or append access to a file object. Similarly, it might require the ability to suspend or terminate a thread object.

When a process opens a handle to an object, the object manager calls the *security reference monitor,* the kernel-mode portion of the security system, sending it the process's set of desired access rights. The security reference monitor checks whether the object's *security descriptor* permits the type of access the process is requesting. If so, the reference monitor returns a set of *granted access rights* that the process is allowed, and the object manager stores them in the object handle it creates. How the security system determines who gets access to which objects is explored in Chapter 6.

Thereafter, whenever the process's threads use the handle, the object manager can quickly check whether the set of granted access rights stored in the handle corresponds to the usage implied by the object service the threads have called. For example, if the caller asked for read access to a section object but then calls a service to write to it, the service fails.

Object Retention

Because all user-mode processes that access an object must first open a handle to it, the object manager can easily track how many of these processes, and even which ones, are using an object. Tracking these handles represents one part in implementing *object retention*—that is, retaining temporary objects only as long as they are in use and then deleting them.

The object manager implements object retention in two phases. The first phase is called *name retention,* and it is controlled by the number of open handles that exist to an object. Every time a process opens a handle to an object, the object manager increments the open handle counter in the object's header. As processes finish using the object and close their handles to it, the object manager decrements the open handle counter. When the counter drops to zero, the object manager deletes the object's name from its global namespace. This deletion prevents new processes from opening a handle to the object.

The second phase of object retention is to stop retaining objects (that is, to delete them) when they are no longer in use. Because operating system code usually accesses objects by using pointers instead of handles, the object manager must also record how many object pointers it has dispensed to operating system processes. It increments a *reference count* for an object each time it gives out a pointer to the object; when kernel-mode components finish using the pointer, they call the object manager to decrement the object's reference count. (For further details on object retention, see the DDK documentation on the functions *ObReferenceObjectByPointer* and *ObDereferenceObject.*)

Figure 3-13 illustrates two event objects that are in use. Process A has the first event open. Process B has both events open. In addition, the first event is being referenced by some kernel-mode structure; thus the reference count is 1. So even if process A and B closed their handles to the first event object, it would remain because its reference count is 1. However, when process B closes its handle to the second event object, the object would be deallocated.

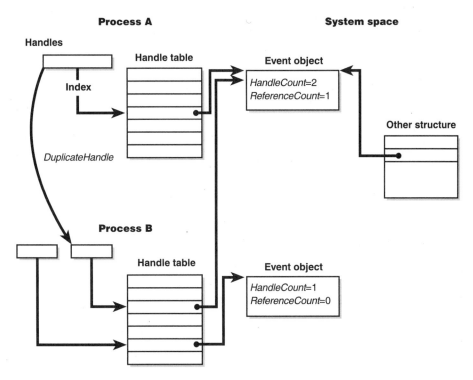

Figure 3-13
Handles and reference counts

So even after an object's open handle counter reaches 0, the object's reference count might remain positive, indicating that the operating system is still using the object. Ultimately, the reference count also drops to 0. When this happens, the object manager deletes the object from memory.

Because of the way object retention works, an application can ensure that an object and its name remain in memory simply by keeping a handle open to the object. Programmers who write applications that contain two or more cooperating processes need not be concerned that one process might delete an object before the other process has finished using it. In addition, closing an application's object handles will not cause an object to be deleted if the operating system is still using it. For example, one process might create a second process to execute a program in the background; it then immediately closes its handle to the process. Because the operating system needs the second process to run the program, it maintains a reference to its process object. Only when the background program finishes executing does the object manager decrement the second process's reference count and then delete it.

Resource Accounting

Resource accounting, like object retention, is closely related to the use of object handles. A positive open handle count indicates that some process is using that resource. It also indicates that some process is being charged for the memory the object occupies. When an object's handle count drops to 0, the process that was using the object should no longer be charged for it.

Many operating systems use a quota system to limit processes' access to system resources. However, the types of quotas imposed on processes are sometimes diverse and complicated, and the code to track the quotas is spread throughout the operating system. For example, in some operating systems, an I/O component might record and limit the number of files a process can open, whereas a memory component might impose a limit on the amount of memory a process's threads can allocate. A process component might limit a user to some maximum number of new processes he or she can create or a maximum number of threads within a process. Each of these limits is tracked and enforced in different parts of the operating system.

In contrast, the Windows NT object manager provides a central facility for resource accounting. Each object header contains an attribute called *quota charges* that records how much the object manager subtracts from a process's allotted paged and/or nonpaged pool quota when a thread in the process opens a handle to the object.

 N O T E Windows NT 5.0 adds significant new capabilities in the areas of quotas. A new object, called a *job,* will allow the grouping of processes together that then share a set of quotas. These quotas will include per-process and per-job user-mode CPU time, minimum and maximum working set size, and number of active processes. It will also allow limiting access to windows outside the job and the clipboard as well as security characteristics. For more information on how quotas will change in Windows NT 5.0, see Chapter 10.

Each process on Windows NT points to a quota structure that records the limits and current values for nonpaged pool, paged pool, and page file usage. However, all the processes in your interactive session share the same quota block (there is no documented way to create processes with their own quota blocks), and system processes, such as services, have no quota limits.

The quotas start at 512 KB for paged pool and 64 KB for nonpaged pool. The limits are "soft," however, in that the system attempts to increase process quotas automatically when they are exceeded. If opening an object will exceed the paged or nonpaged quota, the memory manager is called to see whether the quotas can be increased. The memory manager makes this decision on the basis of the amount of memory remaining in the system pools. If it determines that the quota can't be increased, the open request to the object fails with a "quota exceeded" error. But on most systems, quotas continue to grow as needed.

EXPERIMENT: Viewing Process Quotas

You can view the paged pool, nonpaged pool, and page file current usage, peak usage, and quota (limit) for a process with the Windows NT Resource Kit Process Explode utility, PVIEW.EXE. (Performance Monitor displays only the usage information, not the quotas.) In the following example, the process selected has a peak paged pool usage of 1536 KB, current usage of 1332 KB, and a quota of 1836 KB:

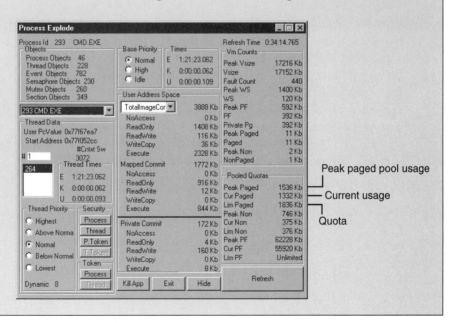

Object Names

An important consideration in creating a multitude of objects is devising a successful system for keeping track of them. The object manager requires the following to help you do so:

- A way to distinguish one object from another
- A method for finding and retrieving a particular object

The first requirement is served by allowing names to be assigned to objects. This is an extension of what most operating systems provide—the ability to name selected resources, files, pipes, or a block of shared memory, for example. The executive, in contrast, allows any resource represented by an object to have a name. The second requirement, finding and retrieving an object, is also satisfied by object names. If the object manager stores objects by name, it can find an object by looking up its name.

Object names also satisfy a third requirement, allowing processes to share objects. The executive's object namespace is a global one, visible to all processes in the system. One process can create an object and place its name in the global namespace, and a second process can open a handle to the object by specifying the object's name. If an object is not meant to be shared in this way, its creator doesn't need to give it a name.

To increase efficiency, the object manager doesn't look up an object's name each time someone uses the object. Instead, it looks up a name under only two circumstances. The first is when a process creates a named object: the object manager looks up the name to verify that it doesn't already exist before storing the new name in the global namespace. The second is when a process opens a handle to a named object: the object manager looks up the name, finds the object, and then returns an object handle to the caller; thereafter, the caller uses the handle to refer to the object. When looking up a name, the object manager allows the caller to select either a case-sensitive or a case-insensitive search, a feature that supports POSIX and other environments that use case-sensitive filenames.

Where the names of objects are stored depends on the object type. Table 3-6 lists the standard object directories found on all Windows NT systems and what types of objects have their names stored there. Of the directories listed, only \BaseNamedObjects and \?? are visible to user programs.

Table 3-6 Standard Object Directories

Directory	Types of Object Names Stored
\??	MS-DOS device names (\DosDevices is a symbolic link to this directory.)
\BaseNamedObjects	Mutexes, events, semaphores, waitable timers, and section objects
\device	Device objects
\driver	Driver objects
\FileSystem	File system driver objects and file system recognizer device objects
\KnownDlls	Section names and path for known DLLs (DLLs mapped by the system at startup time)
\nls	Section names for mapped national language support tables
\ObjectTypes	Names of types of objects
\RPC Control	Port objects used by remote procedure calls (RPCs)
\security	Names of objects specific to the security subsystem
\windows	Win32 subsystem ports and window stations

Because the base kernel objects such as mutexes, events, semaphores, waitable timers, and sections have their names stored in a single object directory, no two of these objects can have the same name, even if they are of a different type. This restriction emphasizes the need to choose names carefully so that they don't collide with other names (for example, prefix names with your company and product name).

Object names are global to a single computer (or to all processors on a multiprocessor computer), but they're not visible across a network. The object manager does, however, supply a hook—called a *parse method*—for accessing named objects that exist on other computers. For example, the I/O manager, which supplies file object services, extends the functions of the object manager to remote files. When asked to open a remote file object, the object manager calls a parse method, which allows the I/O manager to intercept the request and deliver it to a network redirector, a driver that accesses files across the network. Server code on the remote Windows system calls the object manager and the I/O manager on that system to find the file object and return the information back across the network.

EXPERIMENT: Looking at the Base Named Objects

You can see the list of base objects that have names with the Object Viewer utility in the Platform SDK. Run \MSSDK\BIN\WINNT\WIN-OBJ.EXE, and click on \BaseNamedObjects, as shown here:

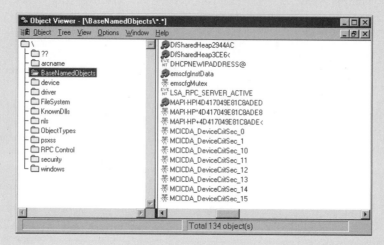

The named objects are shown on the right. The icons indicate the object type. (Waitable timers aren't shown.)

- Mutexes are indicated with a strange-looking bug, because, as I explained earlier, the kernel object that implements mutexes is called a *mutant*. (I'll leave it up to your imagination to decide whether or not this bug resembles a mutant.)

- Sections (Win32 file mapping objects) are shown as a section (slice) of a pie.

- Events don't have an icon—the word "event" is spelled out (but broken into two lines).

- Semaphores are indicated with an icon that resembles a train signal or semaphore.

Object directories The *object directory object* is the object manager's means for supporting this hierarchical naming structure. This object is analogous to a file system directory and contains the names of other objects, possibly even other object directories. The object directory object maintains enough information to translate these object names into pointers to the objects themselves.

The object manager uses the pointers to construct the object handles that it returns to user-mode callers. Both kernel-mode code and user-mode code (such as subsystems) can create object directories in which to store objects. For example, the I/O manager creates an object directory named \Device, which contains the names of objects representing I/O devices.

Symbolic links   In certain file systems (on some UNIX systems, for example), a symbolic link lets a user create a filename or a directory name that, when used, is translated by the operating system into a different file or directory name. Using a symbolic link is a simple method for allowing users to indirectly share a file or the contents of a directory, creating a cross-link between different directories in the ordinarily hierarchical directory structure.

The object manager implements an object called a *symbolic link object,* which performs a similar function for object names in its object namespace. A symbolic link can occur anywhere within an object name string. When a caller refers to a symbolic link object's name, the object manager traverses its object namespace until it reaches the symbolic link object. It looks inside the symbolic link and finds a string that it substitutes for the symbolic link name. It then restarts its name lookup.

One place in which the executive uses symbolic link objects is in translating MS-DOS-style device names into Windows NT internal device names. In MS-DOS, a user refers to floppy and hard disk drives using the names A:, B:, C:, and so on. Moreover, the user can add pseudo drive names with the *subst* (substitute) command or by mapping a drive letter to a network share. Once they are created, these drive names must be visible to all processes on the system.

The Win32 subsystem makes drive letters protected, global data by placing them in the object manager namespace under the \?? object directory. (Prior to Windows NT 4.0, this directory was named \DosDevices; it was renamed \?? for performance reasons, since that name places it first alphabetically.) When the user or an application creates a new drive letter, the Win32 subsystem adds another object under the \?? object directory.

Synchronization

The concept of *mutual exclusion* is a crucial one in operating systems development. It refers to the guarantee that one, and only one, thread can access a particular resource at a time. Mutual exclusion is necessary when a resource doesn't lend itself to shared access or when sharing would result in an unpredictable outcome. For example, if two threads copy a file to a printer port at the same time, their output could be interspersed. Similarly, if one thread reads a memory location while another one writes to it, the first thread will receive unpredictable data. In general, writable resources can't be shared without restrictions, whereas resources that aren't subject to modification can be shared. Figure 3-14 illustrates what happens when two threads running on different processors both write data to a circular queue.

Because the second thread got the value of the queue tail pointer before the first thread had updated it, the second thread inserted its data into the same location that the first thread had used, overwriting data and leaving one queue location empty. Even though this figure illustrates what could happen on a multiprocessor system, the same error could occur on a single-processor system if the operating system were to perform a context switch to the second thread before the first thread updated the queue tail pointer.

Sections of code that access a nonshareable resource are called *critical sections*. To ensure correct code, only one thread at a time can execute in a critical section. While one thread is writing to a file, updating a database, or modifying a shared variable, no other thread can be allowed to access the same resource. The code shown in Figure 3-14 is a critical section that incorrectly accesses a shared data structure without mutual exclusion.

The issue of mutual exclusion, although important for all operating systems, is especially important (and intricate) for a *tightly coupled, symmetric multiprocessing (SMP)* operating system such as Windows NT, in which the same

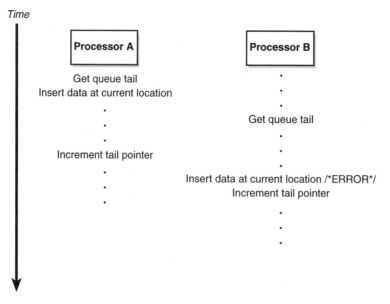

Figure 3-14
Incorrect sharing of memory

system code runs simultaneously on more than one processor, sharing certain data structures stored in global memory. In Windows NT, it is the kernel's job to provide mechanisms that system code can use to prevent two threads from modifying the same structure at the same time. The kernel provides mutual-exclusion primitives that it and the rest of the executive use to synchronize their access to global data structures.

In the following sections, you'll find out how the kernel uses mutual exclusion to protect its global data structures and what mutual-exclusion and synchronization mechanisms the kernel provides to the executive that it, in turn, provides to user mode.

Kernel Synchronization

At various stages during its execution, the kernel must guarantee that one, and only one, processor at a time is executing within a critical section. Kernel critical sections are the code segments that modify a global data structure such as the kernel's dispatcher database or its DPC queue. The operating system can't function correctly unless the kernel can guarantee that threads access these data structures in a mutually exclusive manner.

The biggest area for concern is interrupts. For example, the kernel might be updating a global data structure when an interrupt occurs whose interrupt-handling routine also modifies the structure. Simple single-processor operating systems sometimes prevent such a scenario by disabling all interrupts each time they access global data, but the Windows NT kernel has a more sophisticated solution. Before using a global resource, the kernel temporarily masks those interrupts whose interrupt handlers also use the resource. It does so by raising the processor's IRQL to the highest level used by any potential interrupt source that accesses the global data. For example, an interrupt at dispatch/DPC level causes the dispatcher, which uses the dispatcher database, to run. Therefore, any other part of the kernel that uses the dispatcher database raises the IRQL to dispatch/DPC level, masking dispatch/DPC-level interrupts before using the dispatcher database.

This strategy is fine for a single-processor system, but it's inadequate for a multiprocessor configuration. Raising the IRQL on one processor doesn't prevent an interrupt from occurring on another processor. The kernel also needs to guarantee mutually exclusive access across several processors.

The mechanism the kernel uses to achieve multiprocessor mutual exclusion is called a *spinlock*. A spinlock is a locking mechanism associated with a global data structure, such as the DPC queue shown in Figure 3-15.

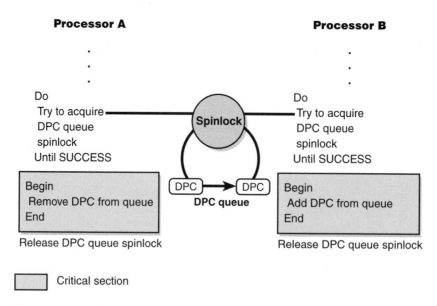

Processor A

Do
  Try to acquire
  DPC queue
  spinlock
  Until SUCCESS

Begin
  Remove DPC from queue
End

Release DPC queue spinlock

Spinlock

DPC → DPC
DPC queue

Processor B

Do
  Try to acquire
  DPC queue
  spinlock
  Until SUCCESS

Begin
  Add DPC from queue
End

Release DPC queue spinlock

☐ Critical section

Figure 3-15
Using a spinlock

Before entering either critical section shown in the figure, the kernel must acquire the spinlock associated with the protected DPC queue. If the spinlock isn't free, the kernel keeps trying to acquire the lock until it succeeds. The spinlock gets its name from the fact that the kernel (and thus, the processor) is held in limbo, "spinning," until it gets the lock.

Spinlocks, like the data structures they protect, reside in global memory. The code to acquire and release a spinlock is written in assembly language for speed and to exploit whatever locking mechanism the underlying processor architecture provides. (For example, on Intel processors, Windows NT uses an instruction that exists only on 486 processors or better; this is one of the reasons that Windows NT doesn't run on Intel 386 platforms anymore.) On many architectures, spinlocks are implemented with a hardware-supported test-and-set operation, which tests the value of a lock variable and acquires the lock in one atomic instruction. Testing and acquiring the lock in one instruction prevents a second thread from grabbing the lock between the time when the first thread tests the variable and the time when it acquires the lock.

When a thread is trying to acquire a spinlock, all other activity ceases on that processor. Therefore, a thread that holds a spinlock is never preempted but is allowed to continue executing so that it will release the lock quickly. The kernel uses spinlocks with great care, minimizing the number of instructions it executes while it holds a spinlock.

The kernel makes spinlocks available to other parts of the executive through a set of kernel functions. Device drivers, for example, require spinlocks in order to guarantee that device registers and other global data structures are accessed by only one part of a device driver (and from only one processor) at a time. Spinlocks are not for use by user programs—user programs should use the objects described in the next section.

Executive Synchronization

Executive software outside the kernel also needs to synchronize access to global data structures in a multiprocessor environment. For example, the memory manager has only one page frame database, which it accesses as a global data structure, and device drivers need to ensure that they can gain exclusive access to their devices. By calling kernel functions, the executive can create a spinlock, acquire it, and release it.

Spinlocks only partially fill the executive's needs for synchronization mechanisms, however. Because waiting on a spinlock literally stalls a processor, spinlocks can be used only under the following strictly limited circumstances:

■ The protected resource must be accessed quickly and without complicated interactions with other code.

■ The critical section code can't be paged out of memory, can't make references to pageable data, can't call external procedures (including system services), and can't generate interrupts or exceptions.

These restrictions are confining and can't be met under all circumstances. Furthermore, the executive needs to perform other types of synchronization in addition to mutual exclusion, and it must also provide synchronization mechanisms to user mode.

The kernel furnishes additional synchronization mechanisms to the executive in the form of kernel objects, known collectively as *dispatcher objects*. The user-visible synchronization objects acquire their synchronization capabilities from kernel dispatcher objects. Each user-visible object that supports synchronization encapsulates at least one kernel dispatcher object. The executive's synchronization semantics are visible to Win32 programmers through the *WaitForSingleObject* and *WaitForMultipleObjects* functions, which the Win32 subsystem implements by calling analogous system services supplied by the object manager. A thread in a Win32 application can synchronize with a Win32 process, thread, event, semaphore, mutex, waitable timer, I/O completion port, or file object.

One other type of executive synchronization object worth noting is called *executive resources*. Executive resources provide both exclusive access (like a mutex) as well as shared read access (multiple readers sharing read-only access to a structure). However, they're available only to kernel-mode code and thus are not accessible from the Win32 API. Resources are not dispatcher objects, but rather data structures allocated directly from nonpaged pool that have their own specialized services to initialize, lock, release, query, and wait on them. The executive resource structure is defined in NTDDK.H, and the executive support routines are documented in the DDK reference documentation.

The remaining subsections describe the implementation details of waiting on dispatcher objects.

Waiting on Dispatcher Objects

A thread can synchronize with a dispatcher object by waiting on the object's handle. Doing so causes the kernel to suspend the thread and change its dispatcher state from running to waiting, as shown in Figure 3-16. The kernel removes the thread from the dispatcher ready queue and no longer considers it for execution.

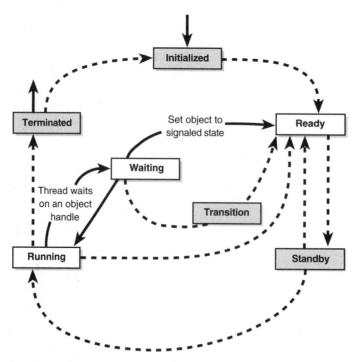

Figure 3-16
Waiting on a dispatcher object

At any given moment, a synchronization object is in one of two states: either the *signaled state* or the *nonsignaled state.* A thread can't resume its execution until the kernel changes its dispatcher state from waiting to ready. This change occurs when the dispatcher object whose handle the thread is waiting on also undergoes a state change, from the nonsignaled state to the signaled state (when a thread sets an event object, for example). To synchronize with an object, a thread calls one of the wait system services supplied by the object manager, passing a handle to the object it wants to synchronize with. The thread can wait on one or several objects and can also specify that its wait should be canceled if it hasn't ended within a certain amount of time. Whenever the kernel sets an object to the signaled state, it checks to see whether any threads are waiting on the object. If they are, the kernel releases one or more of the threads from their waiting state so that they can continue executing.

The following example of setting an event illustrates how synchronization interacts with thread dispatching:

1. A user-mode thread waits on an event object's handle.

2. The kernel changes the thread's scheduling state from ready to waiting and then adds the thread to a list of threads waiting for the event.

3. Another thread sets the event.

4. The kernel marches down the list of threads waiting on the event. If a thread's conditions for waiting are satisfied,* the kernel changes the thread's state from waiting to ready. If it is a variable-priority thread, the kernel might also boost its execution priority.

5. Because a new thread has become ready to execute, the dispatcher reschedules. If it finds a running thread with a priority lower than that of the newly ready thread, it preempts the lower-priority thread and issues a software interrupt to initiate a context switch to the higher-priority thread.

6. If no processor can be preempted, the dispatcher places the ready thread in the dispatcher ready queue to be scheduled later.

---

* Some threads might be waiting for more than one object, so they continue waiting.

What Signals an Object

The signaled state is defined differently for different objects. A thread object is in the nonsignaled state during its lifetime and is set to the signaled state by the kernel when the thread terminates. Similarly, the kernel sets a process object to the signaled state when the process's last thread terminates. In contrast, the timer object, like an alarm, is set to "go off" at a certain time. When its time expires, the kernel sets the timer object to the signaled state.

When choosing a synchronization mechanism, a program must take into account the rules governing the behavior of different synchronization objects. Whether a thread's wait ends when an object is set to the signaled state varies with the type of object the thread is waiting on, as Table 3-7 illustrates.

Table 3-7 Definitions of the Signaled State

Object Type	Set to Signaled State When	Effect on Waiting Threads
Process	Last thread terminates	All released
Thread	Thread terminates	All released
File	I/O operation completes	All released
Event (notification type)	Thread sets the event	All released
Event (synchronization type)	Thread sets the event	One thread released; event object reset
Semaphore	Semaphore count drops to 0	All released
Timer	Set time arrives or time interval expires	All released
Mutex	Thread releases the mutex	One thread released

When an object is set to the signaled state, waiting threads are generally released from their wait states immediately. Some of the kernel dispatcher objects and the system events that induce their state changes are shown in Figure 3-17.

For example, a notification event object (called a manual reset event in the Win32 API) is used to announce the occurrence of some event. When the event object is set to the signaled state, all threads waiting on the event are released. The exception is any thread that is waiting on more than one object at a time; such a thread might be required to continue waiting until additional objects reach the signaled state.

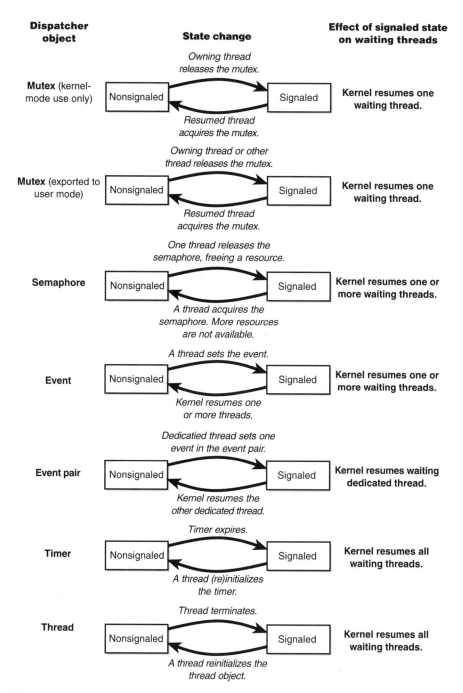

Figure 3-17
Selected kernel dispatcher objects

In contrast to an event object, a mutex object has ownership associated with it. It is used to gain mutually exclusive access to a resource, and only one thread at a time can hold the mutex. When the mutex object becomes free, the kernel sets it to the signaled state and then selects one waiting thread to execute. The thread selected by the kernel acquires the mutex object, and all other threads continue waiting.

This brief discussion was not meant to enumerate all the reasons and applications for using the various executive objects, but rather to list their basic functionality and synchronization behavior. For information on how to put these objects to use in Win32 programs, see the Win32 reference documentation on synchronization objects or Richter's *Advanced Windows*.

Data Structures

Two data structures are key to tracking who is waiting on what: *dispatcher headers* and *wait blocks*. Both of these structures are publicly defined in the DDK include file ntddk.h. The definitions are reproduced here for convenience:

```
typedef struct _DISPATCHER_HEADER {
    UCHAR Type;
    UCHAR Absolute;
    UCHAR Size;
    UCHAR Inserted;
    LONG SignalState;
    LIST_ENTRY WaitListHead;
} DISPATCHER_HEADER;

typedef struct _KWAIT_BLOCK {
    LIST_ENTRY WaitListEntry;
    struct _KTHREAD *RESTRICTED_POINTER Thread;
    PVOID Object;
    struct _KWAIT_BLOCK *RESTRICTED_POINTER NextWaitBlock;
    USHORT WaitKey;
    USHORT WaitType;
} KWAIT_BLOCK, *PKWAIT_BLOCK, *RESTRICTED_POINTER PRKWAIT_BLOCK;
```

The dispatcher header contains the object type, signaled state, and a list of the threads waiting on that object. The wait block represents a thread waiting on an object. Each thread that is in a wait state has a list of the wait blocks that represent the object(s) the thread is waiting on. Each dispatcher object has a list of the wait blocks that represent which threads are waiting on the object. This list is kept so that when a dispatcher object is signaled, the kernel can quickly determine who is waiting on that object. The wait block has a pointer to the object being waited on, a pointer to the thread waiting on the object, and a pointer to the next wait block (if the thread is waiting on more than one object). It also records the type of wait (any or all) as well as the position of that entry in the array of handles passed by the thread on the *WaitForMultipleObjects* call (zero if the thread was waiting on only one object).

Figure 3-18 shows the relationship of dispatcher objects to wait blocks to threads. In this example, thread 1 is waiting on object B, and thread 2 is waiting on objects A and B. If object A is signaled, the kernel will see that because thread 2 is also waiting on another object, it can't be readied for execution. On the other hand, if object B is signaled, the kernel can ready thread 1 for execution right away since it isn't waiting on any other objects.

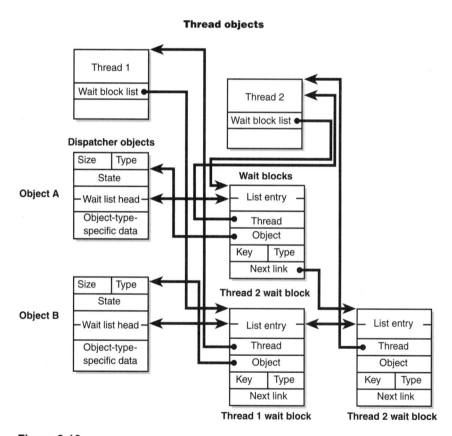

Figure 3-18
Wait data structures

EXPERIMENT: Looking at Wait Queues

Although many process viewer utilities indicate whether a thread is in a wait state (and if so, what kind of wait), you can see the list of objects a thread is waiting on only with the kernel debugger *!thread* command. For example, the following excerpt from the output of a *!process* command shows that the thread is waiting on an event object:

```
> !process
    .
    .
    .
THREAD 80618030  Cid 97.7f  Teb: 7ffde000  Win32Thread: e199cea8
WAIT: (WrUserRequest) UserMode Non-Alertable
        805b4ab0  SynchronizationEvent
```

Although the kernel debugger doesn't have a command for formatting the contents of a dispatcher header, we know the layout (described on page 132), so we can interpret its contents manually:

```
> dd 805b4ab0
0x805B4AB0  00040001 00000000 8061809c 8061809c ..........a...a.
```

From this, we can ascertain that no other threads are waiting on this event object, because the wait list head forward and backward pointers (the third and fourth 32-bit values) point to the same location (a single wait block). Dumping the wait block (at address 0x8061809c) yields the following:

```
> dd 8061809c
0x8061809C  805b4ab8 805b4ab8 80618030 805b4ab0 .J[..J[.0.a..J[.
0x806180AC  8061809c 00010000 00000000 00000000 ..a............
```

The first two 32-bit values point to the list head of the wait blocks in the dispatcher header. The third 32-bit value is the pointer to the thread object. The fourth value points to the dispatcher object itself. The fifth value (0x8061809c) is the pointer to the next wait block. From this, we can conclude that the thread is not waiting on any other objects, since the next wait block field points to the wait block itself.

Windows NT Global Flags

Windows NT has a set of flags stored in a systemwide global variable named *NtGlobalFlag* that enable various internal debugging, tracing, and validation support in the operating system. The system variable *NtGlobalFlag* is initialized from the registry key HKLM\System\CurrentControlSet\Control\Session Manager\GlobalFlag at system boot time. By default, this registry value is 0, so it's likely that on your systems, you're not using any global flags. In addition, each image has a set of *global flags* that also turns on internal tracing and validation code (though the bit layout of these flags is entirely different than the systemwide global flags). Although the use of these flags is not documented or supported for customer use, they can be a useful tool for exploring the internal operation of Windows NT.

Fortunately, the Windows NT Resource Kit (supplement 2 or later) contains a utility named GFLAGS.EXE that allows you to view and change the system global flags (either in the registry or in the running system) as well as image global flags. Gflags has both a command-line and a GUI interface. To see the command-line flags, type *GFLAGS /?*. If you run the utility without any switches, the dialog box shown in Figure 3-19 is displayed.

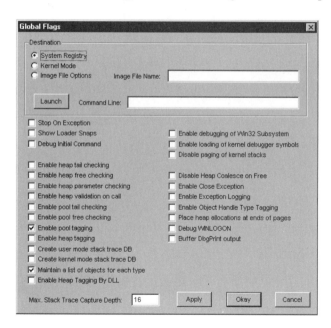

Figure 3-19

Setting system debugging options with Gflags

You can toggle between the settings in the registry (by clicking System Registry) and the current value of the variable in system memory (by clicking Kernel Mode). You must press the Apply button to make the changes. (You'll exit if you press the Okay button.) Although you can change flag settings on the running system, most flags require a reboot to take effect, and there is no documentation on which do and which don't require rebooting. So when in doubt, reboot after changing a global flag.

The Image File Options choice requires that you fill in the filename of a valid executable image. This option is used to change another set of global flags that apply to an individual image (rather than to the whole system). In Figure 3-20, notice that the flags are different than the operating system ones shown in Figure 3-19.

Figure 3-20
Setting image global flags with Gflags

EXPERIMENT: Enabling Image Loader Tracing

To see an example of the detailed tracing information you can obtain by setting global flags, try running GFLAGS on a system booted with the kernel debugger that is connected to a host system running KD or WINDBG.

As an example, try enabling the Show Loader Snaps flag. To do this, select Kernel Mode, click the Show Loader Snaps check box, and click the Apply button. Then run an image on this machine, and in the kernel debugger you'll see volumes of output like the following:

```
LDR: PID: 0xb8 started - 'notepad'
LDR: NEW PROCESS
     Image Path: C:\WINNT\system32\notepad.exe (notepad.exe)
     Current Directory: C:\ddk\bin
     Search Path: C:\WINNT\System32;C:\WINNT\system;C:\WINNT
LDR: notepad.exe bound to comdlg32.dll
LDR: ntdll.dll used by comdlg32.dll
LDR: Snapping imports for comdlg32.dll from ntdll.dll
        :
        :
LDR: KERNEL32.dll loaded. - Calling init routine at 77f01000
LDR: RPCRT4.dll loaded. - Calling init routine at 77e1b6d5
LDR: ADVAPI32.dll loaded. - Calling init routine at 77dc1000
LDR: USER32.dll loaded. - Calling init routine at 77e78037
```

Local Procedure Calls (LPCs)

A local procedure call (LPC) is an interprocess communication facility for high-speed message passing. It is not available through the Win32 API; it is an internal mechanism available only to Windows NT operating system components. Here are some examples of where LPCs are used:

- Remote procedure calls use LPCs to communicate between processes on the same system.

- A few Win32 APIs result in sending messages to the Win32 subsystem process.

- WinLogon uses LPC to communicate with the local security authentication server process, LSASS.

- The security reference monitor (an executive component explained in Chapter 6) uses LPC to communicate with the LSASS process.

EXPERIMENT: Viewing LPC Port Objects

You can see named LPC port objects with the Object Viewer utility in the Platform SDK. Run \mssdk\bin\winobj, and select the root directory. A plug icon identifies the port objects, as shown here:

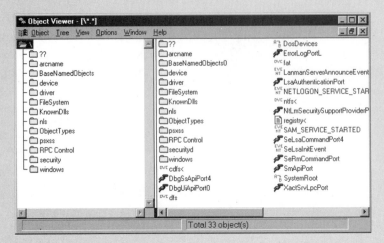

To see the LPC port objects used by RPC, select the \RPC Control directory, as shown here:

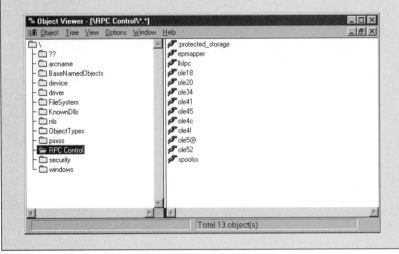

Typically, LPCs are used between a server process and one or more client processes of that server. An LPC connection can be established between two user-mode processes or between a kernel-mode component and a user-mode process. For example, as noted in Chapter 2, Win32 processes send occasional messages to the Win32 subsystem by using LPC. Also, some system processes use LPC to communicate, such as WinLogon and LSASS. An example of a kernel-mode component using LPC to talk to a user process is the communication between the security reference monitor and the LSASS process.

LPC is designed to allow three methods of exchanging messages:

- A message that is shorter than 256 bytes can be sent by calling LPC with a buffer containing the message. This message is then copied from the address space of the sending process into system address space, and from there to the address space of the receiving process.

- If a client and a server want to exchange more than 256 bytes of data, they can choose to use a shared section to which both are mapped. The sender places message data in the shared section and then sends a small message to the receiver with pointers to where the data is to be found in the shared section.

- When a server wants to read or write larger amounts of data than will fit in a shared section, data can be directly read from or written to a client's address space. The LPC component supplies two functions that a server can use to accomplish this. A message sent by the first method is used to synchronize the message passing.

LPC exports a single executive object called the *port object* to maintain the state needed for communication. Although LPC uses a single object type, it has several kinds of ports:

- **Server connection port**   A named port that is a server connection request point. Clients can connect to the server by connecting to this port.

- **Server communication port**   An unnamed port a server uses to communicate with a particular client. The server has one such port per active client.

- **Client communication port**   An unnamed port a particular client thread uses to communicate with a particular server.

- **Unnamed communication port**   An unnamed port created for use by two threads in the same process.

LPC is typically used as follows: A server creates a named server connection port object. A client makes a connect request to this port. If the request is granted, two new unnamed ports, a client communication port and a server communication port, are created. The client gets a handle to the client communication port, and the server gets a handle to the server communication port. The client and the server will then use these new ports for their communication.

A completed connection between a client and a server is shown in Figure 3-21.

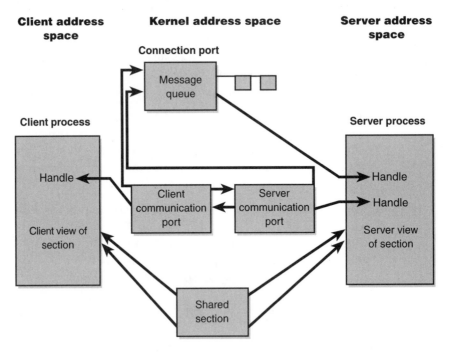

Figure 3-21
Use of LPC ports

Conclusion

In this chapter, we've examined the key base system mechanisms on which the Windows NT executive is built. With this foundation laid, we're ready to explore the individual executive components in more detail, starting with processes and threads.

Processes and Threads

This chapter explains the data structures and algorithms that deal with processes and threads in Microsoft Windows NT 4.0. The first section focuses on the internal structures that make up a process. In the second section, the steps involved in creating a process (and its initial thread) are outlined. Then comes the section on thread internals. The chapter concludes with a description of the thread-scheduling algorithms.

Where there are relevant performance counters or system variables, these are mentioned. Although this book is not a Microsoft Win32 programming book, the process-related and thread-related Win32 functions are listed so that you can pursue additional information on their use.

Because processes and threads touch so many components in Windows NT, a number of terms and data structures (such as working sets, objects and handles, the system memory heaps, and so on) are referred to in this chapter but are explained in detail elsewhere in the book. To fully understand this chapter, you need to be familiar with the terms and concepts explained in Chapter 1 and Chapter 2, such as the difference between a process and a thread, the Windows NT virtual address space layout, the difference between user mode and kernel mode, and the role of key system components such as the executive, kernel, and hardware abstraction layer (HAL).

Process Internals

This section describes the key Windows NT process data structures. Also listed are key system variables, performance counters, and functions and tools that relate to processes.

Data Structures

Each Windows NT process is represented by an executive process (EPROCESS) block. Besides containing many attributes about a process, an EPROCESS block contains and points to a number of other related data structures. For example, each process has one or more threads, represented by executive thread (ETHREAD) blocks. (Thread data structures are explained in the section "Thread Internals" on page 171) The EPROCESS block and its related data structures exist in system space, with the exception of the process environment block (PEB), which exists in the process address space (since it contains information that is modified by user-mode code).

In addition to the EPROCESS block, the Win32 subsystem process (CSRSS) maintains a parallel structure for each Windows NT process that executes a Win32 program. Also, the kernel-mode part of the Win32 subsystem (WIN32K.SYS) has a per-process data structure that is created the first time a thread calls a Win32 USER or GDI function that is implemented in kernel mode.

Figure 4-1 is a simplified diagram of the process and thread data structures. Each data structure shown in the figure is described in detail in this chapter.

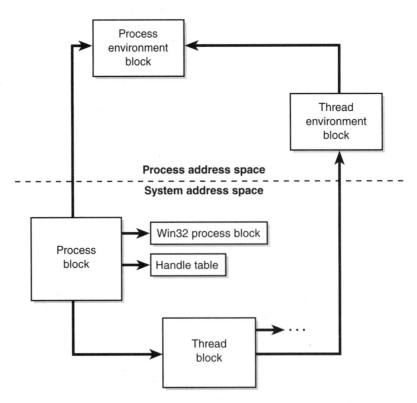

Figure 4-1
Data structures associated with processes and threads

First let's focus on the process block. (We'll get to the thread block in the section "Thread Internals" later in the chapter.) Figure 4-2 shows the key fields in an EPROCESS block.

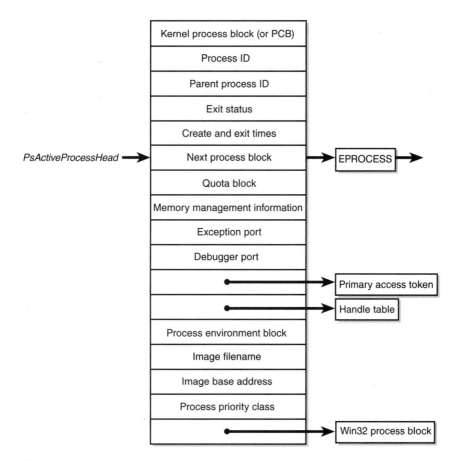

Figure 4-2
Structure of an executive process block

EXPERIMENT: Displaying the Format of an EPROCESS Block

For a list of most of the fields that make up an EPROCESS block and their offsets in hexadecimal, type *!processfields* in the kernel debugger. (To learn how to set up and use the kernel debugger, see page 21 in Chapter 1.) The output looks like this:

```
KDx86> !processfields
 EPROCESS structure offsets:
     Pcb:                              0x0
     ExitStatus:                       0x68
     LockEvent:                        0x6c
     LockCount:                        0x7c
     CreateTime:                       0x80
     ExitTime:                         0x88
     LockOwner:                        0x90
     UniqueProcessId:                  0x94
     ActiveProcessLinks:               0x98
     QuotaPeakPoolUsage[0]:            0xa0
     QuotaPoolUsage[0]:                0xa8
     PagefileUsage:                    0xb0
     CommitCharge:                     0xb4
     PeakPagefileUsage:                0xb8
     PeakVirtualSize:                  0xbc
     VirtualSize:                      0xc0
     Vm:                               0xc8
     LastProtoPteFault:                0xf8
     DebugPort:                        0xfc
     ExceptionPort:                    0x100
     ObjectTable:                      0x104
     Token:                            0x108
     WorkingSetLock:                   0x10c
     WorkingSetPage:                   0x12c
     ProcessOutswapEnabled:            0x130
     ProcessOutswapped:                0x131
     AddressSpaceInitialized:          0x132
     AddressSpaceDeleted:              0x133
     AddressCreationLock:              0x134
     ForkInProgress:                   0x158
     VmOperation:                      0x15c
     VmOperationEvent:                 0x160
     PageDirectoryPte:                 0x164
     LastFaultCount:                   0x168
     VadRoot:                          0x170
     VadHint:                          0x174
```

```
CloneRoot:                           0x178
NumberOfPrivatePages:                0x17c
NumberOfLockedPages:                 0x180
ForkWasSuccessful:                   0x15e
ExitProcessCalled:                   0x186
CreateProcessReported:               0x187
SectionHandle:                       0x188
Peb:                                 0x18c
SectionBaseAddress:                  0x190
QuotaBlock:                          0x194
LastThreadExitStatus:                0x198
WorkingSetWatch:                     0x19c
InheritedFromUniqueProcessId:        0x1a4
GrantedAccess:                       0x1a8
DefaultHardErrorProcessing:          0x1ac
LdtInformation:                      0x1b0
VadFreeHint:                         0x1b4
VdmObjects:                          0x1b8
ProcessMutant:                       0x1bc
ImageFileName[0]:                    0x1dc
VmTrimFaultValue:                    0x1ec
Win32Process:                        0x1f4
Win32WindowStation:                  0x1a0
```

The *!processfields* command shows the format of a process block, not its contents. (The *!process* command actually dumps the contents of a process block. An annotated example of the output from this command is included later in this section, in Figure 4-5, on page 156.) Although some of the field names are self-explanatory, the output doesn't give the data type of the fields, nor does it show the format of the structures that are included within or pointed to by the EPROCESS block (such as the kernel process block, quota block, and so on). By examining the offsets, however, you can at least tell the length of a field. (*Hint:* Fields that are 4 bytes long and refer to some other structure are likely pointers.)

Table 4-1 explains some of the fields in the preceding experiment in more detail and includes references to other places in the book where you can find more information about them. As I've said before and will no doubt say again, processes and threads are such an integral part of Windows NT that it's impossible to talk about them without referring to many other parts of the system. To keep this chapter manageable, however, I've covered those related subjects (such as memory management, security, objects, and handles) elsewhere.

Table 4-1   Contents of the EPROCESS Block

Element	Purpose	Additional Reference
Kernel process (KPROCESS) block	Common dispatcher object header, pointer to the process page directory, list of kernel thread (KTHREAD) blocks belonging to the process, default base priority, quantum, affinity mask, and total kernel and user time for the threads in the process.	Thread scheduling (page 184)
Process identification	Unique process ID, parent process ID, name of image being run, window station process is running on.	
Quota block	Limits on nonpaged pool, paged pool, and page file usage plus current and peak process nonpaged and paged pool usage. (*Note*: This structure can be shared by several processes: all the system processes point to the single systemwide default quota block; all the processes in the interactive session share a single quota block set up by Winlogon [WINLOGON.EXE].)	
Virtual address space descriptors (VAD)	Series of data structures that describes the status of the portions of the address space that exist in the process.	Memory management (Chapter 5)
Working set information	Pointer to working set list (MMWSL structure); current, peak, minimum, and maximum working set size; last trim time; page fault count; memory priority; outswap flags; page fault history.	Memory management (Chapter 5)
Virtual memory information	Current and peak virtual size, page file usage, hardware page table entry for process page directory.	Memory management (Chapter 5)
Exception local procedure call (LPC) port	Interprocess communication channel to which the process manager sends a message when one of the process's threads causes an exception.	Local procedure calls (Chapter 3, page 127)
Debugging LPC port	Interprocess communication channel to which the process manager sends a message when one of the process's threads causes a debug event.	Local procedure calls (Chapter 3, page 127)
Access token (ACCESS_TOKEN)	Executive object describing the security profile of this process.	Security (Chapter 6)
Handle table	Address of per-process handle table.	Object handles (Chapter 3, page 112)

Element	Purpose	Additional Reference
Process environment block (PEB)	Image information (base address, version numbers, module list), process heap information, thread-local storage utilization. (*Note*: The pointers to the process heaps start at the first byte after the PEB.)	Page 166
Win32 subsystem process block (W32PROCESS)	Process details needed by the kernel-mode component of the Win32 subsystem.	

Two key substructures of the executive process block are the kernel process (KPROCESS) block and the process environment block (PEB). The KPROCESS block (which is sometimes called the PCB, or process control block) is illustrated in Figure 4-3 and contains the basic information that the Windows NT kernel needs to schedule threads. (Page directories are covered in Chapter 5, and kernel thread blocks are described in more detail later in this chapter.)

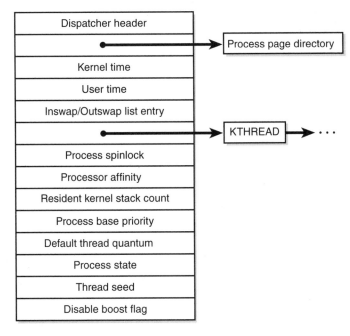

Figure 4-3
Structure of the kernel process block

The PEB, which lives in the user process address space, contains information needed by the image loader, the heap manager, and other Win32 system DLLs that need to be writable from user mode. (The EPROCESS and KPROCESS blocks are accessible only from kernel mode.) The PEB is always mapped at address 0x7FFDF000. The basic structure of the PEB is illustrated in Figure 4-4 and is explained in more detail later in the chapter.

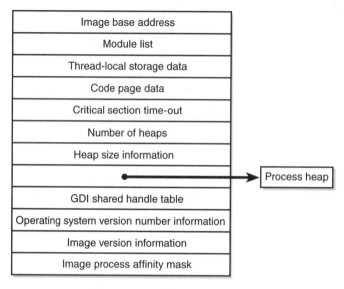

Figure 4-4

Fields of the process environment block

System Variables

A few of the key system global variables that relate to processes are listed in Table 4-2. These variables are referred to later in the chapter, when the steps in creating a process are described.

Performance Counters

Windows NT maintains a number of counters with which you can track the processes running on your system; you can retrieve these counters programmatically or view them with the Performance Monitor utility (PERFMON.EXE). Table 4-3 lists the performance counters relevant to processes (except for memory management–related counters, which are described in Chapter 5).

Table 4-2 **Process-Related System Variables**

Variable	Type	Description
PsActiveProcessHead	Queue header	List head of process blocks
PsIdleProcess	EPROCESS	Idle process block
PsInitialSystemProcess	Pointer to EPROCESS	Pointer to the process block of the initial system process (process ID 2) that contains the system threads
PspCreateProcess-NotifyRoutine	Array of 32-bit pointers	Array of pointers to routines to be called on process creation and deletion (maximum of eight)
PspCreateProcess-NotifyRoutineCount	DWORD	Count of registered process notification routines
PspCidTable	Pointer to HANDLE_TABLE	Handle table for process and thread client IDs

Table 4-3 **Process-Related Performance Counters**

Object: Counter	Function
Process: % Privileged Time	Describes the percentage of time that the threads in the process have run in kernel mode during a specified interval.
Process: % Processor Time	Describes the percentage of CPU time that the threads in the process have used during a specified interval. This count is the sum of % Privileged Time and % User Time.
Process: % User Time	Describes the percentage of time that the threads in the process have run in user mode during a specified interval.
Process: Elapsed Time	Describes the total elapsed time in seconds since this process was created.
Process: ID Process	Returns the process ID. This ID applies only while the process exists, because process IDs are reused.
Process: Thread Count	Returns the number of threads in the process.

Relevant Functions

For reference purposes, the Win32 functions that apply to processes are described in Table 4-4. For further information, consult the Win32 API documentation in the MSDN Library.

Table 4-4 Process-Related Functions

Function	Description
CreateProcess	Creates a new process and thread using the caller's security identification
CreateProcess-AsUser	Creates a new process and thread and its primary thread using an alternate security identification and then executes a specified .EXE
OpenProcess	Returns a handle of the specified process object
ExitProcess	Exits the current process
TerminateProcess	Terminates a process
FlushInstruction-Cache	Empties another process's instruction cache
GetProcessTimes	Obtains another process's timing information, describing how much time the process has spent in user and kernel mode
GetExitCodeProcess	Returns the exit code for another process, indicating how and why the process shut down
GetCommandLine	Returns the command-line string passed to the process
GetCurrent-ProcessID	Returns the ID of the current process
GetProcessVersion	Returns the major and minor versions of the Windows version on which the specified process expects to run
GetStartupInfo	Returns the contents of the STARTUPINFO structure specified during *CreateProcess*
GetEnvironment-Strings	Returns the address of the environment block
GetEnvironment Variable	Returns a specific environment variable
Get/SetProcess-ShutdownParameters	Defines the shutdown priority and number of retries for the current process

Relevant Tools

A number of tools for viewing (and modifying) processes and process information are available. These tools are included within Windows NT itself and within the Windows NT Resource Kit, the Platform Software Development Kit (SDK), and the Device Driver Kit (DDK). The trouble is, you can't get all the information you need with one single tool—most information is available from more than one tool, and the data is sometimes identified by different names (and sometimes assigned different values) in each of the tools. To help you determine which tool to use to get the basic process information you need, consult Table 4-5. This table isn't a comprehensive list of all the information available about a process—for example, you'll find out what tools you can use to gather memory management information in Chapter 5—but if you need the basics, you'll find them here.

> **NOTE** For a dynamic view of process data, use QuickSlice (QSLICE.EXE), the Task Manager (TASKMGR.EXE), or Process Monitor (PMON.EXE)—all other tools listed here take a snapshot of the system and present only a static view.

Table 4-5 Process-Related Tools

Object	Taskman	PerfMon	Pview	Pviewer	Qslice	Pmon	Pstat	Pulist	Tlist	KD !process
Process ID	✓	✓	✓	✓	✓		✓	✓	✓	✓
Image Name	✓		✓	✓	✓	✓	✓	✓	✓	✓
Total CPU Time	✓	✓			✓					
% CPU Time	✓	✓		✓	✓	✓				
Handle Count	✓									
Thread Count	✓	✓	✓	✓	✓	✓	✓			
View Priority Class	✓	✓	✓							
% User Time		✓			✓					
% Privileged Time		✓			✓					
Total User Time		✓					✓			✓
Total Privileged Time		✓					✓			✓
Quota Limits		✓								
Elapsed Time	✓	✓								✓
Creating Process									✓	
Current Directory									✓	
Command Line									✓	
Security ID								✓		

EXPERIMENT: Viewing Process Information

The built-in Windows NT Task Manager provides a quick list of the processes running on the system but not of threads within processes. You can start Task Manager in one of three ways: (1) press Ctrl-Shift-Esc, (2) right-click on the taskbar and select Task Manager, or (3) press Ctrl-Alt-Del and click the Task Manager button. Performance Monitor can also display most (but not all) process and thread information.

Several Windows NT Resource Kit utilities make it easy to get information about currently running processes: QuickSlice (QSLICE.EXE), Process Viewer (PVIEWER.EXE), Task List (TLIST.EXE), Process Status (PSTAT.EXE), Process Monitor (PMON.EXE), and Process User List (PULIST.EXE). Each of these utilities displays overlapping subsets of the information available about processes and threads. (Refer to Table 4-5.)

How do you determine the creator of a process? Although there is no documented Win32 service to retrieve this information, the Windows NT Resource Kit *tlist /t* command can display the "process tree," which shows the relationship of a process to its parent. (It uses an undocumented system service call to get the information.) Here is an example output from *tlist /t*:

```
C:\>tlist /t
System Process (0)
System (2)
 smss.exe (21)
 csrss.exe (24)
 winlogon.exe (35)
 services.exe (41)
  spoolss.exe (69)
  llssrv.exe (94)
  LOCATOR.EXE (96)
  RpcSs.exe (112)
  inetinfo.exe (128)
 lsass.exe (44)
 nddeagnt.exe (119)
Explorer.exe (123) Program Manager
 OSA.EXE (121)
 WINWORD.EXE (117) Microsoft Word - msch02(s).doc
 cmd.exe (72) Command Prompt - tlist /t
  tlist.EXE (100)
```

For an explanation of the system processes shown in this output, see Chapter 3.

Quick Slice gives a quick, dynamic view of the proportions of system and kernel time each of the processes currently running on your system is using. Online, the red part of the bar shows the amount of CPU time spent in kernel mode, and the blue part shows the user-mode time. (Although reproduced below in black and white, the bars in the online display are always red and blue.) The total of all bars shown in the QuickSlice window should add up to 100 percent of CPU time. To run QuickSlice, click the Start button and choose Programs, Resource Kit 4.0, Diagnostics, Quick Slice (or run QLICE.EXE in the Resource Kit directory). For example, try running a graphics-intensive application such as Windows Paint (MSPAINT.EXE). Open Quick Slice and Paint side by side, and draw squiggles in the Paint window. When you do so, MSPAINT.EXE will be running, as shown here:

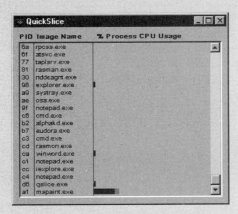

For additional information about the threads in a process, you can also double-click on a process (on either the process name or the colored bar). Here you can see the threads within the process and the relative CPU time used by each thread (not across the system):

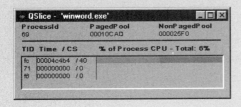

(continued)

Viewing Process Information *continued*

The Process Viewer (PVIEWER.EXE) that comes with the Windows NT Resource Kit permits you to view information about the running processes and threads as well as to kill processes and change process priority classes. You can use this tool to view processes both on the local computer and on remote Windows NT machines across the network. This tool is also available in the Platform SDK and with Visual C++. (In both of these, it's called PVIEW.EXE.) Don't confuse PVIEWER.EXE with PVIEW.EXE in the Windows NT Resource Kit; PVIEW.EXE is a different utility entirely.

The Process Viewer is well documented in the Windows NT Resource Kit tools help file, but here's a quick overview of the options available to you. The basic display of the Process Viewer looks like this:

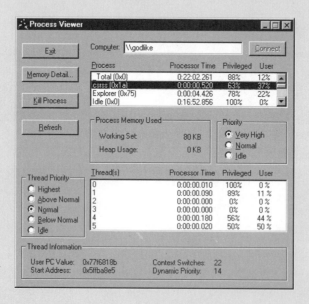

Here's what the various options do:

■ The Computer text box displays the name of the computer whose processes are currently displayed. Click the Connect button to browse for another computer.

- The Memory Detail button shows memory management details about the selected process, such as the amount of memory committed to the process, the size of the working set, and so forth.

- The Kill Process button kills the selected process. Be *very* careful which process you kill, since the process will have no chance to perform any cleanup.

- The Refresh button refreshes the display—Process Viewer does not update the information unless you request it.

- The Processor Time columns in the Process and Thread(s) list boxes show the total processor time the process or thread has used since it was created.

- The Priority collection of radio buttons regulates the selected process's priority class (the Real-time priority class is not shown), and the Thread Priority collection displays the relative thread priorities of the threads within a process.

- At the bottom of the screen, the number of context switches and the thread's dynamic priority, start address, and current PC are displayed.

To see the other displays of process and thread information, try running TLIST.EXE, PSTAT.EXE, PMON.EXE, and PULIST.EXE using the Run command on the Start menu. (None of these utilities are in the Windows NT Resource Kit Start menu folders.)

Kernel Debugger *!process* Command

The *!process* command for the kernel debugger (described in Chapter 1) displays a subset of the information in an EPROCESS block. This output is arranged in two parts for each process. First you see the information about the process, as shown in Figure 4-5. (Not all the fields in the output are labeled here—only the parts germane to this section.)

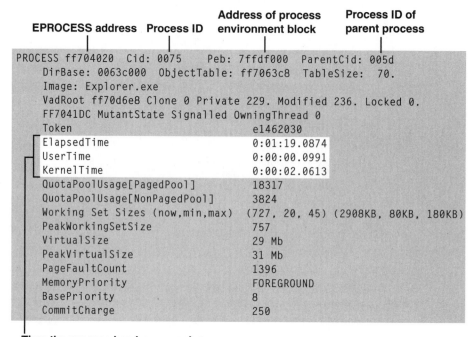

Figure 4-5
Process details of !process *output*

After the basic process output comes a list of the threads in the process. That output is explained in the section "Kernel Debugger *!thread* Output" on page 179. Other commands that display process information include *!handle*, which dumps the process handle table (described in more detail in the section "Object Handles and the Process Handle Table" in Chapter 3 on page 112). Process and thread security structures are described in Chapter 6.

Flow of *CreateProcess*

So far in this chapter, you've seen the structures that are part of a process and the API functions with which you (and the operating system) can manipulate processes. You've also found out how you can use tools to view how processes interact with your system. But how did those processes come into being, and how do they exit once they've fulfilled their purpose? In the following sections, you'll discover how a Win32 process comes to life.

A Win32 process is created when an application calls the Win32 *CreateProcess* function. Creating a Win32 process consists of several stages carried out in three parts of the operating system: the Win32 client-side library KERNEL-32.DLL, the Windows NT executive, and the Win32 subsystem process (CSRSS). Because of the multiple environment subsystem architecture of Windows NT, creating a Windows NT executive process object (which can be used by other subsystems) is separated from the work involved in creating a Win32 process. So, although the following description of the flow of the Win32 *CreateProcess* function is complicated, keep in mind that part of the work is specific to the semantics added by the Win32 subsystem as opposed to the core work needed to create a Windows NT executive process object.

The following list summarizes the main stages of a Win32 *CreateProcess*. The operations performed in each stage are described in detail in the subsequent sections.

1. Open the image file (.EXE) to be executed inside the process.

2. Create the Windows NT executive process object.

3. Create the initial thread (stack, context, and Windows NT executive thread object).

4. Notify the Win32 subsystem of the new process so that it can set up for the new process and thread.

5. Start execution of the initial thread (unless the CREATE_SUSPEN-DED flag was specified).

6. In the context of the new process and thread, complete the initial-ization of the address space (such as load required DLLs) and begin execution of the program.

Figure 4-6 on the next page shows an overview of the stages Windows NT follows to create a process.

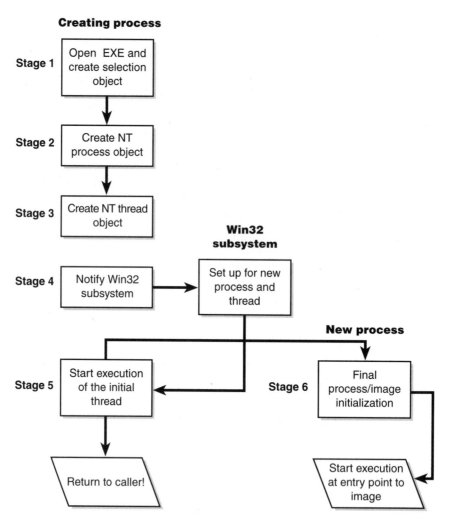

Figure 4-6

The main stages Windows NT follows to create a process

Before describing these stages in more detail, I should mention a few notes that pertain to all the stages.

- In *CreateProcess*, the priority class for the new process is specified as independent bits in the *CreationFlags* parameter. Thus, you can specify more than one priority class for a single *CreateProcess* call. Windows NT resolves the question of which priority class to assign to the process by choosing the lowest-priority class set.

- If no priority class is specified for the new process, the priority class defaults to Normal unless the priority class of the process that created it is Idle, in which case the priority class of the new process will be Idle as well.

- If a Real-time priority class is specified for the new process and the process's caller doesn't have the Increase Scheduling Priority privilege, the High priority class is used instead. In other words, *CreateProcess* doesn't fail just because the caller has insufficient privileges to create the process in the Real-time priority class; the new process just won't have as high a priority.

- All windows are associated with desktops, the graphical representation of your workspace. If no desktop is specified in *CreateProcess*, the process is associated with the caller's current desktop.

Enough background. The steps of *CreateProcess* are described in detail in the following sections.

NOTE Many steps of *CreateProcess* are related to the setup of the process virtual address space and hence refer to many memory management terms and structures, which are defined in Chapter 5.

Stage 1: Opening the Image to Be Executed

As illustrated in Figure 4-7, the first stage in *CreateProcess* is to find the appropriate Win32 image that will run the executable file specified by the caller and to create a section object to later map it into the address space of the new process. If no image name is specified, the first token of the command line (defined to be the first part of the command-line string ending with a space or tab that is a valid file specification) is used as the image filename.

159

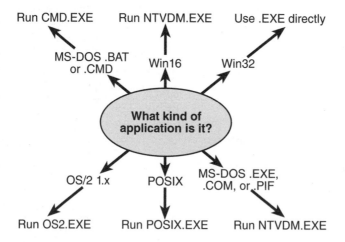

Figure 4-7

Choosing a Win32 image to activate

If the executable file specified is a Win32 .EXE, it is used directly. If it is not a Win32 .EXE (for example, if it's an MS-DOS, a Win16, a POSIX, or an OS/2 application), *CreateProcess* goes through a series of steps to find a Win32 "support image" to run it. This process is necessary because non-Win32 applications are not run directly—Windows NT instead uses one of a few special support images that in turn are responsible for actually running the non-Win32 program. For example, if you attempt to run a POSIX application, *CreateProcess* identifies it as such and changes the image to be run on the Win32 executable file POSIX.EXE. If you attempt to run an MS-DOS or a Win16 executable, the image to be run becomes the Win32 executable NTVDM.EXE. In short, you can't directly create a process that is *not* a Win32 process. If Windows NT can't find a way to resolve the activated image as a Win32 process (as shown in Table 4-6), *CreateProcess* fails.

Specifically, the decision tree that *CreateProcess* goes through to run an image is as follows:

- If the image is an OS/2 1.*x* application, the image to be run changes to OS2.EXE and *CreateProcess* restarts at Stage 1. (OS2.EXE begins only on *x*86-compatible processors; OS/2 images are not supported on RISC processors.)

- If the image is an MS-DOS application with an .EXE, a .COM, or a .PIF extension, a message is sent to the Win32 subsystem to check whether an MS-DOS support process (NTVDM.EXE, specified in the

Table 4-6   Decision Tree for Stage 1 of *CreateProcess*

If the image is a/an	This image will run	And this will happen
POSIX executable file	POSIX.EXE	*CreateProcess* restarts Stage 1
OS/2 1.*x* image	OS2.EXE	*CreateProcess* restarts Stage 1
MS-DOS application with an .EXE, a .COM, or a .PIF extension	NTVDM.EXE	*CreateProcess* restarts Stage 1
Win16 application	NTVDM.EXE	*CreateProcess* restarts Stage 1
Command procedure MS-DOS application with a .BAT or a .CMD extension	CMD.EXE	*CreateProcess* restarts Stage 1

registry key HKLM\System…\Control\WOW\cmdline) has already been created for this session. If a support process has been created, it is used to run the MS-DOS application (the Win32 subsystem sends the message to the VDM (Virtual DOS Machine) process to run the new image) and *CreateProcess* returns. If a support process has not been created, the image to be run changes to NTVDM.EXE and *Create-Process* restarts at Stage 1.

■ If the file to run has a .BAT or a .CMD extension, the image to be run becomes CMD.EXE, the Windows NT command prompt, and *CreateProcess* restarts at Stage 1. (The name of the batch file is passed as the first parameter to CMD.EXE.)

■ If the image is a Win16 (Windows 3.1) executable, *CreateProcess* must decide whether a new VDM process must be created to run it or whether it should use the default systemwide shared VDM process (which might not yet have been created). This decision is controlled by the *CreateProcess* flags CREATE_SEPARATE_WOW_VDM and CREATE_SHARED_WOW_VDM. If these flags are not specified, the default behavior is dictated by the registry field HKLM\System…\Control\WOW\DefaultSeparateVDM. If the application is to be run in a separate VDM, the image to be run changes to the value of HKLM\System…\Control\WOW\wowcmdline and *CreateProcess*

161

restarts at Stage 1. Otherwise, the Win32 subsystem sends a message to see whether the systemwide VDM process exists and can be used. (If the VDM process is running on a different desktop or the VDM process is not running under the same security as the caller, it can't be used and a new VDM process must be created.) If a systemwide VDM process can be used, the Win32 subsystem sends a message to it to run the new image and *CreateProcess* returns. If the VDM process hasn't yet been created (or if it exists but can't be used), the image to be run changes to the VDM support image and *CreateProcess* restarts at Stage 1.

At this point, *CreateProcess* has successfully opened a valid Windows NT executable file and created a section object for it. The object is not mapped into memory yet, but it is open. Just because a section object has been successfully created doesn't mean that the file is a valid Win32 image, however; it could be a DLL or a POSIX executable. If the file is a POSIX executable, the image to be run changes to POSIX.EXE and *CreateProcess* restarts from the beginning of Stage 1. If the file is a DLL, *CreateProcess* fails.

Now that *CreateProcess* has found a valid Win32 executable, it looks in the registry under \Software\Microsoft\Windows NT\CurrentVersion\Image File Execution Options to see whether a subkey with the filename and extension of the executable image (but without the directory and path information—for example, IMAGE.EXE) exists there. If it does, *CreateProcess* looks for a value named Debugger for that key. If the value is not null, the image to be run becomes the value of that key and *CreateProcess* restarts at Stage 1.

TIP You can take advantage of this *CreateProcess* behavior and debug the startup code of Windows NT service processes before they start rather than attach the debugger after starting the service, which doesn't allow you to debug the startup code. If you happen to be feeling mischievous, you can also exploit this behavior to confuse people by causing another file to be run rather than the one they specified.

Stage 2: Creating the Windows NT Executive Process Object

At this point, *CreateProcess* has opened a valid Win32 executable file and created a section object to map it into the new process address space. Next it creates a Windows NT executive process object to run the image by calling the internal system function *NtCreateProcess*. Creating the executive process object involves the following substages:

A. Setting up the EPROCESS block

B. Creating the initial process address space

C. Creating the kernel process block

D. Concluding the setup of the process address space

E. Setting up the PEB

F. Completing the setup of the executive process object

NOTE The only time there won't be a parent process is during system initialization. After that point, a parent process is always required to provide a security context for the new process.

Stage 2A: Setting Up the EPROCESS Block

This substage involves five steps:

1. Allocate and initialize the Windows NT EPROCESS block.

2. Set the new process's quota block to the address of its parent process's quota block, and increment the reference count for the parent's quota block.

3. Store the parent process's process ID in the *InheritedFromUnique-ProcessId* field in the new process object.

NOTE The parent's process ID is stored so that you can determine the creator process. This information is not available through any Win32 function (it's not defined for Win32, although POSIX requires this information), but the Tlist utility in the Windows NT Server Resource Kit uses this information to show the process "tree" when the "/t" qualifier is specified as shown in the experiment "Viewing Process Information" on page 152.

4. Set the new process's exit status to STATUS_PENDING.

5. Create the process's primary access token (a duplicate of its parent's primary token). New processes inherit the security profile of their parent (unless the *CreateProcessAsUser* function is used, which allows specification of a different access token for a new process).

Stage 2B: Creating the Initial Process Address Space

The initial process address space consists of three pages:

- Page directory
- Hyperspace page
- Working set list

To create these three pages, the following steps are taken:

1. Page table entries are created in the appropriate page tables to map the three initial pages listed above.

2. To account for these new pages, the value 3 is deducted from the system variable *MmTotalCommittedPages* and added to *MmProcessCommit*.

3. The systemwide default process minimum working set size (*PsMinimumWorkingSet*) is deducted from *MmResidentAvailablePages*.

4. The page table pages for the nonpaged portion of system space and the system cache are mapped into the process.

5. The process minimum and maximum working set size are set to the values of *PsMinimumWorkingSet* and *PsMaximumWorkingSet*, respectively.

Stage 2C: Creating the Kernel Process Block

The next stage of *CreateProcess* is the initialization of the KPROCESS block, mentioned on page 147, which contains a pointer to a list of kernel threads. (The kernel has no knowledge of handles, so it bypasses the object table.) The kernel process block also points to the process's page table directory (used to keep track of the process's virtual address space), the total time the process's threads have executed, the process's default base-scheduling priority, the default processor affinity for the threads in the process, and the initial value of the process default quantum, which is taken from the value of *PspForegroundQuantum[0]*, the first entry in the systemwide quantum array.

> **NOTE** The initial quantum differs between Windows NT Workstation and Windows NT Server. For more information on thread quantums, turn to their discussion in the section "Thread Scheduling" on page 184.

Stage 2D: Concluding the Setup of the Process Address Space

Setting up the address space for a new process is somewhat complicated, so let's look at what's involved a step at a time. To get the most out of this section, you should have some familiarity with the internals of the Windows NT memory manager, which are described in Chapter 5.

1. The virtual memory manager sets the value of the process's last trim time to the current time. This value is used by the working set manager (which runs in the context of the balance set manager system thread) to determine when to initiate working set trimming.

2. The page frame number (PFN) database for the page directory as well as the page directory entry, which maps hyperspace, are initialized.

3. The memory manager initializes the process's working set list— page faults can now be taken.

4. The major and minor version numbers are copied from the executable file to the EPROCESS block.

5. The section (created when the image file was opened) is now mapped into the new process's address space, and the process section base address is set to the base address of the image.

6. NTDLL.DLL is mapped into the process.

7. The systemwide national language support tables are mapped into the process's address space.

   N O T E   POSIX processes clone the address space of their parents, so they don't have to go through these steps to create a new address space. In the case of POSIX applications, the new process's section base address is set to that of its parent process, and the parent's PEB is cloned for the new process.

8. *CreateProcess* inserts the new process block at the end of Windows NT's list of active processes (*PsActiveProcessHead*).

Stage 2E: Setting Up the PEB

CreateProcess allocates a page for the PEB and initializes a number of fields as shown in Table 4-7.

Table 4-7   Initial Values of the Fields of the PEB

Field	Initial Value
ImageBaseAddress	Base address of section
NumberOfProcessors	*KeNumberProcessors* system variable
NtGlobalFlag	*NtGlobalFlag* system variable
CriticalSectionTimeout	*MmCriticalSectionTimeout* system variable
HeapSegmentReserve	*MmHeapSegmentReserve* system variable
HeapSegmentCommit	*MmHeapSegmentCommit* system variable
HeapDeCommitTotal-FreeThreshold	*MmHeapDeCommitTotalFreeThreshold* system variable
HeapDeCommitFree-BlockThreshold	*MmHeapDeCommitFreeBlockThreshold* system variable
NumberOfHeaps	0
MaximumNumber-OfHeaps	(Size of a page – size of a PEB) / 4
ProcessHeaps	First byte after PEB
OSMajorVersion	*NtMajorVersion* system variable
OSMinorVersion	*NtMinorVersion* system variable
OSBuildNumber	*NtBuildNumber* system variable & 0x3FFF
OSPlatformId	2

If the image file specifies explicit Win32 version values, this information replaces the initial values shown above. The mapping from image version information fields to PEB fields is shown in Table 4-8.

Table 4-8   Win32 Replacements for Initial PEB Values

Field Name	Value Taken from Image Header
OSMajorVersion	OptionalHeader.Win32VersionValue & 0xFF
OSMinorVersion	OptionalHeader.Win32VersionValue >> 8) & 0xFF
OSBuildNumber	OptionalHeader.Win32VersionValue >> 16) & 0x3FFF
OSPlatformId	OptionalHeader.Win32VersionValue >> 30) ^ 0x2

Stage 2F: Completing the Setup of the Executive Process Object

Before the handle to the new process can be returned, a few final setup steps must be completed:

1. The process handle table is initialized; if the duplicate handle flag is set for the parent process, any inheritable handles are copied from the parent's object handle table into the new process. (For more information about object handle tables, see Chapter 3.)

2. If you're running Windows NT Workstation and the image header specifies IMAGE_FILE_AGGRESIVE_WS_TRIM, the PS_WS_TRIM-_FROM_EXE_HEADER flag is set in the process block. If you're running Windows NT Workstation on a small-memory x86 system, the PS_WS_TRIM_BACKGROUND_ONLY_APP flag is set in the process block.

3. If the image header characteristics IMAGE_FILE_UP_SYSTEM-_ONLY flag is set (indicating that the image can run only on a uni-processor system), a single CPU is chosen for all the threads in this new process to run on. This choosing process is done by simply cycling through the available processors—each time this type of image is run, the next processor is used. In this way, these types of images are spread out across the processors evenly.

4. If the image specifies an explicit processor affinity mask (for example, a field in the configuration header), this value is copied to the PEB and later set as the default process affinity mask.

5. If the parent process had an event log section in its PEB, the event log is copied to the new process and a handle is duplicated to the section for the new process.

6. If systemwide auditing of processes is enabled (choose Audit from the Policies menu in the User Manager utility), the process's creation is written to the audit log.

7. The process's creation time is set, the handle to the new process is returned to the caller (*CreateProcess* in KERNEL32.DLL), and execution continues back in user mode.

Stage 3: Creating the Initial Thread and Its Stack and Context

At this point, the Windows NT executive process object is completely set up. It still has no thread, however, so it can't do anything yet. Before the thread can be created, it needs a stack and a context in which to run, so these are set up first. The stack size for the initial thread is taken from the image—there is no way to specify another one.

Now the initial thread can be created, which is done by calling *NtCreate-Thread*. (For a detailed description of how a thread is created, see the section "Flow of *CreateThread*" on page 180.) The thread parameter (which can't be specified in *CreateProcess* but can be specified in *CreateThread*) is the address of the PEB. This parameter will be used by the initialization code that runs in the context of this new thread (as described in Stage 6). However, the thread won't do anything yet—it is created in a suspended state and is not resumed until the process is completely initialized (as described in Stage 5).

Stage 4: Notifying the Win32 Subsystem About the New Process

After all of the necessary executive process and thread objects have been created, KERNEL32.DLL sends a message to the Win32 subsystem so that it can set up for the new process and thread. The message includes the following information:

- Process and thread handles
- Entries in the creation flags
- ID of the process's creator
- Flag indicating whether the process belongs to a Win32 application (so that CSRSS can determine whether or not to show the startup cursor)

The Win32 subsystem performs the following steps when it receives this message:

1. *CreateProcess* duplicates a handle for the process and thread. This step increments the usage count of the process and the thread from 1 (set at creation time) to 2.

2. If a process priority class is not specified, *CreateProcess* sets it to Normal, unless the creating process's priority class was Idle. In that case, it sets the new process priority class to Idle as well.

3. The CSRSS process block is allocated.

4. The new process's exception port is set to be the general function port for the Win32 subsystem so that the Win32 subsystem will

receive a message when an exception occurs in the process. (For further information on exception handling, see Chapter 3.)

5. If the process is being debugged (that is, if it is attached to a debugger process), the process debug port is set to the Win32 subsystem's general function port. This setting ensures that Windows NT will send debug events that occur in the new process (such as thread creation and deletion, exceptions, and so on) as messages to the Win32 subsystem so that it can then dispatch the events to the process that is acting as the new process's debugger.

6. The CSRSS thread block is allocated and initialized.

7. *CreateProcess* inserts the thread in the list of threads for the process.

8. The count of processes in this session is incremented.

9. The process shutdown level is set to x280 (the default process shutdown level—see the documentation for *SetProcessShutdownParameters*).

10. The new process block is inserted into the list of Win32 subsystem-wide processes.

11. The per-process data structure used by the kernel-mode part of the Win32 subsystem (W32PROCESS structure) is allocated and initialized.

12. The application start cursor is displayed. This cursor is the familiar arrow with an hourglass attached—Windows NT's way of saying to the user, "I'm starting something, but you can use the cursor in the meantime." If the process doesn't make a GUI call after 2 seconds, the cursor reverts to the standard pointer. If the process does make a GUI call in the allotted time, *CreateProcess* waits 5 seconds for the application to show a window. After that time, *CreateProcess* will reset the cursor again.

Stage 5: Starting Execution of the Initial Thread

At this point, the process environment has been determined, resources for its threads to use have been allocated, the process has a thread, and the Win32 subsystem knows about the new process. Unless the caller specified the CREATE-_SUSPENDED flag, the initial thread is now resumed so that it can start running and perform the remainder of the process initialization work that occurs in the context of the new process (Stage 6).

Stage 6: Performing Process Initialization in the Context of the New Process

The new thread begins life running the kernel mode thread startup routine *KiThreadStartup*. (For a more detailed description of the thread startup steps leading to this, see the section "Flow of *CreateThread*" on page 180.) The *KiThreadStartup* routine performs the following steps:

1. Lowers the IRQL level from Dispatch level to APC (asynchronous procedure call) level.

2. Enables working set expansion.

3. Queues a user mode APC to the new thread to execute the user-mode thread startup routine *LdrInitializeThunk* inside NTDLL.DLL.

4. Lowers the IRQL level to 0, causing the APC to fire and *LdrInitializeThunk* to be called. The *LdrInitializeThunk* routine initializes the loader, heap manager, NLS tables, TLS array, and critical section structures. It then loads any required DLLs and calls the DLL entry points with the DLL_PROCESS_ATTACH function code.

5. If the process being created is a debuggee, all threads in the process are suspended. (Threads might have been created during step 3.) A create process message is then sent to the process's debug port (the Win32 subsystem function port because this is a Win32 process) so that the subsystem can deliver the process startup debug event (CREATE_PROCESS_DEBUG_INFO) to the appropriate debugger process. *KiThreadStartup* then waits for the Win32 subsystem to get the reply from the debugger (via the *ContinueDebugEvent* function). When the Win32 subsystem replies, all the threads are resumed.

6. Finally, the image begins execution in user mode. This is done by creating a trap frame that specifies the previous mode as user and the address to return to as the main entry point of the image. Thus, when the trap that caused the thread to start execution in kernel mode is dismissed, the program begins running in user mode at the right place.

Thread Internals

Now that we've dissected processes, let's turn our attention to the structure of a thread. Unless explicitly stated otherwise, you can assume that anything in this section applies to both normal user-mode threads and kernel-mode system threads (described in Chapter 3).

Data Structures

At the operating system level, a Windows NT thread is represented by an executive thread (ETHREAD) block, which is illustrated in Figure 4-8 on the next page. The ETHREAD block and the structures it points to exist in the system address space, with the exception of the thread environment block (TEB), which exists in the process address space. In addition, the Win32 subsystem process (CSRSS) maintains a parallel structure for each thread created in a Win32 process. Also, for threads that have called a Win32 subsystem USER or GDI function, the kernel-mode portion of the Win32 subsystem (WIN32K.SYS) maintains a per-thread data structure (called the W32THREAD structure) that is pointed to by the ETHREAD block.

Fibers vs. Threads

Beginning with Service Pack 3 for Windows NT 3.51, Microsoft has included fiber support within Windows NT. Fiber functions were added to the Win32 API set primarily for server applications being ported from UNIX that were designed to schedule their own threads rather than relying on a priority system.

Fibers are subsets of threads contained within a thread object. They are often called "lightweight" threads, and in terms of scheduling, they are invisible to the operating system. Whereas threads are allocated CPU time based on their thread priority (as discussed in the section "Thread Scheduling" on page 184), fibers are not allocated CPU time by the system at all. Instead, the programmer manually schedules the fibers to run. The scheduled fibers won't run unless the thread in which they are contained is scheduled to run; once this condition is met, a fiber within a thread will run until it's finished or until the fiber instructs Windows NT to run another fiber. For further information, see the documentation on the Win32 *ConvertThreadToFiber*, *CreateFiber*, and *SwitchToFiber* functions.

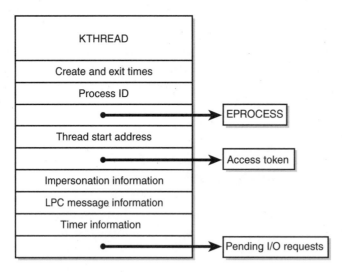

Figure 4-8
Structure of the executive thread block

Most of the fields illustrated in Figure 4-8 are self-explanatory. The first field is the kernel thread (KTHREAD) block. Following that are the thread identification information, the process identification information (including a pointer to the owning process so that its environment information can be accessed), security information in the form of a pointer to the access token and impersonation information, and finally, fields relating to LPC messages and pending I/O requests. As you can see in Table 4-9, some of these key fields are covered in more detail elsewhere in this book.

For more details on the internal structure of an ETHREAD block, you can use the kernel debugger *!threadfields* command to display the offsets in hexadecimal for almost every field in the structure. Although many of the field names are self-explanatory, the output does not give the data type of the fields, nor does it show the format of the structures that are included within or pointed to by the ETHREAD block.

Let's take a closer look at two of the key thread data structures referred to above: the KTHREAD block and the TEB. The KTHREAD block contains the information that the Windows NT kernel needs to access to perform thread scheduling and synchronization on behalf of running threads. Its layout is illustrated in Figure 4-9.

Table 4-9 **Key Contents of the Executive Thread Block**

Element	Description	Additional Reference
KTHREAD block	See Table 4-10	Page 174
Thread time information	Thread create and exit time	
Process identification	Process ID and pointer to EPROCESS block of the process that the thread belongs to	
Start address	Address of thread start routine	
Impersonation information	Access token and impersonation level (if the thread is impersonating a client)	Security (Chapter 6)
LPC information	Message ID that the thread is waiting for and address of message	Local procedure calls (Chapter 3, page 137)
I/O information	List of pending I/O request packets (IRPs)	I/O system (Chapter 7)

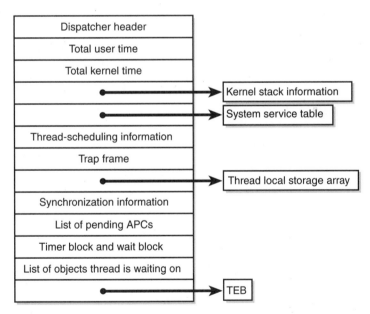

Figure 4-9
Structure of the kernel thread block

The key fields of the KTHREAD block are described briefly in Table 4-10.

Table 4-10 Key Contents of the KTHREAD Block

Element	Description	Additional Reference
Dispatcher header	Because the thread is an object that can be waited on, it starts with a standard kernel dispatcher object header.	Dispatcher objects (Chapter 3, page 127)
Execution time	Total user and kernel CPU time.	
Kernel stack information	Base and upper address of kernel stack.	Memory management (Chapter 5)
Pointer to system service table	Each thread starts out with this field pointing to the main system service table (*KeServiceDescriptorTable*). When a thread first calls a Win32 GUI service, its system service table is changed to one that includes the GDI and USER services in WIN32K.SYS.	System service dispatching (Chapter 3, page 99)
Scheduling information	Base and current priority, quantum, affinity mask, ideal processor, scheduling state, freeze count, suspend count.	Thread scheduling (page 184)
Wait blocks	The thread block contains four built-in wait blocks so that wait blocks don't have to be allocated and initialized each time the thread waits on something. (One is dedicated to timers.)	Synchronization (Chapter 3, page 123)
Wait information	List of objects the thread is waiting on, wait reason, time at which the thread entered the wait state.	Synchronization (page 123)
Mutant list	List of mutant objects owned by the thread.	Synchronization (page 123)
APC queues	List of pending user-mode and kernel-mode APCs, alertable flag.	APC queues (Chapter 3, page 93)
Timer block	Built-in timer block (also a corresponding wait block).	
Queue list	List of queue objects the thread is waiting on.	Synchronization (page 123)
Pointer to TEB	Thread ID, TLS information, PEB pointer, GDI and OpenGL information.	

The TEB, illustrated in Figure 4-10, is the only data structure explained in this section that exists in the process address space (as opposed to the system space).

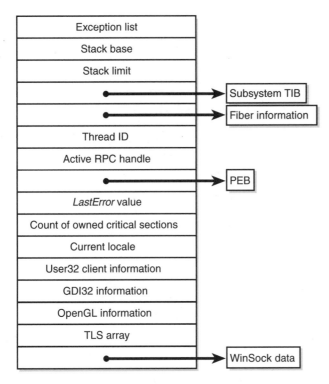

Figure 4-10
Fields of the thread environment block

The TEB stores context information for the image loader and various Win32 DLLs. Because these components run in user mode, they need a data structure writable from user mode. That is why this structure exists in the user address space instead of in the system space, where it would be writable only from kernel mode. You can find the address of the TEB with the kernel debugger *!thread* command.

System Variables

As with processes, a number of Windows NT system variables control how threads run. Table 4-11 shows the kernel-mode system variables that relate to threads.

Table 4-11 Thread-Related System Variables

Variable	Type	Description
PspCreateThread-NotifyRoutine	Array of 32-bit pointers	Array of pointers to routines to be called on during thread creation and deletion (maximum of eight)
PspCreateThread-NotifyRoutineCount	DWORD	Count of registered thread-notification routines

Performance Counters

Most of the key information in the thread data structures is exported as performance counters, which are listed in Table 4-12. You can extract much information about the internals of a thread just by using the standard Performance Monitor utility.

Table 4-12 Thread-Related Performance Counters

Object: Counter	Function
Process: Priority Base	Returns the current base priority of the process. This is the starting priority for threads created within this process.
Thread: % Privileged Time	Describes the percentage of time that the thread has run in kernel mode during a specified interval.
Thread: % Processor Time	Describes the percentage of CPU time that the thread has used during a specified interval. This count is the sum of % Privileged Time and % User Time.
Thread: % User Time	Describes the percentage of time that the thread has run in user mode during a specified interval.
Thread: Context Switches/Sec	Returns the number of context switches per second that the system is executing. The higher this number, the more threads of an equal priority are attempting to execute.
Thread: Elapsed Time	Returns the amount of CPU time (in seconds) that the thread has consumed.
Thread: ID Process	Returns the Process ID of the thread's process. This ID is valid only during the process's lifetime, because process IDs are reused.
Thread: ID Thread	Returns the thread's thread ID. This ID is valid only during the thread's lifetime, because thread IDs are reused.

(continued)

Object: Counter	Function
Thread: Priority Base	Returns the thread's current base priority. This number might be different from the thread's starting base priority.
Thread: Priority Current	Returns the thread's current dynamic priority.
Thread: Start Address	Returns the thread's starting virtual address (*Note*: This address will be the same for most threads.
Thread: Thread State	Returns a value from 0 through 7 relating to the current state of the thread.
Thread: Thread Wait Reason	Returns a value from 0 through 19 relating to the reason why the thread is in a wait state.

Relevant Functions

Table 4-13 shows the Win32 functions for creating and manipulating threads. This table doesn't include functions that have to do with thread scheduling and priorities—those are included in the section "Thread Scheduling" later in this chapter.

Table 4-13 Win32 Thread Functions

Function	Description
CreateThread	Creates a new thread
CreateRemoteThread	Creates a thread in another process
ExitThread	Ends execution of a thread normally
TerminateThread	Terminates a thread
GetExitCodeThread	Gets another thread's exit code
GetThreadTimes	Returns another thread's timing information
Get/SetThreadContext	Returns or changes a thread's CPU registers
GetThreadSelectorEntry	Returns another thread's descriptor table entry (applies only to *x*86 systems)

Relevant Tools

Besides Performance Monitor, several other tools expose various elements of the state of Windows NT threads. (The tools that show thread-scheduling information are listed in the section "Thread Scheduling" on page 184). These are itemized in Table 4-14.

NOTE To display thread details with Tlist, you must type *tlist xxx*, where *xxx* is a process image name or window title. (Wildcards are supported.)

Table 4-14 Thread-Related Tools and Their Functions

Object	Perfmon	Pview	Pviewer	Pstat	Qslice	Tlist	KD !thread
Thread ID	✓	✓		✓		✓	✓
Actual start address	✓	✓	✓	✓			✓
Win32 start address						✓	✓
Current address	✓	✓	✓				✓
Number of context switches	✓	✓	✓	✓			
Total user time		✓		✓			✓
Total privileged time		✓		✓			✓
Elapsed time	✓	✓					✓
Thread state	✓			✓		✓	✓
Reason for wait state	✓			✓		✓	✓
Last error						✓	
Security descriptor			✓				
Access token			✓				
Percentage of CPU time	✓				✓		
Percentage of user time	✓		✓		✓		
Percentage of privileged time	✓		✓		✓		
Address of TEB							✓
Address of ETHREAD							✓
Objects waiting on							✓

Kernel Debugger *!thread* Output

The kernel debugger *!thread* command dumps a subset of the information in the thread data structures. Some key elements of the information displayed by the kernel debugger cannot be displayed by any Windows NT utility: internal structure addresses; priority details; stack information; the pending I/O request list; and, for threads in a wait state, the list of objects the thread is waiting on. (Refer back to Table 4-14.)

To display thread information, use either the *!process* command (which displays all the thread blocks after displaying the process block) or the *!thread* command to dump a specific thread. The output of the thread information, along with some annotations of key fields, is shown in Figure 4-11.

EXPERIMENT: Viewing Thread Information

The following output is the detailed display of a process using the Tlist utility in the Windows NT Resource Kit. Notice that the thread list shows the actual Win32 start address. (All the other utilities that show the thread start address show the actual start address, not the Win32 start address.)

```
C:\> tlist winword
 155 WINWORD.EXE        Microsoft Word - Document1
   CWD:     C:\book\
   CmdLine: "C:\MSOffice\Winword\WINWORD.EXE"
   VirtualSize:    64448 KB    PeakVirtualSize:    106748 KB
   WorkingSetSize: 1104 KB     PeakWorkingSetSize: 6776 KB
   NumberOfThreads: 4
    156 Win32StartAddr:0x5032cfdb LastErr:0x00000000 State:Waiting
    167 Win32StartAddr:0x00022982 LastErr:0x00000000 State:Waiting
    192 Win32StartAddr:0x77fde4b2 LastErr:0x00000000 State:Waiting
    196 Win32StartAddr:0x77fd694a LastErr:0x00000000 State:Waiting
                   0x50000000   WINWORD.EXE
      4.0.1381.4 shp  0x77f60000   ntdll.dll
                   0x50800000   wwintl32.dll
      4.0.1381.4 shp  0x77f00000   KERNEL32.dll
          :
          :
         list of DLLs loaded in process
```

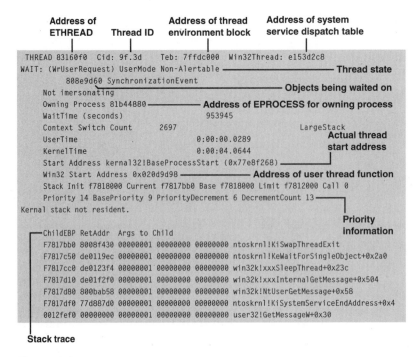

Figure 4-11
Output of !thread

Flow of *CreateThread*

A thread's life cycle starts when a program creates a new thread. The request filters down to the Windows NT executive, where the process manager allocates space for a thread object and calls the kernel to initialize the kernel thread block. The steps in the following list are taken inside the Win32 *CreateThread* function in KERNEL32.DLL to create a Win32 thread. The work that occurs inside the Windows NT executive are substeps of step 3, and the work that occurs in the context of the new thread are substeps of step 7. Because process creation includes creating a thread, some of the information here is repeated from the earlier description of the flow of *CreateProcess*.

1. *CreateThread* creates a user-mode stack for the thread in the process's address space.

2. *CreateThread* initializes the thread's hardware context (CPU architecture–specific). (For further information on the thread context block, see the Win32 API reference documentation on the CONTEXT structure.)

3. *NtCreateThread* is called to create the executive thread object in the suspended state. The following steps execute in kernel mode inside the Windows NT executive and kernel:

   a. The thread count in the process object is incremented.

   b. An executive thread block (ETHREAD) is created and initialized.

   c. A thread ID is generated for the new thread.

   d. The thread's kernel stack is allocated from the nonpaged pool.

   e. The TEB is set up in the user-mode address space of the process.

   f. The thread start address (*KiThreadStartup*) and the user's specified Win32 start address are stored in the ETHREAD block. The thread starts execution in *KiThreadStartup*, which performs thread-specific initialization, and then the actual thread routine specified by the caller of *CreateThread* is invoked.

   g. *KeInitializeThread* is called to set up the KTHREAD block. The thread's initial and current base priorities are set to the process's base priority, and its affinity and quantum are set to that of the process. This function also sets the initial thread ideal processor based on the process thread seed (a random number set during *CreateProcess*). The seed is then incremented so that each thread in the process will have a different ideal processor, assuming the system has more than one. *KeInitializeThread* next sets the thread's state to Initialized and initializes the machine-dependent hardware context for the thread, including the context, trap, and exception frames. The thread's context is set up so that the thread will start in kernel mode at the systemwide startup routine *KiThreadStartup* (described in step 6a).

   h. Any registered systemwide thread creation notification routines are called.

   i. The thread's access token is set to point to the process access token, and an access check is made to determine whether the caller has the right to create the thread. This check will always succeed if you are creating a thread in the local process but might not if you are using *CreateRemoteThread* to create a thread in another process.

4. *CreateThread* notifies the Win32 subsystem about the new thread, and the subsystem does some setup work for the new thread.

5. The thread handle and the thread ID (generated during step 3) are returned to the caller.

6. Unless the caller created the thread with the CREATE_SUSPENDED flag set, the thread is now resumed so that it can be scheduled for execution. When the thread starts running, it executes the following additional steps (in the context of the new thread) before calling the actual user's specified start address. (A flowchart of this final part of thread creation is shown in Figure 4-12.)

a. *KiThreadStartup* lowers the thread's IRQL level from Dispatch level to APC level and then calls the system initial thread routine, *PspUserThreadStartup*. The user-specified thread start address is passed as a parameter to this routine.

b. The system initial thread routine enables working set expansion and then queues a user mode APC to run the image loader initialization routine (*LdrInitializeThunk* in NTDLL.DLL). The IRQL (interrupt request level) is lowered to 0, thus causing the pending APC to fire.

c. The loader initialization routine then performs a number of additional thread-specific initialization steps, such as calling loaded DLLs to notify them of the new thread. (The detailed steps of the initialization of the Win32 subsystem DLLs, such as USER32, KERNEL32, and GDI32, are not covered in this edition of the book.)

d. If the process has a debugger attached, the thread startup routine suspends all other active threads in the process and notifies the Win32 subsystem so that it can deliver the thread startup debug event (CREATE_THREAD_DEBUG_INFO) to the appropriate debugger process. It then waits for the Win32 subsystem to get the reply from the debugger (via the *ContinueDebugEvent* function). When the Win32 subsystem replies, all the threads are resumed.

e. Finally, the main thread begins execution in user mode at the entry point to the image being run. Execution begins when the trap that started the thread execution using a trap frame (built earlier when the kernel thread block was being iniatialized) that specifies previous mode as user and the PC as the start address of the thread is dismissed.

Thread Startup

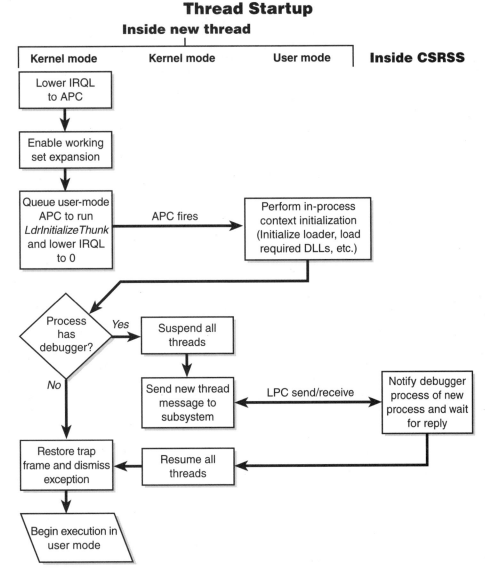

Figure 4-12
In-context thread initialization

Thread Scheduling

This section describes the Windows NT scheduling policies and algorithms. The first subsection gives a condensed description of how scheduling works on Windows NT and a definition of key terms. Then Windows NT priority levels are described from both the Win32 API and the Windows NT kernel points of view. After a review of the relevant Win32 functions and Windows NT utilities and tools that relate to scheduling, the detailed data structures and algorithms that comprise the Windows NT scheduling system are presented.

Overview of Windows NT Scheduling

Windows NT implements a priority-driven, preemptive scheduling system—the highest-priority runnable (*ready*) thread always runs, with the caveat that the thread chosen to run might be limited by the processors on which the thread is allowed to run, a phenomenon called *processor affinity*. By default, threads can run on any available processor, but you can alter processor affinity by using one of the Win32 scheduling functions.

When a thread is selected to run, it runs for an amount of time called a *quantum*. A quantum is the length of time a thread is allowed to run before Windows NT interrupts the thread to find out whether another thread at the same priority level is waiting to run or whether the thread's priority needs to be reduced. Quantum values can vary from thread to thread (and differ between Windows NT Workstation and Windows NT Server). (Quantums are described in more detail on page 195.) A thread might not get to complete its quantum, however. Because Windows NT implements a preemptive scheduler, if another thread with a higher priority becomes ready to run, the currently running thread is preempted before finishing its time slice. In fact, a thread can be selected to run next and be preempted before even beginning its quantum!

The Windows NT scheduling code is implemented in the kernel. There is no single "scheduler" module or routine, however—the code is spread throughout the kernel in which scheduling-related events occur. The routines that perform these duties are collectively called the kernel's *dispatcher*. Thread dispatching occurs at IRQL 2 and is triggered by any of the following events:

- A thread becomes ready to execute—for example, a newly created thread or one just released from the wait state.

- A thread leaves the running state because its time quantum ends, it terminates, or it enters a wait state.

■ A thread's priority changes, either because of a system service call or because Windows NT itself changes the priority value. (See the section "Adjusting Thread Scheduling" on page 204.)

■ The processor affinity of a running thread changes.

At each of these junctions, Windows NT must determine which thread should run next. When Windows NT selects a new thread to run, it performs a *context switch* to it. A context switch is the procedure of saving the volatile machine state associated with a running thread, loading another thread's volatile state, and starting the new thread's execution.

As already noted, Windows NT schedules at the thread granularity. This makes sense when you consider that processes don't run but only provide resources and a context in which their threads run. Because scheduling decisions are made strictly on a thread basis, no consideration is given to what process the thread belongs to. For example, if process *A* has 10 runnable threads and process *B* has 2 runnable threads, and all 12 threads are at the same priority, each thread would receive one-twelfth of the CPU time—Windows NT wouldn't give 50 percent of the CPU to process *A* and 50 percent to process *B*.

To understand the thread-scheduling algorithms, you must first understand the priority levels that Windows NT uses.

EXPERIMENT: Thread-Scheduling State Changes

You can watch thread-scheduling state changes with Performance Monitor. This utility can be useful when you're debugging a multithreaded application if you're unsure about the state of the threads running in the process. To watch thread-scheduling stage changes using Performance Monitor, follow these steps:

1. Run the Notepad utility (NOTEPAD.EXE).

2. Start Performance Monitor. (Select chart view if you're in some other view.)

3. Choose Chart from the Options menu. Change the chart vertical maximum to 7, and click OK. (As you'll see from the explanation text for the performance counter, thread states are numbers from 0 through 7.)

(continued)

Thread-Scheduling State Changes *continued*

4. Click the + (or press Ctrl-I) to bring up the Add Counters dialog box.

5. Select the Thread object, and then select the Thread State counter. Click the Explain button to see the definition of the values.

6. Go to the Instance box and scroll down until you see the Notepad process; select it, and click the Add button.

7. Scroll down in the Instance box to the PerfMon process, select its second thread (thread 1), and add it to the chart by clicking the Add button. You should see something like this:

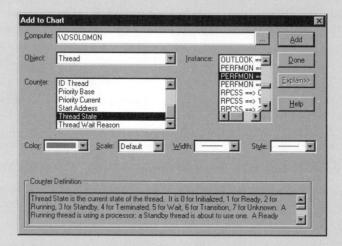

8. Now close the Add To Chart dialog box by clicking Done.

9. You should see the state of the Notepad thread as a 5, which, as shown in the explanation text in the dialog box, represents the wait state. (The thread is waiting for GUI input.) PerfMon, on the other hand, is in the running state (2): the thread you selected is the thread that is gathering the thread states, so when it goes to look at the state of the threads, it is, of course, running.

10. Now bring Notepad to the foreground (Alt-Tab to it or click its icon in the taskbar), and drag it around rapidly across the screen. You should see the thread move from Waiting to Ready

and back. When you see it in the ready state, PerfMon is catching Notepad while it has some window message pending, and the thread that is processing it is ready to run. You should see a display like this:

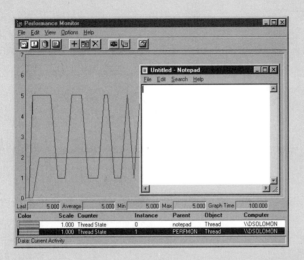

11. Again, you'll never see Notepad in the running state (unless you are on a multiprocessor system) because PerfMon is always in the running state when it gathers the state of the threads you are monitoring.

Priority Levels

As illustrated in Figure 4-13, internally, Windows NT uses 32 priority levels, ranging from 0 through 31. These values divide up as follows:

- Sixteen real-time levels (16–31)
- Fifteen variable levels (1–15)
- One system level (0), reserved for the zero page thread

Thread priority levels are assigned from two different perspectives: those of the Win32 API and those of the Windows NT kernel. The Win32 API first organizes processes by the priority class to which they are assigned at creation

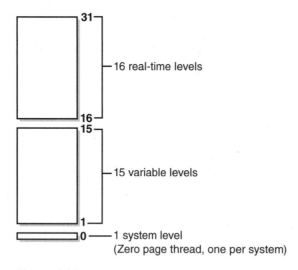

Figure 4-13
Thread priority levels

(Real-time, High, Normal, or Idle) and then by the relative priority of the individual threads within those processes (Time-critical, Highest, Above-normal, Normal, Below-normal, Lowest, and Idle).

To the Win32 API, each thread has a priority based on a combination of its process priority class and its relative thread priority. The mapping from Win32 priority to internal Windows NT numeric priority is shown in Table 4-15.

Table 4-15 Win32 vs. Windows NT Kernel Priorities

		Win32 process priority classes		
		Real time	High	Normal	Idle
	Time critical	31	15	15	15
	Highest	26	15	10	6
Win32 thread priorities	Above normal	25	14	9	5
	Normal	24	13	8	4
	Below normal	23	12	7	3
	Lowest	22	11	6	2
	Idle	16	1	1	1

The priorities shown in Table 4-15 are thread base priorities. The row labeled "Normal" is also the process base priority for the four priority classes. Threads start out inheriting the process base priority, which can be changed with Task Manager (as described in the section "Relevant Tools" on page 190) or with the Win32 *SetProcessPriority* function.

Normally, the process base priority (and hence the starting thread base priority) will be one of the values in the "Normal" row above (24, 13, 8, or 4). Some Windows NT system processes (such as the session manager, service controller, and local security authentication server), however, have a base process priority slightly higher than the default for the Normal class (8). This is so that the threads in these processes will all start at a higher priority than the default value of 8. A system process accomplishes this by using internal Windows NT functions to set its process base priority to a numeric value other than its default starting Win32 base priority.

Whereas a process has only a single priority value (base priority), each thread has two priority values: current and base. As you'll see (in the section "Adjusting Thread Scheduling" on page 204), the current priority for threads in the dynamic range (1 through 15) might be, and often is, higher than the base priority. Threads in the real-time range (16 through 31) never have their priority adjusted by Windows NT, so they always have the same base and current priority.

Win32 Scheduling APIs

The Win32 API functions that relate to thread scheduling are shown in Table 4-16. (For more information, see the Win32 API reference documentation.)

Table 4-16 Scheduling-Related APIs and Their Functions

API	Function
Suspend/ResumeThread	Suspends or resumes a paused thread from execution.
Get/SetPriorityClass	Returns or sets a process's priority class (base priority).
Get/SetThreadPriority	Returns or sets a thread's priority (relative to its process base priority).
Get/SetProcessAffinityMask	Returns or sets a process's affinity mask.
SetThreadAffinityMask	Sets a thread's affinity mask (must be a subset of the process's affinity mask) for a particular set of processors, restricting it to running on those processors.

(continued)

Table 4-16 *continued*

API	Function
Get/SetThreadPriorityBoost	Returns or sets the ability for Windows NT to boost the priority of a thread temporarily (applies only to threads in the dynamic range).
SetThreadIdealProcessor	Establishes a preferred processor for a particular thread but does not restrict the thread to that processor.
Get/SetProcessPriorityBoost	Returns or sets the default priority boost control state of the current process. (This function is used to set the thread priority boost control state when a thread is created.)
SwitchToThread	Yields execution for one quantum to another thread that is ready to run on the current processor.
Sleep	Puts the current thread into a wait state for a specified time interval (figured in milliseconds [msec]). A zero value relinquishes the rest of the thread's quantum.
SleepEx	Causes the current thread to go into a wait state until either an I/O completion callback is completed, an APC is queued to the thread, or the specified time interval ends.

Relevant Tools

As illustrated in Table 4-17, you can view (and change) the base-process priority class with Task Manager, Pview, or Pviewer. You can view the numeric base-process priority value with PerfMon or Pstat. You can view thread priorities with Performance Monitor, Pview, Pviewer, and Pstat. There is no general utility to change relative thread priority levels, however.

Table 4-17   Scheduling-Related Tools

Object	Taskman	PerfMon	Pviewer	Pview	Pstat	KD !thread
Process priority class	✓		✓	✓		
Process base priority		✓			✓	
Thread base priority		✓				
Thread current priority		✓	✓	✓	✓	✓

The only way to specify a starting priority class for a process is with the START command in the Windows NT command prompt.

EXPERIMENT: Examining and Specifying Process and Thread Priorities

Try the following experiment:

1. From the command prompt, type *start/realtime notepad.* Notepad should open.

2. Run Pview, and select NOTEPAD.EXE from the list of processes. You should see a dialog box like the one shown here. (The dynamic priority of the thread in Notepad is 24.)

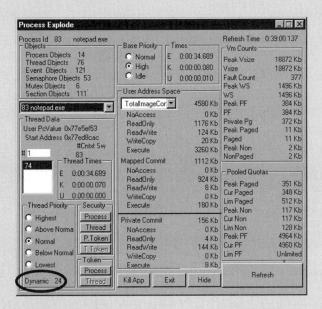

3. The Task Manager can show you similar information. Press Ctrl-Shift-Esc to start the Task Manager, and turn to the Processes tab shown here. Right-click on the Notepad process, and select the Set Priority option, noting that Notepad's process priority class is Realtime, as shown on the following page.

(continued)

Examining and Specifying Process and Thread Priorities *continued*

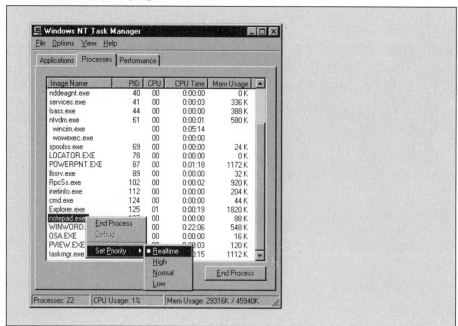

Real-Time Priorities

You can raise or lower thread priorities within the dynamic range in any application; however, you must have the *increase scheduling priority* privilege to enter the real-time range. (If you attempt to move a process into the Real-time priority class and don't have the privilege, the operation doesn't fail—the High class is used.) Be aware that many important Windows NT kernel-mode system threads run in the real-time priority range, so if you spend excessive time running in this range, you might be blocking critical system functions in the memory manager, cache manager, local and network file systems, and even other device drivers. As noted earlier, you won't block hardware interrupts because they have a higher priority than any thread, but you might block system threads from running.

> **NOTE** Although Windows NT has what are called *real-time* priority levels, it is not a true real-time operating system in that it doesn't provide a guaranteed interrupt latency or a way for threads to obtain a guaranteed execution time. For more information, see the MSDN Library article "Real-Time Systems and Microsoft Windows NT."

Interrupt Levels vs. Priority Levels

As illustrated in Figure 4-14, all threads (whether they are running in user mode or kernel mode) run at IRQL 0 or 1. (For a description of how Windows NT uses interrupt levels, see page 86 in Chapter 3.) Threads normally run at IRQL 0. Only kernel mode APCs execute at IRQL 1, since they interrupt the execution of a thread. (For more information on APCs, see page 92 in Chapter 3.) Because of this, no thread, regardless of its priority, blocks hardware interrupts (although high-priority real-time threads can block the execution of important system threads).

Thread-scheduling decisions are made at IRQL 2 (called Dispatch level for thread dispatching). Thus, while the kernel is deciding which thread should run next, no thread can be running and possibly changing scheduling-related information (such as priorities). On a multiprocessor system, access to the thread-scheduling data structures is synchronized by acquiring the Dispatcher spinlock (*KiDispatcherLock*).

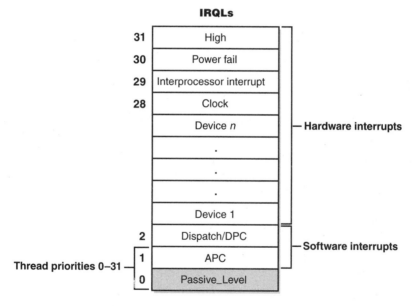

Figure 4-14
Interrupt priorities vs. thread priorities

Thread States

Before you can comprehend the thread-scheduling algorithms and data structures, you need to understand the various execution states that a thread can be in. Figure 4-15 illustrates the state transitions for a Windows NT thread. More details on what happens at each transition are described later in this section.

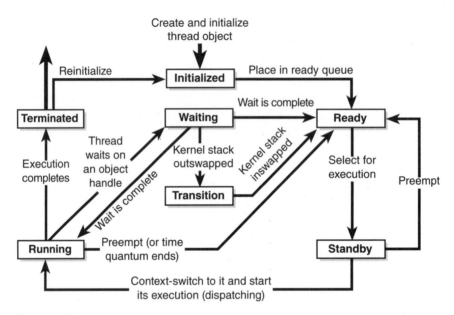

Figure 4-15
Thread states

The thread states are as follows:

- **Ready**   When looking for a thread to execute, the dispatcher considers only the pool of threads in the ready state. These threads are simply waiting to execute.

- **Standby**   A thread in the standby state has been selected to run next on a particular processor. When the correct conditions exist, the dispatcher performs a context switch to this thread. Only one thread can be in the standby state for each processor on the system.

- **Running**   Once the dispatcher performs a context switch to a thread, the thread enters the running state and executes. The thread's execution continues until either the kernel preempts it to run a higher priority thread, its quantum ends, it terminates, or it voluntarily enters the wait state.

■ **Waiting**   A thread can enter the wait state in several ways: a thread can voluntarily wait on an object to synchronize its execution, the operating system (the I/O system, for example) can wait on the thread's behalf, or an environment subsystem can direct the thread to suspend itself. When the thread's wait ends, depending on the priority, the thread either begins running immediately or is moved back to the ready state.

■ **Transition**   A thread enters the transition state if it is ready for execution but its kernel stack is paged out of memory. For example, the thread's kernel stack might be paged out of memory. Once its kernel stack is brought back into memory, the thread enters the ready state.

■ **Terminated**   When a thread finishes executing, it enters the terminated state. Once terminated, a thread object might or might not be deleted. (The object manager sets policy regarding when to delete the object.) If the executive has a pointer to the thread object, it can reinitialize the thread object and use it again.

Quantum

As mentioned earlier in the chapter, a quantum is the amount of time a thread gets to run before Windows NT checks whether another thread at the same priority should get to run. If a thread completes its quantum and there are no other threads at its priority, Windows NT reschedules the thread to run for another quantum.

How long is a quantum? There is no simple answer, because a quantum can vary from thread to thread and from machine to machine. Also, there is no registry setting for a quantum. So how does Windows NT compute a quantum? Several factors come into play:

■ Each thread has a quantum value that represents how long the thread can run until its quantum expires. This value is not a time length but rather a simple integer value, which I'll call *quantum units*.

■ By default, threads start with a quantum value of 6 on Windows NT Workstation and 36 on Windows NT Server. The reason for the longer value on Windows NT Server is because of the assumption that when a server application wakes up as the result of a client request, it should get enough CPU time to complete the request and go back into a wait state. Thus, threads on Windows NT Server run longer so that they can (hopefully) respond to whatever need they are answering within one quantum.

■ Each time the clock interrupts, the clock-interrupt routine deducts a fixed value (3) from the thread quantum. If the thread quantum is 0 or less, the quantum end processing is triggered and another thread might be selected to run. On Windows NT Workstation, since 3 is deducted each time the clock interrupt fires, a thread runs for 2 clock intervals; on Windows NT Server, a thread runs for 12 clock intervals.

■ The length of the clock interval varies according to hardware platform. The frequency of the clock interrupts is up to the HAL, not the kernel. For example, the clock interval for some Intel systems is 10 milliseconds, while for some other systems it is 15 milliseconds. Currently, all Digital Equipment Corporation (DEC) Alpha AXP systems have a clock interval of 7.8125 milliseconds.

■ On Windows NT Workstation, a quantum might be temporarily increased for the threads in the foreground application. Depending on the system setting, one of three quantum values might be added to the base quantum value. (This is described in the section "Quantum Stretching" on page 205.)

■ A quantum is doubled when Windows NT boosts a thread's priority to try to avoid priority inversion. (For more information, see the section "Priority Boosts for CPU Starvation" on page 210.)

■ When a thread comes out of a wait state, its quantum is adjusted. Threads in the real-time range (priority 16 through 31) have their quantum reset to the process default value. Threads in the dynamic priority range (priority 0 through 15) have their quantum decremented by 1. If this adjustment results in a 0 quantum, the quantum is reset to the process default value; if the thread is running with a boosted priority (see page 207), the priority is adjusted accordingly.

Table 4-18 lists the approximate values for the clock interval timer and the corresponding default thread quantums for several different hardware platforms.

Table 4-18   Architectural Differences in Default Quantum

Processor	Clock Interval	Default Quantum on Windows NT Workstation	Default Quantum on Windows NT Server
Typical uniprocessor 486	10 msec	20 msec	120 msec
Typical uniprocessor Pentium, Pentium Pro	15 msec	30 msec	180 msec
Some multiprocessor 486s	10 msec	20 msec	120 msec
Other multiprocessor Intel systems	15 msec	30 msec	180 msec
DEC AXP systems	7.8 msec	15.6 msec	93.6 msec

Scheduling Data Structures

To make thread-scheduling decisions, the kernel maintains a set of data structures known collectively as the *dispatcher database,* which is illustrated in Figure 4-16. The dispatcher database keeps track of which threads are waiting to execute and which processors are executing which threads. The most important structure in the dispatcher database is the *dispatcher ready queue* (located at *KiDispatcherReadyListHead*). This queue is really a series of queues, one queue for each scheduling priority. The queues contain threads that are in the ready state, waiting to be scheduled for execution.

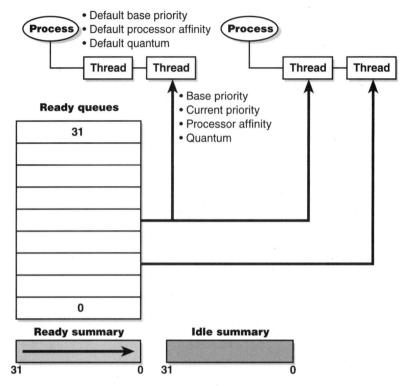

Figure 4-16
Dispatcher database

To speed up the selection of which thread to run or preempt, Windows NT maintains a 32-bit bitmask called the *ready summary* (*KiReadySummary*). Each bit set indicates one or more threads in the ready queue for that priority level. (Bit 0 represents priority 0, and so on.) Windows NT maintains another bitmask, the *idle summary* (*KiIdleSummary*), in which each set bit represents an idle processor.

As noted earlier, thread dispatching takes place at IRQL 2. In addition to preventing other threads from running, being at IRQL 2 synchronizes access to the dispatcher database. On a multiprocessor system, however, changes to the dispatcher database require the additional step of acquiring the kernel dispatcher spinlock (*KiDispatcherLock*).

System Variables

Table 4-19 shows the kernel-mode system variables that are related to thread scheduling.

Table 4-19   Scheduling System Variables

Variable	Type	Description
KiDispatcherLock	Spinlock	Dispatcher spinlock
KeNumber Processors	Byte	Number of processors active in system
KeActiveProcessors	Bitmask (32 bits)	Bitmask of active processors in system
KiIdleSummary	Bitmask (32 bits)	Bitmask of idle processors
KiReadySummary	Bitmask (32 bits)	Bitmask of priority levels that have 1 or more ready threads
KiDispatcherReady ListHead	Array of 32 list entries	List heads for the 32 ready queues
PspForeground Quantum	Array of schar	Note: A quantum is measured in units of clock ticks.
		[0]=default thread quantum value – (6 on Windows NT Workstation, 36 on Windows NT Server)
		[1]=quantum for foreground threads(middle setting) – (12 on Windows NT Workstation, 36 on Windows NT Server)
		[2]=quantum for foreground threads (maximum setting) – (18 on Windows NT Workstation, 36 on Windows NT Server)

Scheduling Scenarios

Windows NT bases the question of "Who gets the CPU?" on thread priority; but how does this work in practice? The following sections illustrate just how priority-driven preemptive multitasking works on the thread level.

Voluntary Switch

First a thread might voluntarily relinquish use of the processor by entering a wait state on some object (such as an event, mutex, semaphore, I/O completion port, process, thread, window message, and so on) by calling one of the many Win32 wait functions (such as *WaitForSingleObject* or *WaitForMultiple-Objects*). Waiting on objects is described in more detail in Chapter 2.

Voluntary switching is roughly equivalent to a thread ordering an item that isn't ready to go at a fast-food counter. Rather than hold up the queue of the other diners, the thread will step aside and let the next thread execute its routine while the first thread's hamburger is being prepared. When the hamburger is ready, the first thread goes to the end of the ready queue of the priority level.

However, as you'll see later in the chapter, most wait operations result in a temporary priority boost so that the thread can pick up its hamburger right away and start eating.

Figure 4-17 illustrates a thread entering a wait state and Windows NT selecting a new thread to run.

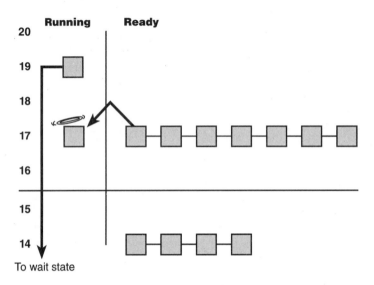

Figure 4-17
Voluntary switching

In Figure 4-17, the top block (thread) is voluntarily relinquishing the processor so that the next thread in the ready queue can run (as represented by the halo it has when in the Running column). Although it might appear from this figure that the relinquishing thread's priority is being reduced, it's not—it's just being moved to the wait queue of the object(s) the thread is waiting on. What about any remaining quantum for the thread? The quantum value is not reset when a thread enters a wait state—in fact, when the wait is satisfied, the thread's quantum value is decremented by 1 quantum unit, equivalent to one-third of a clock interval.

Preemption

In this scheduling scenario, a lower-priority thread is preempted when a higher-priority thread becomes ready to run. This situation might occur for a couple of reasons.

- A higher-priority thread's wait completes. (The event that the other thread was waiting on has occurred.)

- A thread priority is increased or decreased.

In either of these cases, Windows NT must determine whether the currently running thread should still continue to run or whether it should be preempted to allow a higher-priority thread to run.

NOTE Threads running in kernel mode can be preempted by threads running in user mode—the mode in which the thread is running doesn't matter. The thread priority is the determining factor.

When a thread is preempted, it is put at the head of the ready queue for the priority it was running at so that it can finish its quantum when it gets to run again. Although the thread won't get to restart its time slice, it will get to complete any time remaining in its quantum. Figure 4-18 illustrates this situation.

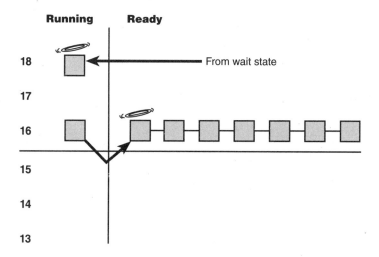

Figure 4-18
Preemptive thread scheduling

In Figure 4-18, a thread with priority 18 emerges from a wait state and repossesses the CPU, causing the thread that had been running (at priority 16) to be bumped to the head of the ready queue. Notice that the bumped thread is not going to the end of the queue but to the beginning; when the preempting thread has finished running, the bumped thread can complete its quantum. In this example, the threads are in the real-time range; as explained in the section "Adjusting Thread Scheduling" on page 204, no dynamic priority boosts are allowed for threads in the real-time range.

If voluntary switching is roughly equivalent to a thread letting another thread place its lunch order while the first thread waits for its meal, preemption is roughly equivalent to a thread being bumped from its place in line because the president of the United States has just walked in and ordered a hamburger. The preempted thread doesn't get bumped to the back of the line but is simply moved aside while the president gets his lunch. As soon as the president leaves, the first thread can resume ordering its meal.

Quantum End

When the running thread exhausts its CPU quantum, Windows NT must determine whether the thread's priority should be decremented and then whether another thread should be scheduled on the processor.

If the thread priority is reduced, Windows NT looks for a more appropriate thread to schedule. (For example, a more appropriate thread would be a thread in a ready queue with a higher priority than the new priority for the currently running thread.) If the thread priority is not reduced, Windows NT selects the next thread in the ready queue at that same priority level and moves the previously running thread to the tail of that queue (giving it a new quantum value and changing its state from running to ready). This case is illustrated in Figure 4-19. If no other thread of the same priority is ready to run, the thread gets to run for another quantum.

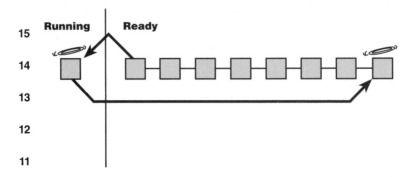

Figure 4-19
Quantum end thread scheduling

The fact that a thread has a quantum does not mean that it must finish the quantum. A thread might voluntarily relinquish control of the CPU before its time slice ends by going into a wait state, or it might be preempted before finishing its time slice by a thread with a higher priority. As discussed earlier, if the thread voluntarily relinquishes the CPU, it will start with a new quantum when it begins running again. If the thread is preempted, however, it moves to the head of the ready queue for the priority it was running at and, later, when it is scheduled again, finishes the remaining time slice it had already begun.

Termination

When a thread finishes running (either because it returned from its main routine, called *ExitThread*, or was killed with *TerminateThread*), it moves from the running state to the terminated state. If there are no handles open on the thread object, the thread is removed from the process thread list and the associated data structures are deallocated and released.

Context Switching

A thread's context and the procedure for context switching vary depending on the architecture of a processor. A typical context switch requires saving and reloading the following data:

- Program counter
- Processor status register
- Other register contents
- User and kernel stack pointers
- A pointer to the address space in which the thread runs (the process's page table directory)

To make a context switch, the kernel saves the old thread's kernel stack pointer in the KTHREAD block and then sets the stack pointer to the new thread's kernel stack address. The kernel then saves the above information about the old the thread by pushing it onto the current thread's kernel-mode stack and updating the stack pointer. The kernel loads the new thread's context and, if the new thread is in a different process, loads the address of its page table directory (so that its address space is available) and flushes the translation buffer cache. If a kernel APC that needs to be delivered is pending, an interrupt at IRQL 1 is requested. Otherwise, control passes to the new thread's restored program counter and the thread resumes execution.

Idle Thread

When no runnable thread exists on a CPU, Windows NT dispatches the per-CPU idle thread. Each CPU is allotted one idle thread since on a multiprocessor system one CPU can be executing a thread while other CPUs might have no threads to execute. Windows NT reports the priority of the idle thread as 0. In reality, however, such threads don't have a priority level because they run only when there are no threads to run. (Remember, only one thread per Windows NT system is actually running at priority 0—the zero page thread.) In fact, the idle loop runs at dispatch level (IRQL 2), polling for work to do: deferred procedure calls (DPCs) to deliver or threads to dispatch to. Although some details of the flow vary between architectures, the basic flow of control of the idle thread is as follows:

1. Enables and disables interrupts (allowing any pending interrupts to be delivered).

2. Checks whether any DPCs (described in Chapter 3) are pending on the processor. If DPCs are pending, clears the pending software interrupt and delivers them.

3. Checks whether a thread has been selected to run next on the processor, and if so, dispatches that thread.

4. Calls the HAL processor idle routine (in case any power management functions need to be performed).

Various Windows NT process viewer utilities report the idle process using different names. Task Manager calls it "System Idle Process," Pview and Pviewer report it as "Idle," Pstat calls it "Idle Process," Tlist calls it "System Process," and Qslice calls it "SystemProcess." The names vary because there is no real process name in the process block; each utility had to pick its own name. No matter what it's called, however, the Idle process is always process ID 0.

Adjusting Thread Scheduling

In some situations, Windows NT adjusts the priority or quantum value of threads. The intent of these adjustments is to improve system throughput and responsiveness. Like any scheduling algorithms, however, these adjustments are not perfect, and they might not be beneficial to all applications.

NOTE Windows NT never boosts the priority of threads in the real-time range (16 through 31)—Windows NT assumes that if you're using the real-time thread priorities, you know what you're doing.

Here are the four types of scheduling adjustments:

- Increasing the quantum for the threads in the foreground process
- Boosting priority upon wait completion
- Boosting priority for threads entering a wait state
- Boosting priority for threads that are not getting any CPU time

Quantum Stretching

The first of these adjustments involves increasing the quantum for threads running inside the foreground application. The *foreground application* is the process that owns the thread that owns the window that is in focus. This adjustment occurs only on Windows NT Workstation and only to interactive processes (processes launched from the interactive session) in the Normal, High, or Real-time priority class.

If you open the System applet in the Control Panel and turn to the Performance tab, you'll see a dialog box like the one shown in Figure 4-20. The Application Performance section has a slider control with three settings: None, in the middle, and Maximum. This setting is stored in the registry in HKLM\System…\Control\PriorityControl\Win32PrioritySeparation. The value is 0, 1, or 2, corresponding to the three selections on the slider bar. (The default setting on all Windows NT systems is Maximum, or 2.)

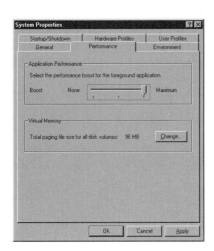

Figure 4-20
Adjusting the foreground application's quantum

If you set the boost to None (the default), the foreground thread's quantum is the system default quantum. If set to the middle notch, the default quantum doubles. And if set to the Maximum setting, the default quantum triples. As mentioned earlier, Windows NT Server uses the same quantum value for foreground and background processes, regardless of the system performance boost setting.

When the foreground window changes, the Win32 subsystem changes the quantum values for all the threads in the foreground process by using the value of the Win32PrioritySeparation registry field as an index into a three-element array named *PspForegroundQuantum*. Each element in the array contains the quantum value that should be used for threads in the foreground process for the three application boost settings in Control Panel. The values of this array are shown in Table 4-20.

Table 4-20 **Quantum Values at Each Boost Setting**

Boost Setting	System Variable	Windows NT Workstation	Windows NT Server
None	*PspForegroundQuantum[0]*	6	36
Middle	*PspForegroundQuantum[1]*	12	36
Maximum	*PspForegroundQuantum[2]*	18	36

Quantum stretching is new to Windows NT 4.0. In earlier versions of Windows NT, the system increased the base priority of the threads in the foreground process by either 1 (middle setting) or 2 (Maximum setting). The problem with this approach was that when a process was brought into the foreground and run, it would completely block execution of background interactive processes because the foreground threads were running at a higher priority than the background threads.

For example, if you started a long-running spreadsheet recalculation and then switched to another application that was CPU-intensive (such as a graphics-intensive game), the spreadsheet process running in the background would get little CPU time even though, from the point of the user, both processes were running at the same priority class. Quantum stretching also does not prevent other background applications from running but does give the one in the foreground a little longer to run before relinquishing the processor. So, while this new method of increasing the quantum of foreground threads instead of their priority can reduce the quick responsiveness of foreground applications in relation to how they ran under Windows NT 3.*x*, it is fairer to background applications. Of course, if you do want to run an interactive application at a higher priority than all other interactive processes, you can always change the priority class to High using Task Manager (or use the *start / high* command from the command prompt).

Priority Boosting After I/Os

Windows NT gives temporary priority boosts upon completion of certain I/O and wait operations so that threads that were waiting on I/O or a kernel object will have more of a chance to run right away and process whatever was being waited on, issue some other I/O or wait request, and go back to sleep.

The amount of boost a thread receives depends on the kind of wait it has just completed. If the thread has finished a long wait for a slow device, it gets a big boost; if the thread had a short wait for a fast device, it gets a smaller boost. Thus, waiting on fast devices such as hard disks or CD-ROMs nets a thread a small boost; waiting on something somewhat slower, such as the network, nets it a larger boost; and waiting on a slow device nets it the largest boost. Boosts are also given when completing a wait on various synchronization objects, such as events or semaphores.

Although it is up to the device driver to specify the priority boost when it completes an I/O request, the values shown in Table 4-21 are the suggested default boost values as defined in \ddk\include\ntddk.h (one of the include files in the Windows NT Device Driver Kit).

Table 4-21 Default Boost Values for Some Devices

Device or Object	Boost
Event, semaphore	1
Disk, CD-ROM, parallel, video	1
Network, mailslot, named pipe, serial	2
Keyboard, mouse	6
Sound	8

As illustrated in Figure 4-21, after the boost is applied, the thread gets to run for one quantum at the elevated priority level. After the thread has completed its quantum, it decays one priority level and then runs another quantum. This cycle continues until the thread's priority level has decayed back to its base priority.

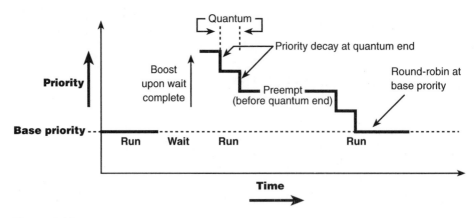

Figure 4-21
Life cycle of a thread

Notice that the boosted thread can still be preempted by another thread with a higher priority, but the interrupted thread gets to finish its time slice at the boosted priority level before it decays to the next lower priority.

As noted earlier, these boosts apply only to threads in the dynamic priority range (0 through 15). No matter how large the boost is, the thread will never be boosted beyond level 15 into the real-time priority range. In other words, a priority-14 thread that receives a boost of 5 will go up to priority 15. A priority-15 thread that receives a boost will remain at priority 15.

Priority Boosts for GUI Threads Entering a Wait State

By default, all threads in processes started in your interactive session have a base priority of 8, the initial priority of a thread in the Normal process priority class. If you look at the current thread priority of a thread waiting for a window message, however, you'll notice the current priority is 14. (To try this, start a copy of Notepad and use PerfMon to examine its current and base priority.) The kernel-mode component of the Win32 subsystem boosts the current priority of threads waiting for user input or window messages to 14 so that when input is available the thread will have a greater chance of running right away—it can process the user input and likely return to a wait state. Unlike the boosts described in the previous section, with this boost, the priority drops immediately back to the base priority of the thread when it finishes its quantum. However, Windows NT doubles the quantum when it grants the priority boost so that when the thread does run, it will run for twice the normal quantum before dropping all the way down to its previous base priority.

EXPERIMENT: Watching Priority Boosts and Decays

Using the CPUSTRES tool in the Win32 SDK (\MSTOOLS\BIN\ CPUSTRES.EXE), you can watch priority boosts in action. Take the following steps:

1. Run \MSTOOLS\BIN\CPUSTRES.EXE.

2. Run Performance Monitor. (Select chart view if you're in some other view.)

3. Click on the Chart menu item, and select Options. Change the chart interval to 0.1 (one-tenth) second and the vertical maximum to 15 (because priority values in the dynamic range only go up to 15).

4. Click the + (or press Ctrl-I) to bring up the Add Counters dialog box.

5. Select the Thread object, and then select both Priority Base Priority Current counters. (Hold down the Ctrl button to select the second counter while keeping the selection of the first counter.)

6. Go to the Instance box, and scroll down the list until you see the CPUSTRES process. Select the second thread. (The first thread is the GUI thread.) You should see something like this:

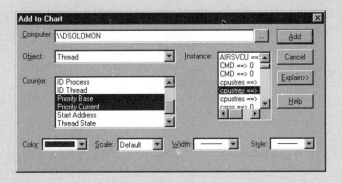

7. Click the Add button, and then click the Done button.

8. Bring CPUSTRES to the foreground. (Alt-Tab to it, or click on its icon in the taskbar.)

9. You should see the current priority being boosted and then decaying back down to the base priority.

Priority Boosts for CPU Starvation

Imagine the following situation: you've got a priority-7 thread that's running, preventing a priority-4 thread from ever getting the CPU; however, a priority-11 thread is waiting on some resource that the priority-4 thread has locked. But because the priority-7 thread in the middle is eating up all the CPU time, the priority-4 thread will never run long enough to finish whatever it's doing and release the resource blocking the priority-11 thread.

What does Windows NT do to address this situation? Once a second, the balance set manager (a system thread that exists primarily to perform memory management functions and is described in more detail in Chapter 5) scans the ready queues for any threads that have been in the ready state (that is, have not run) for longer than 300 clock ticks (approximately 3 to 4 seconds, depending on the clock interval). If it finds such a thread, the balance set manager

EXPERIMENT: Watching Priority Boosts for CPU Starvation

You can watch this priority boost for CPU starvation using the CPU-STRES tool in the Resource Kit and the Platform SDK by following these steps:

1. Run \MSTOOLS\BIN\CPUSTRES.EXE, and make thread 2 active by clicking on the checkbox labeled "Active" underneath thread 2. Change the activity of thread 2 to Maximum.

2. Run Performance Monitor. (Select chart view if you're in some other view.)

3. Choose Chart from the Options menu. Change the chart interval to 0.1 (one-tenth) second and the vertical maximum to 15 (because priority values in the dynamic range only go up through 15).

4. Click the + (or press Ctrl-I) to bring up the Add Counters dialog box.

5. Select the Thread object, and then select both the Priority Base and the Priority Current counters. (Hold down the Ctrl key to select the second counter while keeping the selection of the first counter.)

6. Go to the Instance box, and scroll down until you see the CPUSTRES process. You should see three threads. Select the second thread. (The first thread is the GUI thread, and the

third thread is what the application calls thread 2, which you activated earlier and set to maximum activity.) You should see something like this:

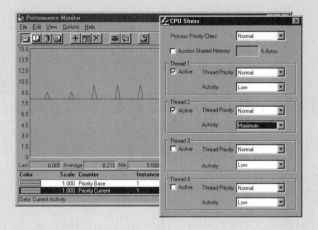

7. Click Add, and then click Done.

8. Bring CPUSTRES to the foreground. (Alt-Tab to it, or click its icon in the taskbar.)

9. Every 4 seconds, you should see the current priority boosted to 14 and then dropped back to 7, as shown here:

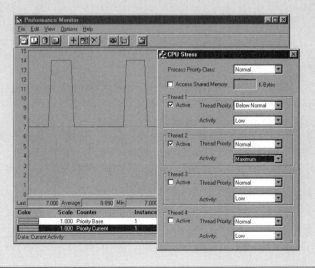

boosts the thread's priority to 15 and gives it double the normal quantum. Once the 2 quantums are up, the thread's priority decays immediately to its original base priority. If the thread wasn't finished and there is a higher priority thread ready to run, the decayed thread will return to the ready queue, where it again becomes eligible for another boost if it remains there for another 300 clock ticks.

The balance set manager doesn't actually scan all ready threads every time it runs. To minimize the CPU time it uses, it scans only 16 ready threads; if there are more threads at that priority level, it remembers where it left off and picks up again on the next pass. Also, it will boost only 10 threads per pass—if it finds 10 threads meriting this particular boost (which would indicate an unusually busy system), it stops the scan at that point and picks up again on the next pass.

Will this algorithm always solve the priority inversion issue? No—it's not perfect by any means. But over time, CPU-starved threads should get enough CPU time to finish whatever processing they were doing and reenter a wait state.

Thread Scheduling on Symmetric Multiprocessing Systems

If scheduling access to system processors is based on thread priority, what happens if you're using more than one processor? In summary, Windows NT attempts to schedule the highest priority runnable threads on all available CPUs. However, several factors influence the choice of which CPU a thread will run on. Before I describe the algorithms, I'll need to define a few terms.

Affinity

Each thread has an *affinity mask* that specifies the processors on which the thread is allowed to run. The thread affinity mask is inherited from the process affinity mask. By default, all processes (and therefore all threads) begin with an affinity mask that is equal to the set of active processors on the system—in other words, all threads can run on all processors.

Two things can alter that:

- A call made by the application to the *SetProcessAffinityMask* or *SetThreadAffinityMask* functions.

- An imagewide affinity mask specified in the image header. (For more information on the detailed format of Windows NT images, see the article "Portable Executable and Common Object File Format Specification" in the MSDN Library.)

Ideal and Next Processor

Each thread has two CPU numbers stored in the kernel thread block:

- *Ideal processor,* or the preferred processor that this thread should run on

- *Next processor,* or the processor on which the thread has been selected to run next (or did run last)

The ideal processor is chosen randomly when a thread is created, based on a seed in the process block. The seed is incremented each time a thread is created so that the ideal processor for each new thread in the process will rotate through the available processors on the system. Windows NT does not change the ideal processor once the thread is created; however, an application can change the ideal processor value for a thread using the *SetThreadIdealProcessor* function.

Choosing a Processor for a Ready Thread

When a thread becomes ready to run, Windows NT first tries to schedule the thread to run on an idle processor. If there is a choice of idle processors, preference is given first to the thread's ideal processor, then to the thread's next processor, then to the currently executing processor (that is, the CPU on which the scheduling code is running). If none of these CPUs are idle, Windows NT picks the first available idle processor by scanning the idle processor mask from lowest to highest CPU number.

If all processors are currently busy and a thread becomes ready, Windows NT looks to see whether it can preempt a thread in the running or standby state on one of the CPUs. Which CPU is examined? The first choice is the thread's ideal processor, and the second choice is the thread's next processor. If neither of those CPUs are in the thread's affinity mask, Windows NT selects the first processor in the active processor mask that the thread can run on.

If the processor selected already has a thread selected to run next (waiting in the standby state to be scheduled) and that thread's priority is less than the priority of the thread being readied for execution, the new thread preempts that thread out of the standby state and becomes the next thread for that CPU. If there is no next thread selected to run for that CPU, Windows NT checks whether the priority of the currently running thread is less than the thread being readied for execution. If so, the currently running thread is marked to be preempted and Windows NT queues an interprocessor interrupt to kick off the currently running thread in favor of this new thread.

NOTE Windows NT does not look at the priority of the current and next threads on all the CPUs—just on the one CPU selected as described above. If no thread can be preempted on that one CPU, the new thread is put in the ready queue for its priority level, where it awaits its turn to get scheduled.

Selecting a Thread to Run on a Specific CPU

In several cases (such as when a thread lowers its priority, changes its affinity, or delays or yields execution), Windows NT must find a new thread to run on the CPU that the currently executing thread was running on. On a single processor system, Windows NT simply picks the first thread in the ready queue, starting with the highest-priority ready queue with at least one thread and working its way down. On a multiprocessor system, however, Windows NT doesn't simply pick the first thread in the ready queue. Instead, it looks for a thread that meets one of the following conditions:

- Ran last on the specified processor
- Has its ideal processor set to the specified processor
- Has been waiting to run for longer than 2 quantums
- Has a priority greater than or equal to 24

Why does it matter which processor a thread was last running on? As usual, the answer is speed—giving preference to the last processor a thread executed on maximizes the chances that thread data remains in the secondary cache of the processor in question.

When the Highest-Priority Ready Threads Are Not Running

As explained in the preceding section, on a multiprocessor system, Windows NT doesn't always select the highest-priority thread to run on a given CPU. Thus, a thread with a higher priority than the currently running thread on a given CPU can become ready but might not immediately preempt the current thread.

Another situation in which the highest-priority thread might not preempt the current thread is when a thread's affinity mask is set as a subset of the available CPUs. In that case, the processors to which the thread has affinity are currently running higher-priority threads and the thread must wait for one of those processors—even if another processor is free or running lower-priority threads that it could otherwise preempt. Windows NT will not move a running thread that could run on a different processor from one CPU to second processor to permit a thread with an affinity for the first processor to run on the first processor.

For example, consider this scenario: CPU 0 is running a priority-8 thread that can run on any processor, and CPU 1 is running a priority-4 thread that can run on any processor. A priority-6 thread that can run on only CPU 0 becomes ready. What happens? Windows NT will not move the priority-8 thread from CPU 0 to CPU 1 (preempting the priority-4 thread) so that the priority-6 thread can run.

Conclusion

In this chapter, we've examined the structure of processes and threads, seen how they are created and destroyed, and looked at how Windows NT decides which threads should run and for how long.

Many references in this chapter are to topics related to memory management. Because threads run inside processes and processes in large part define an address space, the next logical topic is how Windows NT performs virtual and physical memory management—the subjects of Chapter 5.

Memory Management

In this chapter, you'll learn how Microsoft Windows NT implements virtual memory and how it manages the subset kept in physical memory. These jobs involve two primary tasks:

- Translating, or mapping, a process's virtual address space into physical memory so that when a thread running in the context of that process reads or writes to the virtual address space, the correct physical address is updated

- Paging some of the contents of memory to disk when it becomes over-committed—that is, when running threads or system code try to use more physical memory than is currently available—and bringing the contents back into physical memory when needed

Although the details by which the hardware maps virtual memory onto physical memory create some differences in the way Windows NT accomplishes these tasks, in this chapter I'll focus primarily on the platform-independent characteristics of the memory manager that are the same on both *x*86 and Alpha systems. (I'll point out any significant differences as they come up.)

In addition to providing 32-bit virtual memory management, the memory manager provides a core set of services on which the various Windows NT environment subsystems are built. These services include memory mapped files (internally called *section objects*), copy-on-write memory, and support for applications using large, sparse address spaces. In this chapter, I'll summarize these basic services and review pertinent concepts such as reserved versus committed memory and shared memory. I'll also describe the internal structure and components that make up the memory manager, including key data structures and algorithms.

Services the Memory Manager Provides

The memory manager provides a set of system services to environment subsystems to allocate and free virtual memory, share memory between processes, map files into memory, flush virtual pages to disk, retrieve information about a range of virtual pages, change their protection, and lock them into memory.

Like other Windows NT executive services, the memory management services allow their caller to supply a process handle, indicating the particular process whose virtual memory is to be manipulated. The caller can thus manipulate both its own memory or (with the proper permissions) that of another process. For example, as explained in Chapter 4, one process can create another, giving itself the right to manipulate the child process's virtual memory. Thereafter, the parent process can allocate, deallocate, read, and write memory on behalf of the child process by calling virtual memory services and passing a handle to the child process as an argument. This feature is used by subsystems to manage the memory of their client processes, and it is also key for implementing debuggers—since debuggers must be able to read and write to the memory of the process being debugged.

Most of these services are exposed through the Win32 API. The Win32 API has three groups of functions for managing memory in applications: page granularity virtual memory functions (*Virtualxxx*), memory-mapped file functions (*CreateFileMapping, MapViewofFile*), and heap functions (*Heapxxx* and the older interfaces *Localxxx* and *Globalxxx*). (I'll describe the heap manager later in this section.)

The memory manager also provides a number of services to device drivers (and other kernel-mode system code), such as allocating and deallocating physical memory and locking pages in physical memory for direct memory access (DMA) transfers. These functions begin with the prefix *Mm*. In addition, though not strictly part of the memory manager, the executive support routines that begin with *Ex* that are used to allocate and deallocate from the system heaps (paged and nonpaged pool) as well as manipulate look-aside lists. I'll touch on these topics later in this chapter, in the section "System Memory Pools" on page 227.

Although I'll be referring to Win32 functions and kernel-mode memory management and memory allocation routines provided for device drivers, I won't cover the interface and programming details, since this book describes the internal operations of these functions. Refer to the Win32 application programming interface (API) and Device Driver Kit (DDK) documentation on MSDN for a complete description of the available functions and their interfaces.

Reserving and Committing Virtual Memory

Windows NT provides an optional two-phase approach to memory allocation—applications can first *reserve* address space and then *commit* storage in that address space (either in the paging file or by mapping a view of a mapped file). Or they can reserve and commit in the same function call. These services are exposed through the Win32 *VirtualAlloc* and *VirtualAllocEx* functions.

Reserved memory is simply a way for a thread to reserve a range of virtual addresses for future use. You reserve address space, but you commit storage. Accessing reserved memory results in an access violation because there's no committed storage behind the memory to contain or store the data. Committed memory, in contrast, is memory for which the memory manager has corresponding disk storage, called the *backing store*. Accessing committed memory results in the page being brought into physical memory (if it isn't already there).

Pages in a process address space are either free (not committed or reserved, and inaccessible), reserved, or committed. Committed pages are either private (and thus inaccessible to any other process) or mapped into a view of a section (which might or might not be mapped by other processes). Sections are described in the next section as well as in the "Section Objects" section on page 298.

You can decommit storage and/or release address space with the *VirtualFree* or *VirtualFreeEx* functions. The difference between decommittal and release is similar to the difference between reservation and committal—decommitted memory is still reserved, but released memory is neither committed nor reserved. (It's free.)

Using the two-step process of reserving and committing memory can reduce page file usage by deferring committing storage until needed. Reserving memory is a relatively fast and inexpensive operation under Windows NT because it doesn't consume any page file space (a precious system resource) or process page file quota (a limit on the page file space a process can consume). All that need to be updated or constructed are the relatively small internal data structures that represent the state of the process address space. (I'll explain these data structures, called *virtual address space descriptors,* or VADs, later in the chapter.)

Reserving and then committing memory is useful for applications that need a potentially large contiguous memory buffer; rather than committing page file storage for the entire region, the address space can be reserved and then committed later when needed. An application of this technique in the operating system is the user-mode stack for each thread. When a thread is created, a stack is reserved. (1 MB is the default; you can override this size with the *CreateThread* function call or on an imagewide basis by using the /STACK linker flag.) However, only two pages are committed: one for the initial page in the stack and one as a guard page to trap references beyond the end of the committed portion of the stack and automatically expand it.

Windows NT aligns each region of reserved process address space to begin on an integral boundary defined by the value of the system *allocation granularity*, which can be retrieved from the Win32 *GetSystemInfo* function. Currently, this value is 64 KB on all systems. This size was chosen so that if support were added for future processors with large page sizes (for example, up to 64 KB), the risk of requiring changes to applications that made assumptions about allocation alignment would be reduced. (Windows NT kernel-mode code is not subject to the same restrictions; it can reserve memory on the basis of page granularity.)

Finally, when you reserve a region of address space, Windows NT ensures that the size of the region is a multiple of the system page size, whatever that might be. For example, since *x*86 systems use 4-KB pages, if you tried to reserve a region of memory 18 KB in size, the actual amount reserved on an *x*86 system would be 20 KB. (On *x*86 systems only, Windows NT does make use of the 4-MB "large page" feature of the *x*86 architecture to map NTOSKRNL.EXE in system address space.)

Shared Memory and Mapped Files

As is true with most modern operating systems, Windows NT provides a mechanism to share memory among processes and the operating system. *Shared memory* can be defined as memory visible to more than one process or that is present in more than one virtual address space. For example, if two processes compile C programs, it would make sense to load the compiler into memory only once, and when another process invokes it, simply map the second process's virtual addresses to the physical page frames already occupied by the compiler, as illustrated in Figure 5-1.

Each process would still maintain its private memory areas in which to store private data, but the compiler code and unmodified data pages could be shared without harm. As I'll explain later, this kind of sharing happens by default on Windows NT because executable images are mapped as read-only sections and therefore the code portion is never written to and any read/write data is marked copy-on-write. (See the section "Copy-on-Write" on page 224 for more information.)

The underlying primitives in the memory manager used to implement shared memory are called *section objects*. In the Win32 API, they are called *file mapping objects*. The internal structure and implementation of section objects are described later in the chapter (beginning on page 298).

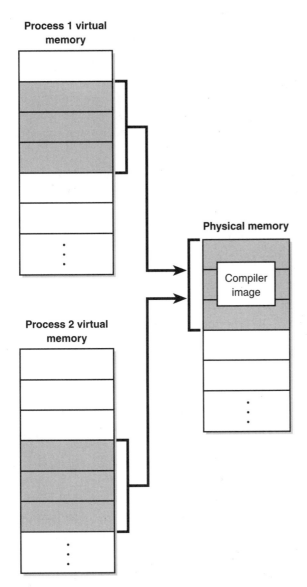

Figure 5-1

Sharing memory between processes

This fundamental primitive in the memory manager is used to map virtual addresses to pages on disk, whether that is in the page file or in some other file that an application wants to access as if it were in memory. A section can be opened by one process or by many; in other words, section objects don't necessarily imply shared memory.

A section object can be connected to an open file on disk (called a mapped file) or to a chunk of the paging file (to provide shared memory). To create a section object, call the Win32 *CreateFileMapping* function, specifying the file handle to map it to (−1 for a page file backed section), and optionally a name and security descriptor. If the section has a name, other processes can open it with *OpenFileMapping.* Or you can grant access to section objects through handle inheritance or handle duplication. Device drivers can also manipulate section objects with the *ZwOpenSection, ZwMapViewOfSection,* and *ZwUnmapViewOfSection* functions. (See the Windows NT DDK documentation for details.)

A Windows NT section object can refer to files that are much larger than can fit in the address space of a process. (If the paging file backs a section object, sufficient space must exist in the paging file to contain it.) Therefore, to access a section object, a process can map only the portion of the section object that it requires (called a *view* of the section) by calling the *MapViewOfFile* function and then specifying the range to map. Mapping views permits processes to conserve address space, since only the views of the section object needed at the time must be mapped into memory.

Win32 applications can use mapped files to conveniently perform I/O to files by simply making them appear in their address space. But user applications aren't the only consumers of section objects: the image loader uses section objects to map executable images, dynamic-link libraries (DLLs), and device drivers into memory, and the cache manager uses them to access data in cached files. (For information on how the cache manager integrates with the memory manager, see Chapter 8.)

How shared memory sections are implemented both in terms of address translation and the internal data structures is explained later in this chapter.

Protecting Memory

Windows NT provides memory protection for processes and the operating system itself so that no user process can inadvertently corrupt the address space of another process (or the operating system itself). Windows NT affords this protection in four primary ways.

First, all systemwide data structures and memory pools used by kernel-mode components of the system can be accessed only while in kernel mode—user-mode threads can't access these pages. If they attempt to do so, the hardware generates a fault, which in turn the memory manager reports to the thread as an access violation.

NOTE In contrast, Microsoft Windows 95 and Microsoft Windows 98 have some pages in system address space that are writable from user mode, thus allowing an errant application to corrupt key system data structures and crash the system.

Second, each process has a separate, private address space, protected from being accessed by any thread belonging to another process (except when shared memory is being used, in which case just the shared pages can be seen by more than one process). Each time a thread references an address, the virtual memory hardware, in concert with the Windows NT memory manager, intervenes and translates the virtual address into a physical one. By controlling how virtual addresses are translated, Windows NT can ensure that threads running in one process don't inappropriately access a page belonging to another process.

Third, in addition to the implicit protection virtual-to-physical address translation offers, all processors supported by Windows NT provide some form of hardware-controlled memory protection (such as read/write, read-only, and so on); the exact details of such protection vary according to the processor. For example, code pages in the address space of a process are marked read-only and are thus protected from modification by user threads. Table 5-1 lists the memory protection options defined in the Win32 API. (See the *VirtualProtect, VirtualProtectEx, VirtualQuery,* and *VirtualQueryEx* functions.)

And finally, shared memory section objects have standard Windows NT access control lists (ACLs) that are checked when processes attempt to open them, thus limiting access of shared memory to those processes with the proper rights. Security also comes into play when a thread creates a section to contain a mapped file. To create the section, the thread must have at least read access to the underlying file object or the operation will fail.

Once a thread has successfully opened a handle to a section, its actions are still subject to the memory manager and the hardware-based page protections described earlier. A thread can change the page-level protection on virtual pages in a section if the change doesn't violate the permissions in the ACL for that section object. For example, the memory manager allows a thread to change the pages of a read-only section to have copy-on-write access, but not to have read/write access. The copy-on-write access is permitted because it has no effect on other processes sharing the data.

These four primary memory protection mechanisms are part of the reason that Windows NT has the reputation of being a robust, reliable operating system that is impervious and resilient to application errors.

Table 5-1 Memory Protection Options Defined in the Win32 API

Attribute	Description
PAGE_NOACCESS	Any attempt to read from, write to, or execute code in this region causes an access violation.
PAGE_READONLY	Any attempt to write to or execute code in memory causes an access violation, but reads are permitted.
PAGE_READWRITE	The page is readable and writable—no action will cause an access violation.
PAGE_EXECUTE*	Any attempt to read from or write to code in memory in this region causes an access violation, but execution is permitted.
PAGE_EXECUTE_READ*	Any attempt to write to code in memory in this region causes an access violation, but executes and reads are permitted.
PAGE_EXECUTE_READWRITE*	The page is readable, writable, and executable—no action will cause an access violation.
PAGE_WRITECOPY	Any attempt to write to memory in this region causes the system to give the process a private copy of the page of physical storage. Attempts to execute code in memory in this region cause an access violation.
PAGE_EXECUTE_WRITECOPY	Any attempt to write to memory in this region causes the system to give the process a private copy of the page of physical storage.
PAGE_GUARD	Any attempt to read from or write to a guard page raises an EXCEPTION_GUARD_PAGE exception and turns off the guard page status. Guard pages thus act as a one-shot alarm.

* Execute-only access is not implemented by the *x*86 or Alpha architecture and so is not supported by Windows NT in any practical sense. Instead, these processors always allow readable pages to be executed.

Copy-On-Write

Copy-on-write page protection is an optimization the memory manager uses to conserve physical memory. When a process maps a copy-on-write view of a section object that contains read/write pages, instead of making a process private copy at the time the view is mapped (as the Digital OpenVMS operating system does), the memory manager defers making a copy of the pages until the page is modified. All modern UNIX systems use this technique as well. For example, as shown in Figure 5-2, two processes are sharing three pages, each marked copy-on-write.

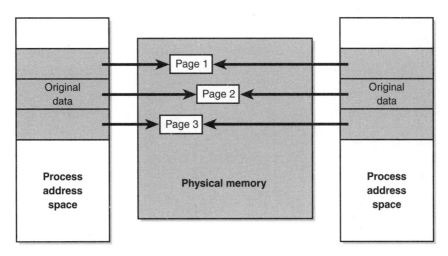

Figure 5-2
The "before" of copy-on-write protection

If a thread in either process writes to the page, a memory management fault is generated. The memory manager sees that the write is to a copy-on-write page, so instead of reporting the fault as an access violation, it allocates a new read/write page in physical memory (backing the page in the paging file), copies the contents of the original page to the new page, updates the corresponding page-mapping information (explained later in this chapter) in this process only to point to the new location, and dismisses the exception, thus causing the instruction that generated the fault to be reexecuted. This time, the write operation succeeds, but as shown in Figure 5-3 on the next page, the newly copied page is now private to the process that did the writing and isn't visible to the other processes still sharing the copy-on-write page. Each new process that writes to that same shared page will also get its own private copy.

Copy-on-write is used to implement breakpoint support in debuggers. For example, by default, code pages start out as read-only. If a programmer sets a breakpoint while debugging a program, however, the debugger must add a breakpoint instruction to the code. It does this by first changing the protection on the page to copy-on-write and then changing the instruction stream. The memory manager then immediately creates a private copy of the code page for the process whose thread set the breakpoint, while other processes continue using the unmodified code page.

Copy-on-write is one example of an evaluation technique known as *lazy evaluation* that the memory manager uses as often as possible. Lazy-evaluation algorithms avoid performing an expensive operation until absolutely required—if the operation is never required, no time is wasted on it.

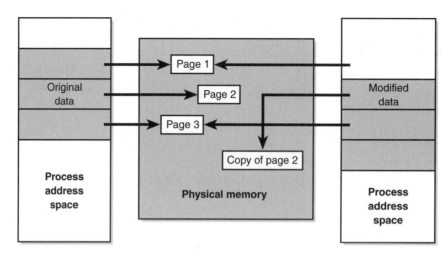

Figure 5-3
The "after" of copy-on-write protection

The POSIX subsystem takes advantage of copy-on-write. Typically, when a UNIX application calls the *fork* function to create another process, the first thing that the new process does is call the *exec* function to reinitialize the address space with an executable program. Instead of copying the entire address space on *fork*, the new process shares the pages in the parent process by marking them copy-on-write. If the child writes to the data, a process private copy is made. If not, the two processes continue sharing and no copying takes place. One way or the other, the memory manager copies only the pages the process tries to write to rather than the entire address space.

To examine the rate of copy-on-write faults, see the Memory: Write Copies/Sec performance counter.

Heap Functions

A heap is a region of one or more pages that can be subdivided and allocated in smaller chunks by a set of functions provided by the *heap manager* (described on page 233). Every process starts out with a default process heap (usually 1 MB in size, unless specified otherwise in the image file by using the /HEAP linker flag). This size is just the initial reserve, however—it will expand automatically as needed. Several Win32 functions that might need to allocate temporary memory blocks as well as Win32 applications use this process default heap. Processes can also create additional private heaps with the *HeapCreate* function. When a process no longer needs a private heap, it can recover the virtual address space by calling *HeapDestroy*. Only a private heap created with *HeapCreate*—not the default heap—can be destroyed during the life of a process.

To allocate memory from the default heap, a thread must obtain a handle to it by calling *GetProcessHeap*. (This function returns the address of the data structure that describes the heap, but callers should never rely on that.) With a heap handle, a thread can then call *HeapAlloc* and *HeapFree* to allocate and free memory blocks from that heap. The heap manager also provides an option for each heap to serialize allocations and deallocations so that multiple threads can call heap functions simultaneously without corrupting heap data structures. The default process heap is set to have this serialization by default (though you can override this on a case-by-case basis). For additional private heaps, a flag passed to *HeapCreate* is used to specify whether serialization should be performed.

For more information on the heap functions, see the Win32 API reference documentation on MSDN or Chapter 9 in Jeffrey Richter's book *Advanced Windows* (third edition, Microsoft Press, 1997).

System Memory Pools

At system initializaton, the memory manager creates two dynamically sized memory pools that the kernel-mode components use to allocate system memory:

- **Nonpaged pool** Consists of ranges of system virtual addresses that are guaranteed to be resident in physical memory at all times and thus can be accessed from any address space without incurring paging I/O.

- **Paged pool** A region of virtual memory in system space that can be paged in and out of the system process's working set. Because of this flexibility, there is no guarantee that an address within the paged portion of the system will not cause a page fault. For this reason, data structures that are accessed at interrupt request levels (IRQLs) at dispatch/DPC level or above must be allocated from nonpaged pool. (IRQLs are explained in Chapter 3.)

Both memory pools are located in the system part of the address space and are mapped to the same virtual address in every process. (In Table 5-9 on page 248, you'll find out where in the system memory they start.) The executive provides routines to allocate and deallocate from these pools; for information on these routines, see the functions that start with *ExAllocatePool* in the Windows NT DDK documentation.

There are two types of nonpaged pools: one for general use and a small one (four pages) reserved for emergency use when nonpaged pool is full and the caller can't tolerate allocation failures. Uniprocessor systems have two paged pools; multiprocessor systems have four. Having more than one paged pool reduces the frequency of system code blocking on simultaneous calls to pool routines.

Both nonpaged and paged pool grow automatically to a system-defined maximum computed at system boot time. The initial size of these pools is also calculated during system initialization and depends on memory size. You can override the initial size of these pools by changing HKLM\System…\Control\ Session Manager\Memory Management\NonPagedPoolSize or \PagedPoolSize from 0 (which causes the system to compute the size) to the size desired in bytes. You can't, however, increase the system-defined maximum size.

The computed sizes are stored in four global system variables, three of which are exposed as performance counters. These three, as well as the two registry keys that can alter the sizes, are listed in Table 5-2.

Table 5-2 System Pool Size Variables and Performance Counters

System Variable	Performance Counter	Registry Key to Override	Description
MmSizeOfNonPaged-PoolInBytes	Memory: Pool Nonpaged Bytes	HKLM\System\…\ Control\SessionManager\ NonPagedPoolSize	Current size of nonpaged pool
MmMaximumNon-PagedPoolInBytes	Not available	Not available	Maximum size of nonpaged pool
MmSizeOfPagedPool-InBytes	Memory: Pool Paged Bytes	HKLM\System\…\Control\ Session Manager\Paged-PoolSize	Maximum (virtual) size of paged pool
MmPagedPoolPage (number of pages)	Memory: Pool Paged Resident Bytes	Not applicable	Current physical (resident) size of paged pool

EXPERIMENT: Monitoring Pool Usage

The Memory performance counter object has separate counters for the size of nonpaged pool and paged pool (both virtual and physical). In addition, the Poolmon utility (shipped in the \support\debug directory on the Windows NT retail CD-ROM as well as in the DDK) allows you to monitor the detailed usage of nonpaged and paged pool. To do so, you must have the internal Enable Pool Tagging option selected. (Pool tagging is always turned on in the checked build.) You should be aware that this option disables pool quota checking, which can result in processes going beyond their paged and nonpaged pool quota. To turn on pool tagging, run the Gflags utility in the Windows NT Resource Kit and select Enable Pool Tagging, as shown here:

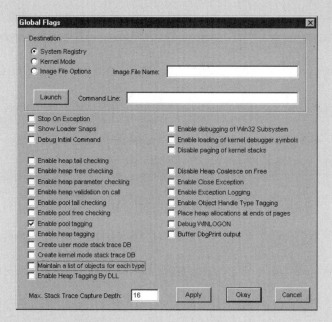

Then click Apply and reboot the system. After the system reboots, run Poolmon; you should see a display like the one at the top of the following page.

(continued)

EXPERIMENT: Monitoring Pool Usage *continued*

```
Command Prompt - poolmon                                              _ □ ✕
Memory:   64692K Avail:     5144K PageFlts:      0   InRam Krnl: 3352K P: 9520K
Commit:   94144K Limit: 182372K Peak: 109420K              Pool N: 2856K P:15376K
Tag  Type     Allocs          Frees           Diff   Bytes        Per Alloc

CM   Paged      9135 (    0)     8731 (    0)    404 5255712 (    0)   13009
Gh 5 Paged   1142563 (  110)  1141356 (    6)   1207 2126880 (    0)    1762
Gcac Paged      5107 (    0)     4985 (    0)    122  807424 (    0)    6618
MnSt Nonp      59080 (    0)    58400 (    0)    680  755328 (    0)    1110
Ggb  Paged      3366 (    0)     3298 (    0)     68  665184 (    0)    9782
Itfd Nonp      80067 (    0)    79897 (    0)    170  526720 (    0)    3098
Ntff Paged     14617 (    0)    13948 (    0)    669  513792 (    0)     768
Cc   Paged     88212 (    0)    87852 (    0)    360  405088 (    0)    1125
Unga Nonp     186863 (   50)   186548 (    0)    315  400512 (    0)    1271
Gh 1 Nonp     790559 (   63)   790334 (    0)    225  309600 (    0)    1376
htDC Nonp       1065 (    0)      971 (    0)     94  235040 (    0)    2500
NtFS Paged      5190 (    0)     5021 (    0)    169  219648 (    0)    1299
Dpsh Paged      4825 (    0)     4776 (    0)     49  202944 (    0)    4141
File Nonp     339280 (    0)   338255 (    0)   1025  196608 (    0)     192
Ntf0 Paged         3 (    0)        0 (    0)      3  196800 (    0)   65536
Gglb Nonp          8 (    0)        0 (    0)      8  177984 (    0)   22248
Fsrt Nonp      54001 (    0)    53241 (    0)    760  174176 (    0)     229
```

The highlighted lines represent changes to the display. (You can disable the highlighting feature.) Type *?* while Poolmon is running to bring up its help screen. You can configure which pools you want to monitor (paged, nonpaged, or both) and the sort order. Also, the command-line options are shown, which allow you to monitor specific structures (or everything but one structure type). For example, the command *poolmon -iCM* will monitor only structures of type CM (the configuration manager, another name for the registry). The columns have the following meanings:

Column	Explanation
Tag	Four-byte tag given to the pool allocation
Type	Pool type (paged or nonpaged pool)
Allocs	Count of all allocations (The number in parentheses shows the difference in the Allocs column since the last update.)
Frees	Count of all Frees (The number in parentheses shows the difference in the Frees column since the last update.)
Diff	Allocs minus Frees
Bytes	Total bytes consumed by this structure type (The number in parentheses shows the difference in the Bytes column since the last update.)
Per Alloc	Size in bytes of a single instance of this structure type

In this example, the CM structure is taking up the most space in paged pool, and Cc structures (cache manager) are taking up the most space in nonpaged pool.

Windows NT also provides a fast memory allocation mechanism called *look-aside lists*. The basic difference between pools and look-aside lists is that although general pool allocations can vary in size, a look-aside list contains only fixed-sized blocks. Look-aside lists can be either pagable or nonpagable, so they are allocated from paged or nonpaged pool. So although the general pools are

EXPERIMENT: Viewing the System Look-Aside Lists

You can display the contents and sizes of the various system look-aside lists with the kernel debugger *!lookaside* command. The following excerpt is from the output of this command:

```
KDx86> !lookaside
 ⋮
 ⋮

Lookaside "Ntfs!NtfsScbDataLookasideList" @ 8021f790 "Ntfs"
    Type      =    0011 PagedPool RaiseIfAllocationFailure
    Current Depth =      0   Max Depth  =        4
    Size          =    320   Max Alloc  =     1280
    AllocateMisses =     0   FreeMisses =        0
    TotalAllocates =     0   TotalFrees =        0
    Hit Rate      =     0%   Hit Rate   =       0%


Total NonPaged currently allocated for above lists =    4864
Total NonPaged potential for above lists           =    4608
Total Paged currently allocated for above lists    =     952
Total Paged potential for above lists              =    2896


ExpSmallNPagedLookasideLists @ 8014bbc0

  Nonpaged 32 bytes @ 8014bbc0
    Current Depth =      4   Max Depth  =        4
    Size          =     32   Max Alloc  =      128
    AllocateHits  =  59574   FreeHits   =    59578
    TotalAllocates =  61419  TotalFrees =    60585
    Hit Rate      =    96%   Hit Rate   =      98%


  Nonpaged 64 bytes @ 8014bbe8
    Current Depth =      4   Max Depth  =        4
    Size          =     64   Max Alloc  =      256
    AllocateHits  =  38009   FreeHits   =    38013
    TotalAllocates =  45042  TotalFrees =    41655
    Hit Rate      =    84%   Hit Rate   =      91%
 ⋮
 ⋮
```

more flexible in terms of what they can supply, look-aside lists are faster because you don't have to search for free memory that fits a varying size allocation (unless the look-aside list is empty, in which case the system must allocate from the normal paged or nonpaged pool). Also, look-aside lists are generally accessed by using fast atomic processor exchange instructions instead of by using mutexes or spinlock acquisition.

By default, eight nonpaged and eight paged look-aside lists are created at system initialization time, with size allocations starting at 32 and going up to 256 in multiples of 32 bytes. Executive components and device drivers can create look-aside lists that match the size of frequently allocated data structures. For information on the functions involved in creating, deleting, and using look-aside lists, see the DDK documentation.

Digging into the Memory Manager

Now that we've reviewed the basic services the memory manager provides, we're ready to begin our exploration of its internal structure and operation.

Components

The memory manager is part of the Windows NT executive and therefore exists in the file NTOSKRNL.EXE. No parts of the memory manager exist in the hardware abstraction layer (HAL). The memory manager consists of the following components:

- A set of executive system services for allocating, deallocating, and managing virtual memory, most of which are exposed through the Win32 API or kernel-mode device driver interfaces.

- A translation-not-valid and access fault trap handler for resolving hardware-detected memory management exceptions and making virtual pages resident on behalf of a process.

- Several support routines that run in the context of six different kernel-mode system threads:

  - ❑ The balance set manager (priority 16), which runs once per second, drives the overall memory management policies, such as working set trimming, aging, and modified page writing. It works in conjunction with system threads to do the actual work.

  - ❑ The process/stack swapper (priority 23) performs both process and kernel thread stack inswapping and outswapping. It is awakened by the balance set manager and by the thread-scheduling code in the kernel when an inswap or outswap operation needs to take place.

❑ The modified page writer (priority 17) writes dirty pages on the modified list back to the appropriate paging files. This thread is awakened when the size of the modified list needs to be reduced.

❑ The mapped page writer (priority 17) writes dirty pages in mapped files to disk. This second modified page writer thread is needed because it can generate page faults that result in requests for free pages. If there were no free pages and there was one modified page writer thread, the system would deadlock waiting for free pages.

❑ The dereference segment thread (priority 18) is responsible for system cache and page file growth.

❑ The zero page thread (priority 0) zeros out pages on the free list so that a cache of zero pages is available to satisfy future demand-zero page faults.

Each of these components is covered in more detail later in the chapter.

Built on top of the memory manager is the Windows NT *heap manager*, a set of functions that allocate and deallocate variable amounts of memory (not on a page-size granularity). A heap is simply a region of reserved address space that is committed and parceled out as needed. The heap manager functions exist in two places: NTDLL.DLL and NTOSKRNL.EXE. The subsystem APIs (such as the Win32 heap APIs) use the copy in NTDLL, and various executive components and device drivers use the copy in NTOSKRNL.

Although not documented, the heap manager supports a number of internal validation checks that you can enable on a systemwide or a per-image basis by using the Gflags utility in the Windows NT Resource Kit. Many of the flags are self-explanatory in terms of what they cause the heap manager to do. In general, enabling these flags will cause invalid use or corruption of the heap to be caught either by returning an error code to the caller or by raising an exception.

Internal Synchronization

Like all other components of the Windows NT executive, the memory manager is fully reentrant and supports simultaneous execution on multiprocessor systems—that is, it doesn't permit two threads to acquire resources in such a way that they corrupt each other's data. To accomplish the goal of being fully re-entrant, the memory manager uses several different internal synchronization mechanisms to control access to its own internal data structures, such as spinlocks and executive resources. (Synchronization objects are discussed in Chapter 3.)

Systemwide resources to which the memory manager must synchronize access include the page frame number (PFN) database (controlled by a spinlock), section objects and the system working set (controlled by executive resources), page file creation (controlled by a mutex), as well as other internal structures. Per-process memory management data structures are synchronized using two mutexes: the working set lock and the address creation lock. The address creation lock is held while the process is being created. The working set lock is held while changes are made to the virtual address space descriptors (VADs) and working set lists. (I'll describe both VADs and working set lists later in this chapter.)

Tuning the Memory Manager

Like most of Windows NT, the memory manager implements a self-tuning approach in that it attempts to provide optimal system performance for varying workloads and system sizes and types. Many internal "knobs" and control values affect policy decisions the memory manager makes in this process of self-tuning. A few are in the registry, but the majority are undocumented global variables accessible only from kernel mode.

> **WARNING** Although you'll find references to many of these knobs, you shouldn't change them. Windows NT has been tested to operate properly for the current possible permutations of these values that can be computed. Changing the registry might render the system unbootable. Changing the value of system variables on a running system can result in unpredictable system behavior, including system hangs or even crashes.

You can find the registry values that affect memory management under the HKLM\System...\Control\Session Manager\Memory Management key. For convenience, they're also listed in Table 5-3. (Windows NT 5.0 supplies additional values.) For more details on these registry values, see the Windows NT Resource Kit Registry Entries help file.

Most of the interesting tuning controls exist as system global variables (look for names beginning with *Mm*) that contain hard-coded, fixed values, or more often, values that are computed at system boot time on the basis of memory size and product type (that is, Windows NT Workstation or Windows NT

Table 5-3 **Registry Variables That Affect the Memory Manager**

Registry Value	Description
ClearPageFileAtShutdown	Specifies whether inactive pages in the paging file are filled with zeros when the system stops. This is a security feature.
DisablePagingExecutive	Specifies whether user-mode and kernel-mode drivers and kernel-mode system code can be paged to disk when not in use. If the value of this entry is 1, drivers and the kernel must remain in physical memory. If the value is set to 0 (the default), they can be paged to disk as needed.
IoPageLockLimit	Specifies the limit of the number of bytes that can be locked for I/O operations. When this value is 0, the system uses the default (512 KB). The maximum value is approximately the equivalent of physical memory minus 7 MB.
LargeSystemCache	Affects whether the file system cache or the working sets of processes are given priority for space in memory. (You can adjust this value only on Windows NT Server.)
NonPagedPoolSize	Indicates initial size of nonpaged pool in bytes. When this value is 0, the system calculates the value.
PagedPoolSize	Indicates maximum size of paged pool in bytes. When the value of this entry is 0, the system calculates the value.
NonPagedPoolQuota	Indicates maximum nonpaged pool that can be allocated by any process (in megabytes). If the value of this entry is set to 0, the system calculates the value.
PagedPoolQuota	Indicates maximum paged pool that can be allocated by any process (in megabytes). If the value of this entry is set to 0, the system calculates the value.
SystemPages	Indicates number of system page table entries reserved for mapping I/O buffers, device drivers, kernel thread stacks, or pages for programmed I/O into the system address space. If the value is 0, the system calculates the value.

Server). Examples of these variables include the sizing of system memory (paged pool, nonpaged pool, system cache, number of system page table entries), page read cluster size, counters that trigger working set trimming, and thresholds for the modified page writer.

The current memory sizes that determine whether Windows NT considers a system to have a small, medium, or large amount of memory are listed in Table 5-4. (These values are likely to increase over time as memory prices continue to fall and the typical memory size on PCs increases.)

Table 5-4   Values That Determine System Memory Size

Size	x86	Alpha
Small	≤19 MB	≤31 MB
Medium	20–32 MB	Can't occur
Large	≥32 MB if Windows NT Workstation ≥64 MB if Windows NT Server	Same as x86

Determining the System Memory Size

Because device drivers (as well as other Windows NT kernel-mode components) might make resource allocation and run-time policy decisions based on these values, the following kernel-mode routines have been provided (and are documented in the DDK):

Function	Description
MmQuerySystemSize	Returns whether the machine has a small, medium, or large amount of available memory.
MmIsThisAnNtAsSystem	Returns TRUE for Windows NT Server and Windows NT Server, Enterprise Edition, and FALSE for Windows NT Workstation. (This routine's name contains a vestige of the original product name planned for Windows NT Server: "Windows NT Advanced Server.")

Examining Memory Usage

The Memory and Process performance counter objects provide access to most of the details about system and process memory utilization. Throughout the chapter, I'll include references to specific performance counters that contain information related to the component being described. For a general overview of how to interpret these counters, see Chapter 12, "Detecting Memory Bottlenecks," in the *Windows NT Workstation Resource Guide.*

Besides Performance Monitor, a number of tools in Windows NT and in the Windows NT Resource Kit display different subsets of memory usage information. I've included relevant examples and experiments throughout the chapter. One particularly interesting experiment, "Accounting for Physical Memory" (on page 288), shows how to account for the physical memory on a Windows NT system by using the available Drivers and Pstat tools. Although you can't track all the memory with 100 percent accuracy, you can get a good idea of how processes and the various components of the operating system use memory.

One word of caution, however—different utilities use varying and sometimes inconsistent or confusing names when displaying memory information. The following experiment illustrates this point. (I'll explain the terms used in this example in subsequent sections.)

EXPERIMENT: Viewing System Memory Information

Both the Task Manager Performance tab and the Windows NT Diagnostics utility (WINMSD.EXE) Memory tab display the same system memory information. The following screen shot shows the Performance tab of the Windows NT Task Manager.

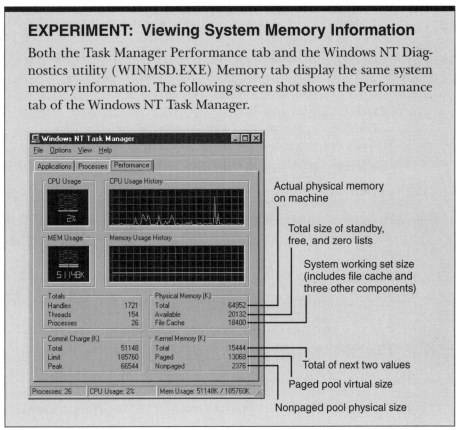

(continued)

237

EXPERIMENT: Viewing System Memory Information *continued*

Both PMON.EXE and PSTAT.EXE (available in the Windows NT Resource Kit as well as in the \support\debug directory on the retail Windows NT CD-ROM) display system and process memory information. The annotations in the output below explain the information reported. (For an explanation of the commit total and limit, see Table 5-7 on page 242.)

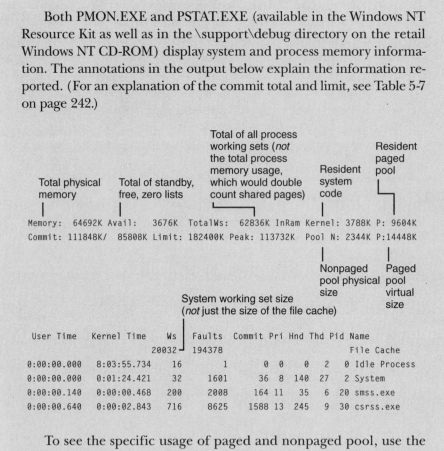

To see the specific usage of paged and nonpaged pool, use the Poolmon utility, which was described in the experiment on page 229.

Address Space Layout

By default, each user process on Windows NT can have up to a 2-GB private address space; the operating system takes the remaining 2 GB. Windows NT Server, Enterprise Edition, has a boot-time option (supported only on *x*86 systems) that allows 3-GB user address spaces. The address space layout for *x*86 systems is shown in Figure 5-4. (The layout on Alpha systems is similar, except the 3-GB user space is not available.)

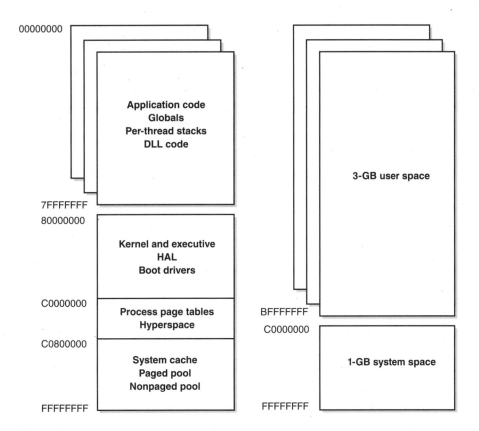

Figure 5-4
x86 *virtual address space layouts*

The 3-GB address space option (enabled by the /3GB flag in BOOT.INI) gives processes a 3-GB address space (leaving 1 GB for system space). This feature was added as a short-term solution to accommodate the need for applications such as database servers to keep more data in memory than could be done with a 2-GB address space. Windows NT 5.0 on Alpha alleviates this restriction with its support for 64-bit large memory addressing.

For a process to access the full 3-GB address space, the image file must have the IMAGE_FILE_LARGE_ADDRESS_AWARE flag set in the image header. Otherwise, Windows NT reserves the third gigabyte so that the application won't see virtual addresses greater than 0x7FFFFFFF. You can set this flag by using IMAGECFG.EXE (in the \support directory on the Windows NT Server, Enterprise Edition, CD-ROM) or by specifying the new linker flag /LARGEADDRESSAWARE when building the executable. This flag has no effect when running the application on a system with a 2-GB user address space.

Virtual Address Space in Windows 95 and Windows 98

The virtual address space for Windows 95 and Windows 98 is organized a bit differently from that of Windows NT. It also provides a 4-GB virtual 32-bit address space, allocating a 2-GB private address space to each process; but it divides the remaining 2 GB between system space (1 GB) and a single shared user space for all shared memory sections (1 GB), as shown in Figure 5-5.

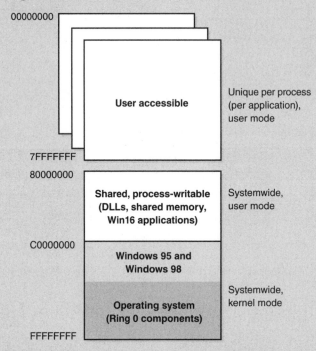

Figure 5-5
Virtual address space layout in Windows 95 and Windows 98

The 1-GB shared region is writable from user mode, so any Win32 process can write to shared memory sections or mapped files, even if they don't have that section object (file mapping object in Win32 terms) open. Windows NT, on the other hand, places shared memory sections inside the private process address space, thus avoiding this security hole. Also, since all MS-DOS and Win16 applications are in this same shared 1-GB region, Win32 processes can corrupt the address space of Win16 and MS-DOS applications in Windows 95 and Windows 98.

NOTE Windows NT 5.0 on Alpha systems supports an extension called *Very Large Memory* (or VLM) that allows user processes to allocate memory beyond the 32-bit address space limit. This support is being provided by a new set of Win32 VLM functions that return a 64-bit pointer. These functions allow a process to allocate up to 28 GB of additional virtual memory and use it to map files (such as large databases) into memory. Only data is allowed in the large memory area, however—not code. Also, pages mapped in this area are not pagable—once the data is read in, it can't be paged out. Thus, VLM doesn't provide true general-purpose 64-bit virtual memory addressing for user processes. However, Microsoft has announced plans to provide a true 64-bit implementation of Windows NT for Alpha and IA64 (Merced) systems. For more information on this and other enhancements coming in Windows NT 5.0, see Chapter 10.

User Address Space Layout

Table 5-5 details the layout of the 2-GB Windows NT user process address space.

Table 5-5 Windows NT User Process Address Space Layout

Range	Size	Function
0x0 through 0xFFFF	64 KB	No-access region to aid programmers in avoiding incorrect pointer references; attempts to access an address within this range will cause an access violation.
0x10000 through 0x7FFEFFFF	2 GB minus at least 192 KB	The private process address space.
0x7FFDE000 through 0x7FFDEFFF	4 KB	Thread environment block (TEB) for first thread. (See Chapter 4.) Additional TEBs are created at the page prior to this page (starting at address 0x7FFDD000 and working backward).
0x7FFDF000 through 0x7FFDFFFF	4 KB	Process environment block (PEB). (See Chapter 4.)
0x7FFE0000 through 0x7FFE0FFF	4 KB	Shared user data page. This read-only page is mapped to a page in system space that contains information such as system time, clock tick count, and version number. This page exists so that this data is directly readable from user mode without requiring a kernel-mode transition.

(continued)

Table 5-5 *continued*

Range	Size	Function
0x7FFE1000 through 0x7FFEFFFF	60 KB	No-access region (remainder of 64-KB region following shared user data page).
0x7FFF0000 through 0x7FFFFFFF	64 KB	No-access region that prevents threads from passing buffers that straddle the user/system space boundary. *MmUserProbeAddress* contains the start of this page.

The system variables shown in Table 5-6 define the range of the user address space.

Table 5-6 Windows NT User Address Space System Variables

System Variable	Description	x86 2-GB User Space	Alpha 2-GB User Space	x86 3-GB User Space
MmHighest-UserAddress	Highest user address (The highest usable address is actually less because of TEBs and PEBs.)	0x7FFEFFFF	0x7FFEFFFF	0xBFFEFFFF
MmUser-ProbeAddress	Highest user address +1 (used in probing accessibility of user buffers)	0x7FFF0000	0x7FFF0000	0xBFFF0000

The performance counters listed in Table 5-7 provide information about total system virtual memory utilization.

Table 5-7 Windows NT Virtual Memory Use Performance Counters

Performance Counter	System Variable	Description
Memory: Committed Bytes	*MmTotalCommittedPages*	The amount of committed private address space that has a backing store
Memory: Commit Limit	*MmTotalCommitLimit*	The amount (in bytes) of memory that can be committed without increasing the size of the paging file (Page files are extensible.)
Memory: % Committed Bytes in Use	*MmTotalCommittedPages* / *MmTotalCommitLimit*	Ratio of committed bytes to commit limit

You can obtain the address space utilization of a single process via the process performance counters in Table 5-8.

**Table 5-8 Windows NT Address Space Use
for Single Process's Performance Counters**

Performance Counter	Description
Process: Virtual Bytes	Total size of the process address space (including shared as well as private pages)
Process: Private Bytes	Size of the private (nonshared) committed address space (same as Process: Page File Bytes)
Process: Page File Bytes	Size of the private (nonshared) committed address space (same as Process: Private Bytes)
Process: Peak Page File Bytes	Peak of Process: Page File Bytes

There is also a performance object named Process Address Space that is not displayed by Performance Monitor. There are 32 counters that identify the address space usage of the selected process. For each of the four types of process address space (Image, Mapped, Reserved, and Unassigned), eight separate counters exist (No Access, Read Only, Read/Write, Write Copy, Executable, Exec Read Only, Exec Read/Write, and Exec Write Copy). In addition, there are counters for the total process address space reserved and free. For even more details about user address space layouts, you can query the Image performance object to report per-image (for example, DLLs) memory utilization.

EXPERIMENT: Viewing Process Memory Utilization

Try examining the various process memory performance counters listed in Tables 5-7 and 5-8 with Performance Monitor. You can also use several other utilities to examine process physical and virtual memory usage.

For example, start Task Manager (type *Ctrl-Shift-Esc*), and click the Processes tab. Then from the View menu, choose Select Columns. Select Memory Usage and Virtual Memory Size, and then click OK. You should see a display like the one at the top of the following page.

Keep in mind that the VM Size column is *not* the process virtual memory size, but rather the process private virtual size (the same as the Process: Private Bytes performance counter described in Table 5-8).

(continued)

Viewing Process Memory Utilization *continued*

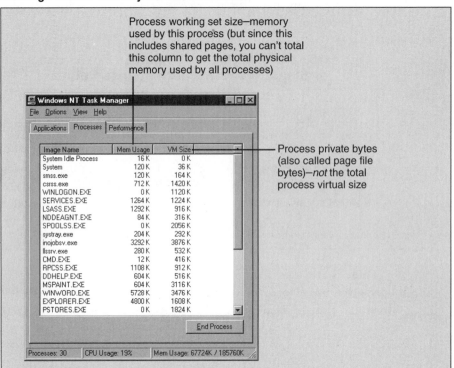

Process working set size—memory used by this process (but since this includes shared pages, you can't total this column to get the total physical memory used by all processes)

Process private bytes (also called page file bytes)—*not* the total process virtual size

Also, as you'll discover in the section on working sets, the Mem Usage column counts shared pages in each process's memory usage total.

The Process Viewer utility (PVIEWER.EXE in the Windows NT Resource Kit; PVIEW.EXE in Visual C++ or the Platform Software Development Kit [SDK]) can display per-process address space details. (The source of this utility is one of the Win32 sample programs on MSDN.) Click the Start button, and work through the Programs, Resource Kit, and Diagnostics menus. Click on Process Viewer, select a process, and click the Memory Detail button. You should see something like the top screen shot on page 245. Try clicking on the User Address Space For list box—you can select the address space used by the image alone or by loaded DLLs.

The Process Explode utility (PVIEW.EXE in the Resource Kit) displays the same information as Process Viewer (in a slightly different form) plus 15 additional process performance counters, including quota information. (See the screen shot at the bottom of page 245.) This utility can also show process and thread security information, as described in Chapter 6.

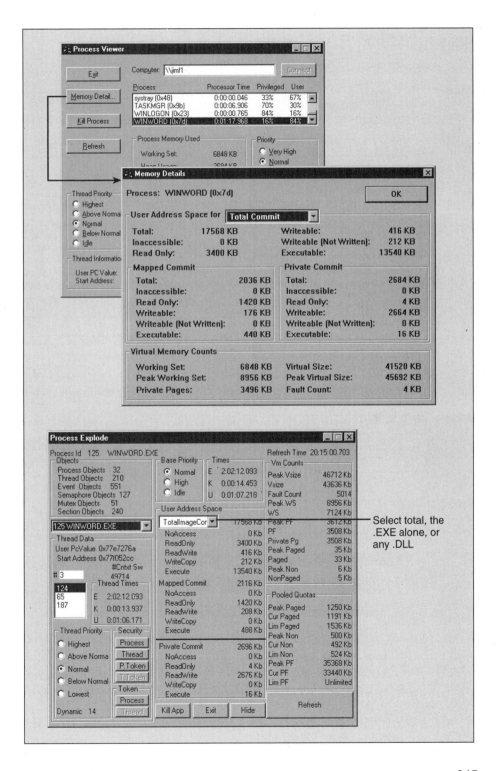

Select total, the
.EXE alone, or
any .DLL

245

System Address Space Layout

This section describes the detailed layout and contents of system space. Figure 5-6 shows the overall structure on *x*86 and Alpha systems with a 2-GB system space. (The details of *x*86 systems with a 1-GB system space are included later in this section.)

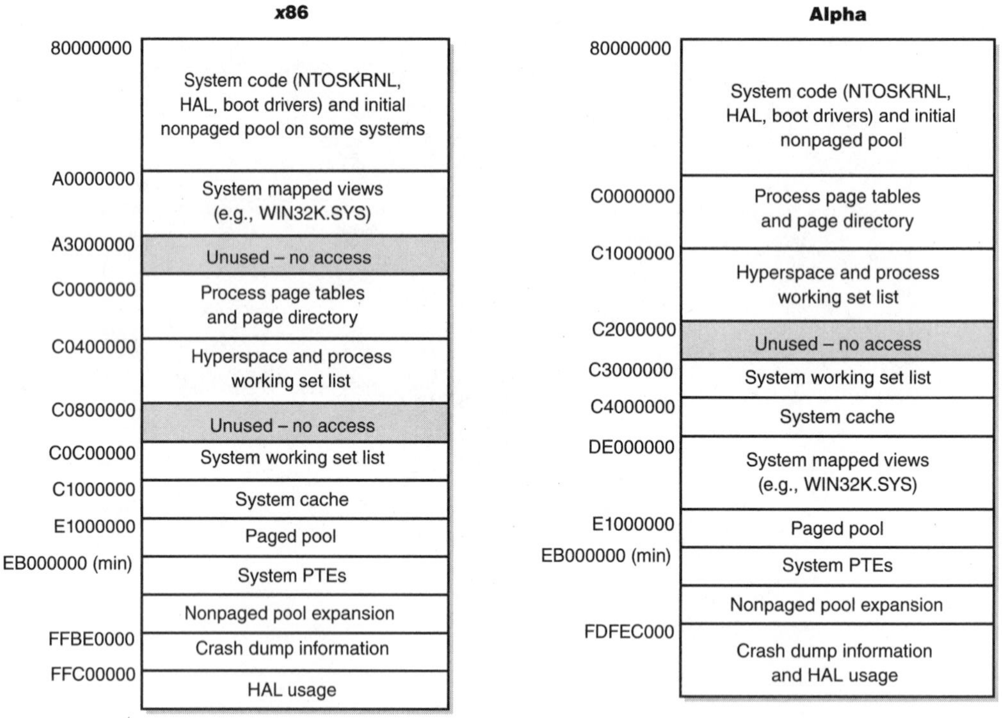

x86

80000000	System code (NTOSKRNL, HAL, boot drivers) and initial nonpaged pool on some systems
A0000000	System mapped views (e.g., WIN32K.SYS)
A3000000	Unused – no access
C0000000	Process page tables and page directory
C0400000	Hyperspace and process working set list
C0800000	Unused – no access
C0C00000	System working set list
C1000000	System cache
E1000000	Paged pool
EB000000 (min)	System PTEs
	Nonpaged pool expansion
FFBE0000	Crash dump information
FFC00000	HAL usage

Alpha

80000000	System code (NTOSKRNL, HAL, boot drivers) and initial nonpaged pool
C0000000	Process page tables and page directory
C1000000	Hyperspace and process working set list
C2000000	Unused – no access
C3000000	System working set list
C4000000	System cache
DE000000	System mapped views (e.g., WIN32K.SYS)
E1000000	Paged pool
EB000000 (min)	System PTEs
	Nonpaged pool expansion
FDFEC000	Crash dump information and HAL usage

Figure 5-6
x86 and Alpha system space layout (not proportional)

Although the order and sizes differ, both architectures have the same basic components in system space:

- **System code**   Contains the operating system image, HAL, and device drivers used to boot the system.

- **System mapped views**   Used to map WIN32K.SYS, the loadable kernel-mode part of the Win32 subsystem, as well as kernel-mode graphics drivers it uses. (See Chapter 2 for more information on WIN32K.SYS.)

- **Process page tables and page directory** Structures that describe the mapping of virtual addresses.

- **Hyperspace** A special region used to map the process working set list and to temporarily map other physical pages for such operations as zeroing a page on the free list (when the zero list is empty and a zero page is needed), invalidating page table entries in other page tables (such as when a page is removed from the standby list), and on process creation to set up a new process's address space.

- **System working set list** The working set list data structures that describe the system working set.[1]

- **System cache** Pages used to map files open in the system cache. (See Chapter 8 for detailed information about the cache manager.)

- **Paged pool** Pagable system memory heap.

- **System page table entries (PTEs)** Pool of system PTEs used to map system pages such as I/O space, kernel stacks, and memory descriptor lists. You can see how many system PTEs are available by examining the value of the Memory: Free System PTEs counter in Performance Monitor.

- **Nonpaged pool** Nonpagable system memory heap, usually existing in two parts—one in the lower end of system space and one in the upper end.

- **Crash dump information** Reserved to record information about the state of a system crash.

- **HAL reserved** System memory reserved for HAL-specific structures.

The rest of this section consists of three tables that list the detailed structure of system space. Table 5-9 on the following page lists the global system variables that contain start and end addresses of various system space regions. Some of these regions are fixed—some are computed at system boot time on the basis

---

1. Internally, the system working set is called the system cache working set. This term is misleading, however, because it includes not only the system cache but also the paged pool, pagable system code and data, and pagable driver code and data.

of memory size and whether the system is running Windows NT Workstation or Windows NT Server. Table 5-10 lists the structure of system space on *x*86 systems. And Table 5-11 on page 250 lists the structure of system space on Alpha systems.

Table 5-9 **System Variables That Describe System Space Regions**

System Variable	Description	*x*86 2-GB System Space	*x*86 1-GB System Space	Alpha 2-GB System Space
MmSystemRange-Start	Start address of system space	0x80000000	0xC0000000	0x80000000
MmSystemCache-WorkingSetList	System working set list	0xC0C00000	0xC0C00000	0xC3000000
MmSystemCache-Start	Start of system cache	0xC1000000	0xC1000000	0xC4000000
MmSystemCache-End	End of system cache	Calculated	Calculated	Calculated
MmPagedPoolStart	Start of paged pool	0xE1000000	0xE1000000	0xE1000000
MmPagedPoolEnd	End of paged pool	Calculated (maximum size is 192 MB)	Calculated (maximum size is 192 MB)	Calculated (maximum size is 240 MB)
MmNonPaged-SystemStart	Start of system PTEs	Calculated (lowest value is 0xEB000000)	Calculated	Calculated (lowest value is 0xEB000000)
MmNonPaged-PoolStart	Start of non-paged pool	Calculated	Calculated	Calculated
MmNonPagedPool-ExpansionStart	Start of non-paged pool expansion	Calculated	Calculated	Calculated
MmNonPagedPool-End	End of non-paged pool	0xFFBE0000	0xFFBE0000	0xFDFE0000

Table 5-10 *x86* System Space

Range	Size	Function
0x80000000 through 0x9FFFFFFF	512 MB	System code used to boot the system (NTOSKRNL.EXE, HAL.DLL, boot drivers) and the initial part of nonpaged pool. On *x86* systems with a 2-GB system space and 32 MB or more of RAM (64 MB in Windows NT 5.0), the first 4 MB is mapped using an *x86* large page PTE.
0xA0000000 through 0xA2FFFFFF	48 MB	Space for system mapped views (currently used to map WIN32K.SYS, the kernel-mode portion of the Win32 subsystem, as well as the kernel-mode graphics drivers it uses).
0xA3000000 through 0xBFFFFFFF	464 MB	Unused on most Windows NT systems (will be used by Terminal Server on Windows NT 5.0).
0xC0000000 through 0xC03FFFFF	4 MB	Process page tables (page directory is at 0xC0300000 and is 4 KB in size). This is per-process data mapped in system space.
0xC0400000 through 0xC07FFFFF	4 MB	Working set list and hyperspace. This is per-process data mapped in system space.
0xC0800000 through 0xC0BFFFFF	4 MB	Unused.
0xC0C00000 through 0xC0FFFFFF	4 MB	System working set list.
0xC1000000 through 0xE0FFFFFF	512 MB (maximum)	System cache (size calculated at boot time).
0xE1000000 through 0xECFFFFFF*	192 MB (maximum)	Paged pool (size calculated at boot time).
0xEB000000 through 0xFFBDFFFF	331.875 MB (339,840 KB)	System PTEs and nonpaged pool (size calculated at boot time).
0xFFBE0000 through 0xFFFFFFFF	4.125 MB (4224 KB)	Crash dump structures and private HAL data structures.

* Because paged pool is limited by the start address of the region containing nonpaged pool and the system PTEs, it can go beyond address 0xEB000000 only if those addresses aren't used.

Table 5-11 **Alpha System Space**

Range	Size	Function
0x80000000 through 0xBFFFFFFF	1024 MB	System code used to boot the system (NTOSKRNL.EXE, HAL.DLL, boot drivers) and the initial part of nonpaged pool
0xC0000000 through 0xC01FFFFF	2 MB	Process page tables (The page directory is at 0xC01800000 and is 8 KB in size, though only 1 KB is used.)
0xC0200000 through 0xC0FFFFFF	14 MB	Unused
0xC1000000 through 0xC1FFFFFF	16 MB	Working set list and hyperspace
0xC20000000 through 0xC2FFFFFF	16 MB	Unused (in Windows NT 5.0, used for VLM PTEs)
0xC3000000 through 0xC3FFFFFF	16 MB	System working set list
0xC4000000 through 0xDDFFFFFF	416 MB (maximum)	System cache (size calculated at boot time)
0xDE000000 through 0xE0FFFFFF	48 MB	Space for system mapped views (currently used only to map WIN32K.SYS, the kernel-mode portion of the Win32 subsystem)
0xE1000000 through 0xEFFFFFFF*	240 MB (maximum)	Paged pool (size calculated at boot time)
0xEB000000 through 0xFDFE0000	304.125 MB (311,424 KB)	System PTEs and nonpaged pool (size calculated at boot time)
0xFDFE0000 through 0xFFFFFFFF	31.875 MB (32,640 KB)	Crash dump structures and private HAL data structures

* Because paged pool is limited by the start address of the region containing nonpaged pool and the system PTEs, it can go beyond address 0xEB000000 only if those addresses aren't used.

Address Translation

Now that you've seen how Windows NT structures the 32-bit virtual address space, let's look at how it maps these address spaces to real physical pages.[2] I'll describe what happens when such a translation doesn't resolve to a physical memory address (paging) and explain how Windows NT manages physical memory via working sets and the page frame database.

---

2. The CPU hardware architecture dictates much of what is described in this section. For more details on the structures used to perform address translation, see the appropriate processor hardware documentation (such as the *Intel486 Microprocessor Family Programmer's Reference Manual* or the *Alpha AXP Architecture Reference Manual*).

User applications reference 32-bit virtual addresses. The CPU, using data structures the memory manager creates and maintains, translates virtual addresses into physical addresses. For example, Figure 5-7 shows three consecutive virtual pages mapped to three physically discontiguous pages.

The dashed line connecting the virtual pages to the PTEs in Figure 5-7 represents the indirect relationship between virtual pages and physical memory. Virtual addresses are not mapped directly to physical ones. Instead, as you'll discover in this section, each virtual address is associated with a system-space structure called a *page table entry* (*PTE*), which contains the physical address to which the virtual one is mapped.

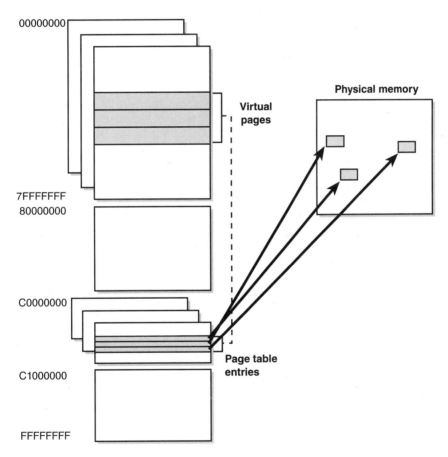

Figure 5-7
Mapping virtual addresses to physical memory

NOTE Kernel-mode code (such as device drivers) can reference physical memory addresses by mapping them to virtual addresses. For more information, see the memory descriptor list (MDL) support routines described in the DDK documentation.

Throughout the remainder of this section, I'll explain the details of how Windows NT accomplishes this mapping.

Translating a Virtual Address

Windows NT uses a two-level page table structure (as defined in the *x*86 and Alpha architectures) to translate virtual to physical addresses. A 32-bit virtual address is interpreted as three separate components—the page directory index, the page table index, and the byte index—that are used as indexes into the structures that describe page mappings, as illustrated in Figure 5-8.

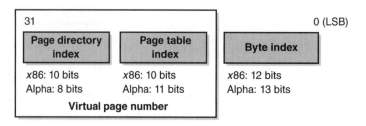

Figure 5-8
Components of a 32-bit virtual address

The differences in field width between the *x*86 and Alpha platforms are dictated by the page size for each platform. For example, on *x*86 systems, the byte index is 12 bits, since pages are 4096 bytes (2^{12} = 4096). On Alpha systems, the byte index is 13 bits, since pages are 8192 bytes (2^{13} = 8192).

The *page directory index* is used to locate the page table in which the virtual address's PTE is located. The *page table index* is used to locate the PTE, which, as mentioned earlier, contains the physical address to which a virtual page maps. The *byte index* finds the proper address within that physical page. Figure 5-9 shows the relationship of these three values and how they are used to map a virtual address into a physical address.

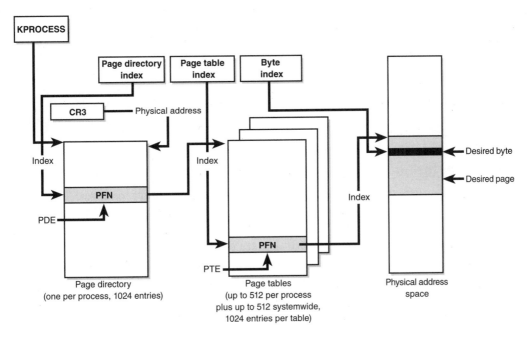

Figure 5-9
Translating a valid virtual address (x86-specific)

The following basic steps are involved in translating a virtual address:

1. The memory management hardware locates the page directory for the current process. On each process context switch, the hardware is told the address of a new process page directory, typically by the operating system setting a special CPU register.

2. The page directory index is used as an index into the page directory to locate the page directory entry that describes the location of the page table needed to map the virtual address.

3. The page table index is used as an index into the page table to locate the PTE that describes the location of the virtual page in question.

4. The PTE is used to locate the page. If the page is valid, it contains the physical page number, or page frame number, of the page in physical memory that contains the virtual page. If the page is not valid, the memory management fault handler locates the page and tries to make it valid. (See the section on page fault handling on page 265.) If the page can't be made valid (for example, because of

a protection fault), the fault handler generates an access violation or a bug check.

5. When the PTE is pointed to a valid page, the byte index is used to locate the address of the desired data within the physical page.

Now that you have the overall picture, let's look at the detailed structure of page directories, page tables, and PTEs.

Page Directories

Each process has a single *page directory*, a page the memory manager creates to map the location of all page tables for that process. The physical address of the process page directory is stored in the kernel process (KPROCESS) block but is also mapped virtually at address 0xC0300000 on *x86* systems (0xC0180000 on Alpha systems), since nearly all code running in kernel mode references virtual addresses, not physical ones. (For more detailed information about KPROCESS and other process data structures, refer to Chapter 4.)

The CPU knows the location of the page directory page because a special register (CR3 on *x86*, PDR on Alpha) inside the CPU that is loaded by the operating system contains the physical address of the page directory. Each time a context switch occurs to a thread that is in a different process than that of the currently executing thread, this register is loaded from KPROCESS by the context-switch routine in the kernel. Context switches between threads in the same process do not result in reloading the physical address of the page directory because all threads within the same process share the same process address space.

The page directory is composed of *page directory entries* (*PDEs*), each of which is currently 4 bytes long and describes the state and location of all the possible page tables for that process. (As described later in the chapter, page tables are created on demand, so the page directory for most processes points only to a small set of page tables.) The format of a PDE is not repeated here, since it is mostly the same as a hardware PTE (shown on page 258).

On *x86* systems, 1024 page tables are required to describe the full 4-GB virtual address space. The process page directory that maps these page tables contains 1024 PDEs. Therefore, the page directory index needs to be 10 bits wide ($2^{10} = 1024$). On Alpha systems, only 256 page tables are needed to map 4 GB, because pages are twice as large as on *x86* systems (and each page table maps twice as many pages).

EXPERIMENT: Examining the Page Directory and PDEs

You can see the physical address of the currently running process's page directory by examining the DirBase field in the *!process* kernel debugger output:

Physical address of PDE

```
KDx86> !process
PROCESS 80145880  Cid: 0000    Peb: 00000000  ParentCid: 0000
    DirBase: 00030000 ObjectTable: 80695668 TableSize: 126.
    Image: Idle
    VadRoot 0 Clone 0 Private 0. Modified 0. Locked 0.
    80145A3C MutantState Locked OwningThread 0
    Process Lock Owned by Thread 0
    .
    .
    .
```

You can see the page directory's virtual address by examining the kernel debugger output for the PTE of a particular virtual address, as shown here:

Virtual address of PDE

Contents of PDE

```
KDx86> !pte 50001
00050001 -  PDE at C0300000        PTE at C0000140
         contains 00700067         contains 00E63047
      pfn 00700  --DA--UW       pfn 00E63   --D--UWV
```

PFN of page **State and**
table page **protection of**
page table
page

The PTE part of the kernel debugger output is defined in the section "Page Table Entries" on the following page.

Process and System Page Tables

Before referencing a byte within a page with the byte offset, the CPU first needs to be able to find the page that contains the desired byte of data. To do this, the operating system constructs another page of memory that contains the mapping information needed to find the desired page containing the data. This page of mapping information is called a *page table*. Because Windows NT provides a private address space for each process, each process has its own set of process page tables to map that private address space, since the mappings will be different for each process.

The page tables that describe system space are shared among all processes, however. When a process is created, system space page directory entries are initialized to point to the existing system page tables. But as shown in Figure 5-10, not all processes have the same view of system space. For example, if paged pool expansion requires the allocation of a new system page table, the memory manager doesn't go back and update all the process page directories to point to the new system page table. Instead, it updates the process page directories when the processes reference the new virtual address.

Thus, a process can take a page fault when referencing paged pool that is in fact physically resident because its process page directory doesn't yet point to the new system page table that describes the new area of pool. Page faults don't occur when accessing nonpaged pool, even though it too can be expanded, because Windows NT builds enough system page tables to describe the maximum size during system initialization.

System PTEs are not an infinite resource—Windows NT calculates how many system PTEs to allocate based on the memory size. You can see how many system PTEs are available by examining the value of the Memory: Free System PTEs counter in Performance Monitor. You can also override the calculation made at boot time by setting the registry value HKLM\System...\Control-\Session Manager\SystemPages to the number of PTEs you want. However, the maximum that Windows NT will allocate is 50,000 on *x86* systems and 20,000 on Alpha systems.

Page Table Entries

As mentioned earlier, page tables are composed of an array of page table entries (PTEs). You can use the *!pte* command in the kernel debugger to examine PTEs. (See the experiment "Translating Addresses" on page 263.) Valid PTEs (the kind we'll be discussing here; invalid PTEs are covered in a later section) have

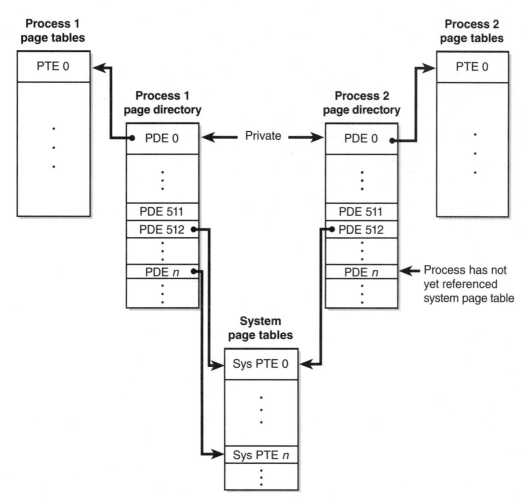

Figure 5-10
System and process-private page tables

two main fields: the page frame number (PFN) of the physical page containing the data or of the physical address of a page in memory, and some flags that describe the state and protection of the page, as shown in Figure 5-11.

NOTE In reality, hardware PTEs on Alpha systems are 64 bits in size. But since Windows NT assumes a 32-bit PTE, what the memory manager views as the 32-bit "hardware PTE" shown in Figure 5-11 is interpreted by the PALcode to construct the real 64-bit hardware PTE.

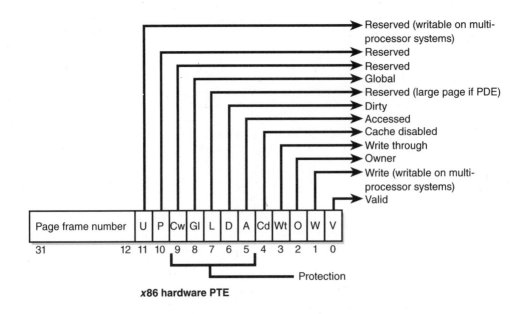

x86 hardware PTE

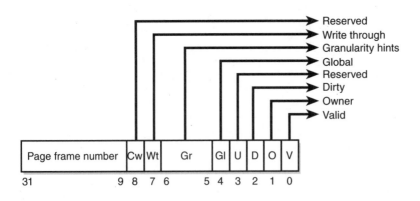

Alpha hardware PTE

Figure 5-11
Valid hardware PTEs

As you'll see later, the bits labeled Reserved in Figure 5-11 are used only when the PTE is not valid (the bits are interpreted by software). Table 5-12 briefly describes the hardware-defined bits in a valid PTE. Notice that not all bits apply to both platforms—those that don't are marked N/A.

Table 5-12 **PTE Status and Protection Bits**

Name of Bit	Meaning on *x86*	Meaning on Alpha
Accessed	Page has been read.	N/A
Cache Disabled	Disables caching for that page.	N/A
Dirty	Page has been written to.	Before a page has been written to, this bit serves as a write-protect bit. After a page has been written to, this bit indicates that the page has been written to.
Global	Translation applies to all processes. (For example, a translation buffer flush won't affect this PTE.)	Translation applies to all processes. (For example, a translation buffer flush won't affect this PTE.)
Granularity Hints	N/A	Provides for mapping translations larger than the standard page size (8 KB), since these large pages must be virtually and physically aligned.
Large Page	Indicates that the PDE maps a 4-MB page (used to map NTOSKRNL).	N/A
Owner	Indicates whether user-mode code can access the page or whether the page is limited to kernel-mode access.	Indicates whether user-mode code can access the page or whether the page is limited to kernel-mode access.
Valid	Indicates whether the translation maps to a page in physical memory.	Indicates whether the translation maps to a page in physical memory.
Write Through	Disables caching of writes to this page so that changes are immediately flushed to disk.	Disables caching of writes to this page so that changes are immediately flushed to disk.
Write	On uniprocessor systems, indicates whether the page is read/write or read-only; on multiprocessor systems, indicates whether the page is writable. (The Write bit is stored in a reserved bit in the PTE.)	N/A

Two bits worth describing in more detail relate to the differences in the way page protection and access information is represented on *x*86 and Alpha systems. On *x*86 systems, a hardware PTE contains a Dirty bit and an Accessed bit. The Accessed bit is clear if a physical page represented by the PTE hasn't been read or written; the processor sets this bit when the page is first read or written. The processor sets the Dirty bit only when a page is first written. In addition to those two bits, the *x*86 architecture has a Write bit that provides page protection—when this bit is clear, the page is read-only; when it is set, the page is read/write. If a thread attempts to write to a page with the Write bit clear, a memory management exception occurs and the memory manager's access fault handler (described in the next section) must determine whether the thread can write to the page (for example, if the page was really marked copy-on-write) or whether an access violation should be generated.

The Alpha platform uses these bits differently. First, it doesn't implement an Accessed or a Write bit in hardware. Second, the meaning of the Dirty bit differs from its meaning on *x*86 systems in that it's used for write protection. If this bit is clear, the page has never been written to and therefore might be read-only. If it's set, the page has been written to and therefore must have been a read/write page. When a thread attempts to write to a page on which the Dirty bit isn't set, a memory management exception occurs. Windows NT differentiates between a read-only page and a read/write page that hasn't been written to yet by using a reserved bit in the PTE (the Write bit) to store the protection of the page. In that way, it can determine whether the thread should be permitted to write to the page or whether an access violation should be generated.

Hardware PTEs on multiprocessor *x*86 systems have an additional Write bit implemented in software that is intended to avoid stalls when flushing the PTE cache (called the translation look-aside buffer) across processors. Basically, it serves the same function as the Dirty bit does on the Alpha platform, indicating that a page has been written to by a thread running on some processor or another.

On the hardware platforms currently supported by Windows NT, PTEs are always 4 bytes (32 bits) in size, so the number of PTEs per page table depends on the page size. On *x*86 systems, each page table contains 1024 PTEs (4096 bytes per page at 4 bytes per PTE) and therefore can map 1024 pages, for a total of 4 MB of data pages. On Alpha systems, each page table contains 2048 PTEs (8192/4), mapping a maximum of 2048 pages (a total of 16 MB of data pages).

The virtual address's page table index field indicates which PTE within the page table maps the data page in question. On *x*86 systems, the page table index is 10 bits wide, allowing you to reference up to 1024 PTEs. On Alpha systems, the page table index is 11 bits, because each page table contains 2048 PTEs. However, because Windows NT provides a 4-GB private virtual address space, more than one page table is needed to map the entire address space. To calculate the number of page tables required to map the entire 4-GB process virtual address space, divide 4 GB by the virtual memory mapped by a single page table. Recall that each page table on an *x*86 system maps 4 MB of data pages. Therefore, on *x*86 systems, 1024 page tables (4 GB/4 MB) are required to map the full 4-GB address space. On Alpha systems, each page table maps 16 MB, so only 256 page tables (4 GB/16 MB) are required.

Byte Within Page

Once the memory manager has found the physical page in question, it must find the requested data within that page. This is where the byte index field comes in. The byte index field tells the CPU which byte of data in the page you want to reference. On *x*86 systems, the byte index is 12 bits wide, allowing you to reference up to 4096 bytes of data (the size of a page). On current Alpha systems, the page size is 8192 bytes of data, so the byte index field is 13 bits wide.

Translation Look-Aside Buffer

As we've learned so far, each address translation requires two lookups: one to find the right page table in the page directory and one to find the right entry *in* the page table. Because doing two additional memory lookups for every reference to a virtual address would result in unacceptable system performance, most CPUs cache address translations so that repeated accesses to the same addresses don't have to be retranslated. Both the *x*86 and Alpha processors provide such a cache in the form of an array of associative memory called the *translation look-aside buffer,* or TLB. Associative memory, such as the TLB, is a vector whose cells can be read simultaneously and compared to a target value. In the case of the TLB, the vector contains the virtual-to-physical page mappings of the most recently used pages and the type of page protection applied to each page, as shown in Figure 5-12. Each entry in the TLB is like a cache entry, whose tag holds portions of the virtual address and whose data portion holds a physical page number, protection field, valid bit, and usually a dirty

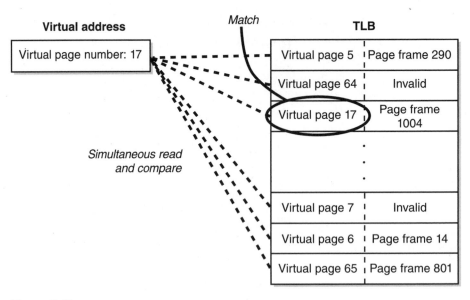

Figure 5-12
Accessing the translation look-aside buffer

bit indicating the condition of the page to which the cached PTE corresponds. If a PTE's global bit is set, the TLB entry is not invalidated on process context switches.

Virtual addresses that are used frequently are likely to have entries in the TLB, which provides extremely fast virtual-to-physical address translation and, therefore, fast memory access. If a virtual address isn't in the TLB, it might still be in memory, but multiple memory accesses are needed to find it, which makes the access time slightly slower. If a virtual page has been paged out of memory or if the memory manager changes the PTE, the memory manager must explicitly invalidate the TLB entry. If a process accesses it again, a page fault occurs and the memory manager brings the page back into memory and re-creates an entry for it in the TLB.

To maximize the amount of common code, the memory manager treats all PTEs the same whenever possible, whether they are maintained by hardware or by software. For example, the memory manager calls a kernel routine when a PTE changes from invalid to valid. The job of this routine is to load this new PTE into the TLB in whatever hardware-specific manner the architecture requires. On Alpha systems, the software loads the new PTE. On x86 systems, the code is a NO-OP since the processor loads the TLB without any intervention from the software.

EXPERIMENT: Translating Addresses

To clarify how address translation works, let's go through a real example of translating a virtual address on an *x*86 system, using the available tools in the kernel debugger to examine page directories, page tables, and PTEs. In this example, we'll use a process that has virtual address 0x50001 currently mapped to a valid physical address. In later examples, you'll see how to follow address translation for invalid addresses with the kernel debugger.

First let's convert 0x50001 to binary and break it into the three fields that are used to translate an address. In binary, 0x50001 is 101.0000.0000.0000.0001. Breaking into the component fields yields the following:

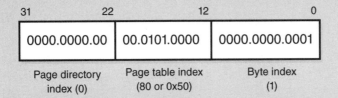

31	22	12	0
0000.0000.00	00.0101.0000	0000.0000.0001	

| Page directory index (0) | Page table index (80 or 0x50) | Byte index (1) |

To start the translation process, the CPU needs the physical address of the process page directory, stored in the CR3 register while a thread in that process is running. You can display this address either by examining the CR3 register itself or by dumping the KPROCESS block for the process in question using the *!process* command, as shown here:

```
KDx86> !process
PROCESS 81555020   Cid:  0099    Peb:  7ffdf000  ParentCid:  0094
    DirBase: 012f0000  ObjectTable:  80695ba8  TableSize:  46.
    Image: IEXPLORE.EXE
       .
       .                    ───── Physical address of page directory
       .
kdx86> r cr3
Cr3: 012F0000 ───
```

(continued)

EXPERIMENT: Translating Addresses *continued*

In this case, the page directory is stored at physical address 0x12-F0000. As shown in the preceding illustration, the page directory index field in this example is 0. Therefore, the PDE is at physical address 0x12F0000.

The kernel debugger *!pte* command displays the PDE and PTE that describe a virtual address, as shown here:

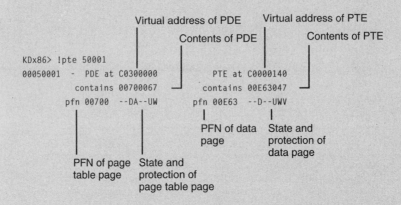

In the first column, the kernel debugger displays the PDE and in the second column the PTE. Notice that the PDE address is shown as a virtual address, not a physical address—as noted earlier, the process page directory starts at virtual address 0xC0300000 on *x*86 systems. Because we're looking at the first PDE in the page directory, the PDE address is the same as the page directory address.

The PTE is at virtual address 0xC0000140. You can compute this address by multiplying the page table index (0x50 in this example) by the size of a PTE: 0x50 multiplied by 4 equals 0x140. Because the memory manager maps page tables starting at 0xC0000000, adding 140 yields the virtual address shown in the kernel debugger output: 0xC0000140. The page table page is at PFN 0x700, and the data page is at PFN 0xe63.

The PTE flags are displayed to the right of the PFN number. For example, the PTE that describes the page being referenced has flags of D---UWV. *D* here stands for dirty (the page has been modified), *U* for user-mode page (as opposed to a kernel-mode page), *W* for writable page (rather than read-only), and *V* for valid. (The PTE represents a valid page in physical memory.)

Page Fault Handling

In the preceding section, you saw how address translations are resolved when the PTE is valid. When the PTE valid bit is clear, this indicates that the desired page is for some reason not (currently) accessible to the process. This section describes the types of invalid PTEs and how references to them are resolved.

A reference to an invalid page is called a *page fault*. The kernel trap handler (introduced in Chapter 3 on page 81) dispatches this kind of fault to the memory manager fault handler (*MmAccessFault*) to resolve. This routine runs in the context of the thread that incurred the fault and is responsible for attempting to resolve the fault (if possible) or raise an appropriate exception. These faults can be caused by a variety of conditions, as listed in Table 5-13.

Table 5-13 **Reasons for Access Faults**

Reason for Fault	Result
Accessing a page that is not resident in memory but is on disk in a page file or mapped file	Allocate a physical page and read the desired page from disk and into the working set
Accessing a page that is on the standby or modified list	Transition the page to the process or system working set
Accessing a page that has no committed storage (for example, reserved address space or address space that is not allocated)	Access violation
Accessing a page from user mode that can be accessed only in kernel mode	Access violation
Writing to a page that is read-only	Access violation
Accessing a demand-zero page	Add a zero-filled page to the process working set
Writing to a guard page	Guard-page violation (if a reference to a user-mode stack, perform automatic stack expansion)
Writing to a copy-on-write page	Make process-private copy of page and replace original in process or system working set

(continued)

Table 5-13 *continued*

Reason for Fault	Result
Referencing a page in system space that is valid but not in the process page directory (for example, if paged pool expanded after the process page directory was created)	Copy page directory entry from master system page directory structure and dismiss exception (This fault is never pointed to by hardware.)
On a multiprocessor system, writing to a page that is valid but hasn't yet been written to	Set dirty bit in PTE

The following section described the four basic kinds of invalid PTEs that are processed by the access fault handler. Following that is an explanation of a special case of invalid PTEs, prototype page table entries, which are used to implement (potentially) shared pages.

Invalid PTEs

The following list details the four kinds of invalid PTEs and their structure. (The *x*86 format is shown; the Alpha format is similar but not exactly the same in all cases.) Some of the flags are the same as those for a hardware PTE as described in Table 5-12 on page 259.

- **Page file**   The desired page resides within a paging file. An in-page operation is initiated, as illustrated here:

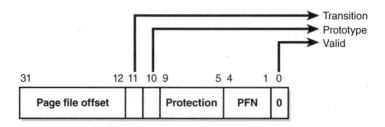

- **Demand zero**   The desired page must be satisfied with a page of zeros. The pager looks at the zero page list. If the list is empty, the pager takes a page from the standby list and zeros it. The PTE format is the same as the page file PTE shown above, but the page file number and offset are zeros.

■ **Transition** The desired page is in memory on either the standby, modified, or modified-no-write list. The page is removed from the list and added to the working set, as shown here:

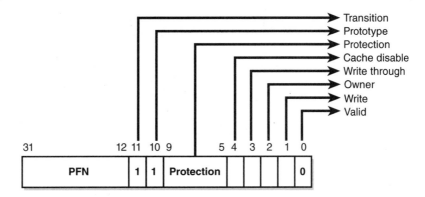

■ **Unknown** The PTE is zero, or the page table doesn't yet exist. In both cases, this means you should examine the virtual address descriptors (VADs) to determine whether this virtual address has been reserved. If so, page tables are built to represent the newly committed address space. (See the discussion of VADs on page 273.)

Prototype PTEs

If a page can be shared between two processes, the memory manager relies on a software structure called *prototype page table entries* (*prototype PTEs*) to map these potentially shared pages. An array of prototype PTEs is created when a section object is first created. These prototype PTEs are part of the *segment* structure, described at the end of this chapter.

When a process first references a page mapped to a view of a section object (recall that the VADs are created only when the view is mapped), the memory manager uses the information in the prototype PTE to fill in the real PTE used for address translation in the process page table.

When a shared page is made valid, both the process PTE and the prototype PTE point to the physical page containing the data. To track the number of process PTEs that reference a valid shared page, a counter in the *PFN database entry* (described on page 285) is incremented. Thus, the memory manager can determine when a shared page is no longer referenced by any page table and thus can be made invalid and moved to a transition list or written out to disk.

When a page is invalidated, the PTE in the process page table is filled in with a special PTE that points to the prototype PTE entry that describes the page, as shown in Figure 5-13.

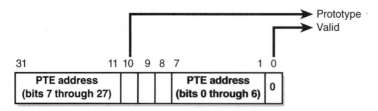

Figure 5-13
Structure of an invalid PTE that points to the prototype PTE

Thus, when the page is later accessed, the memory manager can locate the prototype PTE using the information encoded in this PTE, which in turn describes the page being referenced. A shared page can be in one of five different states as described by the prototype PTE entry:

- **Active/valid**   The page is in physical memory as a result of another process that accessed it.

- **Transition**   The desired page is in memory on the standby or modified list.

- **Demand zero**   The desired page should be satisfied with a page of zeros.

- **Page file**   The desired page resides within a page file.

- **Mapped file**   The desired page resides within a mapped file.

Although the format of these prototype PTE entries is the same as that of the real PTE entries described earlier in the chapter, these prototype PTEs are not used for address translation—they are a layer between the page table and the page frame database and never appear directly in page tables. (The only type of "real" PTE that doesn't show up in a prototype PTE entry is the prototype PTE entry itself.)

By having all the accessors of a potentially shared page point to a prototype PTE to resolve faults, the memory manager can manage shared pages without needing to update the page tables of each process sharing the page. For example, a shared code or data page might be paged out to disk at some point. When the memory manager retrieves the page from disk, it needs only to update the prototype PTE to point to the page's new physical location—the PTEs in each of the processes sharing the page remain the same (with the valid bit clear and still pointing to the prototype PTE).

Figure 5-14 illustrates two virtual pages in a mapped view. One is valid, and the other is invalid and in the page file. As shown, the first page is valid and is pointed to by the process PTE and the prototype PTE. The second page is in the paging file—the prototype PTE contains its exact location. The process PTE (and any other processes with that page mapped) points to this prototype PTE.

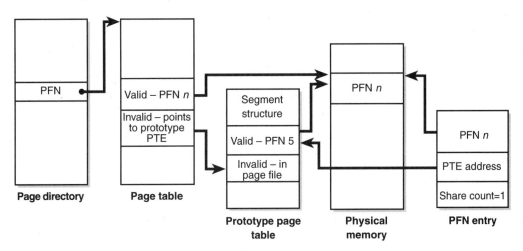

Figure 5-14
Prototype page table entries

In-Paging I/O

In-paging I/O occurs when a read operation must be issued to a file (paging or mapped) to satisfy a page fault. Also, since page tables are pagable, the processing of a page fault can incur additional page faults when the system is loading the page table page that contains the PTE or the prototype PTE that describes the original page being referenced.

The in-page I/O operation is synchronous—that is, the thread waits on an event until the I/O completes—and is not interruptible by asynchronous procedure call (APC) delivery. The pager uses a special modifier in the I/O request function to indicate paging I/O. Upon completion of paging I/O, the I/O system sets an event, which wakes up the pager and allows it to continue in-page processing.

While the paging I/O operation is in progress, the faulting thread does not own any critical memory management synchronization objects. This allows other threads within the process to issue virtual memory functions and handle page faults while the paging I/O takes place. But it also exposes a number of interesting conditions that the pager must recognize when the I/O completes:

- Another thread in the same process or a different process could have faulted the same page (called a collided page fault and described in the next section).

- The page could have been deleted (and remapped) from the virtual address space.

- The protection on the page could have changed.

- The fault could have been for a prototype PTE, and the page that maps the prototype PTE could be out of the working set.

The pager handles these conditions by saving enough state on the thread's kernel stack before the paging I/O request such that when the request is complete, it can detect these conditions and, if necessary, dismiss the page fault without making the page valid. When the faulting instruction is reissued, the pager is again invoked and the PTE is reevaluated in its new state.

Collided Page Faults

The case when another thread or process faults a page that is currently being in-paged is known as a *collided page fault*. The pager detects and handles collided page faults optimally since they are common occurrences in multithreaded systems. If another thread or process faults the same page, the pager detects the collided page fault, noticing that the page is in transition and that a read is in progress. (This information is in the PFN database entry.) In this case, the pager issues a wait operation on an event specified in the PFN database entry. The thread that first issued the I/O needed to resolve the fault initialized this event.

When the I/O operation completes, all threads waiting on the event have their wait satisfied. The first thread to acquire the PFN database lock is responsible for performing the in-page completion operations. These operations consist of checking I/O status to ensure the I/O operation completed successfully, clearing the read-in-progress bit in the PFN database, and updating the PTE element.

When subsequent threads acquire the PFN database lock to complete the collided page fault, the pager recognizes that the initial updating has been performed as the read-in-progress bit is clear and checks the in-page error flag in the PFN database element to ensure that the in-page I/O completed successfully. If the in-page error flag is set, the PTE is not updated and an in-page error exception is raised in the faulting thread.

Page Files

Windows NT 4.0 supports up to 16 paging files on *x*86 systems and 16 on Alpha systems. When the system boots, the session manager process (described in Chapter 2) reads the list of page files to open by examining the registry value HKLM\System...\Control\Session Manager\Memory Management\Paging-Files. Once open, the page files can't be deleted while the system is running, because the System process (also described in Chapter 2) maintains an open handle to each page file.

EXPERIMENT: Viewing System Page Files

To view the list of page files, look in the registry at HKLM\System...\ Control\Session Manager\Memory Management\PagingFiles. To add or remove page files, use Control Panel's System applet. Click the Performance tab, and click the Virtual Memory Change button.

To add a new page file, Control Panel uses the (internal only) *NtCreate-PagingFile* system service defined in NTDLL.DLL. Page files are always created as noncompressed files (even if the directory they are in is compressed). To keep new page files from being deleted, a handle is duplicated into the System process so that when the handle to the new page file is closed by the creating process, the page file will still be open by another process.

The memory management system keeps track of page file usage on a global basis, termed *commitment,* and on a per-process basis as *page file quota.* Commitment and page file quota are charged whenever virtual addresses that require backing store from the paging file are committed. Once the global commit limit has been reached, allocating virtual memory will fail.

The performance counters listed in Table 5-14 allow you to examine page file usage on a system-wide or per-page-file basis.

Table 5-14   Page File Performance Counters

Performance Counter	Description
Memory: Committed Bytes	Number of bytes of virtual (not reserved) memory that has been committed.
Memory: Commit Limit	Number of bytes of virtual memory that can be committed without having to extend the paging file(s); if the paging file(s) can be extended, this limit is soft.
Paging File: % Usage	Percentage of the paging file committed.
Paging File: % Usage Peak	Highest percentage of the paging file committed.

EXPERIMENT: Viewing Page File Usage with Task Manager

You can also view system page file and memory usage performance counters with Task Manager by clicking its Performance tab. You'll see the following counters related to page files:

Total virtual memory that has committed storage

Maximum virtual memory without extending page file

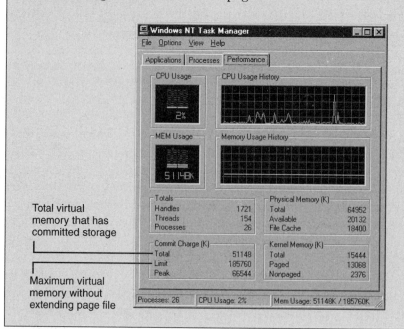

Virtual Address Descriptors

The memory manager uses a demand-paging algorithm to know when to load pages into memory, waiting until some thread references an address and incurs a page fault before retrieving the page from disk. Like copy-on-write, demand paging is a form of lazy evaluation—waiting to perform a task until it is required.

The memory manager uses lazy evaluation not only to bring pages into memory but also to construct the page tables required to describe new pages. For example, when a thread commits a large region of virtual memory with *VirtualAlloc*, the memory manager could immediately construct the page tables required to access the entire range of allocated memory. But what if some of that range is never accessed? Creating page tables for the entire range would be a wasted effort. Instead, the memory manager waits to create a page table until a thread incurs a page fault, and then it creates a page table for that page. This method significantly improves performance for processes that reserve and/or commit a lot of memory but access it sparsely.

With the lazy-evaluation algorithm, allocating even large blocks of memory is a fast operation. This performance gain is not without its trade-offs, however: when a thread allocates memory, the memory manager must respond with a range of addresses for the thread to use. Because the memory manager doesn't build page tables until the thread actually accesses the memory, it can't look there to determine which virtual addresses are free. To solve this problem, the memory manager maintains another set of data structures to keep track of which virtual addresses have been reserved in the process's address space and which have not. These data structures are known as *virtual address descriptors* (*VADs*). For each process, the memory manager maintains a set of VADs that describes the status of the process's address space. VADs are structured as a self-balancing binary tree to make lookups efficient. A diagram of a VAD tree is shown in Figure 5-15 on the following page.

When a process reserves address space or maps a view of a section, the memory manager creates a VAD to store any information supplied by the allocation request, such as the range of addresses being reserved, whether the range will be shared or private, whether a child process can inherit the contents of the range, and the page protection applied to pages in the range.

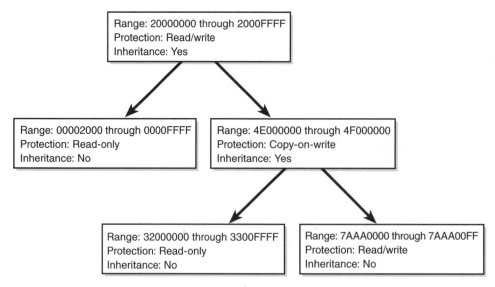

Figure 5-15
Virtual address descriptors

When a thread first accesses an address, the memory manager must create a PTE for the page containing the address. To do so, it finds the VAD whose address range contains the accessed address and uses the information it finds

EXPERIMENT: Viewing Virtual Address Descriptors

You can use the kernel debugger's *!vad* command to view the VADs for a given process. First find the address of the root of the VAD tree with the *!process* command. Then specify that address to the *!vad* command, as shown in the following example:

```
KDx86> !process 73
Searching for Process with Cid == 73
PROCESS 80568020 Cid: 0073    Peb: 7ffdf000  ParentCid: 002b
    DirBase: 022a4000  ObjectTable: 805fc008  TableSize:  30.
    Image: atsvc.exe
    VadRoot 80565108 Clone 0 Private 84. Modified 91. Locked 0.
```

```
KDx86> !vad 80565108
VAD      level     start       end      commit
805650e8 ( 1)      10000     10fff          1 Private     READWRITE
805650c8 ( 2)      20000     20fff          1 Private     READWRITE
80565108 ( 0)      30000    12ffff          3 Private     READWRITE
80568d48 ( 3)     130000    130fff          1 Private     READWRITE
80568d28 ( 2)     140000    23ffff          5 Private     READWRITE
805688e8 ( 4)     240000    24ffff          0 Mapped      READWRITE
80568828 ( 3)     250000    265fff          0 Mapped      READONLY
805687e8 ( 5)     270000    293fff          0 Mapped      READONLY
805687a8 ( 4)     2a0000    2e0fff          0 Mapped      READONLY
80568768 ( 6)     2f0000    2f2fff          0 Mapped      READONLY
80568748 ( 5)     300000    30ffff          2 Private     READWRITE
80568728 ( 7)     310000    70ffff         16 Private     READWRITE
80568708 ( 6)     710000    710fff          1 Private     READWRITE
805f8148 ( 7)     720000    7e7fff          0 Mapped      EXECUTE_READ
805f5d68 ( 8)     7f0000    832fff          0 Mapped      READONLY
80568668 ( 9)     850000    b4ffff          0 Mapped      EXECUTE_READ
80568628 (10)     b50000    b50fff          1 Private     READWRITE
805685e8 (11)     b60000    b60fff          1 Private     READWRITE
805686a8 (12)     b70000    b8ffff          1 Private     READWRITE
80565c88 (13)     b90000    c8ffff          2 Private     READWRITE
80565b68 (14)     c90000    d8ffff          2 Private     READWRITE
8056bec8 ( 1)    1070000   1078fff          2 Mapped  Exe EXECUTE_WRITECOPY
805f0808 ( 7)   5f810000  5f816fff          2 Mapped  Exe EXECUTE_WRITECOPY
80568948 ( 6)   777e0000  777ecfff          2 Mapped  Exe EXECUTE_WRITECOPY
805689c8 ( 5)   77800000  77839fff          3 Mapped  Exe EXECUTE_WRITECOPY
80568988 ( 6)   77840000  77848fff          2 Mapped  Exe EXECUTE_WRITECOPY
80568ac8 ( 4)   77dc0000  77dfdfff          7 Mapped  Exe EXECUTE_WRITECOPY
805f18a8 ( 7)   77e00000  77e05fff          2 Mapped  Exe EXECUTE_WRITECOPY
80568a08 ( 6)   77e10000  77e61fff          2 Mapped  Exe EXECUTE_WRITECOPY
80568a88 ( 5)   77e70000  77ec3fff          2 Mapped  Exe EXECUTE_WRITECOPY
80568a48 ( 6)   77ed0000  77efbfff          2 Mapped  Exe EXECUTE_WRITECOPY
80568ca8 ( 3)   77f00000  77f5dfff          3 Mapped  Exe EXECUTE_WRITECOPY
805f7348 ( 2)   77f60000  77fbbfff          5 Mapped  Exe EXECUTE_WRITECOPY
80568ce8 ( 4)   78000000  78046fff          8 Mapped  Exe EXECUTE_WRITECOPY
805688a8 ( 5)   7f5f0000  7f7effff          0 Mapped      EXECUTE_READ
80565168 ( 3)   7ffb0000  7ffd3fff          0 Mapped      READONLY
80567808 ( 7)   7ffdc000  7ffdcfff          1 Private     EXECUTE_READWRITE
805f0c28 ( 6)   7ffdd000  7ffddfff          1 Private     EXECUTE_READWRITE
80565088 ( 5)   7ffde000  7ffdefff          1 Private     EXECUTE_READWRITE
80565128 ( 4)   7ffdf000  7ffdffff          1 Private     EXECUTE_READWRITE

Total VADs:    40  average level:   6  maximum depth: 14
```

to fill in the PTE. If the address falls outside the range covered by the VAD, the memory manager knows that the thread did not allocate the memory before attempting to use it and therefore generates an access violation.

Working Sets

In the last several sections, we've concentrated on the virtual view of a Windows NT process—page tables, PTEs, and virtual address space descriptors. In the remainder of this chapter, I'll explain how Windows NT keeps a subset of virtual addresses in physical memory.

As you'll recall, the term used to describe a subset of virtual pages resident in physical memory is called a *working set.* There are two kinds of working sets—process working sets and the system working set.

 NOTE The kernel extensions to support Terminal Server for Windows NT (which supports multiple independent interactive user sessions on a single Windows NT server system) add a third type of working set: the session working set. A session consists of a set of processes as well as a system working set for kernel-mode session-specific data structures allocated by the kernel-mode part of the Win32 subsystem (WIN32K.SYS).

Before examining the details of each type of working set, let's look at the overall policy for deciding which pages are brought into physical memory and how long they remain. After that, we'll explore the two types of working sets.

Paging Policies

Virtual memory systems generally define three policies that dictate how (or when) paging is performed: a fetch policy, a placement policy, and a replacement policy.

A *fetch policy* determines when the pager brings a page from disk into memory. One type of fetch policy attempts to load the pages a process will need before it asks for them. Other fetch policies, called *demand-paging policies,* load a page into physical memory only when a page fault occurs. In a demand-paging system, a process incurs many page faults when its threads first begin executing, because the threads reference the initial set of pages they need to get going. Once this set of pages is loaded into memory, the paging activity of the process decreases.

NOTE To optimize the startup time of an image, a tool named the Working Set Tuner has been provided in the Platform SDK. This utility reorders the pages in an executable image, placing them in the order in which they are referenced during image startup and thus decreasing load time.

The Windows NT memory manager uses a demand-paging algorithm with "clustering" to load pages into memory. When a thread receives a page fault, the memory manager loads into memory the faulted page plus a small number of pages surrounding it. This strategy attempts to minimize the number of paging I/Os a thread will incur. Because programs, especially large ones, tend to execute in small regions of their address space at any given time, loading clusters of virtual pages reduces the number of disk reads. The values that determine the default page read cluster size are listed in Table 5-15. Notice that the values differ for data pages and code pages.

Table 5-15   Page Fault Clustering Values

Memory Size	Cluster Size for Data Page	Cluster Size for Code Page
Small	0	1
Medium	1	2
Large	3	7

When a thread receives a page fault, the memory management system must also determine where in physical memory to put the virtual page. The set of rules it uses to do this is called a *placement policy*. Windows NT considers the size of CPU memory caches when choosing page frames to minimize unnecessary thrashing of the cache.

If physical memory is full when a page fault occurs, a *replacement policy* is used to determine which virtual page must be removed from memory to make room for the new page. Common replacement policies include *least recently used* (*LRU*) and *first in, first out* (*FIFO*). The LRU algorithm requires the virtual memory system to track when a page in memory is used. When a new page frame is required, the page that hasn't been used for the greatest amount of time is paged to disk and its frame is freed to satisfy the page fault. The FIFO algorithm is somewhat simpler; it removes the page that has been in physical memory for the greatest amount of time, regardless of how often it's been used.

Replacement policies can be further characterized as either global or local. A global replacement policy allows a page fault to be satisfied by any page frame, whether or not that frame is owned by another process. For example, a global replacement policy using the FIFO algorithm would locate the page that has been in memory the longest and would free it to satisfy a page fault; a local replacement policy would limit its search for the oldest page to the set of pages already owned by the process that incurred the page fault. Global replacement policies make processes vulnerable to the behavior of other processes—an ill-behaved application can undermine the entire operating system by inducing excessive paging activity in all processes.

On multiprocessor *x*86 systems and on all Alpha systems, Windows NT implements a variation of a local FIFO replacement policy. On uniprocessor *x*86 systems, it implements something closer to a least recently accessed policy (known as the *clock algorithm*, as implemented in some versions of Berkeley UNIX). It allocates a number of page frames (dynamically adjusted) to each process, called the *process working set* (or in the case of pagable system code and data, to the *system working set*). When a process working set reaches its limit and/ or a working set needs to be trimmed because of demands for physical memory from other processes, the memory manager removes pages from the working set until it has determined there are enough free pages. How Windows NT determines whether there are enough pages is explained in the next section.

Process Working Sets

Every process starts with the same default working set minimum and maximum. These values, which are listed in Table 5-16, are calculated at system initialization time and are based strictly on the size of physical memory. (For an explanation of small, medium, and large memory systems, see page 236.)

**Table 5-16 Default Minimum and Maximum
Working Set Sizes in Pages**

Memory Size	Default Minimum Working Set Size (in Pages)	Default Maximum Working Set Size (in Pages)
Small	20	45
Medium	30	145
Large	50	345

You can change these default values on a per-process basis with the Win32 *SetProcessWorkingSetSize* function, though you must have the "increase scheduling priority" user right to do this. The maximum working set size can't exceed the systemwide maximum calculated at system initialization time and stored in the global variable *MmMaximumWorkingSetSize*. This value is set to be the number of available pages (the size of the zero, free, and standby list) at the time the computation is made minus 512 pages. However, this computed value has a fixed limit of 1984 MB for both *x*86 and Alpha systems or 3008 MB on an *x*86 system running with a 3-GB user space.

When a page fault occurs, the process's working set limits and the amount of free memory on the system are examined. If conditions permit, the memory manager allows a process to grow to its working set maximum (or beyond—the maximum can be exceeded if enough free pages are available). If the process reaches its limit and requires more pages, the memory manager removes one of the process's pages for each new page fault the process generates.

When physical memory runs low, the memory manager uses a technique called *automatic working set trimming* to increase the amount of free memory available in the system. The working set trimmer, a routine that runs in the context of the balance set manager (described on page 281), examines each process in memory, comparing the current size of its working set to its minimum working set value. When it finds processes using more than their minimums, it removes some pages from their working sets, making the pages available for other uses. If the amount of free memory is still too low, the memory manager continues removing pages from processes' working sets until it achieves a minimum number of free pages on the system. If since the last time a process was trimmed it has incurred more than a few page faults, it becomes exempt from trimming, the theory being that if the memory manager makes a mistake and trims pages that were being used, it won't trim any more out until the next periodic trim cycle (6 seconds later). With the Win32 *SetProcessWorkingSetSize* function mentioned earlier, you can also initiate working set trimming of your own process, for example, after the initialization in your application takes place.

The algorithm to determine which pages to remove from a working set is different on a single-processor *x*86 system than on a multiprocessor *x*86 system or an Alpha system. On a single-processor *x*86 system, the memory manager tries to remove pages that haven't been accessed recently. It does this by checking the accessed bit in the hardware PTE to see whether the page has been accessed. If the bit is clear, the page is removed from the working set. If the bit is set, the memory manager clears it and goes on to examine the next page in the working set. In this way, if the accessed bit is clear the next time the working set manager examines the page, it knows that the page hasn't been accessed since the last time it was examined. This scan for pages to remove continues through the working set list until either the number of desired pages has been removed or the scan has returned to the starting point. (The next time the working set is trimmed, the scan picks up where it left off last.)

On a multiprocessor *x*86 system and on all Alpha systems, the working set manager does not check the access bit; clearing it would require invalidating TLB entries on other processors, which would result in unnecessary TLB cache misses by threads in the same process that might be running on other processors. Thus, on a multiprocessor system, pages are removed from the working set without regard to the state of the accessed bit.

NOTE The algorithm for working set trimming is being improved in Windows NT 5.0 to be more intelligent when deciding which pages to remove from a working set.

As a process incurs page faults, if enough memory is available, the memory manager expands the working set. If memory is tight, the memory manager decides whether or not to expand the working set, depending on the process's page fault rate. If, however, the process incurs no page faults for a period of time, either the code the process's threads are executing fits comfortably within the process's minimum working set or none of the process's threads are executing.

EXPERIMENT: Viewing Process Working Set Sizes

You can use Performance Monitor to examine process working set sizes by looking at the following performance counters:

Counter	Description
Process: Working Set	Current size of the selected process's working set in bytes
Process: Working Set Peak	Peak size of the selected process's working set in bytes
Process: Page Faults/Sec	Number of page faults for the process that occur each second

Several other process viewer utilities (such as Task Manager, Pview, Pviewer, and so on) also display the process working set size.

You can also get the total of all the process working sets by selecting _Total process in the instance box in Performance Monitor. This process isn't real—it's simply a total of the process-specific counters for all processes currently running on the system. The total you see is misleading, however, because the size of each individual process working set includes pages being shared by other processes. Thus, if two or more processes share a page, the page is counted in each process's working set.

Balance Set Manager and Swapper

Working set expansion and trimming take place in the context of a system thread called the *balance set manager* (routine *KeBalanceSetManager*). The balance set manager is created during system initialization. Although the balance set manager is technically part of the kernel, it calls the memory manager's working set manager to perform working set analysis and adjustment.

The balance set manager waits on two different event objects: an event that is signaled when a periodic timer set to fire once per second expires and an internal working set manager event that the memory manager signals at various points when it determines that working sets need to be adjusted. For example, if the system is experiencing a high page fault rate or the free list is too small, the working set manager wakes up the balance set manager so that it will call the memory manager to begin trimming working sets. When memory is more plentiful, the working set manager will permit faulting processes to gradually increase the size of their working sets by faulting pages back into memory, but the working sets will grow only as needed.

When the balance set manager wakes up as the result of its 1-second timer expiring, it takes the following four steps:

1. Every *fourth* time the balance set manager wakes up because its 1-second timer has expired, it signals an event that wakes up another system thread called the swapper (routine *KeSwapProcessOrStack*).

2. It then checks the look-aside lists and adjusts their depths if necessary (to improve access time).

3. It looks for threads that might warrant having their priority boosted because they are CPU starved. (See the section "Priority Boosts for CPU Starvation" in Chapter 4 on page 210)

4. Call the memory manager's working set manager. (The working set manager has its own internal counters that regulate when to perform working set trimming and how aggressively to trim.)

The swapper is also awakened by the scheduling code in the kernel if a thread that needs to run has its kernel stack swapped out or if the process that contains the thread has its working set swapped out. The swapper looks for threads that have been in a wait state for a specified amount of time (3 seconds on small memory systems, 7 seconds on medium or large memory systems). If it finds one, it marks the thread's kernel stack to be swapped out to the paging file so as to reclaim its physical memory, operating on the principle that, if a thread's been waiting that long, it's going to be waiting even longer. When the last thread in a process has its kernel stack removed from memory, the process working set is marked to be entirely outswapped. That is why, for example, processes that have been idle for a long time (such as WinLogon is after you log on) can have a zero working set size.

Some of the system variables that affect working set expansion and trimming are listed in Table 5-17. The values of these variables are fixed, and you can't change them without using the kernel debugger or writing a device driver.

Table 5-17   Working Set–Related System Control Variables

Variable	Value	Description
MmWorkingSetSize-Increment	6	The number of pages to add to a working set if there are sufficient available pages and the working set is below its maximum.
MmWorkingSetSize-Expansion	20	The number of pages by which to expand the maximum working set if it is at its maximum and there are sufficient available pages.
MmWsExpand-Threshold	90	The number of pages that must be available to expand the working set above its maximum.
MmPagesAboveWs-Threshold	37	If memory is getting short and *MmPagesAboveWsMinimum-* is above this value, trim working sets.
MmWsAdjustThreshold	45	The number of pages required to be freed by working set reduction before working set reduction is attempted.
MmWsTrimReduction-Goal	29	The total number of pages to reduce by working set trimming.

System Working Set

Just as processes have working sets, the pagable code and data in the operating system are managed by a single *system working set*. Five different kinds of pages can reside in the system working set:

- System cache pages
- Paged pool
- Pagable code in NTOSKRNL.EXE
- Pagable code in device drivers
- System mapped views (sections mapped at 0xA0000000, such as WIN32K.SYS)

You can examine the size of the system working set or the size of the five components that contribute to it with the performance counters or system variables shown in Table 5-18. Keep in mind that the performance counter values are in bytes whereas the system variables are measured in terms of pages.

Table 5-18 System Working Set Performance Counters

Performance Counter (in Bytes)	System Variable (in Pages)	Description
Memory: Cache Bytes*	*MmSystemCacheWs- .WorkingSetSize*	Total size of system working set (including the cache, paged pool, pagable NTOSKRNL and driver code, and system mapped views); this is *not* the size of the system cache alone, even though the name implies that it is.
Memory: Cache Bytes Peak	*MmSystemCacheWs.Peak*	Peak system working set size.
Memory: System Cache Resident Bytes	*MmSystemCachePage*	Physical memory consumed by the system cache.
Memory: System Code Resident Bytes	*MmSystemCodePage*	Physical memory consumed by pagable code in NTOSKRNL.EXE.
Memory: System Driver Resident Bytes	*MmSystemDriverPage*	Physical memory consumed by pagable device driver code.
Memory: Paged Pool Resident Bytes	*MmPagedPoolPage*	Physical memory consumed by paged pool.

* Internally, this working set is called the system *cache* working set, even though the system cache is just one of four different components in it. Thus, several utilities think they are displaying the size of file cache when they are displaying the total size of the system working set.

You can also examine the paging activity in the system working set by examining the Memory: Cache Faults/Sec performance counter, which describes page faults that occur in the system working set (both hard and soft). The system variable that contains the value for this counter is *MmSystemCache-Ws.PageFaultCount*.

The minimum and maximum system working set size is computed at system initialization time based on the amount of physical memory on the machine and whether the system is running Windows NT Workstation or Windows NT Server. The initial values, which are listed in Table 5-19, are chosen based on system memory size.

Table 5-19 Minimum and Maximum Size of System Working Set

Memory Size	System Working Set Minimum (in Pages)	System Working Set Maximum (in Pages)
Small	388	500
Medium	688	1150
Large	1188	2050

These numbers are further altered if the registry field HKLM\System...\Control\Session Manager\Memory Management\LargeSystemCache is set to 1 (the default is 0) and the number of available pages (*MmAvailablePages*, as described on page 298) is greater than 350 plus 6 MB (a total of 1886 pages on *x*86 systems and 1118 pages on Alpha systems). In this case, the system working set maximum is set to available pages minus 4 MB. If this value is greater than the maximum working set size supported by Windows NT (1984 MB for normal *x*86 and Alpha systems or 3008 MB on an *x*86 system running with a 3-GB user space), the system working set maximum is reduced to that maximum value minus 5 pages.

Windows NT then checks to see whether the new system working set maximum is greater than the virtual size of the system cache—if it is, the working set is reduced to the virtual size of the system cache. In other words, the system working set could potentially expand to use all of the virtual memory reserved for the system cache. (See Chapter 8 for more information about the virtual size of the system cache.)

Finally, a check is made to determine whether the difference between the system working set minimum and maximum is less than 500 pages. If it is, the working set minimum is reduced to the working set maximum minus 500 pages.

The final calculated working set minimum and maximum are then stored in the system variables shown in Table 5-20. (These variables are not available through any performance counter.)

Table 5-20 System Variables That Store Working Set Minimums or Maximums

Variable	Type	Description
MmSystemCacheWsMinimum or *MmSystemCacheWs.MinimumWorkingSetSize*	ULONG	Minimum working set size
MmSystemCacheWsMaximum or *MmSystemCacheWs.MaximumWorkingSetSize*	ULONG	Maximum working set size

Page Frame Database

Whereas working sets describe the resident pages owned by a process or the system, the *page frame database* describes the state of each page in physical memory. Pages are in one of eight states, as shown in Table 5-21.

Table 5-21 Page States

Status	Description
Active (also called valid)	The page is part of a working set (either a process working set or the system working set), and a valid PTE points to it.
Transition	A temporary state for a page that is not owned by a working set and is not on any paging list. A page is in this state when an I/O is in progress to the page. The PTE is encoded so that collided page faults can be recognized and handled properly.
Standby	The page previously belonged to a working set but was removed. The page was not modified since it was last made resident. The PTE still refers to the physical page but is marked invalid and in transition.
Modified	The page previously belonged to a working set but was removed. However, the page was modified while it was in use and its contents haven't yet been written to disk. The PTE still refers to the physical page but is marked invalid and in transition.
Modified no write	Same as a modified page, except that it has been marked so that the memory manager's modified page writer won't write it to disk. The cache manager marks pages as modified no write at the request of file system drivers. NTFS uses this for pages containing file system metadata so that it can first ensure transaction log entries are flushed to disk before the pages they are protecting are written to disk. (NTFS transaction logging is explained in Chapter 9.)
Free	The page is free but has dirty data in it. (Dirty pages can't be given as a user page to a user process without being initialized with zeros.)
Zeroed	The page is free and has been initialized with zeros by the zero page thread.
Bad	The page has generated parity or other hardware errors and can't be used.

The PFN database consists of an array of structures numbered from 0 through the number of physical pages of memory on the system (minus 1). The page frame database and its relationship to page tables are shown in Figure 5-16. As this figure shows, valid PTEs point to entries in the page frame database, and the page frame database entries (for nonprototype PFNs) point back to the page table that is using them. For prototype PFNs, they point back to the prototype PTE.

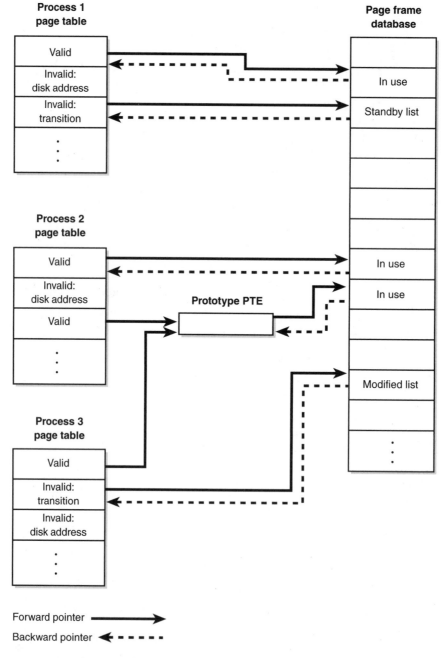

Figure 5-16
Page tables and the page frame database

Of the page states listed in Table 5-21 on page 285, six are organized into linked lists so that the memory manager can quickly locate pages of a specific type. (Active/valid pages and transition pages aren't in any systemwide page list.) Figure 5-17 shows an example of how these entries are linked together.

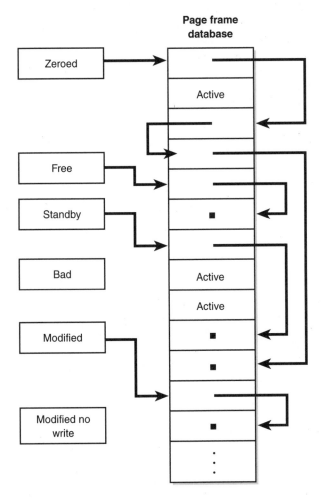

Figure 5-17
Page lists in the PFN database

EXPERIMENT: Accounting for Physical Memory

With the Windows NT Resource Kit tools and Performance Monitor, you can come close to accounting for all of physical memory. To add up the memory on your machine, run Performance Monitor and add the following counters:

- **Total process working set size**   To add this counter, select the Process: Working Set Size counter for the _Total process. Remember that the process working set size is larger than the actual total process memory utilization since shared pages are counted in each process working set.

- **Total system working set size**   To add this counter, select Memory: Cache Bytes. As you'll see, this counter is more than just the cache size—it includes three other components, all of which comprise the system working set.

- **Size of nonpaged pool**   Add this counter by selecting Memory: Pool Nonpaged Bytes.

- **Size of the free, zero, and standby lists**   Specify the sizes of these lists by selecting Memory: Available Bytes.

Your graph now contains a representation of all of physical memory except for two components:

- Nonpaged operating system and driver code

- The modified and modified no write paging lists

Although there is no way to get the exact size of the nonpaged operating system and driver code, you can obtain an estimate by totaling the first two columns of the loaded kernel-mode module list from the Drivers or Pstat utility and then subtracting the size of WIN32K.SYS. (The image sections in WIN32K.SYS are marked nonpaged, but the loader has special case code that marks them all as pagable.) A sample of the output from the Drivers utility is shown at the top of the next page. (Pstat's output is similar but includes the address of the loaded module in system space.) In this example, the total nonpaged system code and data is 2,453,536 (code) + 218,656 (data) − 1,162,624 (WIN32K.SYS code) − 40,064 (WIN32K.SYS data) = 1,469,504 bytes, or about 1.5 MB.

```
ModuleName     Code    Data    Bss   Paged    Init        LinkDate
----------------------------------------------------------------------------
ntoskrnl.exe  282816   42112     0  435392   84352   Sat May 10 21:11:27 1997
    hal.dll    24992    4224     0    9920   21120   Mon Mar 10 13:40:06 1997
  atapi.sys    20736    1088     0       0     768   Thu Apr 10 12:06:59 1997
SCSIPORT.SYS    9824      32     0   15552    2208   Mon Mar 10 13:42:27 1997
cpq32fs2.sys   62080     288     0       0     640   Mon Aug 12 23:19:00 1996
   Disk.sys     3328       0     0    7072    1600   Thu Apr 24 19:27:46 1997
 CLASS2.SYS     7040       0     0    1632    1152   Thu Apr 24 19:23:43 1997
   Ntfs.sys    68160    5408     0  269632    8704   Thu Apr 17 19:02:31 1997
 Floppy.SYS     1088     672     0    7968    6112   Tue Jul 16 21:31:09 1996
  Cdrom.SYS    12608      32     0    3072    3104   Tue Jul 16 21:31:29 1996
 Fs_Rec.SYS       64       0     0    2912    1152   Mon Mar 10 13:51:19 1997
   Null.SYS        0       0     0     288     416   Tue Jul 16 21:31:21 1996
 KSecDD.SYS     1280     224     0    3456    1024   Wed Jul 17 17:34:19 1996
   Beep.SYS     1184       0     0       0     704   Wed Apr 23 12:19:43 1997
auddrive.SYS   15296     320     0   17632   11008   Wed Sep 04 14:09:02 1996
i8042prt.sys   10784      32     0       0   10976   Mon Apr 21 13:03:54 1997
mouclass.sys    1984       0     0       0    3968   Mon Mar 10 13:43:11 1997
kbdclass.sys    1952       0     0       0    3840   Tue Jul 16 21:31:16 1996
VIDEOPRT.SYS    2080     128     0   11296    2752   Mon Mar 10 13:41:37 1997
  mga64.sys     1920   68768     0   30112    6880   Tue Aug 27 06:26:50 1996
    vga.sys      128      32     0   10784     832   Tue Jul 16 21:30:37 1996
   Msfs.SYS      864      32     0   15328    1664   Mon Mar 10 13:45:01 1997
   Npfs.SYS     6560     192     0   22624    3200   Mon Mar 10 13:44:48 1997
   NDIS.SYS    11744     704     0   96768    4640   Thu Apr 17 19:19:45 1997
SYSMGMT.SYS    66784     352     0      32   46528   Wed Sep 18 23:19:00 1996
 win32k.sys  1162624   40064     0       0    6400   Fri Apr 25 18:17:32 1997
  NTDLL.DLL   237568   20480     0       0       0   Fri Apr 11 13:38:50 1997
----------------------------------------------------------------------------
     Total  2453536  218656     0 1568032  311264
```

The size of the individual paging lists is available only from the kernel debugger *!memusage* command. The following excerpt is from the output from this command:

```
KDx86> !memusage
  loading PFN database....................
          Zeroed:    645 (  2580 kb)
            Free:      4 (    16 kb)
         Standby:   2185 (  8740 kb)
        Modified:    590 (  2360 kb)
 ModifiedNoWrite:      0 (     0 kb)
    Active/Valid:   6815 ( 27260 kb)
      Transition:      0 (     0 kb)
         Unknown:      0 (     0 kb)
           TOTAL:  10239 ( 40956 kb)
```

The last figure you need to complete this exercise of accounting for all of physical memory is the size of the modified and modified no write lists, which in this case comes out to approximately 2.3 MB (2360 KB).

289

In the next section, you'll find out how these lists are used to satisfy page faults and how pages move to and from the various lists.

Page List Dynamics

Figure 5-18 shows a state diagram for page frame transitions. For simplicity, the modified no write list is not shown.

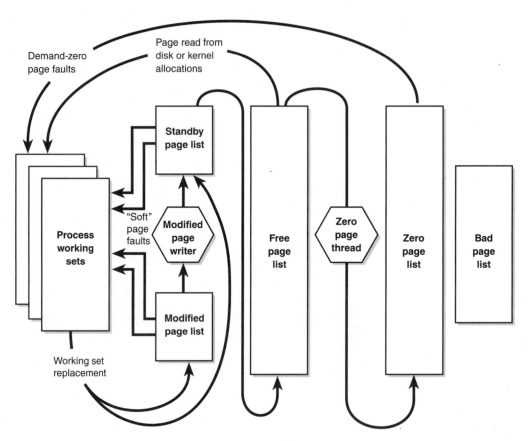

Figure 5-18
State diagram for page frames

Page frames move between the paging lists in the following ways:

■ When the memory manager needs a zero-initialized page to service a demand-zero page fault (a reference to a page that is defined to be all zeros, or to a user-mode committed private page that has never been accessed), it first attempts to get one from the zero page list; if the list is empty, it gets one from the free page list and zeros the page. If the free list is empty, it goes to the standby list and zeros that page.

One reason zero-initialized pages are required is to meet C2 security requirements. C2 specifies that user-mode processes must be given initialized page frames to prevent them from reading a previous process's memory contents. Therefore, the memory manager gives user-mode processes zeroed page frames unless the page is being read in from a mapped file. If that's the case, the memory manager uses nonzeroed page frames, initializing them with the data off the disk.

The zero page list is populated from the free list by a system thread called the *zero page thread* (thread 0 in the System process). It waits on an event object to signal it to go to work. When the free list has eight or more pages, this event is signaled. However, the zero page thread will run only if all other threads are not running, because the zero page thread runs at priority 0 and the lowest priority that a user thread can be set to is 1.

■ When the memory manager doesn't require a zero-initialized page, it goes first to the free list; if that is empty, it goes to the zeroed list. If the zeroed list is empty, it goes to the standby list. Before the memory manager can use a page frame from the standby or modified list, it must first backtrack and remove the reference from the invalid PTE (or prototype PTE) that still points to the page frame. Since entries in the page frame database contain pointers back to the previous user's page table (or to a prototype PTE for shared pages), it can quickly find the PTE and make the appropriate change.

■ When a process has to give up a page out of its working set (either because it referenced a new page and its working set was full, its working set was trimmed by the memory manager, or the process exits), the page goes to the standby list if the page was clean (not modified) or to the modified list if the page was modified while it was resident.

EXPERIMENT: Viewing Page Fault Behavior

With the PFMON tool in the Windows NT Resource Kit, you can watch page fault behavior as it occurs. Soft faults refer to a page fault satisfied from one of the transition lists. Hard faults can be either a disk-read or a demand-zero fault. The following example is a portion of output you'll see if you start Microsoft Notepad with Pfmon and then exit. Be sure to notice the summary of page fault activity at the end.

```
C:\> pfmon notepad
SOFT: KiUserApcDispatcher : KiUserApcDispatcher
SOFT: LdrInitializeThunk : LdrInitializeThunk
SOFT: 0x77f61016 :  : 0x77f61016
SOFT: 0x77f6105b :  : fltused+0xe00
HARD: 0x77f6105b :  : fltused+0xe00
SOFT: LdrQueryImageFileExecutionOptions : LdrQueryImageFileExecutionOptions
SOFT: RtlAppendUnicodeToString : RtlAppendUnicodeToString
SOFT: RtlInitUnicodeString : RtlInitUnicodeString
  :
  :

    notepad.dbg Caused     8 faults had   17 Soft    3 Hard faulted VA's
     ntdll.dbg Caused   183 faults had   48 Soft    5 Hard faulted VA's
   comdlg32.dbg Caused     7 faults had   12 Soft    5 Hard faulted VA's
   kernel32.dbg Caused    53 faults had   45 Soft    3 Hard faulted VA's
     user32.dbg Caused    56 faults had   53 Soft    2 Hard faulted VA's
      gdi32.dbg Caused    22 faults had   19 Soft    2 Hard faulted VA's
   advapi32.dbg Caused    12 faults had   21 Soft    3 Hard faulted VA's
     rpcrt4.dbg Caused     3 faults had   11 Soft    2 Hard faulted VA's
     shell32.dbg Caused   10 faults had   22 Soft    4 Hard faulted VA's
    comctl32.dbg Caused    5 faults had   12 Soft    2 Hard faulted VA's
```

When the modified list gets too big, or if the size of the zeroed and standby lists falls below a minimum threshold (as indicated by the kernel variable *MmMinimumFreePages*, which is computed at system boot time), a system thread called the *modified page writer* is awakened to write pages back to disk and move the pages to the standby list.

Modified Page Writer

The modified page writer is responsible for limiting the size of the modified page list by writing pages to their backing store locations when the list becomes too big. It consists of two system threads: one to write out modified pages (*MiModifiedPageWriter*) to the paging file and a second one to write modified pages to mapped files (*MiMappedPageWriter*). Two threads are required to avoid creating a deadlock, which would occur if the writing of mapped file pages caused a page fault that in turn required a free page when no free pages were available (thus requiring the modified page writer to create more free pages). By having the modified page writer perform mapped file paging I/Os from a second system thread, that thread can wait without blocking regular page file I/O.

Both threads run at priority 17 and, after initialization, wait on separate event objects to trigger their operation. The modified page writer event is set when the number of modified pages exceeds the maximum value computed at system initialization (*MmModifiedPageMaximum*). It is also set by the working set management code when the number of available pages (*MmAvailablePages*) goes below *MmMinimumFreePages*.

Table 5-22 shows the number of pages that trigger the waking of the modified page writer to reduce the size of the modified list and how many pages it leaves on the list. As with other memory management variables, this value is computed at system boot time and depends on the amount of physical memory.

Table 5-22 **Modified Page Writer Values**

Memory Size	Modified Page Threshold	Retain Modified Pages
Small	100	40
Medium	150	80
Large	300	150
>33 MB (special case)	400	800

When invoked, the modified page writer attempts to write as many pages as possible to the backing store with a single I/O request. It accomplishes this by examining the original PTE field of the PFN database elements for pages on the modified page list to locate pages in contiguous locations in the backing store. Once a list is created, the pages are removed from the modified list, an I/O request is issued, and at successful completion of the I/O request, the pages are placed at the tail of the standby list.

Pages that are in the process of being written can be referenced to disk. When this happens, the reference count and the share count in the PFN entry that represents the physical page are incremented to indicate that the page is being used by another process. When the I/O operation completes, the modified page writer notices that the share count is no longer 0 and doesn't place the page on the standby list.

PFN Data Structures

Although PFN entries are of fixed length, they can be in several different states, depending on the state of the page. Thus, individual fields have different meanings depending on the state. The states of a PFN entry are shown in Figure 5-19.

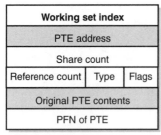

PFN for a page in a
working set

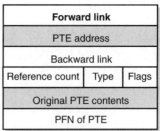

PFN for a page on the standby
or the modified list

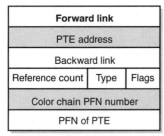

PFN for a page on the
zero or free list

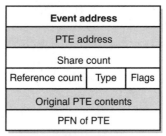

PFN for a page with a
I/O in progess

Figure 5-19
States of PFN entries

Several fields are the same for several of the PFN types, but others are specific to a given type of PFN. The following fields appear in more than one PFN type:

- **PTE address** Virtual address of the PTE that points to this page.

- **Reference count** The number of references to this page. The reference count is incremented when a page is first added to a working set and/or when the page is locked in memory for I/O (for example, by a device driver). The reference count is decremented when the share count becomes 0 or when pages are unlocked from memory. When the reference count becomes 0, the page is no longer owned by a working set, and depending on its status, the PFN entry that describes the page is updated to add the page to the free, standby, or modified list.

■ **Type** The type of page represented by this PFN (active/valid, transition, standby, modified, modified no write, free, zeroed, bad, and transition).

■ **Flags** The information contained in the flags field is shown in Table 5-23 on the following page.

■ **Original PTE contents** All PFN entries contain the original contents of the PTE that pointed to the page (which could be a prototype PTE). Saving the contents of the PTE allows it to be restored when the physical page is no longer resident.

■ **PFN of PTE** Physical page number of the page table page containing the PTE that points to this page.

The remaining fields are specific to the type of PFN. For example, the first PFN in Figure 5-19 represents a page that is active and part of a working set. The share count field represents the number of PTEs that refer to this page. (Pages marked read-only or copy-on-write can be shared by multiple processes.) For page table pages, this field is the number of valid PTEs in the page table. As long as the share count is greater than 0, the page is not eligible for removal from memory.

The working set index field is an index into the process (or system) working set list where the virtual address that maps this physical page resides. If the page is a private page, the working set index field refers directly to the entry in the working set list, since the page is mapped only at a single virtual address. In the case of a shared page, the working set index is a hint that is guaranteed to be correct only for the first process that made the page valid. (Other processes will try to use the same index where possible.) The process that initially sets this field is guaranteed to refer to the proper index and doesn't need to add a working set list hash entry referenced by the virtual address into its working set hash tree. This guarantee reduces the size of the working set hash tree and makes searches faster for these particular direct entries.

The second PFN in Figure 5-19 is for a page on either the standby or the modified list. In this case, the forward and backward link fields link the elements of the list together within the list. This linking allows pages to be easily manipulated to satisfy page faults. When a page is on one of the lists, the share

Table 5-23 Flags Within PFN Entries

Flag	Meaning
Modified state	Indicates whether the page was modified. (If the page is modified, its contents must be saved to disk before removing it from memory.)
Prototype PTE	Indicates that the PTE referenced by the PFN entry is a prototype PTE. (For example, this page is sharable.)
Parity error	Indicates that the physical page contains parity or error correction control errors.
Read in progress	Indicates that an in-page operation is in progress for the page. The first DWORD contains the address of the event object that will be signaled when the I/O is complete; also used to indicate the first PFN for nonpaged pool allocations.
Write in progress	Indicates that a page write operation is in progress. The first DWORD contains the address of the event object that will be signaled when the I/O is complete; also used to indicate the last PFN for nonpaged pool allocations.
Start of nonpaged pool	For nonpaged pool pages, indicates that this is the first PFN for a given nonpaged pool allocation.
End of nonpaged pool	For nonpaged pool pages, indicates that this is the last PFN for a given nonpaged pool allocation.
In-page error	Indicates that an I/O error occurred during the in-page operation on this page. (In this case, the first field in the PFN contains the error code.)

count is by definition 0 (since the page is not in use by any working set) and therefore can be overlaid with the backward link. However, the reference count might not be 0, since an I/O could be in progress for this page (for example, when the page is being written to disk).

The third PFN in Figure 5-19 on page 294 is for a page on the free or zeroed list. Besides being linked together within the two lists, these PFN entries use an additional field to link physical pages by "color," their location in the processor memory cache. Windows NT attempts to minimize unnecessary thrashing of CPU memory caches by mapping virtually contiguous pages to pages that are physically contiguous in the cache. It achieves this optimization by avoiding using the same cache entry for two different pages wherever possible. For processors with direct mapped caches, optimally using the hardware's capabilities can result in a significant performance advantage.

The fourth PFN in Figure 5-19 on page 294 is for a page that has an I/O in progress (for example, a page read). While the I/O is in progress, the first field points to an event object that will be signaled when the I/O completes. If an in-page error occurs, this field contains the Windows NT error status code representing the I/O error. This PFN type is used to resolve collided page faults.

EXPERIMENT: Viewing PFN Entries

You can examine individual PFN entries with the kernel debugger *!pfn* command. You first need to supply the PFN as an argument. (For example, *!pfn* 0 shows the first entry, *!pfn* 1 shows the second, and so on.) In the following example, the PTE for virtual address 0x50000 is displayed, followed by the PFN that contains the page directory and then the actual page:

```
KDx86> !pte 50000
00050000  - PDE at C0300000        PTE at C0000140
          contains 00700067        contains 00DAA047
       pfn 00700 --DA--UWV     pfn 00DAA --D---UWV

KDx86> !pfn 700
    PFN address 827CD800
    flink        00000004  blink /
 share count 00000010  pteaddress C0300000
    reference count 0001                        color 0
    restore pte 00000080  containing page      00030  Active    M
    Modified

KDx86> !pfn daa
    PFN address 827D77F0
    flink        00000077  blink /
 share count 00000001  pteaddress C0000140
    reference count 0001                        color 0
    restore pte 00000080  containing page      00700  Active    M
    Modified
```

In addition to the PFN database, the system variables in Table 5-24 describe the overall state of physical memory.

Table 5-24   System Variables That Describe Physical Memory

Variable	Description
MmNumberofPhysicalPages	Total number of physical pages available on the system
MmAvailablePages	Total number of available pages on the system—the sum of the pages on the zeroed, free, and standby lists
MmResidentAvailablePages	Total number of physical pages that would be available if every process were at its minimum working set size

Section Objects

As you'll remember from the section on shared memory earlier in the chapter, the *section object,* which the Win32 subsystem calls a *file-mapping object,* represents a block of memory that two or more processes can share. A section object can be mapped to the paging file or to another file on disk.

The executive uses sections to load executable images into memory, and the cache manager uses them to access data in a cached file. (See Chapter 8 for more information on how the cache manager uses section objects.) You can also use section objects to map a file into a process address space. The file can then be accessed as a large array by mapping different views of the section object and reading or writing to memory rather than to the file (an activity called *mapped file I/O*). When the program accesses an invalid page (one not in physical memory), a page fault occurs and the memory manager automatically brings the page into memory from the mapped file. If the application modifies the page, the memory manager writes the changes back to the file during its normal paging operations (or the application can flush a view using the Win32 *FlushViewOfFile* function).

Section objects, like other objects, are allocated and deallocated by the object manager. The object manager creates and initializes an object header, which it uses to manage the objects; the memory manager defines the body of the section object. The memory manager also implements services that user-mode threads can call to retrieve and change the attributes stored in the body of section objects. The structure of a section object is shown in Figure 5-20.

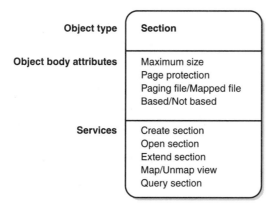

Figure 5-20
A section object

Table 5-25 summarizes the unique attributes stored in section objects.

Table 5-25 **Section Object Body Attributes**

Attribute	Purpose
Maximum size	The largest size to which the section can grow in bytes; if mapping a file, the maximum size is the size of the file.
Page protection	Page-based memory protection assigned to all pages in the section when it is created.
Paging file/Mapped file	Indicates whether the section is created empty (backed by the paging file) or loaded with a file (backed by the mapped file).
Based/Not based	Indicates whether a section is a based section, which must appear at the same virtual address for all processes sharing it, or a nonbased section, which can appear at different virtual addresses for different processes.

EXPERIMENT: Viewing Section Objects

With the Object Viewer (WINOBJ.EXE in the Platform SDK), you can see the list of sections that have global names. As explained in Chapter 3, these names are stored in the object manager directory \BaseNamed-Objects.

With the Windows NT Resource Kit OH (Open Handles) tool, you can list the open handles to section objects. The following command displays all open handles to objects of type *section*, whether or not they have names. (A section must have a name only if other processes need to open it by name.)

```
c:\> oh -t section -a
  2 System         Section       012c
 23 smss.exe        Section       0004
 23 smss.exe        Section       0020
 31 csrss.exe       Section       0004
 31 csrss.exe       Section       001c \NLS\NlsSectionLocale
 31 csrss.exe       Section       0020 \NLS\NlsSectionUnicode
 31 csrss.exe       Section       0030
 31 csrss.exe       Section       0038 \NLS\NlsSectionUnicode
 31 csrss.exe       Section       003c \NLS\NlsSectionLocale
 31 csrss.exe       Section       0044 \NLS\NlsSectionCType
 31 csrss.exe       Section       004c \NLS\NlsSectionCType
 31 csrss.exe       Section       0050
 31 csrss.exe       Section       0054 \NLS\NlsSectionSortkey
 31 csrss.exe       Section       005c \NLS\NlsSectionSortkey
 31 csrss.exe       Section       0064 \NLS\NlsSectionSortTbls
 31 csrss.exe       Section       006c \NLS\NlsSectionSortTbls
 37 WINLOGON.EXE    Section       0004
 37 WINLOGON.EXE    Section       0018
 43 SERVICES.EXE    Section       0004
 43 SERVICES.EXE    Section       0030
 43 SERVICES.EXE    Section       0100
 43 SERVICES.EXE    Section       011c
 43 SERVICES.EXE    Section       0138
 46 LSASS.EXE       Section       0004
 46 LSASS.EXE       Section       0028
```

The data structures maintained by the memory manager that describe mapped sections are shown in Figure 5-21. These structures ensure that data read from mapped files is consistent, regardless of the type of access (open file, mapped file, and so on).

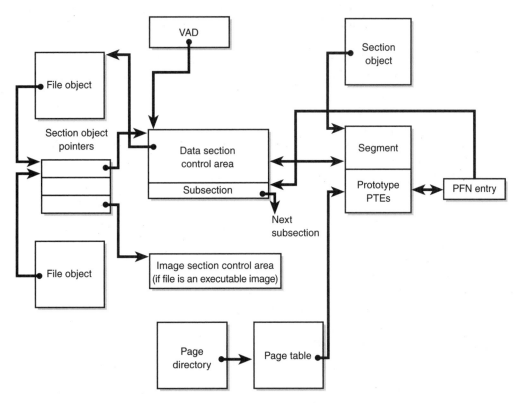

Figure 5-21
Internal section structures

For each open file (represented by a file object), there is a single *section object pointers* structure. (This structure is also discussed in Chapter 8). This structure is the key to maintaining data consistency for all types of file access as well as to providing caching for files. The section object pointers structure points to one or two *control areas*. One control area is used to map the file when it is accessed as a data file, and one is used to map the file when it is run as an executable image. A control area in turn points to *subsection* structures that describe the mapping information for each section of the file (read-only, read-write, copy-on-write, and so on). The control area also points to a *segment* structure allocated in paged pool that contains the prototype PTEs used to map to the actual pages mapped by the section object. As described earlier in the chapter, process page tables point to these prototype PTEs, which in turn map the pages being referenced.

Although Windows NT ensures that any process that accesses (reads or writes) a file will always see the same, consistent data, there is one case in which two copies of pages of a file can reside in physical memory (but even in this case, all accessors get the latest copy and data consistency is maintained). This can happen when an image file has been accessed as a data file (having been read or written) and then run as an executable image (for example, when an image is linked and then run—the Linker had the file open for data access, and then when the image was run, the image loader mapped it as an executable). Internally, the following actions occur:

1. When the image file is created, a data control area is created to represent the data pages in the image file being read or written.

2. When the image is run and the section object is created to map the image as an executable, the memory manager finds that the section object pointers for the image file point to a data control area and flushes the section. This step is necessary to ensure that any modified pages have been written to disk before accessing the image through the image control area.

3. The memory manager then creates a control area for the image file.

4. As the image begins execution, its (read-only) pages are faulted in from the image file.

Because the pages mapped by the data control area might still be resident (on the standby list), this is the one case in which two copies of the same data are in two different pages in memory. However, this duplication does not result in a data consistency issue, because, as mentioned, the data control area has already been flushed to disk, so the pages read from the image are up to date.

EXPERIMENT: Viewing Control Areas

To find the address of the control area structures for a file, you must first get the address of the file object in question. You can obtain this address by dumping the process handle table with the *!handle* command and noting the object address of a file object. Although the kernel debugger *!file* command displays the basic information in a file object, it doesn't display the pointer to the section object pointers structure. However, since file objects are defined in the public DDK header file \ddk\inc\ntddk.h, you can look up the offset (0x20 in Windows NT 4.0). So, simply examine the pointer at offset 0x20 into the file object, and you'll have the section object pointers structure. That structure is also defined in ntddk.h. It consists of three 32-bit pointers: a pointer to the data control area, a pointer to the shared cache map (explained in Chapter 8), and a pointer to the image control area. From the section object pointers structure, you can obtain the address of a control area for the file (if one exists) and feed that address into the *!ca* command.

Another technique is to display the list of all control areas with the *!memusage* command. The following excerpt is from the output of this command.

```
KDx86> !memusage
 loading PFN database.....................
           Zeroed:    645 (  2580 kb)
             Free:      4 (    16 kb)
          Standby:   2185 (  8740 kb)
         Modified:    590 (  2360 kb)
  ModifiedNoWrite:      0 (     0 kb)
     Active/Valid:   6815 ( 27260 kb)
       Transition:      0 (     0 kb)
          Unknown:      0 (     0 kb)
            TOTAL:  10239 ( 40956 kb)

 Usage Summary in KiloBytes (Kb):
 Control Valid Standby Dirty Shared Locked PageTables  name
 8054e9a8     8    360     0      0      0        0  mapped_file( eudora32.dll )
 8055a5a8     0    792     0      0      0        0  mapped_file( MM2048.DAT )
 8062d8e8  2080     44     0      0      0        0     No Name for File
 80607328   180    256     0     84      0        0  mapped_file( OLE32.DLL )
 8062e9a8   948     32     0      0      0        0     No Name for File
 805ed208     8      0     0      0      0        0  mapped_file( MSV1_0.DLL )
```

(continued)

EXPERIMENT: Viewing Control Areas *continued*

The "Control" column points to the control area structure that describes the mapped file. You can display control areas, segments, and subsections with the kernel debugger *!ca* command. This output is from a *!ca* command:

```
kd> !ca ffb6b208
ControlArea @ffb6b208
  Segment:    e17d2008    Flink           0    Blink:             0
  Section Ref      1      Pfn Ref         1    Mapped Views:      1
  User Ref         0      Subsections     1    Flush Count:       0
  File Object ff35e548    ModWriteCount   0    System Views:      1
  Flags (8080) File WasPurged

   File: \TEMP\ICD1.tmp\com\ms\win32\MIXERCONTROLDETAILS_LISTTEXT.class


Segment @ e17d2008:
  Base address     0     Total Ptes      100   NonExtendPtes:    100
  Image commit     0     ControlArea ffb6b208 SizeOfSegment:   0  100000
  Image Base       0     Committed         0   PTE Template:    4fdcd2
  Based Addres     0     ProtoPtes   e17d2040 Image Info:        0


Subsection 1. @ ffb6b238
  ControlArea: ffb6b208   Starting Sector 0 Number Of Sectors 100
  Base Pte     e17d2040   Ptes In subsect       100 Unused Ptes        0
  Flags             60    Sector Offset           0 Protection         6
```

Conclusion

In this chapter, we've examined how the Windows NT memory manager implements 32-bit virtual memory management. As with most 32-bit operating systems, each process is given access to a private 32-bit address space, protecting one process's memory from another's but allowing processes to share memory efficiently and securely. Advanced capabilities, such as the inclusion of mapped files and the ability to sparsely allocate memory, are also available. The Win32 environment subsystem makes most of the memory manager's capabilities available to applications through the Win32 API.

The memory manager's implementation relies on lazy-evaluation techniques whenever possible to avoid performing time-consuming and unnecessary operations unless they are required. It is also self-tuning, adapting to both large multiprocessor servers as well as uniprocessor desktop workstations.

One aspect of the memory manager that I didn't describe in this chapter is its tight integration with the cache manager, which I'll cover in Chapter 8. But before we get to that, let's take a closer look at the Windows NT security mechanisms.

CHAPTER SIX

Security

As mentioned in Chapter 1, Microsoft Windows NT provides a comprehensive, configurable set of security services that meets the requirements of the U.S. government Department of Defense C2 level for trusted operating systems. In 1995, two stand-alone configurations of Windows NT Server and Workstation 3.5 were formally certified at the C2 level by the United States National Computer Security Center (NCSC). (See *http://www.radium.ncsc.mil/tpep/epl* for more details.) In 1996, Windows NT Server and Windows NT Workstation 3.51 in both stand-alone and networked configurations were certified at the F-C2/E3 level by the UK Information Technology Security Evaluation and Certification (ITSEC) board. This evaluation is equivalent to the U.S. C2 evaluation. (For more information on the ITSEC evaluation, see *http://www.itsec.gov.uk*.) Windows NT 4.0 is currently under evaluation by both the U.S. NCSC and ITSEC.

Here are the security services and their required basic features:

- A *secure logon facility* requires users to identify themselves by entering a unique logon identifier and a password before they are allowed access to the system.

- *Discretionary access control* allows the owner of a resource to determine who can access the resource and what they can do with it. The owner grants rights that permit various kinds of access to a user or to a group of users.

- *Security auditing* affords the ability to detect and record security-related events or any attempts to create, access, or delete system resources. Logon identifiers record the identities of all users, making it easier to trace anyone who performs an unauthorized action.

- *Memory protection* prevents unauthorized processes from accessing the private virtual memory of another process. In addition, Windows NT guarantees that when a page of physical memory is allocated to a user process, that page will never contain dirty data from another process.

Windows NT meets these requirements through its security subsystem and related components.

To fully understand this chapter, you'll need to be familiar with security terms such as users, groups, domains, security IDs, access control lists, access tokens, user rights, and security auditing. Because this is an internals book, I'm not going to explain these user-visible objects and mechanisms or the Win32 programming interfaces that manage them. Also, because security is one of the areas that is being significantly enhanced and changed in Windows NT 5.0, I've gone into less detail in this chapter than in other chapters in this book.

Windows NT 5.0 ▶   **NOTE**   Windows NT 5.0 extends the security model in several key ways, particularly in distributed systems environments. Briefly, the enhancements include integration with the new Active Directory to provide scalable, flexible account management for large domains, allowing fine-grain access control and delegation of administration; Kerberos version 5 authentication protocol, a mature Internet security standard as the default protocol for network authentication, providing a foundation for authentication interoperability, and authentication using public key certificates; secure channels based on Secure Sockets Layer 3.0; and CryptoAPI version 2.0, delivering industry-standard protocols for data integrity and privacy across public networks. For more information on the security enhancements in Windows NT 5.0, see Chapter 10.

Several existing sources describe Windows NT security in great detail:

- For a description of Windows NT security from the user's and administrator's perspective, see the chapters "Working with User and Group Accounts," "Managing User Work Environments," "Managing Shared Resources and Resource Security," and "Monitoring Events" in the *Windows NT Server Concepts and Planning Manual* (available in the \support\books directory on the Windows NT Server CD-ROM as well as on MSDN Library and TechNet).

- The *Windows NT Workstation Resource Guide* contains an even more in-depth description of Windows NT security, specifically in Chapter 6 ("Security") and Appendix B ("Security in a Software Development Environment").

- For a detailed description of security from the programmer's perspective, see the security section of the Platform Software Development Kit (SDK) documentation as well as the variety of security programming articles and sample programs on MSDN Library. The kernel-mode interface to security functions (such as *SeAccessCheck*) is described in the Windows NT Device Driver Kit (DDK) documentation.

- The interface between the local server authority server (LSASS) and authentication packages is described in a help file that comes with the Windows NT DDK (\ddk\hlp\lsaauth.hlp).

So without repeating the information in the above sources, in this chapter, I'll focus on describing the internal components involved in providing security on Windows NT.

Security System Components

Here are some of the components and databases that implement Windows NT security:

- **Security reference monitor (SRM)**   A component in the Windows NT executive (NTOSKRNL.EXE) that is responsible for performing security access checks on objects, manipulating privileges (user rights), and generating any resulting security audit messages.

- **Local security authority (LSA) server**   A user-mode process running the image LSASS.EXE that is responsible for the local system security policy (such as which users are allowed to log on to the machine, password policies, the list of privileges granted to users and groups, and the system security auditing settings), user authentication, and sending security audit messages to the Event Log.

- **LSA policy database**   A database that contains the system security policy settings. This database is stored in the registry under HKEY-_LOCAL_MACHINE\Security. It includes such information as what domains are trusted to authenticate logon attempts, who has permission to access the system and how (interactive, network, and service logons), who is assigned which privileges, and what kind of security auditing is to be performed.

- **Security accounts manager (SAM) server**   A set of subroutines responsible for managing the database that contains the usernames and groups defined on the local machine or for a domain (if the system is a domain controller). The SAM runs in the context of the LSASS process.

- **SAM database** A database that contains the defined users and groups, along with their passwords and other attributes. This database is stored in the registry under HKEY_LOCAL_MACHINE\SAM.

- **Default authentication package** A dynamic-link library (DLL) named MSV1_0.DLL that runs in the context of the LSASS process that implements Windows NT authentication. This DLL is responsible for checking whether a given username and password match what is specified in the SAM database, and if they do, returning the information about that user.

- **Logon process** A user-mode process running WINLOGON.EXE that is responsible for capturing the username and password, sending them to the LSA for verification, and creating the initial process in the user's session.

- **Network logon service** A user-mode service inside the process SERVICES.EXE that responds to network logon requests. Authentication is handled as local logons are, by sending them to the LSASS process for verification.

Figure 6-1 shows the relationships among these components and the databases they manage.

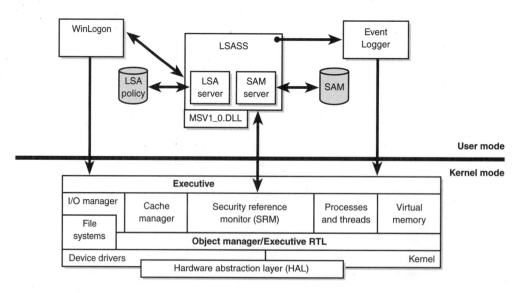

Figure 6-1

Windows NT security components

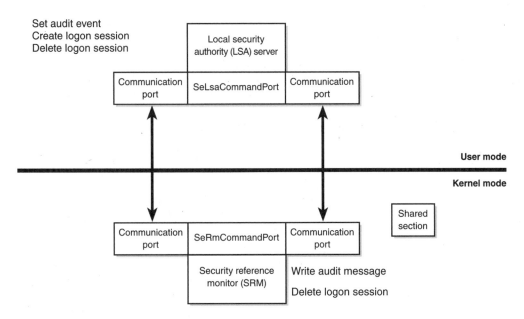

Figure 6-2
Communication between the SRM and the LSA

The SRM, which runs in kernel mode, and the LSA, which runs in user mode, communicate using the local procedure call (LPC) facility described in Chapter 3. During system initialization, the SRM creates a port, named *SeRmCommandPort*, to which the LSA connects. When the LSA process starts, it creates an LPC port named *SeLsaCommandPort*. The SRM connects to this port, resulting in the creation of private communication ports. The SRM creates a shared memory section for messages longer than 256 bytes, passing a handle in the connect call. Once the SRM and the LSA connect to each other during system initialization, they no longer listen on their respective connect ports. Therefore, a later user process has no way to connect successfully to either of these ports for malicious purposes—the connect request will never complete. The communication ports used by the SRM and the LSA are unnamed and thus can't be opened by another process.

Figure 6-2 shows the communication paths as they exist after system initialization.

Protecting Objects

Protecting objects is the essence of discretionary access control and auditing. The objects that can be protected on Windows NT include files, devices, mailslots, named and anonymous pipes, processes, threads, events, mutexes, semaphores, waitable timers, access tokens, window stations, desktops, network shares, services, registry keys, and printers.

Because system resources that are exported to user mode (and hence require security validation) are implemented as objects, the Windows NT object manager is a key gate at which security access checks are performed. To control who can manipulate an object, the security system must first be sure of each user's identity. This need to guarantee the user's identity is the reason that Windows NT requires authenticated logon before accessing any system resources. When a thread opens a handle to an object, the object manager and the security system use the caller's security identification to determine whether the caller should be given the handle it is requesting.

The following sections examine object protection from two perspectives: controlling which users can access which objects and identifying a user's security information.

Security Descriptors and Access Control

All securable objects are assigned *security descriptors* when they are created. A security descriptor controls who has what access to the object. It consists of the following main attributes:

- **Owner SID**   The owner's security ID[1]

- **Group SID**   The security ID of the primary group for the object (used only by POSIX)

- **Discretionary access control list (DACL)**   Specifies who has what access to the object

- **System access control list (SACL)**   Specifies which operations by which users should be logged in the security audit log

---

1. The format and structure of security IDs are described in the security section of the Platform SDK documentation.

WindowsNT5.0▶ **N O T E** Windows NT 5.0 offers a new set of Win32 API security functions to manipulate security information for objects. For more information about these functions, see the description of *Set/Get-SecurityInfoEx, Set/GetNamedSecurityInfoEx, ConvertSecurityDescriptorToAccess,* and the new ACTRL_ACCESS structure in the Platform SDK documentation in MSDN Library.

An *access control list* (ACL) is made up of an ACL header and zero or more *access control entry* (ACE) structures. An ACL with zero ACEs is called a *null ACL* and indicates that no user has access to the object.

In a DACL, each ACE contains a security ID and an access mask. Two types of ACEs can appear in a DACL: access allowed and access denied. As you would expect, the access-allowed ACE grants access to a user, and the access-denied ACE denies the access rights specified in the access mask. The accumulation of access rights granted by individual ACEs forms the set of access rights granted by an ACL. If no DACL is present in a security descriptor, everyone has full access to the object. On the other hand, if the DACL is *null* (has 0 ACEs), no user has access to the object.

An SACL contains only one type of ACE, called a system audit ACE, which specifies which operations performed on the object by specific users or groups should be audited. (The audit information is stored in the system audit log.) Both successful and unsuccessful attempts can be audited. If the SACL is null, no auditing takes place on the object. (Security auditing is described later in this chapter.)

Figure 6-3 is a simplified picture of a file object and its ACL.

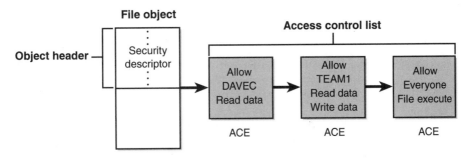

Figure 6-3
Access control list (ACL)

As shown in Figure 6-3, the first ACE allows DAVEC to read the file. The second ACE allows members of the group TEAM1 to have read and write access, and the third ACE grants all other users (Everyone) execute access.

Assigning ACLs

To determine which ACL to assign to a new object, the security system applies one of three mutually exclusive rules, in the following order:

1. If a caller explicitly provides a security descriptor when creating the object, the security system applies it to the object.

2. If a caller doesn't supply a security descriptor and the object has a name, the security system looks at the security descriptor in the object directory in which the new object name is stored. Some of the object directory's ACEs might be marked as inheritable[2], meaning that they should be applied to new objects created in the object directory. If any of these inheritable ACEs are present, the security system forms them into an ACL, which it attaches to the new object. (Separate flags indicate ACEs that should be inherited only by container objects rather than by objects that are not containers.)

3. If neither of the first two cases occurs, the security system retrieves the default ACL from the caller's access token and applies it to the new object. Several subsystems on Windows NT have hard-coded DACLs that they assign on object creation (for example, services, LSA, and SAM objects).

Determining Access

Two algorithms are used for validating access to an object:

- One to determine the maximum access allowed to the object (which can be done with the new Windows NT 5.0 Win32 function *GetEffectiveRightsFromAcl*).

- One to determine whether a specific desired access is allowed (which can be done with the Win32 *AccessCheck* function and the new Windows NT 5.0 functions *AccessCheckByType** and *TrusteeAccessToObject*).

---

2. For a description of ACE inheritance rules, see the Platform SDK documentation.

The first algorithm builds a granted-access mask and a denied-access mask by examining the entries in the ACL as follows:

1. If the object has no DACL, the object has no protection and the security system grants all access.

2. If the caller has the take-ownership privilege, the security system grants the write-owner access before examining the DACL.

3. If the caller is the owner of the object, the read-control and write-DACL access rights are granted.

4. For each access-denied ACE that contains a SID that matches one in the caller's access token, the ACE's access mask is added to the denied-access mask.

5. For each access-allowed ACE that contains a SID that matches one in the caller's access token, the ACE's access mask is added to the granted-access mask being computed, unless that access has been denied.

When all the entries in the DACL have been examined, the computed granted-access mask is returned to the caller as the maximum allowed access to the object.

The second algorithm is used to determine whether a specific access request can be granted, based on the caller's access token. Each open function in the Win32 API that deals with securable objects has a parameter that specifies the desired access mask. To determine whether the caller has access, the following steps are performed:

1. If the object has no DACL, the object has no protection and the security system grants the desired access.

2. If the caller has the take-ownership privilege, the security system grants the write-owner access before examining the DACL. The security system grants write-owner access if it was the only access requested.

3. If the caller is the owner of the object, the read-control and write-DACL access rights are granted. If these rights were the only access rights requested, access is granted without examining the DACL.

4. Each ACE in the DACL is examined from first to last. If the SID in the ACE matches an *enabled* SID (SIDs can be enabled and disabled) in the caller's access token (whether that be the primary SID or a group SID), the ACE is processed. If it is an access-allowed ACE, the rights in the access mask in the ACE are granted; if all the requested access rights have been granted, the access check succeeds. If it is an access-denied ACE and any of the requested access rights are in the denied-access rights, access is denied to the object.

5. If the end of the DACL is reached and some of the requested access rights still haven't been granted, access is denied.

Both access-validation algorithms rely on the fact that access-denied ACEs are placed before access-allowed ACEs. This arrangement is done by convention—the raw Win32 ACL functions allow building an ACL with the ACEs out of order. (The ACL functions added in Windows NT 4.0 automatically place ACEs in the correct order.)

Windows NT 5.0 ▶ **NOTE** In Windows NT 5.0, the order of ACEs is more complicated because of the introduction of object-specific ACEs and automatic inheritance. Noninherited ACEs go before inherited ACEs. Within the noninherited ACEs and inherited ACEs, the ACEs are placed according to ACE type: access-denied ACEs that apply to the object itself, followed by access-denied ACEs that apply to a subobject of the object, followed by access-allowed ACEs that apply to the object itself, followed by access-allowed ACEs that apply to a subobject of the object. For more information, see the description of the new Windows NT 5.0 Win32 security functions in the Platform SDK reference documentation in MSDN Library.

Because it wouldn't be efficient for the security system to process the DACL every time a process uses a handle, this check takes place only when a handle is opened, not each time the handle is used. Also keep in mind that because kernel-mode code uses pointers rather than handles to access objects, the access check is not performed when the operating system uses objects. In other words, the Windows NT executive "trusts" itself in a security sense.

Once a process successfully opens a handle, the security system can't revoke the access rights that have been granted, even if the object's DACL changes. This capability would require a complete security check each time a handle is used rather than only when the handle is originally created. Storing granted access rights directly in handles improves performance significantly, especially for objects with long DACLs attached.

Access Tokens and Impersonation

An *access token* is the data structure that contains the security identification of a process or a thread: its security ID (SID), the list of groups that the user is a member of, and the list of privileges that are enabled and disabled. Because access tokens are exported to user mode, a number of Win32 functions create and manipulate them. (See the Platform SDK reference documentation for details about the Win32 functions that relate to access tokens.) Internally, the kernel-mode access-token structure is an object the object manager allocates that the executive process block or the thread block points to. You can examine access-token objects with the Pview utility and the kernel debugger, as demonstrated in experiments later in this section.

Each process has a primary access token that it inherits from its creating process. At logon, the LSASS process verifies that the username and password match the information stored in the SAM. If they do, it returns an access token to WinLogon, which then assigns that access token to the initial process in the user's session. (You'll find more information on the logon process and security in the section "Logon" on page 321.) Further processes created in the user's session inherit this access token. You can also generate an access token by using the Win32 *LogonUser* function. You can then use this access token to create a process with a specific access token by using the Win32 *CreateProcessAsUser* function.

Individual threads can also have their own access tokens—if they are *impersonating* a client. This capability allows threads to have a different access token than that of the process. For example, server processes typically impersonate client processes so that a server process (which is likely running with administrative rights) can perform operations on behalf of the client using the client's security profile rather than its own. A client process can limit the level of impersonation that a server process can perform by specifying a *security quality of service* (*SQOS*) when connecting to the server. For examples of the variations of impersonation that are possible, see the SECURITY_ANONYMOUS, SECURITY_IDENTIFICATION, and SECURITY_IMPERSONATION flags that can be specified with the Win32 *CreateFile* function.

By default, a thread doesn't have its own access token unless it requests one using the Win32 *ImpersonateSelf* function, which clones the process primary access token and assigns it to the thread. Once a thread has its own access token, it can use one of the four Win32 impersonation functions to take on the security token of a client on whose behalf the thread is about to operate. These functions are *ImpersonateNamedPipeClient, RpcImpersonateClient, DdeImpersonate-Client,* and *ImpersonateLoggedOnUser.* If the security support provider interface is being used, the *ImpersonateSecurityContext* function is another way to impersonate a client access token. For details about the interfaces to these functions, see the Platform SDK reference documentation as well as the technical articles explaining how to apply them, both in MSDN Library.

Figure 6-4 illustrates the basic process and thread security structures. In the figure, notice that the process object and the thread objects have security descriptors, as do the access-token objects themselves. Also in this figure, thread 2 has an impersonation token. (Thread 1 defaults to the process access token.)

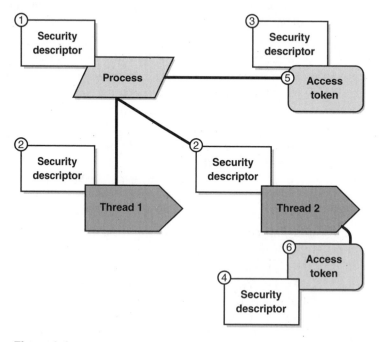

Figure 6-4
Process and thread security structures

The following experiments demonstrate how to view process access tokens, security descriptions, and security descriptors for access tokens.

EXPERIMENT: Viewing Process and Thread Security Information

You can view process and thread security descriptors and access tokens with the Windows NT Resource Kit Process Explode utility, PVIEW-.EXE (not to be confused with PVIEW.EXE in the Platform SDK and Visual C++, which is a different utility). The numbering of the six buttons in the Security and Token sections of the Pview utility match up with the process and thread security structures shown in Figure 6-4.

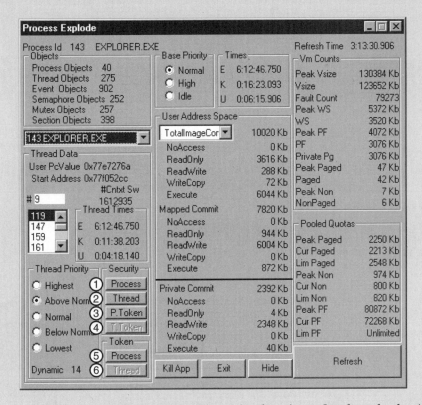

In this example, buttons 4 (security descriptor for thread token) and 6 (thread access token) are grayed out (disabled) because the currently selected thread (number 119) has no thread-specific access token.

EXPERIMENT: Viewing Access Tokens with the Kernel Debugger

The kernel debugger *!tokenfields* command displays the format of an internal access-token object. Although this structure differs from the user-mode access-token structure returned by Win32 API security functions, the fields are similar. For further information on access tokens, see the description in the Platform SDK documentation.

The following output is from the kernel debugger's *!tokenfields* command:

```
kd> !tokenfields
 TOKEN structure offsets:
    TokenSource:          0x0
    AuthenticationId:     0x18
    ExpirationTime:       0x20
    ModifiedId:           0x28
    UserAndGroupCount:    0x30
    PrivilegeCount:       0x34
    VariableLength:       0x38
    DynamicCharged:       0x3c
    DynamicAvailable:     0x40
    DefaultOwnerIndex:    0x44
    DefaultDacl:          0x58
    TokenType:            0x5c
    ImpersonationLevel:   0x60
    TokenFlags:           0x64
    TokenInUse:           0x65
    ProxyData:            0x68
    AuditData:            0x6c
    VariablePart:         0x70
```

You can examine the access token for a process with the *!token* command. You'll find the address of the token in the output of the *!process* command, as shown here:

```
kd> !process 6b
Searching for Process with Cid == 6b
PROCESS ffb96960  Cid: 006b    Peb: 7ffdf000  ParentCid: 0028
    DirBase: 006c4000  ObjectTable: ffbb2c68  TableSize:  30.
    Image: atsvc.exe
    VadRoot ffbb60c8 Clone 0 Private 84. Modified 99. Locked 0.
    FFB96B1C MutantState Signalled OwningThread 0
    Token                                  e198fbf0
    :
    :
```

```
kd> !token e198fbf0
TOKEN e198fbf0  Flags: 1  Source *SYSTEM*  AuthentId (0, 3e7)
    Type:                 Primary (IN USE)
    Token ID:             26f1
    Modified ID:          (0, 13a9)
    SidCount:             3
    Sids:                 e198fd50
    PrivilegeCount:       20
    Privileges:           e198fc60
```

Many system processes run under a special access token named SYSTEM. This account is not the same as the Administrators account in the SAM, although it does have similar privileges. Figure 6-5 shows the contents of the SYSTEM access token using the Windows NT Resource Kit Process Explode utility (\NTRESKIT\PVIEW.EXE).

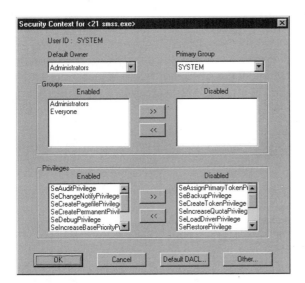

Figure 6-5
SYSTEM access token

A process running under the SYSTEM access token has several restrictions. For example, it doesn't have domain credentials, which means it has limited or no access to network resources. Also, it can't share objects with other non-SYSTEM user processes unless it creates them using either a DACL, which allows a user or group of users access to the object, or a NULL DACL, which allows everyone access. For more information about security for Windows NT service processes, see the Platform SDK documentation section "About Services."

Security Auditing

The object manager can generate audit events as a result of an access check, and Win32 functions available to user applications can generate them directly. Kernel-mode code is always allowed to generate an audit event. Processes that call audit system services, however, must have the *SeAuditPrivilege* privilege to successfully generate an audit record. This requirement prevents a malicious user-mode program from flooding the Security Log.

The audit policy of the local system controls the decision to audit a particular type of security event. The audit policy, called the local security policy, is one part of the security policy the LSA maintains on the local system. The LSA sends messages to the SRM to inform it of the auditing policy at system initialization time and when the policy changes. The LSA is responsible for receiving audit records from the SRM, editing them, and sending the records to the Event Log. The LSA (instead of the SRM) sends these records because it adds pertinent details, such as the information needed to more completely identify the process that is being audited.

The SRM sends these audit events via its LPC connection to the LSA. The Event Logger then writes the audit event to a Security Log. In addition to audit events passed by the SRM, both the LSA and the SAM generate audit records that the LSA sends directly to the Event Logger. Figure 6-6 depicts this overall flow.

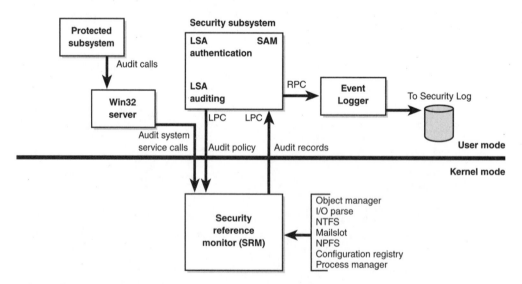

Figure 6-6
Flow of security audit records

Audit records are put on a queue to be sent to the LSA as they are received—they are not submitted in batches. The audit records are moved from
the SRM to the security subsystem in one of two ways. If the audit record is small
(less than the maximum LPC message size), it is sent as an LPC message. The
audit records are copied from the address space of the SRM to the address
space of the LSASS process. If the audit record is large, the SRM uses shared
memory to make the message available to LSASS and simply passes a pointer
in an LPC message.

Logon

Logon occurs through the interaction of the logon process (WinLogon), the
LSA, one or more authentication packages, and the SAM. Authentication packages are DLLs that perform authentication checks. MSV1_0 is the Windows NT
authentication package for interactive logon.

WinLogon is a trusted process responsible for managing security-related
user interactions. It coordinates logon, starts the user's shell at logon, handles
logoff, and manages various other operations relevant to security, including
entering passwords at logon, changing passwords, and locking and unlocking
the workstation. The WinLogon process must ensure that operations relevant
to security are not visible to any other active processes. For example, WinLogon
guarantees that an untrusted process can't get control of the desktop during
one of these operations and thus gain access to the password.

WinLogon is the only process that intercepts logon requests from the
keyboard. It makes calls to the LSA to authenticate the user attempting to log
on. If the user is authenticated, the logon process activates a logon shell on
behalf of that user. The interaction between the components involved in logon
is illustrated in Figure 6-7.

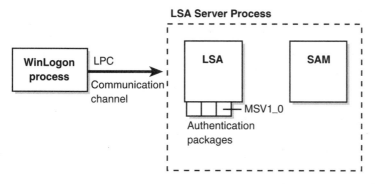

Figure 6-7
Components involved in logon

As mentioned in Chapter 2, the identification and authentication aspects of the logon process are implemented in a replaceable DLL named *GINA* (Graphical Identification and Authentication). The standard Windows NT GINA DLL, MSGINA.DLL, implements the default Windows NT logon interface. However, developers can provide their own GINA DLL to implement other identification and authentication mechanisms in place of the standard Windows NT user name/password method. In addition, WinLogon can load additional network provider DLLs that need to perform secondary authentication. This capability allows multiple network providers to gather identification and authentication information all at one time during normal logon. For more information on GINA, see the documentation in MSDN Library.

WinLogon Initialization

During system initialization, before any user applications are active, WinLogon performs certain steps to ensure that it controls the workstation once the system is ready for the user:

- Creates and opens a window station to represent the keyboard, mouse, and monitor. WinLogon creates a security descriptor for the station that has one and only one ACE containing only the WinLogon SID. This unique security descriptor ensures that no other process can access the workstation unless explicitly allowed by WinLogon.

- Creates and opens three desktops: an application desktop, a WinLogon desktop, and a screen saver desktop. The security on the WinLogon desktop is created so that only WinLogon can access that desktop. The other two desktops allow both WinLogon and users to access them. This arrangement means that any time the WinLogon desktop is active, no other process has access to any active code or data associated with the desktop. Windows NT uses this feature to protect the secure operations that involve passwords and locking and unlocking the desktop.

- Establishes an LPC connection with the LSA. This connection will be used for exchanging information during logon, logoff, and password operations and is made by calling *LsaRegisterLogonProcess*.

- Calls *LsaLookupAuthenticationPackage* to get an association ID for MSV1_0, which will be used for authentication operations when a logon is attempted.

WinLogon then performs certain Windows operations to set up the window environment:

- Initializes and registers a window class data structure that associates a WinLogon procedure with the window it subsequently creates.

- Registers the secure attention sequence (SAS) hot-key sequence associating it with the window just created, guaranteeing that WinLogon's window procedure is called whenever the user enters the SAS. This measure prevents Trojan horse programs from gaining control of the screen when the SAS is entered.

- Registers the window so that the procedure associated with this window gets called if a user logs off or if the screen saver times out. The Win32 subsystem checks to verify that the process requesting notification is the WinLogon process.

Once the WinLogon desktop is created during initialization, it becomes the active desktop. When the WinLogon desktop is active, it is always locked. WinLogon unlocks it only to switch to the application desktop or to the screen saver desktop. (Only the WinLogon process can lock or unlock a desktop.)

User Logon Steps

Logon begins when a user presses the SAS (Ctrl-Alt-Delete). After the SAS is pressed, WinLogon switches to the secure desktop and prompts for username and password. WinLogon also creates a unique local group for this user that it assigns to this instance of the desktop (keyboard, screen, and mouse). WinLogon passes this group to the LSA as part of the *LsaLogonUser* call. If the user is successfully logged on, this group will be included in the logon process token— a step that protects access to the desktop. For example, another user logging on to the same account but on a different system will be unable to write to the first user's desktop because this second user won't be in the first user's group.

When the username and password have been entered, WinLogon calls the LSA, passing the logon information and specifying which package is to receive them for authentication (as mentioned earlier, MSV1_0 implements Windows NT authentication; all the authentication packages on the system are defined in the registry at HKLM\System\CurrentControlSet\Control\Lsa). The LSA calls the authentication package based on this information, passing the logon information through.

The MSV1_0 authorization package takes the username and password information and sends a request to the SAM to retrieve the account information, including the password, the groups to which the user belongs, and any account restrictions. MSV1_0 first checks the account restrictions, such as hours or type of accesses allowed. If the user can't log on because of the restrictions in the SAM database, the logon call fails and MSV1_0 returns a failure status to the LSA.

MSV1_0 then compares the password and username to that stored by SAM. If the information matches, MSV1_0 generates a unique identifier for the logon session (called a logon user ID, or LUID) and creates the logon session by calling the LSA associating this unique identifier with the session, passing the information needed to ultimately create an access token for the user. (Recall that an access token includes the user's SID; group SIDs; and user profile information, such as home directory.)

Then, the LSA looks in the local policy database for this user's allowed access—interactive, network, or service process. If the requested logon doesn't match the allowed access, the logon attempt will be terminated. The LSA deletes the newly created logon session by cleaning up any of its data structures and then returns failure to WinLogon, which in turn displays an appropriate message to the user. If the requested access is allowed, the LSA adds any additional security IDs (such as Everyone, Interactive, and the like). It then checks its policy database for any granted privileges for all the IDs for this user and adds these privileges to the user's access token.

When the LSA has accumulated all the necessary information, it calls the executive to create the access token. The executive creates a primary access token for an interactive or a service logon and an impersonation token for a network logon. After the access token is successfully created, the LSA duplicates the token, creating a handle that can be passed to WinLogon, and closes its own handle. If necessary, the logon operation is audited. At this point, the LSA returns success to WinLogon along with a handle to the access token, the LUID for the logon session, and the profile information, if any, that was returned by MSV1_0.

Conclusion

Windows NT provides an extensive array of security functions that meet the key requirements of both government agencies and commercial installations. In this chapter, we've taken a brief tour behind the scenes of the internal components behind these security features. As mentioned, the Platform SDK and Windows NT Resource Kit describe Windows NT security from the programmer's and system administrator's points of view in great detail.

In the next chapter, we'll look at the last major executive component considered in this book: the I/O system.

CHAPTER SEVEN

The I/O System

The Microsoft Windows NT I/O system is a component of the Windows NT executive and therefore resides in the file NTOSKRNL.EXE. It accepts I/O requests (from both user-mode and kernel-mode callers) and delivers them, in a different form, to I/O devices. Between the user-mode I/O functions and the actual I/O hardware lie several discrete system components, including file system drivers, filter drivers, and low-level device drivers. (Network device drivers are beyond the scope of this book.)

The design goals for the Windows NT I/O system included the following:

- Make I/O processing fast on both single and multiprocessor systems

- Protect shareable resources using the standard Windows NT security mechanisms (described in Chapter 6)

- Meet the requirements for I/O services dictated by the Microsoft Win32, OS/2, and POSIX subsystems

- Provide services to make device driver development as easy as possible and allow drivers to be written in a high-level language

- Allow device drivers to be added or removed from the system dynamically

- Provide support for multiple installable file systems, including the FAT, the CD-ROM file system (CDFS), and the Windows NT file system (NTFS)

- Provide mapped file I/O capabilities for image activation, file caching, and application use

In this chapter, we'll first examine the structure and components of the I/O system and the various types of device drivers. We'll then look at the key data structures that describe devices, device drivers, and I/O requests. Finally, we'll go over the steps necessary to complete I/O requests as they move through the system.

NOTE This chapter does *not* contain enough information for you to write Windows NT device drivers. Its purpose is simply to explain the structure and key components of the I/O system, the types of device drivers, and the way I/O processing occurs. For details on writing device drivers, consult the Windows NT Device Driver Kit (DDK) documentation on MSDN Library (or on MSDN Online).

I/O System Structure and Model

On Windows NT, programs perform I/O on virtual files. A *virtual file* refers to any source or destination for I/O that is treated as if it were a file (such as files, directories, pipes, and mailslots.) All data that is read or written is regarded as a simple stream of bytes directed to these virtual files. User-mode applications (whether they be Win32, POSIX, or OS/2) call documented functions, which in turn call internal I/O subsystem functions to read from a file, write to a file, and perform other operations. The I/O manager dynamically directs these virtual file requests to the appropriate device driver. Figure 7-1 illustrates this basic structure, along with the other key components that comprise the Windows NT I/O system.

The components shown in Figure 7-1 have the following roles:

- The I/O subsystem API is the internal executive system services (such as *NtReadFile* and *NtWriteFile*) that subsystem DLLs call to implement a subsystem's documented I/O functions.

- The I/O manager is responsible for driving the processing of I/O requests.

- Kernel-mode device drivers translate I/O requests into specific control requests to hardware devices.

- Kernel-mode device drivers translate I/O requests into specific control requests to hardware devices.

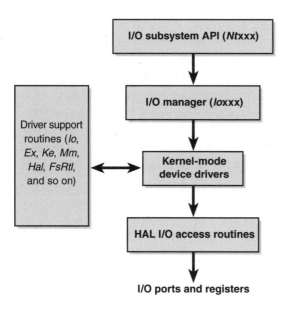

Figure 7-1

I/O system structure

- Driver support routines are called by device drivers to accomplish their I/O requests.

- Hardware abstraction layer (HAL) I/O access routines insulate device drivers from variations in the hardware platform, allowing them to be binary portable across a given architecture family and source portable across the hardware architectures that Windows NT supports.

In the following sections, we'll be looking at some of these components more closely, examining the I/O manager in more detail, reviewing the basic I/O services visible in the Win32 API, and covering the various types of device drivers and the key I/O system data structures.

NOTE Windows NT 5.0 introduces some major changes to the I/O system and device driver architecture, namely Plug and Play and power management. Driver initialization is quite different in the Plug and Play world. For a brief review of these new features, see Chapter 10. For a detailed description of how the I/O system will be enhanced, refer to the Windows NT 5.0 DDK documentation.

I/O Manager

The *I/O manager* defines the orderly framework, or model, within which I/O requests are delivered to device drivers. The I/O system is *packet driven*. Most I/O requests are represented by an *I/O request packet* (*IRP*), which travels from one I/O system component to another. (As you'll discover on page 330, fast I/O is the exception; it doesn't use IRPs.) An IRP is a data structure that controls how the I/O operation is processed at each stage. (You'll find more information about IRPs on page 348.)

The I/O manager creates an IRP that represents each I/O operation, passing the IRP to the correct driver and disposing of the packet when the I/O operation is complete. In contrast, a driver receives an IRP, performs the operation the IRP specifies, and either passes the IRP back to the I/O manager for completion or on to another driver (via the I/O manager) for further processing.

In addition to creating and disposing of IRPs, the I/O manager supplies code that is common to different drivers and that the drivers call to carry out their I/O processing. By consolidating common tasks in the I/O manager, individual drivers become simpler and more compact. For example, the I/O manager provides a function that allows one driver to call other drivers. It also manages buffers for I/O requests, provides time-out support for drivers, and records which installable file systems are loaded into the operating system. These support routines are documented in the DDK.

The I/O manager also provides flexible I/O services that allow environment subsystems, such as Win32 and POSIX, to implement their respective I/O functions. These services include sophisticated services for asynchronous I/O that allow developers to build scalable high-performance server applications.

The uniform, modular interface that drivers present allows the I/O manager to call any driver without requiring any special knowledge of its structure or internal details. Drivers can also call each other (via the I/O manager) to achieve layered, independent processing of an I/O request.

I/O Functions

Besides the normal open, close, read, and write functions, the Windows NT I/O system provides several advanced features, such as asynchronous I/O and mapped files.

> **NOTE** Many other file-related and I/O-related functions in the Win32 API, such as *LockFile* (byte range locking), *CopyFile* and *Move-File* (high-performance file copying), *CancelIo*, *FlushFileBuffers*, directory manipulation, and file search functions are not detailed in this chapter. For a complete list of the Win32 file and I/O functions available in the Win32 API, see the section "Files and I/O" in the Platform SDK documentation.

Asynchronous I/O

Most I/O operations that applications issue are *synchronous;* that is, the device performs the data transfer and returns a status code when the I/O is complete. The program can then access the transferred data immediately. When used in their simplest form, the Win32 *ReadFile* and *WriteFile* functions are executed synchronously. They complete an I/O operation before returning control to the caller.

Asynchronous I/O allows an application to issue an I/O request and then continue executing while the device transfers the data. This type of I/O can improve an application's throughput because it allows the application to continue with other work while an I/O operation is in progress. To use asynchronous I/O, you must specify the FILE_FLAG_OVERLAPPED flag on the Win32 *CreateFile* function. Of course, after issuing asynchronous I/O operations, the thread must be careful not to access any data from the I/O operation until the device driver has finished the data transfer. The thread must synchronize its execution with the completion of the I/O request by waiting on a handle to some synchronization object (whether that is an event object, an I/O completion port, or the file object itself) that will be signaled when the I/O is complete. (For information on how to use these objects, see the Platform SDK documentation.)

Regardless of the type of I/O request, internally I/O operations represented by IRPs are performed asynchronously; that is, once an I/O request has been initiated, the device driver returns to the I/O system. Whether or not the I/O system returns to the caller depends on whether the file was opened for asynchronous I/O. Figure 7-2 illustrates the flow of control when a read operation is initiated. Notice that the wait is done in kernel mode by the *NtReadFile* function depending on the overlapped flag in the file object.

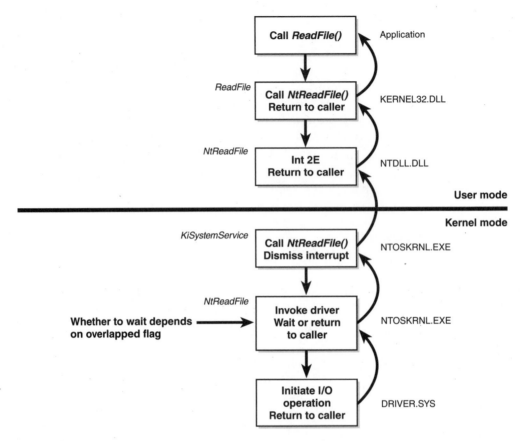

Figure 7-2
Control flow for an I/O operation

You can test the status of a pending asynchronous I/O with the Win32 *HasOverlappedIoCompleted* function. If you're using I/O completion ports, you can use the *GetQueuedCompletionStatus* function.

Fast I/O

Fast I/O is a special mechanism that allows the I/O system to bypass generating an IRP and instead go directly to the file system driver or cache manager to complete an I/O request. (Fast I/O is described in detail in Chapter 8.)

Mapped File I/O and File Caching

Mapped file I/O is an important feature of the I/O system, one that the I/O system and the memory manager produce jointly. (See Chapter 5 for details on how mapped files are implemented.) *Mapped file I/O* refers to the ability to view a file residing on disk as part of a process's virtual memory. A program can access the file as a large array without buffering data or performing disk I/O. The program accesses memory, and the memory manager uses its paging mechanism to load the correct page from the disk file. If the application writes to its virtual address space, the memory manager writes the changes back to the file as part of normal paging.

Mapped file I/O is available to user mode through the Win32 *CreateFileMapping* and *MapViewOfFile* functions. Within the operating system, mapped file I/O is used for important operations such as file caching and image activation (loading and running executable programs). The other major consumer of mapped file I/O is the cache manager. File systems use the cache manager to map file data in virtual memory to provide better response time for I/O-bound programs. As the caller uses the file, the memory manager brings accessed pages into memory. Whereas most caching systems allocate a fixed number of bytes for caching files in memory, the Windows NT cache grows or shrinks depending on how much memory is available. This size variability is possible because the cache manager relies on the memory manager to automatically expand (or shrink) the size of the cache, using the normal working set mechanisms explained in Chapter 5. By taking advantage of the memory manager's paging system, the cache manager avoids duplicating the work that the memory manager already performs. (The workings of the cache manager are explained in detail in Chapter 8.)

Scatter/Gather I/O

Windows NT also supports a special kind of high-performance I/O that is called *scatter/gather*, available via the Win32 *ReadFileScatter* and *WriteFileScatter* functions. These functions allow an application to issue a single read or write from more than one buffer in virtual memory to a contiguous area of a file on disk. To use scatter/gather I/O, the file must be opened for noncached I/O, the user buffers being used have to be page-aligned, and the I/Os must be asynchronous (overlapped).

Device Drivers

Windows NT supports several types of device drivers. Figure 7-3 shows the relationship between the Win32 I/O functions and the three main categories of device drivers.

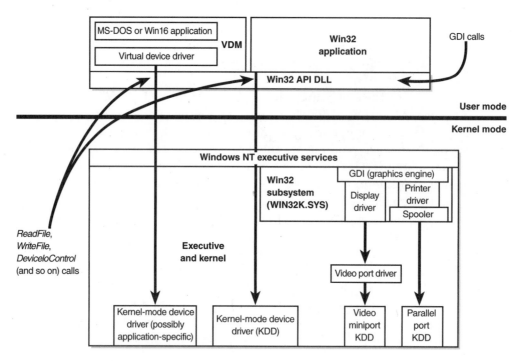

Figure 7-3

Types of device drivers

- *Virtual device drivers* (VDDs) are used to emulate 16-bit MS-DOS applications. They trap what an MS-DOS application thinks are references to I/O ports and translates them into native Win32 I/O functions. Because Windows NT is a fully protected operating system, user-mode MS-DOS applications can't access hardware directly and thus must go through a real kernel-mode device driver.

- Win32 subsystem *display drivers* and *printer drivers* translate device-independent graphics (GDI) requests into device-specific requests. These drivers are collectively called *kernel-mode graphics drivers*. Display drivers are paired with a video miniport driver to complete video display support. Each video miniport driver provides hardware-level support for its associated display driver.

■ *Kernel-mode device drivers* are the only type of driver that can directly control and access hardware devices.

In this chapter, the focus is on kernel-mode device drivers. For more information on VDDs or graphics device drivers, consult the DDK documentation.

There are several types of kernel-mode device drivers:

■ Low-level *hardware device drivers* directly control and access hardware devices.

■ *Class drivers* implement the I/O processing for a particular class of devices, such as disk, tape, or CD-ROM.

■ *Port drivers* implement the processing of an I/O request specific to a type of I/O port, such as SCSI.

■ *Miniport drivers* map a generic I/O request to a type of port into a adapter type, such as a specific SCSI adapter.

■ *File system drivers* accept I/O requests to files and satisfy the requests by issuing their own, more explicit, requests to physical device drivers.

■ *File system filter drivers* intercept I/O requests, perform additional processing, and pass them on to lower-level drivers. Examples include FTDISK.SYS (the fault-tolerant disk driver).

Figure 7-4 on the following page shows the relationships among the various types of kernel-mode device drivers.

NOTE File system drivers are not currently documented in the DDK. However, an Installable File System Kit that contains the header file needed to build file systems as well as sample source code for several local and network file system drivers is available from Microsoft. For more information about this kit, visit *http://www.microsoft.com/hwdev/ntifskit.*

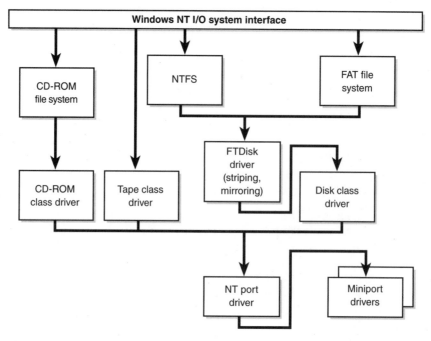

Figure 7-4
Driver structure

An example will help demonstrate how these device drivers work. A file system driver accepts a request to write data to a particular file. It translates the request into a request to write a certain number of bytes to the disk at a particular "logical" location. It then passes this request to a simple disk driver. The disk driver, in turn, translates the request into a cylinder/track/sector location on the disk and manipulates the disk heads to retrieve the data. This layering is illustrated in Figure 7-5.

This figure illustrates the division of labor between two layered drivers. The I/O manager receives a write request that is relative to the beginning of a particular file. The I/O manager passes the request to the file system driver, which translates the write operation from a file-relative operation to a starting location (a sector boundary on the disk) and a number of bytes to read. The file system driver calls the I/O manager to pass the request to the disk driver, which translates the request to a physical disk location and transfers the data.

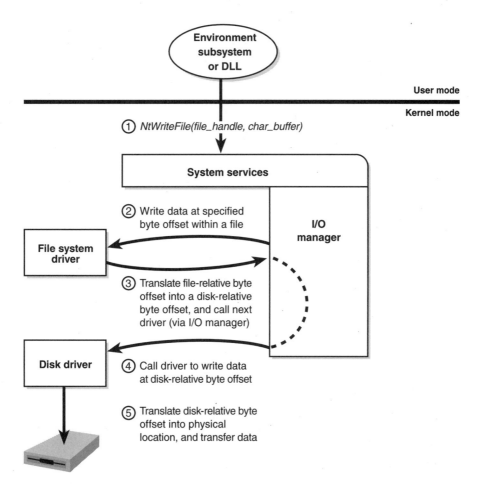

Figure 7-5
Layering a file system driver and a disk driver

Because all drivers—both device drivers and file system drivers—present the same framework to the operating system, another driver can easily be inserted into the hierarchy without altering the existing drivers or the I/O system. For example, several disks can be made to seem like a very large single disk by adding a driver. Such a driver actually exists in Windows NT to provide fault-tolerant disk support. This logical, multivolume driver is located between the file system and the disk drivers, as shown in Figure 7-6.

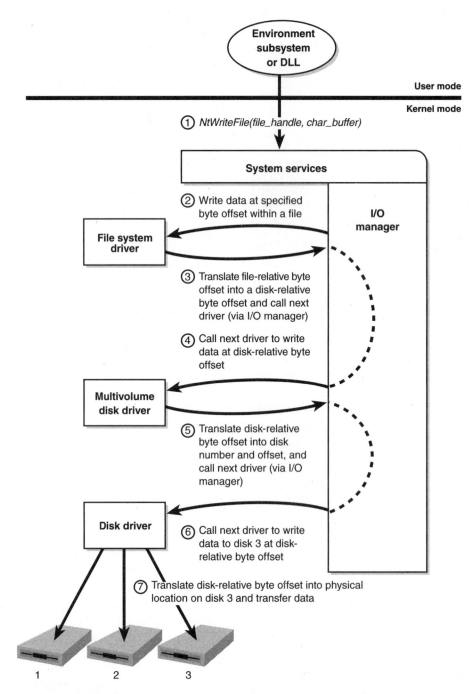

Figure 7-6
Adding a layered driver

EXPERIMENT: Viewing the Loaded Driver List

Although you can see which drivers have been loaded by going to the
Control Panel Devices applet, you won't be able to see the driver names
there. To display the list of loaded kernel-mode drivers, you'll need to
use the Drivers utility in the Windows NT Resource Kit or the Pstat
utility (shipped in the Windows NT Resource Kit and also available in
the \support\debug directory on a Windows NT CD-ROM). Pstat lists
the drivers at the end of its display. (It first lists all the processes and
threads in the system.) The only difference in the output of the two
utilities is that Pstat shows the load address of the driver in system
address space. The following output is from Pstat:

```
C:\>pstat
  :
  : (Process and thread list display not shown)

  ModuleName Load Addr   Code    Data    Paged            LinkDate
  -------------------------------------------------------------------
  ntoskrnl.exe 80100000  282816  42112   435392 Sat May 10 21:11:27 1997
      hal.dll 80001000   24992   4224     9920 Mon Mar 10 13:40:06 1997
    atapi.sys 80012000   20736   1088        0 Thu Apr 10 12:06:59 1997
  SCSIPORT.SYS 801db000    9824     32    15552 Mon Mar 10 13:42:27 1997
   cpq32fs2.sys 801e3000  62080    288        0 Mon Aug 12 23:19:00 1996
      Disk.sys 80018000    3328      0     7072 Thu Apr 24 19:27:46 1997
    CLASS2.SYS 8001c000    7040      0     1632 Thu Apr 24 19:23:43 1997
      Ntfs.sys 801f3000   68160   5408   269632 Thu Apr 17 19:02:31 1997
    Floppy.SYS f8e98000    1088    672     7968 Tue Jul 16 21:31:09 1996
     Cdrom.SYS f8ea8000   12608     32     3072 Tue Jul 16 21:31:29 1996
    Fs_Rec.SYS f910a000      64      0     2912 Mon Mar 10 13:51:19 1997
      Null.SYS f91ce000       0      0      288 Tue Jul 16 21:31:21 1996
  VIDEOPRT.SYS f8ef0000    2080    128    11296 Mon Mar 10 13:41:37 1997
     mga64.sys fe4ce000    1920  68768    30112 Tue Aug 27 06:26:50 1996
       vga.sys f90a8000     128     32    10784 Tue Jul 16 21:30:37 1996
  :
  : (Partial display)
```

If you're looking at a crash dump (or live system) with the kernel
debugger, you can get a similar display with the kernel debugger *!driver*
command.

Structure of a Driver

The I/O system drives the execution of device drivers. Device drivers consist of a set of routines that are called to process the various stages of an I/O request. Figure 7-7 illustrates the key driver-function routines.

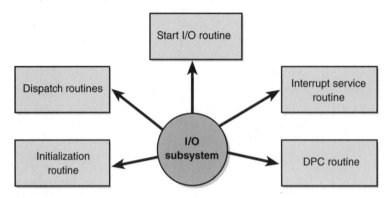

Figure 7-7
Primary device driver routines

These five main device driver routines are shown in Figure 7-7:

- **An initialization routine** The I/O manager executes a driver's initialization routine when it loads the driver into the operating system. The routine creates system objects that the I/O manager uses to recognize and access the driver.

- **A set of dispatch routines** Dispatch routines are the main functions that a device driver provides. Some examples are open, close, read, and write and any other capabilities the device, file system, or network supports. When called on to perform an I/O operation, the I/O manager generates an IRP and calls a driver through one of the driver's dispatch routines.

- **A start I/O routine** The driver can use a start I/O routine to initiate a data transfer to or from a device.

- **An interrupt service routine (ISR)** When a device interrupts, the kernel's interrupt dispatcher transfers control to this routine. In the Windows NT I/O model, ISRs run at a high device interrupt request level (IRQL), so they perform as little work as possible to avoid blocking lower-level interrupts unnecessarily. An ISR queues a deferred procedure call (DPC), which runs at a lower IRQL, to execute the remainder of interrupt processing. (Only drivers for interrupt-driven devices have ISRs; a file system, for example, doesn't have one.)

■ **An interrupt-servicing DPC routine** A DPC routine performs most of the work involved in handling a device interrupt after the ISR executes. The DPC routine executes at an IRQL that is lower than that of the ISR to avoid blocking other interrupts unnecessarily. A DPC routine initiates I/O completion and starts the next queued I/O operation on a device.

Although the following routines are not shown in Figure 7-7, they are found in many types of device drivers:

■ **One or more completion routines** A layered driver might have completion routines that will notify it when a lower-level driver finishes processing an IRP. For example, the I/O manager calls a file system's completion routine after a device driver finishes transferring data to or from a file. The completion routine notifies the file system about the operation's success, failure, or cancellation, and it allows the file system to perform cleanup operations.

■ **A cancel I/O routine** If an I/O operation can be cancelled, a driver can define one or more cancel I/O routines. The cancel routine that the I/O manager calls can vary depending on how far along the operation has progressed when it is cancelled. The IRP records that cancel I/O routines are active at any given time.

■ **An unload routine** An unload routine releases any system resources a driver is using so that the I/O manager can remove them from memory. A driver can be loaded and unloaded while the system is running.

■ **A system shutdown notification routine** This routine allows driver cleanup on system shutdown.

■ **Error-logging routines** When unexpected errors occur (for example, when a disk block goes bad), a driver's error-logging routines note the occurrence and notify the I/O manager. The I/O manager writes this information to an error log file.

Synchronization

Drivers must synchronize their access to global driver data for two main reasons:

- The execution of a driver can be preempted by higher-priority threads and time-slice (or quantum) expiration or interrupted by interrupts.

- On multiprocessor systems, Windows NT can run driver code simultaneously on more than one processor.

Without synchronization, corruption could occur—for example, because device driver code running at a low IRQL when a caller initiates an I/O operation can be interrupted by a device interrupt, causing the device driver's ISR to execute while its own device driver is already running. If the device driver was modifying data that its ISR also modifies, such as device registers, heap storage, or static data, the data can become corrupted when the ISR executes. Figure 7-8 illustrates this problem.

To avoid this situation, a device driver written for Windows NT must synchronize its access to any data that the device driver shares with its ISR. Before attempting to update shared data, the device driver must lock out all other threads (or CPUs, in the case of a multiprocessor system) to prevent them from updating the same data structure.

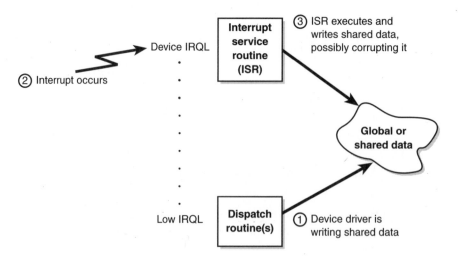

Figure 7-8
Data corruption in a device driver

The Windows NT kernel provides special synchronization routines that device drivers must call when they access data that their ISRs also access. These kernel-synchronization routines keep the ISR from executing while the shared data is being accessed. On a single CPU system, these routines raise the IRQL to a specified level before updating a structure. On a multiprocessor system, however, since a driver can execute on two or more processors at once, this technique is not enough to block other accessors. Therefore, another mechanism, *spinlocks,* is used to lock a structure for exclusive access from a particular CPU. (Spinlocks are explained in the section "Kernel Synchronization" in Chapter 3.)

By now, you should realize that although ISRs require special attention, any data that a device driver uses is subject to being accessed by the same device driver running on another processor. Therefore, it is critical for device driver code to synchronize its use of any global or shared data (or any accesses to the physical device itself). If that data is used by the ISR, the device driver must use kernel-synchronization routines; otherwise, the device driver can use a kernel spinlock.

Data Structures

Four primary data structures represent I/O requests: file objects, driver objects, device objects, and I/O request packets (IRPs).

Each of these structures is defined in the DDK header file \DDK\INC\ NTDDK.H as well as in the DDK documentation. You can display each of them with the kernel debugger using the *!file, !devobj, !drvobj,* and *!irp* commands.

File Objects

Files clearly fit the criteria for objects in Windows NT: they are system resources that threads in two or more user-mode processes can share; they can have names; they are protected by object-based security; and they support synchronization. Although most shared resources in Windows NT are memory-based resources, most of those that the I/O system manages are located on physical devices or are actual physical devices. Despite this difference, shared resources in the I/O system, like those in other components of the Windows NT executive, are manipulated as objects. (See Chapter 2 for a description of the object manager and Chapter 6 for information on object security.)

File objects provide a memory-based representation of shareable physical resources (except named pipes and mailslots, which are memory-based rather than physical resources). File objects also represent these resources in the Windows NT I/O system. Table 7-1 lists some of the file object's attributes. For specific field declarations and sizes, see the structure definition for FILE-_OBJECT in NTDDK.H.

Table 7-1   **File Object Attributes**

Attribute	Purpose
Filename	Identifies the physical file that the file object refers to
Byte offset	Identifies the current location in the file (valid only for synchronous I/O)
Share mode	Indicates whether other callers can open the file for read, write, or delete operations while this caller is using it
Open mode	Indicates whether I/O will be synchronous or asynchronous, cached or noncached, sequential or random, and so on
Pointer to device object	Indicates the type of device on which the file resides
Pointer to the volume parameter block	Indicates the volume, or partition, that the file resides on
Pointer to section object pointers	Indicates a root structure that describes a mapped file
Pointer to private cache map	Identifies which parts of the file are cached by the cache manager and where they reside in the cache

When a caller opens a file or a simple device, the I/O manager returns a handle to a file object. Figure 7-9 illustrates what occurs when a file is opened.

In this example, a C program calls the run-time library function *fopen*, which in turn calls the Win32 *CreateFile* function. The Win32 subsystem DLL (in this case, KERNEL32.DLL) then calls the native *NtCreateFile* function in NTDLL.DLL. The routine in NTDLL.DLL contains the appropriate instruction to cause a transition into kernel mode to the system service dispatcher, which then calls the real *NtCreateFile* routine in NTOSKRNL.EXE. (See Chapter 3 for more information about system service dispatching.)

Like other executive objects, file objects are protected by a security descriptor that contains an access control list (ACL). The I/O manager consults the security subsystem to determine whether the file's ACL allows the process to access the file in the way its thread is requesting. If it does, the object manager grants the access and associates the granted access rights with the file handle that it returns. If this thread or another thread in the process needs to perform additional operations not specified in the original request, the thread must open another handle, which prompts another security check. (See Chapter 6 for more information about object protection.)

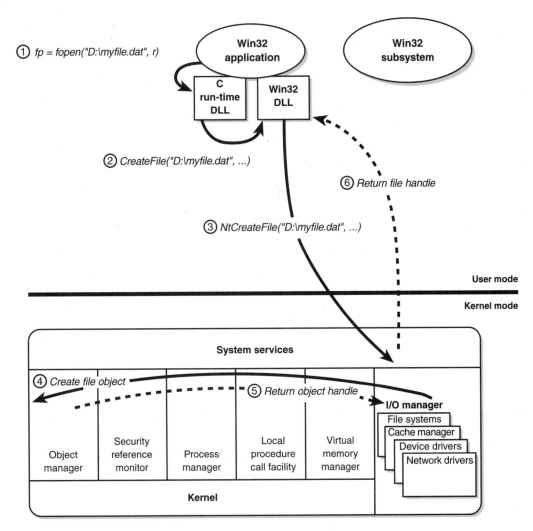

Figure 7-9
Opening a file object

Because a file object is a memory-based representation of a shareable resource and not the resource itself, it is different from other executive objects. A file object contains only data that is unique to an object handle, whereas the file itself contains the data or text to be shared. Each time a thread opens a file handle, a new file object is created with a new set of handle-specific attributes. For example, the attribute byte offset refers to the location in the file at which the next read or write operation using that handle will occur. Each thread that opens a handle to a file has a private byte offset even though the underlying file is shared. A file object is also unique to a process, except when a process duplicates a file handle to another process or when a child process inherits a file handle from a parent process. In these situations, the two processes have separate handles that refer to the same file object.

Although a file handle might be unique to a process, the underlying physical resource is not. Therefore, as when using any shared resource, threads must synchronize their access to shareable files, file directories, or devices. If a thread is writing to a file, for example, it should specify exclusive write access when opening the file handle to prevent other threads from writing to the file at the same time. Alternatively, by using the Win32 *LockFile* function, it could lock portions of the file while writing to it.

Driver Objects and Device Objects

When a thread opens a handle to a file object, the I/O manager must determine from the file object's name which driver (or drivers) it should call to process the request. Furthermore, the I/O manager must be able to locate this information the next time a thread uses the same file handle. The following system objects fill this need:

- A *driver object* represents an individual driver in the system and records for the I/O manager the address of each of the driver's dispatch routines (entry points).

- A *device object* represents a physical, logical, or virtual device on the system and describes its characteristics, such as the alignment it requires for buffers and the location of its device queue to hold incoming I/O request packets.

The I/O manager creates a driver object when a driver is loaded into the system, and it then calls the driver's initialization routine, which fills in the object with the driver's entry points. The initialization routine also creates one device object for each device to be operated by this driver. It hangs the device objects off the driver object, as shown in Figure 7-10.

When a file is opened, the filename includes the name of the device object on which the file resides. For example, the name \Device\Floppy0\myfile.dat refers to the file *myfile.dat* on the floppy disk drive A. The substring \Device-\Floppy0 is the name of the internal Windows NT device object representing

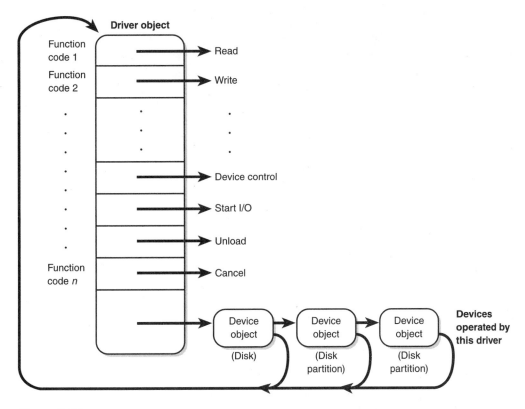

Figure 7-10
The driver object

that floppy disk drive. When opening myfile.dat, the I/O manager creates a file object and stores a pointer to the Floppy0 device object in the file object and then returns a file handle to the caller. Thereafter, when the caller uses the file handle, the I/O manager can find the Floppy0 device object directly. Keep in mind that internal Windows NT device names can't be used in Win32 applications—instead, the device name must appear in a special directory in the object manager's namespace, \?? (formerly named \DosDevices). This directory contains symbolic links to the real, internal Windows NT device names. Device drivers are responsible for creating links in this directory so that their devices will be accessible to Win32 applications. You can examine or even change these links programmatically with the Win32 *QueryDosDevice* and *Define-DosDevice* functions.

345

EXPERIMENT: Viewing Win32 Device Name to Windows NT Device Name Mappings

You can examine the symbolic links that define the Win32 device name-space with the Object Viewer utility in the Platform SDK (\mssdk\bin\winnt\winobj.exe). Run Winobj, and click on the \?? directoryz, as shown here:

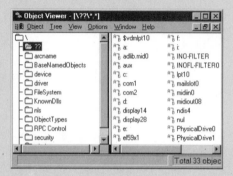

Notice the symbolic links on the right. Try double clicking on the device c:. You should see something like this:

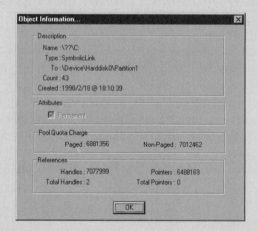

The C: is a symbolic link to the internal device named \Device\Harddisk0\Partition1, or the first logical partition on the first hard drive in the system. The com1 is a symbolic link to \Device\Serial0, and so forth. Try creating your own links with the Subst command at the command prompt.

As Figure 7-10 on page 345 illustrates, a device object points back to its driver object, which is how the I/O manager knows which driver routine to call when it receives an I/O request. It uses the device object to find the driver object representing the driver that services the device. It then indexes into the driver object using the function code supplied in the original request; each function code corresponds to a driver entry point.

A driver object often has multiple device objects associated with it. The list of device objects represents the physical, logical, and virtual devices that the driver controls. For example, each partition of a hard disk has a separate device object that contains partition-specific information. However, the same hard disk driver is used to access all partitions. When a driver is unloaded from the system, the I/O manager uses the queue of device objects to determine which devices will be affected by the removal of the driver.

Using objects to record information about drivers prevents the I/O manager from needing to know details about individual drivers. The I/O manager merely follows a pointer to locate a driver, which provides a layer of portability and allows new drivers to be loaded easily. Representing devices and drivers with different objects also makes it easy for the I/O system to assign drivers to control additional or different devices if the system configuration changes.

EXPERIMENT: Displaying Driver and Device Objects

You can display driver and device objects with the kernel debugger *!devobj* and *!drvobj* commands. In the following example, a device object is displayed. The device object output contains the address of the corresponding driver object. Notice that the *!drvobj* command displays a small subset of the information contained in a driver object structure.

```
kd> !devobj ff671030
Device object is for:
 NamedPipe \FileSystem\Npfs  DriverObject ff672970
Current Irp 00000000 RefCount 91 Type 00000011 DevExt ff6710e8
Device queue is not busy.
kd> !drvobj ff672970
Driver object is for:
 \FileSystem\Npfs
Device Object list:
ff671030
```

I/O Request Packet

The IRP is where the I/O system stores information it needs to process an I/O request. When a thread calls an I/O service, the I/O manager constructs an IRP to represent the operation as it progresses through the I/O system. The I/O manager stores a pointer to the caller's file object in the IRP.

Figure 7-11 shows the relationship between an IRP and the file, device, and driver objects described in the preceding sections. Although this example shows an I/O request to a single-layered device driver, most I/O operations are not this direct; they involve one or more layered drivers. This case will be shown later in this section.

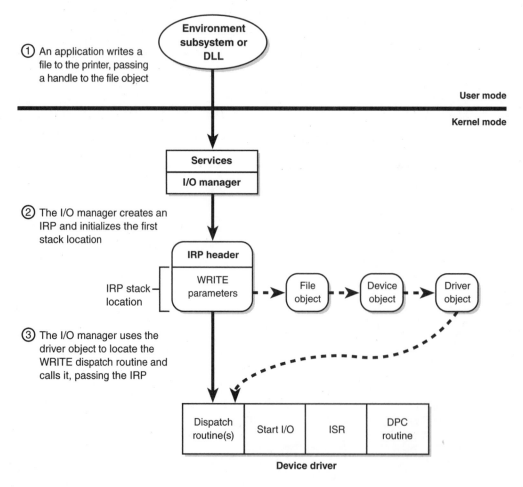

Figure 7-11
Data structures involved in a single-layered driver I/O request

An IRP consists of two parts: a fixed portion (called a header) and one or more stack locations. The fixed portion contains information such as the type and size of the request, whether the request is synchronous or asynchronous, a pointer to a buffer for buffered I/O, and state information that changes as the request progresses. An IRP stack location contains a function code, function-specific parameters, and a pointer to the caller's file object.

While active, each IRP is stored in an IRP queue associated with the thread that requested the I/O. This arrangement allows the I/O system to find and free any outstanding IRPs if a thread terminates or is terminated with outstanding I/O requests. For more information on IRPs and the system routines that process them, see the DDK documentation.

EXPERIMENT: Examining IRPs and the Thread IRP Queue

You can examine the pending IRPs for a thread with the *!thread* command in the kernel debugger. This command shows the address and basic information for each pending IRP, but not the details. If you want to display the detailed contents, you can do so with the *!irp* command. In the following example, a *!process* command has been issued, and it displays the threads in a process. One of the threads has an I/O pending, as indicated by the IRP shown in the thread IRP list. The address of the IRP is then fed to the *!irp* command. The I/O in this example is to a named pipe.

```
THREAD ffbbb020  Cid 46.2b  Teb: 7ffdc000  Win32Thread: 00000000
WAIT: (UserRequest) UserMode Non-Alertable
            ffbbc400  NotificationEvent
            ffbbb6e4  NotificationEvent
        IRP List:
            ff6edb28: (0006,00b8) Flags: 00000800  Mdl: 00000000
  :
  :
kd> !irp ff6edb28
Irp is active with 2 stacks 2 is current
 No Mdl Thread ffbbb020:  Irp stack trace.
 cmd flg cl Device    File      Completion-Context
   0   0  0 00000000 00000000 00000000-00000000
             Args: 00000000 00000000 00000000 00000000
 >  d   0  1 ff671030 ffbbb688 00000000-00000000    pending
        \FileSystem\Npfs
             Args: 00000000 00000000 00110008 00000000
```

I/O Processing

Now that we've covered the structure and types of drivers and the data structures that support them, let's look at how I/O requests flow through the system. I/O requests pass through several predictable stages of processing. The stages vary depending on whether the request is destined for a device operated by a single-layered driver or for a device reached through a multilayered driver. Because processing varies further depending on whether the caller specified synchronous or asynchronous I/O, let's first consider these two types of I/O.

I/O Request to a Single-Layered Driver

This section traces a synchronous I/O request to a single-layered kernel-mode device driver. Handling a synchronous I/O to a single-layered driver consists of six steps:

1. The I/O request passes through a subsystem DLL.

2. The subsystem DLL calls the I/O manager's *NtWriteFile* service.

3. The I/O manager sends the request in the form of an IRP to the driver (a device driver, in this case).

4. The driver starts the I/O operation.

5. When the device completes the operation and interrupts the CPU, the device driver services the interrupt.

6. The I/O manager completes the I/O request.

These six steps are illustrated in Figure 7-12.

Now that we've seen how an I/O is initiated, let's take a closer look at interrupt processing and I/O completion.

Servicing an Interrupt

After an I/O device completes a data transfer, it interrupts for service and the Windows NT kernel, I/O manager, and device driver are called into action. Figure 7-13 on page 352 illustrates the first phase of the process. (Chapter 3 describes the interrupt dispatching mechanism, including DPCs. I've included a brief summary here since DPCs are key to I/O processing.)

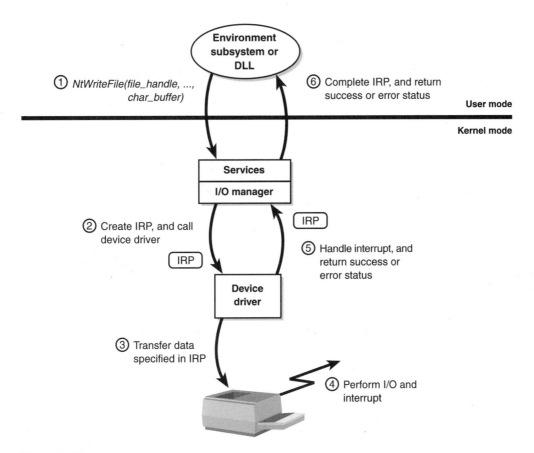

Figure 7-12
Queuing and completing a synchronous request

When a device interrupt occurs, the processor transfers control to the kernel trap handler, which indexes into its interrupt dispatch table to locate the ISR for the device. ISRs on Windows NT typically handle device interrupts in two steps. When an ISR is first invoked, it usually remains at device IRQL only long enough to capture the device status and then stop the device's interrupt. It then queues a DPC and exits, dismissing the interrupt. Later, when the DPC routine is called, the device finishes processing the interrupt. When that's done, the device calls the I/O manager to complete the I/O and dispose of the IRP. It might also start the next I/O request that is waiting in the device queue.

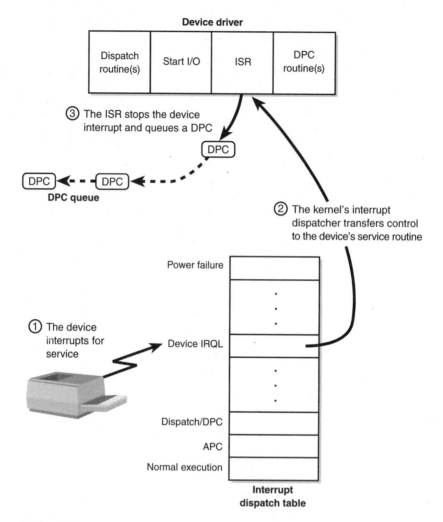

Figure 7-13
Servicing a device interrupt (phase 1)

The advantage of using a DPC to perform most of the device servicing is that any blocked interrupt whose priority lies between the device IRQL and the dispatch/DPC IRQL is allowed to occur before the lower-priority DPC processing occurs. Intermediate-level interrupts are thus serviced more promptly than they otherwise would be. This second phase of an I/O (the DPC processing) is illustrated in Figure 7-14.

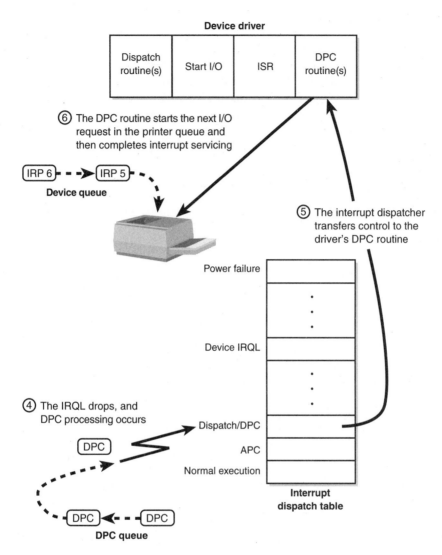

Figure 7-14
Servicing a device interrupt (phase 2)

Completing an I/O Request

After a device driver's DPC routine has executed, some work still remains before the I/O request can be considered finished. This third stage of I/O processing is called *I/O completion,* and what it entails varies with different I/O operations. For example, all the I/O services record the outcome of the operation in an *I/O status block,* a data structure supplied by the caller. Similarly, some services that perform buffered I/O require the I/O system to return data to the calling thread.

In both cases, the I/O system must copy some data that is stored in system memory into the caller's virtual address space. To gain access to the caller's virtual address space, the I/O manager must transfer the data "in the context of the caller's thread," that is, while the caller's thread is executing. It does so by queueing a kernel-mode asynchronous procedure call (APC) to the thread. This process is illustrated in Figure 7-15.

As explained in Chapter 3, APCs execute in the context of a particular thread, whereas a DPC executes in arbitrary thread context, meaning that the DPC routine can't touch the user-mode process address space. Remember too that DPCs have a higher software interrupt priority than APCs.

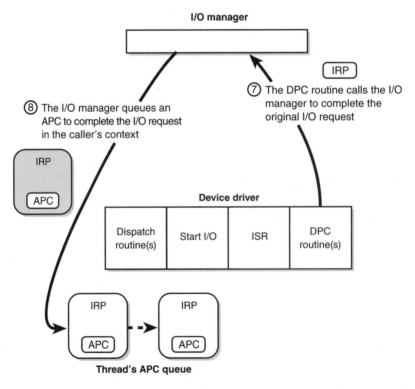

Figure 7-15
Completing an I/O request (phase 1)

The next time that thread begins to execute at low IRQL, the pending APC is delivered. The kernel transfers control to the I/O manager's APC routine, which copies the data (if any) and the return status into the original caller's address space, frees the IRP representing the I/O operation, and sets the caller's file handle (or caller-supplied event or I/O completion port) to the signaled state. The I/O is now considered complete. The original caller or any other threads that are waiting on the file (or other object) handle are released from their waiting state and readied for execution.

Figure 7-16 illustrates the second stage of I/O completion.

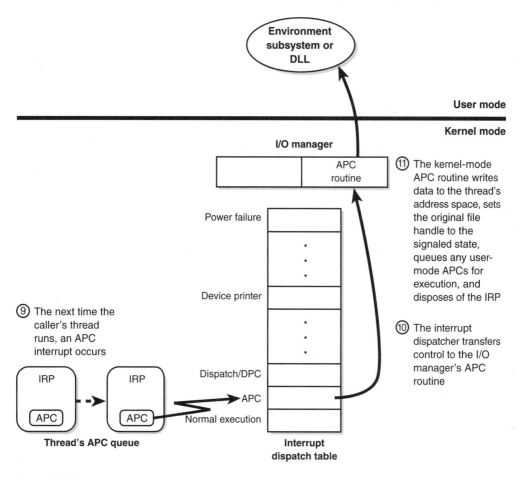

Figure 7-16
Completing an I/O request (phase 2)

355

A final note about I/O completion: the asynchronous I/O functions *Read-FileEx* and *WriteFileEx* allow a caller to supply a user-mode APC as a parameter. If the caller does so, the I/O manager queues this APC to the caller as the last step of I/O completion. This feature allows a caller to specify a subroutine to be called when an I/O request is complete. As explained in the Platform SDK documentation for these functions, user-mode APC completion routines execute in the context of the requesting thread and are delivered only when the thread enters an alertable wait state (such as calling the Win32 *SleepEx*, *WaitForSingleObjectEx*, or *WaitForMultipleObjectsEx* function).

I/O Requests to Layered Drivers

The preceding section showed how an I/O request to a simple device controlled by a single device driver is handled. I/O processing for file-based devices or for requests to other layered drivers happens in much the same way. The major difference is, obviously, that one or more additional layers of processing are added to the model.

Figure 7-17 shows how an asynchronous I/O request travels through layered drivers. It uses an example of a disk controlled by a file system.

Once again, the I/O manager receives the request and creates an I/O request packet to represent it. This time, however, it delivers the packet to a file system driver. The file system driver exercises great control over the I/O operation at that point. Depending on the type of request the caller made, the file system can send the same IRP to the device driver or it can generate additional IRPs and send them separately to the device driver.

The file system is most likely to reuse an IRP if the request it receives translates into a single straightforward request to a device. For example, if an application issues a read request for the first 512 bytes in a file stored on a floppy disk, the FAT file system would simply call the disk driver, asking it to read one sector from the floppy disk, beginning at the file's starting location.

To accommodate its reuse by multiple drivers in a request to layered drivers, an IRP contains a series of *IRP stack locations*. These data areas, one for every driver that will be called, contain the information that each driver needs in order to execute its part of the request—for example, function code, parameters, and driver context information. As Figure 7-17 illustrates, additional stack locations are filled in as the IRP passes from one driver to the next. You can think of an IRP as being similar to a stack in the way data is added to it and removed from it during its lifetime. However, an IRP is not associated with any

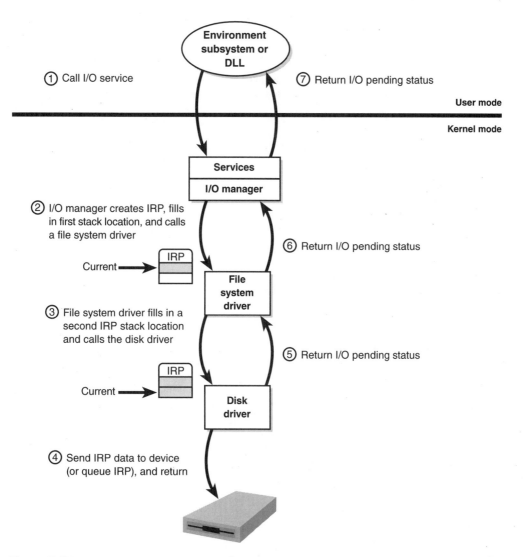

Figure 7-17

Queuing an asynchronous request to layered drivers

particular process, and its allocated size doesn't grow and shrink. The I/O manager allocates an IRP from nonpaged system memory at the beginning of the I/O operation.

After the disk driver finishes a data transfer, the disk interrupts and the I/O completes, as shown in Figure 7-18.

357

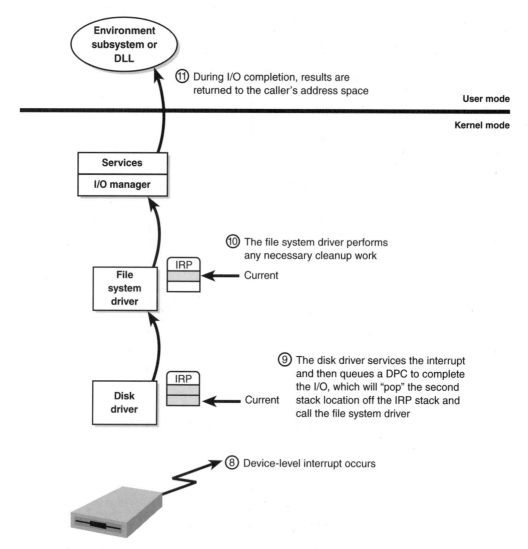

Figure 7-18
Completing a layered I/O request

As an alternative to reusing a single IRP, a file system can establish a group of *associated* IRPs that work in parallel on a single I/O request. For example, if the data to be read from a file is dispersed across the disk, the file system driver might create several IRPs, each of which reads some portion of the request from a different sector. This queueing is illustrated in Figure 7-19.

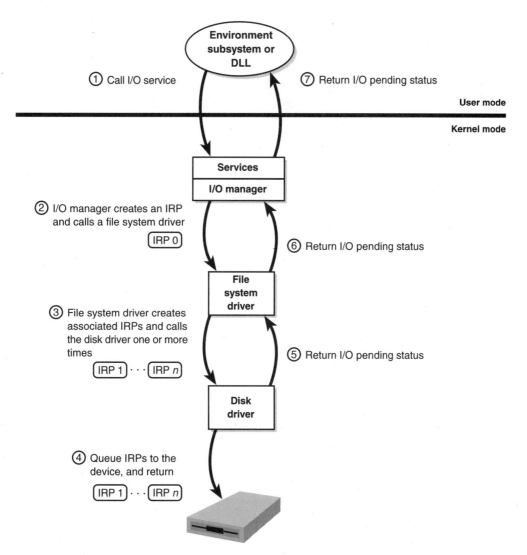

Figure 7-19
Queueing associated IRPs

The file system driver delivers the associated IRPs to the device driver, which queues them to the device. They are processed one at a time, and the file system driver keeps track of the returned data. When all the associated IRPs complete, the I/O system completes the original IRP and returns to the caller, as shown in Figure 7-20.

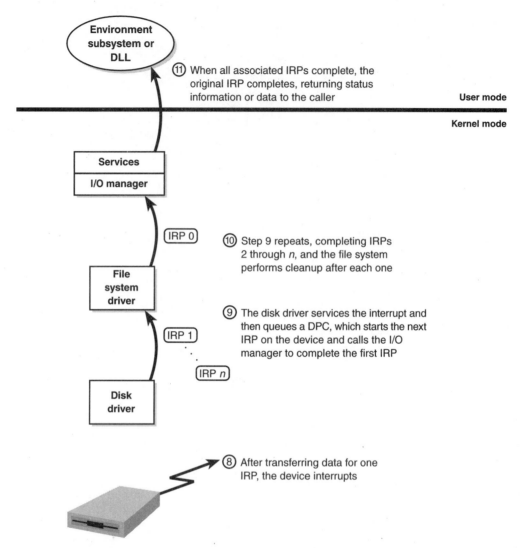

Figure 7-20
Completing associated IRPs

Conclusion

The I/O system defines the model of I/O processing on Windows NT and performs functions that are common to or required by more than one driver. Its chief responsibility is to create IRPs representing I/O requests and to shepherd the packets through various drivers, returning results to the caller when an I/O is complete. The I/O manager locates various drivers and devices by using I/O system objects, including driver and device objects. Internally, the Windows NT I/O system operates asynchronously to achieve high performance and provides both synchronous and asynchronous I/O capabilities to user-mode applications.

Device drivers include not only traditional hardware device drivers but also file system, network, and layered filter drivers. All drivers have a common structure and communicate with one another and the I/O manager by using common mechanisms. The I/O system interfaces allow drivers to be written in a high-level language to lessen development time and to enhance their portability. Because drivers present a common structure to the operating system, they can be layered one on top of another to achieve modularity and reduce duplication between drivers. Also, all Windows NT device drivers should be designed to work correctly on multiprocessor systems.

In the next chapter, we'll look at the last core executive component examined in detail this book: the Windows NT cache manager.

Cache Manager

The Microsoft Windows NT cache manager is a set of kernel-mode functions and system threads that cooperate with the memory manager to provide data caching for all Windows NT file system drivers (both local and network). In this chapter, I'll explain how the Windows NT cache manager, including its key internal data structures and functions, works; how it is sized at system initialization time; how it interacts with other elements of the operating system; and how you can observe its activity through performance counters. I'll also describe the four flags on the Win32 *CreateFile* function that affect file caching.

> **NOTE** None of the internal functions of the cache manager are outlined in this chapter beyond the depth required to explain how the cache manager works. The programming interfaces to the cache manager are defined in the *Windows NT Installable File System* (IFS) kit. As of this writing, the kit includes the C header files that define the interfaces as well as sample file system drivers, including the source code to the FAT file system and a network redirector. Future versions of the kit might include more complete documentation of the interfaces. For more information about the IFS kit, see *http:// microsoft.com/hwdev/ntifskit*.

Key Features of the Windows NT Cache Manager

The Windows NT cache manager has several key features:

- Supports all file system types (both local and network), thus removing the need for each file system to implement its own cache management code

- Uses the memory manager to control what parts of what files are in physical memory (trading off demands for physical memory between user processes and the operating system)

■ Caches data on a virtual block basis (offsets within a file)—in contrast to most caching systems, which cache on a logical block basis (offsets within a disk partition)—allowing for intelligent read-ahead and high-speed access to the cache without involving file system drivers (This method of caching, called *fast I/O*, is described later in the chapter.)

■ Supports "hints" passed by applications at file open time (such as random vs. sequential access, temporary file creation, and so on)

■ Supports recoverable file systems (for example, those that use transaction logging) to recover data after a system failure

Although I'll talk more throughout this chapter about how these features are used in the cache manager, in this section I'll introduce you to the concepts behind these features.

Single, Centralized System Cache

Some operating systems rely on each individual file system to cache data, a practice that results either in duplicated caching and memory management code in the operating system or in limitations on the kinds of data that can be cached. In contrast, Windows NT offers a centralized caching facility that caches all externally stored data, whether on local hard disks, floppy disks, network file servers, or CD-ROMs. Any data can be cached, whether it's user data streams (the contents of a file and the ongoing read and write activity to that file) or file system *metadata* (such as directory and file headers). As you'll discover in this chapter, the method Windows NT uses to access the cache depends on the type of data being cached.

The Memory Manager

One unusual aspect of the Windows NT cache manager is that it never knows how much cached data is actually in physical memory. This statement might sound strange, since the purpose of a cache is to keep a subset of frequently accessed data in physical memory as a way to improve I/O performance. The reason Windows NT cache manager doesn't know how much data is in physical memory is that it accesses data by mapping views of files into system virtual address spaces, using standard *section objects* (*file mapping objects* in Win32 terminology). (Section objects are the basic primitive of the memory manager and are explained in detail in Chapter 5.) As addresses in these mapped views are accessed, the memory manager pages in blocks that are not in physical memory. And when memory demands dictate, the memory manager pages data out of the cache and back to the files that are open in (mapped into) the cache.

By caching on the basis of a virtual address space using mapped files, the cache manager avoids generating read or write I/O request packets to access the data for files it is caching. Instead, it simply copies data to or from the virtual addresses where the portion of the cached file is mapped and relies on the memory manager to fault in (or out) the data into (or out of) memory as needed. This process allows the memory manager to make global trade-offs on how much memory to give to the system cache versus to the user processes. (The cache manager also initiates I/O, such as lazy writing, which is described later in the chapter; however, it calls the memory manager to write the pages.) Also, as you'll learn in the next section, this design makes it possible for processes that open cached files to see the same data as do those processes mapping the same file into their user address spaces.

Cache Coherency

One important function of a cache manager is to ensure that any process accessing cached data will get the most recent version of that data. A problem can arise when one process opens a file (and hence the file is cached) while another process maps the file into its address space directly (using the Win32 *MapViewOfFile* function). This potential problem doesn't occur under Windows NT because both the cache manager and the user applications that map files into their address spaces use the same memory management file mapping services. Because the memory manager guarantees that it has only one representation of each unique mapped file (regardless of the number of section objects or mapped views), it maps all views of a file (even if they overlap) to a single set of pages in physical memory, as shown in Figure 8-1. (For more information on how the memory manager works with mapped files, see Chapter 5.)

So, for example, if Process 1 has a view of the file mapped into its address space and Process 2 is accessing the same view via the system cache, Process 2 will see any changes that Process 1 makes as they're made, not as they're flushed. The memory manager won't flush *all* user-mapped pages—only those that it knows have been written to (because they have the modified bit set). Therefore, any process accessing a file under Windows NT always sees the most up-to-date version of that file, even if some processes have the file open through the I/O system and others have the file mapped into their address space using the Win32 file mapping functions.

NOTE Cache coherency is a little more difficult for network redirectors than for local file systems because network redirectors must implement additional flushing and purge operations to ensure cache coherency when accessing network data.

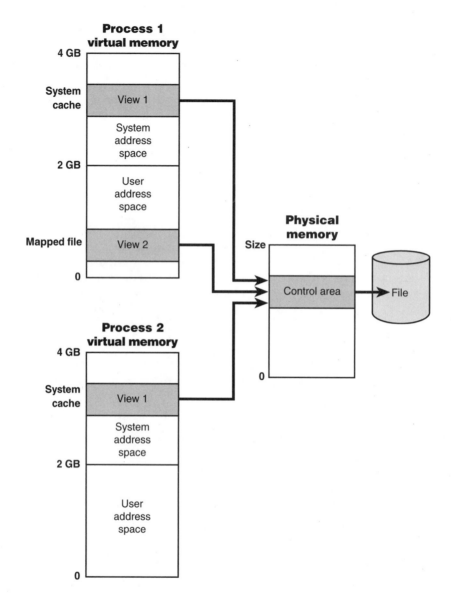

Figure 8-1
Coherent caching scheme

Virtual Block Caching

Most operating system cache managers (including Novell NetWare, OpenVMS, OS/2, and most UNIX systems) cache data on the basis of *logical blocks*. With this method, the cache manager keeps track of which blocks of a disk partition are in the cache. The Windows NT cache manager, in contrast, uses a method known as *virtual block caching*, in which the cache manager keeps track of which parts of which *files* are in the cache. The cache manager is able to monitor these file portions by mapping 256-KB views of files into system virtual address spaces, using special system cache routines found in the memory manager. This approach has the following key benefits:

- It opens up the possibility of doing intelligent read-ahead; because the cache tracks which parts of which files are in the cache, it can predict where the caller might be going next.

- It allows the I/O system to bypass going to the file system for requests for data that is already in the cache (fast I/O). Because the cache manager knows which parts of which files are in the cache, it can return the address of cached data to satisfy an I/O request without having to call the file system.

Details of how intelligent read-ahead and fast I/O work are provided later in this chapter.

Stream-Based Caching

Windows NT's cache manager is also designed to do *stream caching,* as opposed to file caching. A *stream* is a sequence of bytes within a file. Some file systems, such as NTFS, allow a file to contain more than one stream; the cache manager accommodates such file systems by caching each stream independently. NTFS can exploit this feature by organizing its master file table (described in Chapter 9) into streams and by caching these streams as well. In fact, although the Windows NT cache manager might be said to cache files, it in fact caches streams (all files have at least one stream of data) identified by both a filename and, if more than one stream exists in the file, a stream name.

Recoverable File System Support

Recoverable file systems such as NTFS are designed to reconstruct the disk volume structure after a system failure. This capability means that I/O operations in progress at the time of a system failure must be either entirely completed or entirely backed out from the disk when the system is restarted. Half-completed I/O operations can corrupt a disk volume and even render an entire volume inaccessible. To avoid this problem, a recoverable file system maintains a log file in which it records every update it intends to make to the file system structure (the file system's metadata) before it writes the change to the volume. If the system fails, interrupting volume modifications in progress, the recoverable file system uses information stored in the log to reissue the volume updates.

> **NOTE** The term *metadata* applies only to changes in the file system structure: file and directory creation, renaming, and deletion.

To guarantee a successful volume recovery, every log file record documenting a volume update must be completely written to disk before the update itself is applied to the volume. Because disk writes are cached, the cache manager and the file system must work together to ensure that the following actions occur, in sequence:

1. The file system writes a log file record documenting the volume update it intends to make.

2. The file system calls the cache manager to flush the log file record to disk.

3. The file system writes the volume update to the cache; that is, it modifies its cached metadata.

4. The cache manager flushes the altered metadata to disk, updating the volume structure. (Actually, log file records are batched before being flushed to disk, as are volume modifications.)

When a file system writes data to the cache, it can supply a *logical sequence number* (*LSN*) that identifies the record in its log file, which corresponds to the cache update. The cache manager keeps track of these numbers, recording the lowest and highest LSNs (representing the oldest and newest log file records) associated with each page in the cache. In addition, data streams that are protected by transaction log records are marked as "no write" by NTFS so that the modified page writer won't inadvertently write out these pages before the corresponding log records are written. (When the modified page writer sees a page marked this way, it moves the page to a special list that the cache manager then flushes at the appropriate time, such as when lazy writer activity takes place.)

When it prepares to flush a group of dirty pages to disk, the cache manager determines the highest LSN associated with the pages to be flushed and reports that number to the file system. The file system can then call the cache manager back, directing it to flush the log file up to the high-water mark represented by the reported LSN. *After* the cache manager flushes the log file up to that LSN, it flushes the corresponding volume structure updates to disk, thus ensuring that it records what it's going to do before actually doing it. These interactions between the file system and the cache manager guarantee the recoverability of the disk volume after a system failure.

Cache Structure

Because the Windows NT system cache manager caches data on a virtual basis, it is given a region of system virtual address spaces to manage (instead of a region of physical memory). The cache manager then divides each address space region into 256-KB slots called *views*, as shown in Figure 8-2 on the following page. (For a detailed description of the layout of system space, see Chapter 5.)

At a file's first I/O (read or write) operation, the cache manager maps a 256-KB view of the 256-KB-aligned region of the file that contains the requested data into a free slot in the system cache. For example, if 10 bytes starting at an offset of 300,000 bytes were read into a file, the view that would be mapped would begin at offset 262144 (the second 256-KB-aligned region of the file) and extend for 256 KB.

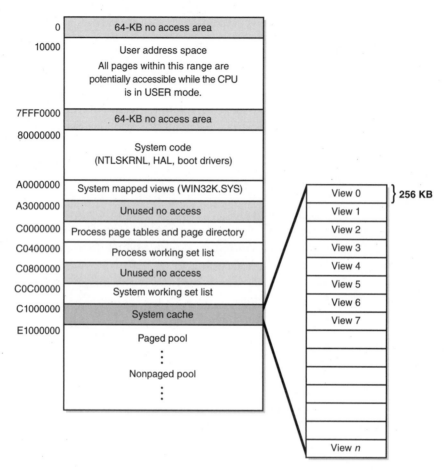

Figure 8-2
System cache address space (Intel-specific)

The cache manager maps views of files into slots in the cache on a round-robin basis, mapping the first requested view into the first 256-KB slot, the second view into the second 256-KB slot, and so forth, as shown in Figure 8-3. In this example, File B was mapped first, File A second, and File C third, so File B's mapped chunk occupies the first slot in the cache. Notice that although File C is only 100 KB (and thus smaller than one of the views in the system cache), it requires its own 256-KB slot in the cache.

Views of files remain mapped into the system cache until all handles to the file they correspond to are closed. A view is marked active, however, only during a read or write operation to or from the file. If the cache manager needs to map a view of a file and there are no more free slots in the cache, it will unmap

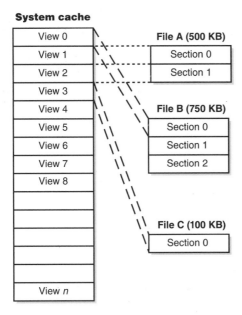

Figure 8-3
Files of varying sizes mapped into the system cache

the oldest inactive view and use that slot. If no views are available, an I/O error is returned, indicating that insufficient system resources were available to perform the operation. Given that views are marked active only during a read or write operation, however, this scenario is extremely unlikely since thousands of files would have to be accessed simultaneously for this situation to occur.

Cache Size

In the following sections, I'll explain how Windows NT computes the size of the system cache (both virtually and physically). As with most calculations related to memory management, the size of the system cache depends on a number of factors, including memory size and which version of Windows NT is running.

Cache Virtual Size

The virtual size of the system cache is a function of the amount of physical memory installed. The default size is 64 MB on *x*86 systems and 128 MB on Alpha systems. If the system has more than 4032 pages of physical memory (16 MB on *x*86 systems, 32 MB on Alpha systems), the cache size is set to 128 MB plus 64 MB for each additional 1024 pages: 4 MB on *x*86 systems and 8 MB on Alpha systems. (As always, details such as these are subject to change in future releases.) For example, an *x*86 system with 64 MB of physical memory has 16,384 pages. Using the above algorithm, the virtual size of the system cache for this computer will be:

128 MB + (16384 pages − 4032 pages) / 1024 pages * 64 MB = 900 MB

Table 8-1 shows the minimum and maximum virtual size of the system cache, along with the start and end addresses.

Table 8-1   Size and Location of System Data Cache

Platform	Address Range	Minimum/Maximum Virtual Size
*x*86 2-GB system space	0xC1000000-E0FFFFFF	64–512 MB
*x*86 1-GB system space	0xC1000000-DCFFFFFF	64–448 MB
Alpha 2-GB system space	0xC4000000-DDFFFFFF	128–416 MB

Table 8-2 lists the system variables that contain the virtual size and address of the system cache.

Table 8-2   System Variables for the Virtual Size and Address of the System Cache

System Variable	Description
MmSystemCacheStart	Starting virtual address of cache
MmSystemCacheEnd	Ending virtual address of cache
MmSizeOfSystemCacheInPages	Maximum size of cache in pages

Cache Physical Size

As mentioned earlier, one of the key differences in the design of the Windows NT cache manager from that of other operating systems is the delegation of physical memory management to the global memory manager. Because of this, the existing code that handles working set expansion and trimming as well as manages the modified and standby list is also used to control the size of the system cache, dynamically balancing demands for physical memory between processes and the operating system.

The system cache doesn't have its own working set but rather shares a single system set that includes cache data, paged pool, pageable NTOSKRNL code, and pageable driver code. As explained in the section "System Working Set" in Chapter 5 (on page 282), this single working set is called internally the *system cache working set* even though the system cache is just one of the components that contribute to it. For the purposes of this book, I'll refer to this working set simply as the *system working set*.

You can examine the physical size of the system cache compared to that of the total system working set as well as page fault information on the system working set by examining the performance counters or system variables listed in Table 8-3.

Table 8-3 System Variables for the Physical Size of the System Cache and Page Fault Information

Performance Counter (in bytes)	System Variable (in pages)	Description
Memory: System Cache Resident Bytes	*MmSystemCachePage*	Physical memory consumed by the system cache.
Memory: Cache Bytes	*MmSystemCacheWs.WorkingSetSize*	Total size of the system working set (including the cache, paged pool, and pageable code). This is *not* the size of the cache (as the name implies)!
Memory: Cache Bytes Peak	*MmSystemCacheWs.Peak*	Peak system working set size.
Memory: Cache Faults/Sec	*MmSystemCacheWs.PageFaultCount*	Page faults in the system working set (not just the cache).

Most utilities that claim to display the size of the system cache (such as Task Manager, Pview, Pstat, Pmon, Perfmtr, and so on) in fact display the total system working set size, not just the cache size. The reason for this inaccuracy is that the performance counter Memory: Cache Bytes (see Table 8-3) returns the total system working set size, which includes the system cache, paged pool, and pageable system code, even though the name and explanatory text imply that it represents just the cache size. For example, if you start Task Manager (by pressing Ctrl-Shift-Esc) and click the Performance tab, the field named File Cache is actually the system working set size, as you can see in Figure 8-4.

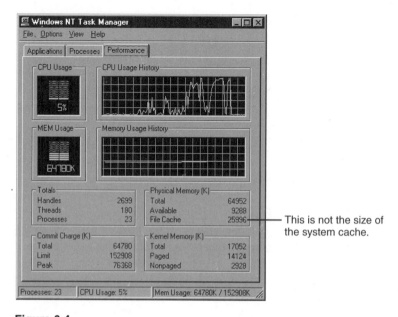

This is not the size of the system cache.

Figure 8-4
The Windows NT Task Manager does not report the size of the system cache

A number of internal system variables control working set expansion and trimming, such as *MmWorkingSetReductionMaxCacheWs*, *MmWorkingSetReductionMinCacheWs*, *MmWorkingSetVolReductionMaxCacheWs*, and *MmPeriodicAgressiveCacheWsMin*. Although I don't cover these variables in detail in this book, in Chapter 5, I do describe the memory manager's general policies for working set management.

Cache Data Structures

The cache manager uses these data structures to keep track of cached files:

■ Each 256-KB slot in the system cache is described by a virtual address control block.

■ Each separately opened cached file has a private cache map, which contains information used to control read-ahead (discussed later in the chapter).

■ Each cached file has a single shared cache map structure, which points to slots in the system cache that contain mapped views of the file.

These structures and their relationships are described in the next sections.

Systemwide Cache Data Structures

The cache manager keeps track of the state of the views in the system cache using an array of data structures called *virtual address control blocks* (*VACBs*). During system initialization, the cache manager allocates a single chunk of nonpaged pool to contain all the VACBs required to describe the system cache. It stores the address of the VACB array in the variable *CcVacbs*. Each VACB represents one 256-KB view in the system cache, as shown in Figure 8-5. The structure of a VACB is shown in Figure 8-6.

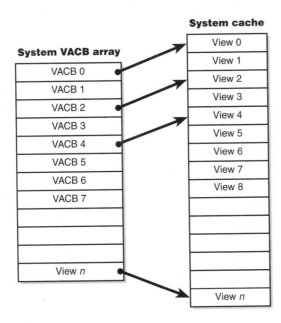

Figure 8-5
System VACB array

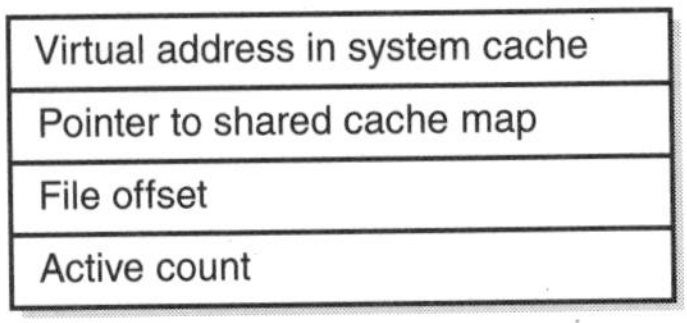

| Virtual address in system cache |
| Pointer to shared cache map |
| File offset |
| Active count |

Figure 8-6
VACB structure

As you can see in Figure 8-6, the first field in a VACB is the virtual address of the data in the system cache. The second field is a pointer to the shared cache map structure, which identifies which file is cached. The third field identifies the offset within the file at which the view begins (always based on a 256-KB granularity). Finally, the VACB contains the number of references to the view, that is, how many active reads or writes are accessing the view. During an I/O operation on a file, the file's VACB reference count is incremented and then decremented when the I/O operation is over. For access to file system metadata, the active count represents how many file system drivers have the pages in that view locked into memory.

Per-File Cache Data Structures

Each open handle to a file has a corresponding file object. (File objects are explained in detail in Chapter 7.) If the file is cached, the file object points to a *private cache map* structure that contains the location of the last two reads so that the cache manager can perform intelligent read-ahead (described in the section "Intelligent Read-Ahead" on page 382). In addition, all the private cache maps for a file object are linked together.

Each cached file (as opposed to file object) has a *shared cache map* structure that describes the state of the cached file, including its size and (for security reasons) its valid data length. (The function of the valid data length field is explained in the section "Write-Back Caching and Lazy Writing" on page 379) The shared cache map also points to the *section object pointers* (maintained by the memory manager), which describe the file's mapping into virtual memory, the list of private cache maps associated with that file, and any VACBs that describe currently mapped views of the file in the system cache. (See page 301 in Chapter 5 for more about section object pointers.) The relationships among these per-file cache data structures are illustrated in Figure 8-7.

When asked to read from a particular file, the cache manager must determine the answers to two questions:

1. Is the file in the cache?

2. If so, which VACB, if any, refers to the requested location?

In other words, the cache manager must find out whether a view of the file at the desired address is mapped into the system cache. If no VACB contains the desired file offset, the requested data is not currently mapped into the system cache.

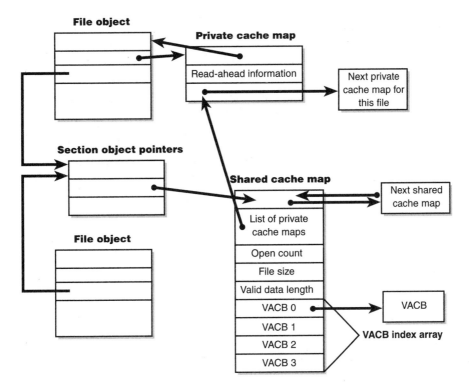

Figure 8-7
Per-file cache data structures

To keep track of which views for a given file are mapped into the system cache, the cache manager maintains an array of pointers to VACBs, the *VACB index array*. The first entry in the VACB index array refers to the first 256 KB of the file, the second entry to the second 256 KB, and so on. The diagram in Figure 8-8 on the following page shows four different sections of three different files that are currently mapped into the system cache.

When a process accesses a particular file in a given location, the cache manager looks in the appropriate entry in the file's VACB index array to see whether the requested data has been mapped into the cache. If the array entry is nonzero (and hence contains a pointer to a VACB), the area of the file being referenced is in the cache. The VACB, in turn, points to the location in the system cache where the view of the file is mapped. If the entry is zero, the cache manager must find a free slot in the system cache (and therefore a free VACB) to map the required view.

377

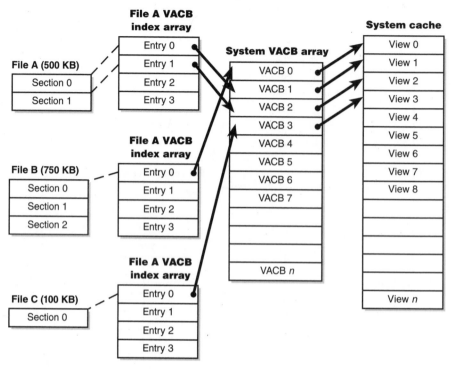

Figure 8-8
VACB index arrays

As a size optimization, the shared cache map contains a VACB index array that is 4 entries in size. Since each VACB describes 256 KB, this small fixed-size array can describe a file of up to 1 MB. If a file is larger than 1 MB, a separate VACB index array is allocated from nonpaged pool, based on the size of the file divided by 256 KB and rounded up in the case of a remainder. The shared cache map then points to this separate structure.

Cache Operation

In this section, you'll see how the cache manager implements reading and writing file data on behalf of file system drivers. Keep in mind that the cache manager is involved in file I/O only when a file is opened (for example, using the Win32 *CreateFile* function). Mapped files do not go through the cache manager, nor do files opened with the FILE_FLAG_NO_BUFFERING flag set.

Write-Back Caching and Lazy Writing

The Windows NT cache manager implements a write-back cache with lazy write. This means that data written to files is first stored in memory in cache pages and then written to disk later. Thus, write operations are allowed to accumulate for a short time and are then flushed to disk all at once, reducing the overall number of disk I/O operations.

The cache manager must explicitly call the memory manager to flush cache pages because the memory manager writes memory contents to disk only when demand for physical memory exceeds supply, as is appropriate for volatile data. Cached file data, however, represents nonvolatile disk data. If a process modifies cached data, the user expects the contents to be reflected on disk in a timely manner.

The decision about how often to flush the cache is an important one. If the cache is flushed too frequently, system performance will be slowed by unnecessarily increased I/O. If the cache is flushed too rarely, you risk losing modified file data in the case of a system failure (a loss especially irritating to users who know that they asked the application to save the changes) and running out of physical memory (because it's being used by an excess of modified pages).

To balance these concerns, once per second a system thread created by the cache manager—the *lazy writer*—queues one quarter of the dirty pages in the system cache to be written to disk. The I/O operations are actually performed by system worker threads from the systemwide critical worker thread pool.

NOTE For C2-secure file systems (such as NTFS), the cache manager provides a means for the file system to track when and how much data has been written to a file. After the lazy writer flushes dirty pages to the disk, the cache manager notifies the file system, instructing it to update its view of the valid data length for the file.

You can examine the activity of the lazy writer by examining the cache performance counters or system variables listed in Table 8-4.

Table 8-4 System Variables for Examining the Activity of the Lazy Writer

Performance Counter (frequency)	System Variable (count)	Description
Cache: Lazy Write Flushes/Sec	*CcLazyWriteIos*	Number of lazy writer flushes
Cache: Lazy Write Pages/Sec	*CcLazyWritePages*	Number of pages written by the lazy writer

Calculating the Dirty Page Threshold

The *dirty page threshold* is the number of pages that the system cache keeps in memory before waking up the lazy writer system thread to write out pages back to the disk. This value is computed at system initialization time and depends on physical memory size and the value of the registry key \System...\Control\ SessionManager\Memory Management\LargeSystemCache. This key is 0 by default on both Windows NT Workstation and Windows NT Server. It can be adjusted only on Windows NT Server systems, by modifying the properties of the server's network service within the Network applet in Control Panel. (Even though this service exists on Windows NT Workstation, its parameters can't be adjusted.) Figure 8-9 shows the dialog box you use when modifying the properties of the Server network service.

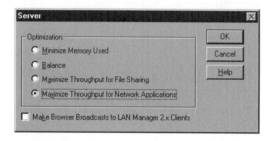

Figure 8-9
Server dialog box, which is used to modify the amount of memory allocated for local and network applications in Windows NT Server

The setting shown in Figure 8-9, Maximize Throughput For Network Applications, is the default—the LargeSystemCache key is 0. Changing the setting to Maximum Throughput For File Sharing would change the value of Large-SystemCache from 0 to 1. The settings Minimize Memory Used and Balance change LargeSystemCache back to 0. Although each of the four settings in the Server dialog box affect the behavior of the file server service, they also modify the value of LargeSystemCache, which affects the system cache in general (for both local and network file access).

Table 8-5 contains the algorithm used to calculate the dirty page threshold. The calculations in Table 8-5 are overridden if the system maximum working set size is greater than 4 MB—and it often is. (See page 284 in Chapter 5 to find out how the memory manager chooses system working set sizes, that is, how it determines whether the size is small, medium, or large.) When the maximum working set size exceeds 4 MB, the dirty page threshold is set to the value of the system maximum working set size minus 2 MB.

Table 8-5 Algorithm for Calculating the Dirty Page Threshold

System Memory Size	Dirty Page Threshold
Small	Physical pages / 8
Medium	Physical pages / 4
Large and registry LargeSystemCache=0	Sum of the above two values
Large and registry LargeSystemCache=1	Same as preceding entry; however, if the computed value is less than the size of physical memory, the dirty page threshold is set to the size of physical memory.

Disabling Lazy Writing for a File

If you create a temporary file by specifying the FILE_ATTRIBUTE_TEMP-ORARY flag on the Win32 *CreateFile* function, the lazy writer won't write dirty pages to the disk unless there is a severe shortage of physical memory. This characteristic of the lazy writer improves system performance—the lazy writer doesn't immediately write data to a disk that might ultimately be discarded.

Forcing the Cache to Write Through to Disk

Because some applications can't tolerate even momentary delays between writing a file and seeing the updates on disk, the cache manager also supports write-through caching on a per-file basis; changes are written to disk as soon as they're made. To turn on write-through caching, set the FILE_FLAG_WRITE-_THROUGH flag when opening a file. Alternatively, a thread can explicitly flush an open file using the Win32 *FlushFileBuffers* function when it reaches a point at which the data needs to be written to disk. You can observe cache flush operations that are the result of write-through I/O requests or explicit calls to *FlushFileBuffers* via the performance counters or system variables shown in Table 8-6.

Table 8-6 System Variables for Viewing Cache Flush Operations

Performance Counter (frequency)	System Variable (count)	Description
Cache: Data Flushes/Sec	*CcDataFlushes*	Number of times cache pages were flushed explicitly or because of write through
Cache: Data Flush Pages/Sec	*CcDataPages*	Number of pages flushed explicitly or because of write through

Flushing Mapped Files

If the lazy writer must write data to disk from a view that's also mapped into another process's address space, the situation becomes a little more complicated because the cache manager will only know about the pages it has modified. (Pages modified by another process are known only to that process because the modified bit in the page table entries for modified pages are kept in the process private page tables.) To address this situation, the memory manager informs the cache manager when a user maps a file. When such a file is flushed in the cache (for example, as a result of a call to the Win32 *FlushFileBuffers* function), the cache manager writes the dirty pages in the cache and then notices that the file is also mapped by another process. It then flushes the entire view of the section in order to write out pages that might have been modified by the second process. If a user maps a view of a file that is also open in the cache, when the view is unmapped, the modified pages are marked as dirty so that when the lazy writer thread later flushes the view, those dirty pages will be written to disk. This procedure works as long as the sequence occurs in the following order:

1. A user unmaps the view.

2. A process flushes file buffers.

If this sequence is not followed, you can't predict which pages will be written to disk.

Intelligent Read-Ahead

The Windows NT cache manager uses the principle of spatial locality to perform *intelligent read-ahead* by predicting what data the calling process is likely to read next based on the data that it is reading currently. Because the system cache is based on virtual addresses, which are contiguous for a particular file, it doesn't matter whether they're juxtaposed in physical memory. File read-ahead for logical block caching is an impossibility because that cache system is based on the relative positions of the accessed data on the disk, and of course, files are not necessarily stored contiguously on disk.

The two types of read-ahead—virtual address read-ahead and asynchronous read-ahead with history—are explained in the next two sections. You can examine read-ahead activity by using the Cache: Read Aheads/Sec performance counter or the *CcReadAheadIos* system variable.

Virtual Address Read-Ahead

Recall from Chapter 5 that when the memory manager resolves a page fault, it reads into memory several pages near the one explicitly accessed, a method called *in-page clustering*. For applications that read sequentially, this *virtual address read-ahead* operation reduces the number of disk reads necessary to retrieve data. The only disadvantage to the memory manager's method is that because this read-ahead is done in the context of resolving a page fault it must be performed synchronously, while the thread waiting on the data being paged back into memory is waiting. The cache manager improves on this scheme for cached files by prereading their data asynchronously. When called to retrieve cached data, the cache manager first accesses the requested virtual page to satisfy the request and then queues an additional I/O request to retrieve additional data to a system worker thread. The worker thread then executes in the background, reading additional data in 64-KB blocks in anticipation of the caller's next read request. The preread pages are faulted into memory while the program continues executing so that when the caller requests the data, it's already in memory.

Asynchronous Read-Ahead with History

The virtual address read-ahead performed by the cache manager improves I/O performance, but its benefits are limited to sequentially accessed data. To extend read-ahead benefits to certain cases of randomly accessed data, the cache manager maintains a history of the last two read requests in the private cache map for the file handle being accessed, a method known as *asynchronous read-ahead with history*. If a pattern can be determined from the caller's apparently random reads, the cache manager extrapolates it. For example, if the caller reads page 4000 and then page 3000, the cache manager assumes that the next page the caller will require is page 2000 and prereads it.

> **NOTE** Although a caller must issue a minimum of three read operations to establish a predictable sequence, only two are stored in the private cache map.

To make read-ahead even more efficient, the Win32 *CreateFile* function provides a flag indicating sequential file access: FILE_FLAG_SEQUENTIAL_SCAN. If this flag is set, the cache manager doesn't keep a read history for the caller for prediction but instead performs sequential read-ahead. It also reads ahead three times as much data (192 KB instead of 64 KB) using a separate I/O operation for each read. As the caller continues reading, the cache manager prereads additional blocks of data, always staying about 192 KB ahead of the caller. Although the asynchronous read-ahead with history technique uses more memory than the standard read-ahead, it minimizes disk I/O and further improves the performance of applications reading large amounts of cached sequential data. The Cache: Read Aheads/Sec performance counter indicates sequential access read-ahead operations.

For applications that have no predictable read pattern, the FILE_FLAG-_RANDOM_ACCESS flag can be specified when the file is open. This flag instructs the cache manager not to attempt to predict where the application is reading next and thus disables read-ahead. This flag isn't currently implemented in Windows NT 4.0, however, but it will be in Windows NT 5.0. In the meantime, applications that know they are doing random file I/O should specify this flag now, even though it won't affect the cache manager until Windows NT 5.0.

Windows NT 5.0 ▶   **NOTE**   The FILE_FLAG_RANDOM_ACCESS flag, which is currently ignored, will be supported by the cache manager in Windows NT 5.0.

System Threads

As mentioned earlier, the cache manager performs lazy write and read-ahead I/O operations by submitting requests to the common critical system worker thread pool. However, it does limit the use of these threads to one less than the total number of critical worker system threads for small and medium memory systems (two less than the total for large memory systems).

Internally, the cache manager organizes its work requests into two lists (though these are serviced by the same set of executive worker threads):

- The *express queue* is used for read-ahead operations.

- The *regular queue* is used for lazy write scans (for dirty data to flush), write behinds, and lazy closes.

To keep track of the work items the worker threads need to perform, the cache manager creates its own internal *look-aside list*, a fixed-length list of worker queue item structures. (Look-aside lists are discussed in Chapter 5.) The number of worker queue items depends on system size: 32 for small-memory systems, 64 for medium-memory systems, 128 for large-memory Windows NT Workstation systems, and 256 for large-memory Windows NT Server systems.

Fast I/O

Whenever possible, reads and writes to cached files are handled by a high-speed mechanism named fast I/O. Fast I/O is a means of reading or writing a cached file without going through the work of generating an I/O request packet (IRP), as described in Chapter 7. With fast I/O, the I/O manager calls the file system driver's fast I/O routine to see whether I/O can be satisfied directly from the cache manager without generating an IRP.

Because the Windows NT cache manager keeps track of which blocks of which files are in the cache, file system drivers can use the cache manager to access file data simply by copying to or from pages mapped to the actual file being referenced without going through the overhead of generating an IRP.

Fast I/O doesn't always occur. For example, the first read or write to a file requires setting up the file for caching (mapping the file into the cache and setting up the cache data structures, as explained in the section "Cache Data Structures" on page 374). Also, if the caller specified an asynchronous read or write, fast I/O isn't used since the caller might be stalled during paging I/O operations required to satisfy the buffer copy to or from the system cache and thus not really providing the requested asynchronous I/O operation. But even on a synchronous I/O, the file system driver might decide that it can't process the I/O operation using the fast I/O mechanism, say, for example, if the file in question has a locked range of bytes (as a result of calls to the Win32 *LockFile* and *UnlockFile* functions). Because the cache manager doesn't know what parts of what files are locked, the file system driver must check the validity of the read or write, which requires generating an IRP. The decision tree for fast I/O is shown in Figure 8-10 on the following page.

These steps are involved in servicing a read or a write with fast I/O:

1. A thread performs a read or write operation.

2. If the file is cached and the I/O is synchronous, the request passes to the fast I/O entry point of the file system driver. If the file is not cached, the file system driver sets up the file for caching so that the next time, fast I/O can be used to satisfy a read or write request.

3. If the file system driver's *fast I/O* routine determines that fast I/O is possible, it calls the cache manager read or write routine to access the file data directly in the cache. (If fast I/O is not possible, the file system driver returns to the I/O system, which then generates an IRP for the I/O and eventually calls the file system's regular read routine.)

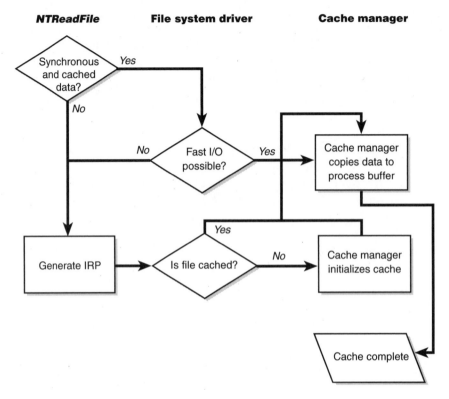

Figure 8-10
Fast I/O decision tree

4. The cache manager translates the supplied file offset into a virtual address in the cache.

5. For reads, the cache manager copies the data from the cache into the buffer of the process requesting it; for writes, it copies the data from the buffer to the cache.

6. One of the following actions occurs:

   ❑ For reads, the read-ahead information in the caller's private cache map is updated.

   ❑ For writes, the dirty bit of any modified page in the cache is set so that the lazy writer will know to flush it to disk.

   ❑ For write-through files, any modifications are flushed to disk.

NOTE The fast I/O path is not limited to occasions when the requested data already resides in physical memory. As noted in steps 5 and 6 of the preceding list, the cache manager simply accesses the virtual addresses of the already opened file where it expects the data to be. If a cache miss occurs, the memory manager dynamically pages the data into physical memory.

The performance counters or system variables listed in Table 8-7 can be used to determine the fast I/O activity on the system.

Table 8-7 System Variables for Determining Fast I/O Activity

Performance Counter (frequency)	System Variable (count)	Description
Cache: Synch Fast Reads/Sec	*CcFastReadWait*	Synchronous reads that were handled as fast I/O requests
Cache: Async Fast Reads/Sec	*CcFastReadNoWait*	Asynchronous reads that were handled as fast I/O requests (These are always zero because asynchronous fast reads aren't done in Windows NT.)
Cache: Fast Read Resource Misses/Sec	*CcFastReadResourceMiss*	Fast I/O operations that couldn't be satisfied because of resource conflicts (This situation can occur with FAT but not with NTFS.)
Cache: Fast Read Not Possibles/Sec	*CcFastReadNotPossible*	Fast I/O operations that couldn't be satisfied (The file system driver decides; for example, files with byte range locks can't use fast I/O.)

Cache Support Routines

The first time a file is accessed, the file system driver is responsible for determining whether some part of the file is mapped in the system cache. If not, it must call the *CcInitializeCacheMap* function to set up the per-file data structures described in the preceding section.

Once a file is set up for cached access, the file system driver calls one of several functions to access the data in the file. There are three primary methods for accessing cached data, each intended for a specific situation.

- The first method (copy read) copies user data between cache buffers in system space and a process buffer in user space.

- The second method (mapping and pinning) reads and writes data directly to cache buffers using virtual addresses.

- The third method (physical memory access) reads and writes data directly to cache buffers using physical addresses.

File system drivers must provide two versions of the file read operation—cached and noncached—to prevent an infinite loop when the memory manager processes a page fault. When the memory manager resolves a page fault by calling the file system to retrieve data from the file (via the device driver, of course), it must specify this noncached read operation by setting the "no cache" flag in the IRP.

The next three sections explain these cache access mechanisms, their purpose, and how they are used.

Copying to and from the Cache

Because the system cache is in system space, it is mapped into the address space of every process. As with all system space pages, however, cache pages are not accessible from user mode, since that would be a potential security hole. (For example, a process might not have the rights to read a file whose data is currently contained in some part of the system cache.) Thus, user application file reads and writes to cached files must be serviced by kernel-mode routines that copy data between the cache's buffers in system space and the application's buffers residing in the process address space. The functions that file system drivers can use to perform this operation are listed in Table 8-8.

Table 8-8   Kernel-Mode Functions for Copying to and from the Cache

Function	Description
CcCopyRead	Copies a specified byte range from the system cache to a user buffer
CcFastCopyRead	Faster variation of *CcCopyRead* but limited to 32-bit file offsets and synchronous reads (used by NTFS, not FAT)
CcCopyWrite	Copies a specified byte range from a user buffer to the system cache
CcFastCopyWrite	Faster variation of *CcCopyWrite* but limited to 32-bit file offsets and synchronous, non-write-through writes (used by NTFS, not FAT)

You can examine read activity from the cache via the performance counters or system variables listed in Table 8-9.

Table 8-9 System Variables for Examining Read Activity from the Cache

Performance Counter (frequency)	System Variable (count)	Description
Cache: Copy Read Hits %	(*CcCopyReadWait* + *CcCopyReadNoWait*) / (*CcCopyReadWait* + *CcCopyReadNoWait*) + (*CcCopyReadWaitMiss* + *CcCopyReadNoWaitMiss*)	Percentage of copy reads to parts of files that were in the cache (A copy read can still generate paging I/O—the Memory: Cache Faults/Sec counter reports page fault activity for the system working set but includes both hard and soft page faults, so the counter still doesn't indicate actual paging I/O caused by cache faults.)
Cache: Copy Reads/Sec	*CcCopyReadWait* + *CcCopyReadNoWait*	Total copy reads from the cache
Cache: Synch Copy Reads/Sec	*CcCopyReadWait*	Synchronous copy reads from the cache
Cache: Async Copy Reads/Sec	*CcCopyReadNoWait*	Asynchronous copy reads from the cache

Caching with the Mapping and Pinning Interfaces

Just as user applications read and write data in files on a disk, file system drivers need to read and write the data that describes the files themselves (the metadata, or volume structure data). However, since the file system drivers run in kernel mode, they could, if the cache manager were properly informed, modify data directly in the system cache. To permit this optimization, the cache manager provides the functions shown in Table 8-10 on the following page. These functions permit the file system drivers to find where in virtual memory the file system metadata resides, thus allowing direct modification without the use of intermediary buffers.

If a file system driver needs to read file system metadata in the cache, it calls the cache manager's mapping interface to obtain the virtual address of the desired data. The cache manager touches all the requested pages to bring them into memory and then returns control to the file system driver. The file system driver can then access the data directly.

Table 8-10 Functions for Finding Metadata Locations

Function	Description
CcMapData	Maps the byte range for read access
CcPinRead	Maps the byte range for read/write access
CcPreparePinWrite	Prepares a page to be written to
CcPinMappedData	Pins a previously mapped buffer
CcSetDirtyPinnedData	Notifies the cache manager that the data has been modified
CcUnpinData	Releases the pages so that they can be removed from memory

If the file system driver needs to modify cache pages, it calls the cache manager's pinning services, which keep the pages being modified in memory. The pages are not actually locked into memory (such as when a device driver locks pages for direct memory access transfers). Instead, the memory manager's mapped page writer (explained in Chapter 5) sees that these pages are pinned and doesn't write the pages to disk until they are unpinned (released) by the file system driver. When the pages are released, the cache manager flushes any changes to disk and releases the cache view that the metadata occupied.

The mapping and pinning interfaces solve one thorny problem of implementing a file system: buffer management. Without directly manipulating cached metadata, a file system must predict the maximum number of buffers it will need when updating a volume's structure. By allowing the file system to access and update its metadata directly in the cache, the cache manager eliminates the need for buffers, simply updating the volume structure in the virtual memory provided by the memory manager. The only limitation the file system encounters is the amount of available memory.

You can examine pinning and mapping activity in the cache via the performance counters or system variables listed in Table 8-11.

Caching with the Direct Memory Access Interfaces

In addition to the mapping and pinning interfaces used to access metadata directly in the cache, the cache manager provides a third interface to cached data: *direct memory access (DMA)*. These DMA functions are used to read from or write to cache pages without intervening buffers, such as when a network file system is doing a transfer over the network.

Table 8-11 **System Variables for Examining Pinning and Mapping Activity**

Performance Counter (frequency)	System Variable (count)	Description
Cache: Data Map Hits %	(*CcMapDataWait* + *CcMapDataNoWait*) / (*CcMapDataWait* + *CcMapDataNoWait*) + (*CcMapDataWaitMiss* + *CcMapDataNoWaitMiss*)	Percentage of data maps to parts of files that were in the cache (A copy read can still generate paging I/O.)
Cache: Data Maps/Sec	*CcMapDataWait* + *CcMapDataNoWait*	Total data maps from the cache
Cache: Synch Data Maps/Sec	*CcMapDataWait*	Synchronous data maps from the cache
Cache: Async Data Maps/Sec	*CcMapDataNoWait*	Asynchronous data maps from the cache
Cache: Data Map Pins/Sec	*CcPinMappedDataCount*	Number of requests to pin mapped data
Cache: Pin Read Hits %	(*CcPinReadWait* + *CcPinReadNoWait*) / (*CcPinReadWait* + *CcPinReadNoWait*) + (*CcPinReadWaitMiss* + *CcPinReadNoWaitMiss*)	Percentage of pinned reads to parts of files that were in the cache (A copy read can still generate paging I/O.)
Cache: Pin Reads/Sec	*CcPinReadWait* + *CcPinReadNoWait*	Total pinned reads from the cache
Cache: Synch Pin Reads/Sec	*CcPinReadWait*	Synchronous pinned reads from the cache
Cache: Async Pin Reads/Sec	*CcPinReadNoWait*	Asynchronous pinned reads from the cache

The DMA interface returns to the file system the *physical* addresses of cached user data (rather than the *virtual* addresses, which the mapping and pinning interfaces return), which can then be used to transfer data directly from physical memory to a network device. Although small amounts of data (1 KB to 2 KB) can use the usual buffer-based copying interfaces, for larger transfers, the DMA interface can result in significant performance improvements for a network server processing file requests from remote systems.

To describe these references to physical memory, a *memory descriptor list* (*MDL*) is used. (MDLs are described in Chapter 5.) The four separate functions described in Table 8-12 create the cache manager's DMA interface.

Table 8-12   Functions That Create the DMA Interface

Function	Description
CcMdlRead	Returns an MDL describing the specified byte range
CcMdlReadComplete	Frees the MDL
CcMdlWrite	Returns an MDL describing a specified byte range (possibly containing zeros)
CcMdlWriteComplete	Frees the MDL and marks the range for writing

You can examine MDL activity from the cache via the performance counters or system variables listed in Table 8-13.

Table 8-13   System Variables for Examining MDL Activity from the Cache

Performance Counter (frequency)	System Variable (count)	Description
Cache: MDL Read Hits %	(*CcMdlReadWait* + *CcMdlReadNoWait*) / (*CcMdlReadWait* + *CcMdlReadNoWait*) + (*CcMdlReadWaitMiss* + *CcMdlReadNoWaitMiss*)	Percentage of MDL reads to parts of files that were in the cache (References to pages satisfied by an MDL read can still generate paging I/O.)
Cache: MDL Reads/Sec	*CcMdlReadWait* + *CcMdlReadNoWait*	Total MDL reads from the cache
Cache: Synch MDL Reads/Sec	*CcMdlReadWait*	Synchronous MDL reads from the cache
Cache: Async MDL Reads/Sec	*CcMdlReadNoWait*	Asynchronous MDL reads from the cache

Write Throttling

Windows NT must determine whether the scheduled writes will affect system performance and then schedule any delayed writes. First it asks whether a certain number of bytes can be written right now without hurting performance and blocks that write if necessary. Then it sets up callback for automatically writing the bytes when writes are again permitted. Once it is notified of an impending write operation, the cache manager determines how many dirty pages are in the cache and how much physical memory is available. If few physical pages are free, the cache manager momentarily blocks the file system thread that is requesting to write data to the cache. The cache manager's lazy writer flushes some of the dirty pages to disk and then allows the blocked file system thread to continue. This *write throttling* prevents system performance from degrading because of a lack of memory when a file system or network server issues a large write operation.

Write throttling is also useful for network redirectors transmitting data over slow communication lines. For example, suppose a local process writes a large amount of data to a remote file system over a 1200-baud line. The data isn't written to the remote disk until the cache manager's lazy writer flushes the cache. If the redirector has accumulated lots of dirty pages that are flushed to disk at once, the recipient could receive a network time-out before the data transfer completes. By using the *CcSetDirtyPageThreshold* function, the cache manager allows network redirectors to set a limit on the number of dirty cache pages they can tolerate, thus preventing this scenario. By limiting the number of dirty pages, the redirector ensures that a cache flush operation won't cause a network time-out.

Conclusion

The Windows NT cache manager provides a high-speed, intelligent mechanism for reducing disk I/O and increasing overall system throughput. By caching on the basis of virtual blocks, the Windows NT cache manager can perform intelligent read-ahead. By relying on the global memory manager's mapped file primitive to access file data, the cache manager can provide the special fast I/O mechanism to reduce the CPU time required for read and write operations and also leave all matters related to physical memory management to the single Windows NT global memory manager, thus reducing code duplication and increasing efficiency.

Windows NT File System (NTFS)

This chapter details the internal structure and operation of the Microsoft Windows NT File System (hereafter referred to as NTFS). After reviewing the NTFS design goals and major features, I'll describe the NTFS on-disk structure and explain how NTFS implements transaction-based file system recovery. Finally, I'll cover the implementation of the optional fault tolerance support.

 N O T E   Some of the exciting NTFS extensions being introduced in Windows NT 5.0 are noted throughout this chapter. For a complete list of these new extensions, see Chapter 10.

NTFS Design Goals and Features

In 1988, Microsoft already supported two file systems—the FAT file system for MS-DOS and Microsoft Windows and the high-performance file system (HPFS) for OS/2. Unfortunately, both of these file systems suffered from limitations that made them either less reliable than a file system for Windows NT should be or unable to handle the large system configurations that were expected to run the Windows NT operating system. After careful consideration, the Windows NT team decided to create a new file system—NTFS. Although the design for NTFS was new, it was influenced by FAT and HPFS as well as by certain features required by the POSIX standard.

The following section describes the requirements that drove the design of NTFS. The subsequent section examines the advanced features of NTFS.

High-End File System Requirements

MS-DOS uses the FAT file system, which was originally designed for floppy disks of a relatively small size, generally 1 MB or less. As hard disks became the standard storage device for personal computers and over time grew larger, they began to stretch the limits of the FAT file system. The OS/2 operating system introduced HPFS to address some of the limitations of the FAT file system. For example, HPFS greatly improved file access times for large directories and could be used on hard disks up to 4 GB in size. HPFS was later expanded to support disk sizes up to 2 TB (terabytes), or approximately 2 trillion bytes.

The FAT file system worked well for small disks, and HPFS added some new capabilities, greater file access efficiency, and support for larger media. However, neither file system was suitable for mission-critical applications that required recoverability, security, data redundancy and fault tolerance, and support for even larger storage media than HPFS provided.

Recoverability

As far as disk I/O is concerned, personal computer users have tended to care most about speed—above all, they've usually just wanted to get their work done fast. As Windows NT moves the personal computer into more businesses and corporations, however, the reliability of the data stored on the system becomes increasingly important relative to the speed with which a user can access data on a disk drive. In other words, if the system fails and a disk drive is corrupted or becomes inaccessible, the speed of the preceding I/O operations is largely irrelevant.

To address the requirement for reliable data storage and data access, NTFS provides file system recovery based on a transaction-processing model. *Transaction processing* is a technique for handling modifications to a database so that system failures don't affect the correctness or integrity of the database. The basic tenet of transaction processing is that some database operations, called transactions, are all-or-nothing propositions. (A *transaction* is defined as an I/O operation that alters file system data or changes the volume's directory structure.) The separate disk updates that make up the transaction must be executed *atomically*; that is, once the transaction begins to execute, all of its disk updates must be completed. If a system failure interrupts the transaction, the part that has been completed must be undone, or *rolled back*. The rollback operation returns the database to a previously known and consistent state, as if the transaction had never occurred.

NTFS uses the transaction-processing model to implement its file system recovery feature. If a program initiates an I/O operation that alters the structure of the NTFS—that is, changes the directory structure, extends a file, allocates space for a new file, and so on—NTFS treats that operation as an atomic transaction. It guarantees that the transaction is either completed or, if the system fails while executing the transaction, rolled back. The details of how NTFS does this is explained in the section "Recoverability Support" on page 426.

In addition, NTFS uses redundant storage for vital file system information so that if one location on the disk goes bad, NTFS can still access the volume's critical file system data. This redundancy of file system data contrasts with the on-disk structures of both the FAT file system and HPFS, which have single sectors containing critical file system data. If a read error occurs in one of these sectors, an entire volume is lost.

Security

Data security is crucial to customers who process private or sensitive information—banks, hospitals, and national defense–related agencies, for example. Such customers need guarantees that their data will be secure from unauthorized access.

Security in NTFS is derived directly from the Windows NT object model. (For more information on NTFS security, see Chapter 6.) An open file is implemented as a file object with a security descriptor stored on disk as a part of the file. Before a process can open a handle to any object, including a file object, the Windows NT security system verifies that the process has appropriate authorization to do so. The security descriptor, combined with the requirement that a user log on to the system and provide an identifying password, ensures that no process can access a file unless given specific permission to do so by a system administrator or by the file's owner. (For more information about security descriptors, see the section on page 310 in Chapter 6, and for more details about file objects, see the section on page 341 in Chapter 7.)

Data Redundancy and Fault Tolerance

In addition to recoverability of file system data, some customers require that their own data not be endangered by a power outage or catastrophic system failure. The NTFS recovery capabilities do ensure that the file system on a volume remains accessible, but they make no guarantees for complete recovery of user files. For applications that can't risk losing file data, data redundancy provides an extra level of protection.

The Windows NT layered driver model (explained in Chapter 7) is used to provide fault tolerant disk support. NTFS communicates with a fault tolerant disk driver, which in turn communicates with a hard disk driver to write data to disk. This communication allows a Windows NT system to establish fault tolerant disk storage by installing an additional driver. The fault tolerant driver can *mirror,* or duplicate, data from one disk onto another disk so that a redundant copy can always be retrieved. This support is commonly called *RAID level 1.* The fault tolerant driver also allows data to be written in *stripes* across three or more disks, using the equivalent of one disk to maintain parity information. If the data on one disk is lost or becomes inaccessible, the driver can reconstruct the disk's contents by means of exclusive-OR operations. This support is called *RAID level 5.*

Large Disks and Large Files

Engineering and other scientific applications often store and process extremely large quantities of information. Hard disks with over 8 GB of storage and disk arrays with 100 GB to 500 GB of storage are no longer uncommon. NTFS supports very large disks and large files more efficiently than does either the FAT file system or HPFS.

Until the introduction of Microsoft Windows 95 OSR2, the FAT file system used a table 16 bits wide to record the allocation status of a disk volume. Because a volume is divided into same-sized allocation units—called *clusters*—and each cluster must be uniquely numbered using 16 bits, FAT can support a maximum of 2^{16}, or 65,536, clusters per volume (although the FAT reserves some of this space for itself). A single FAT volume is limited to containing 65,518 files (the maximum number of available clusters), regardless of the disk size.

Windows NT 5.0 ▶ **NOTE** Windows NT 5.0 will support FAT32, the enhanced version of FAT shipped as part of Microsoft Windows 95 OEM Service Release 2 (as well as Microsoft Windows 98). FAT32 alleviates some of the restrictions of the FAT16 design by allowing smaller clusters (4 KB for drives up to 8 GB) as well as support for hard disk sizes larger than 2 GB. FAT32 also has the ability to relocate the root directory and use the backup copy of the FAT instead of the default copy. The boot record on FAT32 drives has been expanded to include a backup of critical data structures, making FAT32 partitions less susceptible to a single point of failure than are existing FAT16 volumes. Finally, the root directory on a FAT32 drive is now an ordinary cluster chain, so it can be located anywhere on the drive. For this reason, the previous limitations on the number of root directory entries no longer exist.

HPFS uses 32 bits to enumerate its allocation units, a strategy that yields 2^{32}, or over 4 billion, numbers. HPFS uses signed numbers, however, which reduces this number to 2 billion possible allocation units on an HPFS volume. Rather than clusters, HPFS allocates disk space in terms of physical sectors, each set at 512 bytes. This lack of flexibility can be a problem, particularly in Asian markets, where disk drives commonly have a hardware sector size of 1024 bytes. HPFS can't be used on such drives because disks can't allocate space in increments smaller than their hardware sector size. HPFS is also limited to a maximum file size of 4 GB.

NTFS allocates clusters and uses 64 bits to number them, which results in a possible 2^{64} (over 16,000,000,000,000,000,000, or 16 billion billion) clusters, each up to 64 KB. Each file can be 2^{64} bytes long, which should satisfy data storage requirements for some time to come. As in the FAT file system, the cluster size in NTFS is adjustable, but it is not required to grow proportionally to the disk size. NTFS uses a cluster size of 512 bytes on small disks and a maximum cluster size of 64 KB on large disks. Although NTFS uses a 64-bit (8-byte) disk address to represent each run (disk allocation), it "encodes" the addresses so that they occupy only 3 to 5 bytes per run. (Look ahead to Figure 9-17 to see an example of address encoding.) HPFS uses 12 bytes to represent each run.

Additional Features in NTFS

In addition to NTFS being recoverable, secure, reliable, and efficient for mission-critical systems, it includes the following advanced features that allow it to support a broad range of applications.

Multiple Data Streams

In NTFS, each unit of information associated with a file, including its name, its owner, its time stamps, its contents, and so on, is implemented as a file attribute (object attribute). Each attribute consists of a single *stream*, that is, a simple sequence of bytes. This generic implementation makes it easy to add more attributes (and therefore more streams) to a file. Because a file's data is "just another attribute" of the file and because new attributes can be added, NTFS files (and file directories) can contain multiple data streams.

An NTFS file has one default data stream, which has no name. An application can create additional, named data streams and access them by referring to their names. To avoid altering the Microsoft Win32 I/O APIs, which take a string as a filename argument, the name of the data stream is specified by appending a colon (:) to the filename. Because the colon is a reserved character, it can serve as a separator between the filename and the data stream name, as illustrated in this example:

```
myfile.dat:stream2
```

Each stream has a separate allocation size (how much disk space has been reserved for it), an actual size (how many bytes the caller has used), and a valid data length (how much of the stream has been initialized). In addition, each stream is given a separate file lock that is used to lock byte ranges and to allow concurrent access. To reduce processing overhead, sharing is done per file rather than per stream.

The one component in Windows NT that uses multiple data streams is the Apple Macintosh file server support that comes with Windows NT Server. Macintosh systems use two streams per file— one to store data and the other to store resource information, such as the file type and the icon used to represent the file. Because NTFS allows multiple data streams, a Macintosh user can copy an entire Macintosh folder (analogous to a directory) to a Windows NT Server, and another Macintosh user can copy the folder from the server without losing resource information. Other applications can use the multiple data stream feature as well. A backup utility, for example, might use an extra data stream to store backup-specific time stamps on files. Or an archival utility might implement hierarchical storage in which files that are older than a certain date or that haven't been accessed for a specified period of time are moved to tape. The utility could copy the file to tape, set the file's default data stream to 0, and add a data stream that specifies the name and location of the tape on which the file is stored.

Unicode-Based Names

Like Windows NT as a whole, NTFS is fully Unicode enabled, using Unicode characters to store names of files, directories, and volumes. Unicode, a 16-bit character-coding scheme, allows each character in each of the world's major languages to be uniquely represented, which aids in moving data easily from one country to another. Unicode is an improvement over traditional representation of international characters—using a double-byte coding scheme that stores some characters in 8 bits and others in 16 bits, a technique that requires loading various code pages to establish the available characters. Because Unicode has a unique representation for each character, it doesn't depend on which code page is loaded. Each directory and filename in a path name can be as many as 255 characters long and can contain Unicode characters, embedded spaces, and multiple periods.

General Indexing Facility

The NTFS architecture is structured to allow indexing of file attributes on a disk volume. This structure enables the file system to efficiently locate files that match certain criteria—for example, all the files in a particular directory. The FAT file system indexes filenames but doesn't sort them, making lookups in large directories slow. HPFS indexes and sorts filenames as NTFS does, but the design of NTFS allows for indexing other file attributes as well.

 NOTE In Windows NT 5.0, NTFS is being extended to index other attributes, such as object IDs (enterprise-wide unique identifiers for files). For more information on the additional indexing capabilities planned for the NTFS in Windows NT 5.0, see Chapter 10.

Dynamic Bad-Cluster Remapping

Ordinarily, if a program tries to read data from a bad-disk sector, the read operation fails and the data in the allocated cluster becomes inaccessible. If the disk is formatted as a fault tolerant NTFS volume, however, the Windows NT fault tolerant driver dynamically retrieves a good copy of the data that was stored on the bad sector and then sends NTFS a warning that the sector is bad. NTFS allocates a new cluster, replacing the cluster in which the bad sector resides, and copies the data to the new cluster. It flags the bad cluster and no longer uses it. This data recovery and dynamic bad-cluster remapping is an especially useful feature for file servers and fault tolerant systems or for any application that can't afford to lose data. If the fault tolerant driver isn't loaded when a sector goes bad, NTFS still replaces the cluster and doesn't reuse it, but it can't recover the data that was on the bad sector.

POSIX Support

As explained in Chapter 1, one of the mandates for Windows NT was to fully support the POSIX.1 standard. In the file system area, the POSIX standard requires support for case-sensitive file and directory names, a "file-change-time" time stamp (which is different than the MS-DOS "time-last-modified" stamp), and hard links (multiple directory entries that point to the same file). NTFS implements each of these features.

EXPERIMENT: Creating a Hard Link

To create a hard link, use the ln utility in the Windows NT Resource Kit. For example, type the following lines of code:

```
C:\>cd \ntreskit\posix
C:\NTRESKIT\POSIX>dir ln.exe
 Volume in drive C has no label.
 Volume Serial Number is 28BC-F247
 Directory of C:\NTRESKIT\POSIX
03/01/98  12:00a              90,960 LN.EXE
               1 File(s)      90,960 bytes
                         317,863,936 bytes free

C:\NTRESKIT\POSIX>ln ln.exe foo.exe
ln: ln.exe: No such file or directory

C:\NTRESKIT\POSIX>ln LN.EXE foo.exe
```

The second to last command failed because the POSIX subsystem processes filenames as case-sensitive (Win32 does not). So in the last command, referencing LN.EXE (uppercase letters) worked and created the hard link—a directory entry called "foo.exe" was created to point to the same file that LN.EXE points to. If you delete LN.EXE, the file remains because there is still a link to it (foo.exe). When the last link to a file is deleted, the space for the file itself is released.

NTFS Internal Structure

As described in Chapter 7, in the framework of the Windows NT I/O system, NTFS and other file systems are loadable device drivers that run in kernel mode. They are invoked indirectly by applications that use Win32 or other I/O APIs (such as POSIX). As Figure 9-1 shows, the Windows NT environment subsystems call Windows NT system services, which in turn locate the appropriate loaded drivers and call them. (For a description of system service dispatching, see page 99 in Chapter 3.)

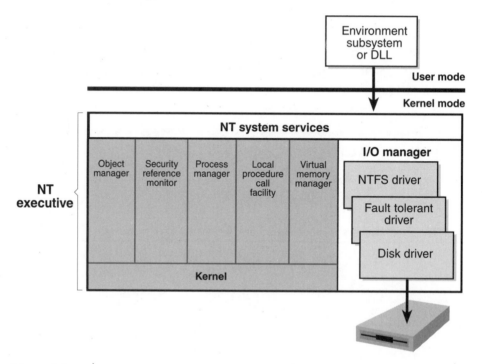

Figure 9-1
Components of the Windows NT I/O system

The layered drivers pass I/O requests to one another by calling the Windows NT executive's I/O manager. Relying on the I/O manager as an intermediary allows each driver to maintain independence so that it can be loaded or unloaded without affecting other drivers. In addition, the NTFS driver interacts with the three other NT executive components, shown in the left side of Figure 9-2, that are closely related to file systems.

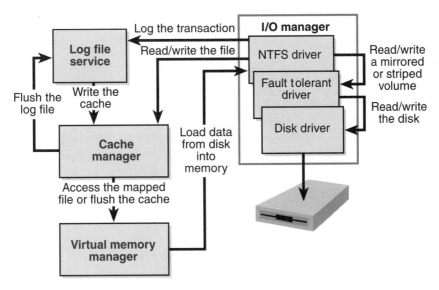

Figure 9-2
NTFS and related components

The *log file service* (*LFS*) is the part of NTFS that provides services for maintaining a log of disk writes. The log file it writes is used to recover an NTFS-formatted volume in the case of a system failure.

The *cache manager* is the component of the Windows NT executive that provides systemwide caching services for NTFS and other file system drivers, including network file system drivers (servers and redirectors). All file systems implemented for Windows NT access cached files by mapping them into virtual memory and then accessing the virtual memory. The cache manager provides a specialized file system interface to the Windows NT *virtual memory manager* for this purpose. When a program tries to access a part of a file that is not loaded into the cache (a *cache miss*), the memory manager calls NTFS to access the disk driver and obtain the file contents from disk. The cache manager optimizes disk I/O by using its *lazy writer,* a set of system threads that call the memory manager to flush cache contents to disk as a background activity (asynchronous disk writing). (For a complete description of the cache manager, see Chapter 8.)

NTFS participates in the Windows NT object model by implementing files as objects. This implementation allows files to be shared and protected by the object manager, the component of Windows NT that manages all executive-level objects. (The object manager is described on page 101 in Chapter 3.)

An application creates or accesses a file just as it does other Windows NT objects: by means of object handles. By the time an I/O request reaches NTFS, the Windows NT object manager and security system have already verified that the calling process has the authority to access the file object in the way it is attempting to. The security system has compared the caller's access token to the entries in the access control list for the file object. (See Chapter 6 for more information about access control lists.) The I/O manager has also transformed the file handle into a pointer to a file object. NTFS uses the information in the file object to access the file on disk.

Figure 9-3 shows the data structures that link a file handle to the file system's on-disk structure.

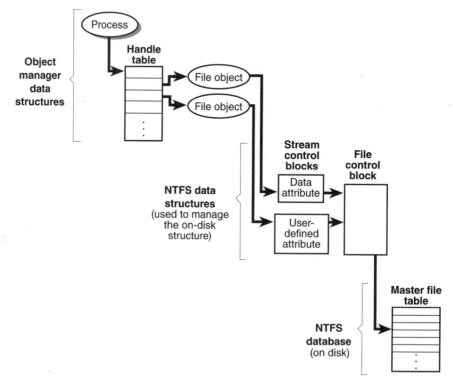

Figure 9-3
NTFS data structures

By the time the I/O system calls NTFS, the handle has been translated to a pointer to a file object. NTFS then follows several pointers to get from the file object to the location of the file on disk. As Figure 9-3 shows, a file object, which represents a single call to the open-file system service, points to a *stream control block* (*SCB*) for the file attribute that the caller is trying to read or write. In Figure 9-3, a process has opened both the data attribute and a user-defined attribute for the file. The SCBs represent individual file attributes and contain information about how to find specific attributes within a file. All the SCBs for a file point to a common data structure called a *file control block* (*FCB*). The FCB contains a pointer (actually, a file reference, explained in the section "File Reference Numbers" later in this chapter) to the file's record in the disk-based master file table (or MFT), which is described in detail in the following section.

NTFS On-Disk Structure

This section describes the on-disk structure of an NTFS volume, including how disk space is divided and organized into clusters, how files are organized into directories, how the actual file data and attribute information is stored on disk, and finally, how NTFS data compression works.

Volumes

The structure of NTFS begins with a volume. A *volume* corresponds to a logical partition on a disk, and it is created when you format a disk or part of a disk for NTFS. You can also create a fault tolerant volume that spans multiple disks by using the Windows NT Disk Administrator utility.

A disk can have one volume or several. NTFS handles each volume independently of the others. Three sample disk configurations for a 150-MB hard disk are illustrated in Figure 9-4.

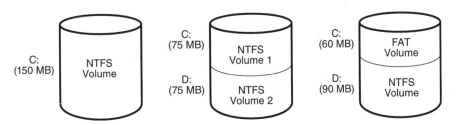

Figure 9-4
Sample disk configurations

A volume consists of a series of files plus any additional unallocated space remaining on the disk partition. In the FAT file system, a volume also contains areas specially formatted for use by the file system. An NTFS volume, however, stores all file system data, such as bitmaps and directories, and even the system bootstrap, as ordinary files.

Clusters

NTFS is like the FAT file system in that it uses the cluster as its fundamental unit of disk allocation. The cluster size on a volume, or the *cluster factor,* is established when a user formats the volume with either the Format command or the Disk Administrator utility. The cluster factor varies with the size of the volume, but it is an integral number of physical sectors, always a power of 2 (1 sector, 2 sectors, 4 sectors, 8 sectors, and so on), as shown in Figure 9-5. The cluster factor is expressed as the number of bytes in the cluster, such as 512 bytes, 1 KB, or 2 KB.

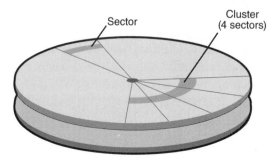

Figure 9-5
Sectors and a cluster on a disk

Internally, NTFS refers only to clusters and is unaware of a disk's sector size. NTFS uses the cluster as its unit of allocation in order to maintain its independence from physical sector sizes. This independence allows NTFS to efficiently support very large disks by using a larger cluster size or to support nonstandard disks that have a sector size other than 512 bytes. On a larger volume, use of a larger cluster size can reduce fragmentation and speed allocation, at a small cost in terms of wasted disk space. The Format command (available from the Windows NT command prompt) as well as the Format command on the Tools menu in Disk Administrator choose a default cluster size based on the volume size, but you can override this size.

> **NOTE** The default cluster size for small disks (up to 512 MB) is 512 bytes (or the hardware sector size if it is larger than 512 bytes). For disks up to 1 GB, the default cluster size is 1 KB. For disks between 1 GB and 2 GB, the default cluster size is 2 KB. For disks larger than 2 GB, the default cluster size is 4 KB. This default balances the inherent trade-off between the disk fragmentation that can occur with too small a cluster size and the wasted space (internal fragmentation) that can occur with too large a cluster size.

NTFS refers to physical locations on a disk by means of *logical cluster numbers* (*LCNs*). LCNs are simply the numbering of all clusters from the beginning of the volume to the end. To convert an LCN to a physical disk address, NTFS multiplies the LCN by the cluster factor to get the physical byte offset on the volume, as the disk driver interface requires. NTFS refers to the data within a file by means of *virtual cluster numbers* (*VCNs*). VCNs number the clusters belonging to a particular file from 0 through m. VCNs are not necessarily physically contiguous, however; they can be mapped to any number of LCNs on the volume.

Master File Table (MFT)

In NTFS, all data stored on a volume is contained in a file, including the data structures used to locate and retrieve files, the bootstrap data, and the bitmap that records the allocation state of the entire volume (the NTFS metadata). Storing everything in files allows the file system to easily locate and maintain the data, and each separate file can be protected by a security descriptor. In addition, if a particular part of the disk goes bad, NTFS can relocate the metadata files to prevent the disk from becoming inaccessible.

The *master file table* (MFT) is the heart of the NTFS volume structure. The MFT is implemented as an array of file records. The size of each file record is fixed at 1 KB, regardless of cluster size. (The structure of a file record is described in the "File Records" section on page 410.) Logically, the MFT contains one row for each file on the volume, including a row for the MFT itself. In addition to the MFT, each NTFS volume includes a set of *metadata files* containing the information that is used to implement the file system structure. Each of these NTFS metadata files has a name that begins with a dollar sign ($), although the signs are hidden. For example, the filename of the MFT is $MFT. The rest of the files on an NTFS volume are normal user files and directories, as shown in Figure 9-6 on the following page.

Usually, each MFT record corresponds to a different file. If a file has a large number of attributes or becomes highly fragmented, however, more than one file record might be needed. In such cases, the first record, which stores the locations of the others, is called the *base file record*.

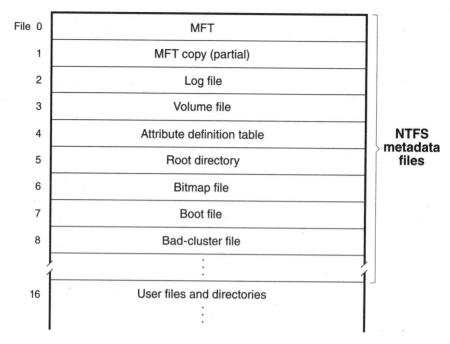

File 0	MFT	
1	MFT copy (partial)	
2	Log file	
3	Volume file	
4	Attribute definition table	NTFS metadata files
5	Root directory	
6	Bitmap file	
7	Boot file	
8	Bad-cluster file	
16	User files and directories	

Figure 9-6
File records for NTFS metadata files in the MFT

When it first accesses a volume, NTFS must *mount* it—that is, prepare it for use. To mount the volume, NTFS looks in the boot file (defined on page 409) to find the physical disk address of the MFT. The MFT's own file record is the first entry in the table; the second file record points to a file located in the middle of the disk called the *MFT mirror* (filename $MFTMirr) that contains a copy of the first few rows of the MFT. This partial copy of the MFT is used to locate metadata files if part of the MFT file can't be read for some reason.

Once NTFS finds the file record for the MFT, it obtains the VCN-to-LCN mapping information in the file record's data attribute, decompresses it, and stores it in memory. This mapping information tells NTFS where the runs composing the MFT are located on the disk. NTFS then decompresses the MFT records for several more metadata files and opens the files. Next, NTFS performs its file system recovery operation (described in the section "Recovery" on page 436), and finally, it opens its remaining metadata files. The volume is now ready for user access.

As the system runs, NTFS writes to another important metadata file, the *log file* (filename $LogFile). NTFS uses the log file to record all operations that affect the NTFS volume structure, including file creation or any commands, such as Copy, that alter the directory structure. The log file is used to recover an NTFS volume after a system failure.

Another entry in the MFT is reserved for the root directory (also known as "\"). Its file record contains an index of the files and directories stored in the root of the NTFS directory structure. When NTFS is first asked to open a file, it begins its search for the file in the root directory's file record. After opening a file, NTFS stores the file's MFT file reference so that it can directly access the file's MFT record when it reads and writes the file later.

NTFS records the allocation state of the volume in the *bitmap file* (filename $Bitmap). The data attribute for the bitmap file contains a bitmap, each of whose bits represents a cluster on the volume, identifying whether the cluster is free or has been allocated to a file.

Another important system file, the *boot file* (filename $Boot), stores the Windows NT bootstrap code. For the system to boot, the bootstrap code must be located at a specific disk address. During formatting, however, the Format utility defines this area as a file by creating a file record for it. Creating the boot file allows NTFS to adhere to its rule of making everything on the disk a file. The boot file as well as NTFS metadata files can be individually protected by means of the security descriptors that are applied to all Windows NT objects. Using this "everything on the disk is a file" model also means that the bootstrap can be modified by normal file I/O, although the boot file is currently protected from editing.

EXPERIMENT: Viewing NTFS Metadata Files

Since the NTFS metadata files are regular NTFS files, they can be seen with the directory command if you use the /a:h (hidden) qualifier and type the correct name of the file, as shown here:

```
C:\>dir/a:h $mft
 Volume in drive C has no label.
 Volume Serial Number is 28BC-F247

 Directory of C:\

03/06/97  06:11p             1,035,264 $MFT
```

NTFS also maintains a *bad-cluster file* (filename $BadClus) for recording any bad spots on the disk volume and a file known as the *volume file* (filename $Volume), which contains the volume name, the version of NTFS for which the volume is formatted, and a bit that when set signifies that a disk corruption has occurred and must be repaired by the Chkdsk utility. (The Chkdsk utility is covered in more detail later in the chapter.) Finally, NTFS maintains a file containing an *attribute definition table* (filename $AttrDef) that defines the attribute types supported on the volume and indicates whether they can be indexed, recovered during a system recovery operation, and so on.

File Reference Numbers

A file on an NTFS volume is identified by a 64-bit value called a *file reference*. The file reference consists of a file number and a sequence number. The file number corresponds to the position of the file's file record in the MFT minus 1 (or to the position of the base file record minus 1 if the file has more than 1 file record). The file reference sequence number, which is incremented each time an MFT file record position is reused, enables NTFS to perform internal consistency checks. A file reference is illustrated in Figure 9-7.

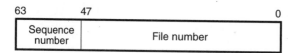

Figure 9-7
File reference

Files Records

Instead of viewing a file as just a repository for textual or binary data, NTFS stores files as a collection of attribute/value pairs, one of which is the data it contains (called the *unnamed data attribute*). Other attributes that comprise a file include the filename, time stamp information, security descriptor, and possibly additional named data attributes. Figure 9-8 illustrates an MFT record for a small file.

Each file attribute is stored as a separate stream of bytes within a file. Strictly speaking, NTFS doesn't read and write files—it reads and writes attribute streams. NTFS supplies these attribute operations: create, delete, read (byte range), and write (byte range). The read and write services normally operate on the file's unnamed data attribute. However, a caller can specify a different data attribute by using the named data stream syntax.

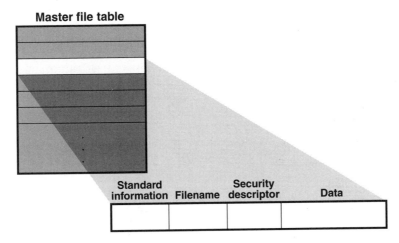

Figure 9-8
MFT record for a small file

Table 9-1 lists the standard attributes for files on an NTFS volume. (Not all attributes are present for every file.)

Table 9-1   Standard Attributes for NTFS Files

Attribute	Description
Standard information	File attributes such as read-only, archive, and so on; time stamps, including when the file was created or last modified; and how many directories point to the file (its *hard link count*).
Filename	The file's name in Unicode characters. A file can have multiple filename attributes, as it does when a POSIX hard link to a file exists or when a file with a long name has an automatically generated "short name" for access by MS-DOS and 16-bit Microsoft Windows applications.
Security descriptor	The security data structure that protects the file from unauthorized access. The security descriptor attribute specifies who owns the file and who can access it.

(continued)

Table 9-1 *continued*

Attribute	Description
Data	The contents of the file. In NTFS, a file has one default unnamed data attribute and can have additional named data attributes; that is, a file can have multiple data streams. A directory has no default data attribute but can have optional named data attributes.
Index root, index	Three attributes used to implement filename allocation, bitmap indexes for large directories (directories only).
Attribute list	A list of the attributes that make up the file and the file reference of the MFT file record in which each attribute is located. This seldom-used attribute is present when a file requires more than one MFT file record.

Windows NT 5.0 ▶ **NOTE**   To save disk space, security descriptors in Windows NT 5.0 are stored in a central file and referenced by each file record.

Each attribute in a file record has a name (optional) and a value. NTFS identifies an attribute by its name in uppercase letters preceded by a dollar sign ($), such as $FILENAME or $DATA. An attribute's value is the byte stream composing the attribute. For example, the value of the $FILENAME attribute is the file's name; the value of the $DATA attribute is whatever bytes the user stored in the file. These attribute names, however, actually correspond to numeric type codes, which NTFS uses to order the attributes within a file record. The file attributes in an MFT record are ordered by these type codes (numerically in ascending order), with some attribute types appearing more than once—if a file has multiple data attributes, for example, or multiple filenames.

Filenames

Both NTFS and FAT allow each filename in a path to be as many as 255 characters long. Filenames can contain Unicode characters as well as multiple periods and embedded spaces. However, the FAT file system supplied with MS-DOS is limited to 8 (non-Unicode) characters for its filenames, followed by a period and a 3-character extension. Figure 9-9 provides a visual representation of the different *file namespaces* Windows NT supports and shows how they intersect.

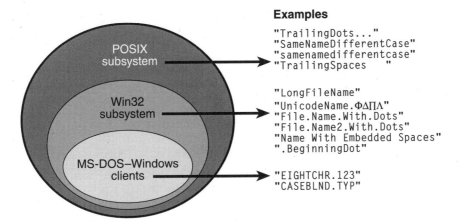

Examples

```
"TrailingDots..."
"SameNameDifferentCase"
"samenamedifferentcase"
"TrailingSpaces    "

"LongFileName"
"UnicodeName.ΦΔΠΛ"
"File.Name.With.Dots"
"File.Name2.With.Dots"
"Name With Embedded Spaces"
".BeginningDot"

"EIGHTCHR.123"
"CASEBLND.TYP"
```

Figure 9-9
Windows NT file namespaces

The POSIX subsystem requires the biggest namespace of all the application execution environments that Windows NT supports, and therefore the NTFS namespace is equivalent to the POSIX namespace. The POSIX subsystem can create names that are not visible to Win32 and MS-DOS applications, including names with trailing periods and trailing spaces. Ordinarily, creating a file using the large POSIX namespace is not a problem because you would do that only if you intended that file to be used by the POSIX subsystem or by POSIX client systems.

The relationship between 32-bit Windows (Win32) applications and MS-DOS–Windows applications is a much closer one, however. The Win32 area in Figure 9-9 represents filenames that the Win32 subsystem can create on an NTFS volume but that MS-DOS and 16-bit Windows applications can't see. This group includes filenames longer than the 8.3 format of MS-DOS names, those containing Unicode (international) characters, those with multiple period characters or a beginning period, and those with embedded spaces. When a file is created with such a name, NTFS automatically generates an alternate, MS-DOS-style filename for the file. Windows NT displays these short names when you use the */x* option with the Dir command.

The MS-DOS filenames are fully functional aliases for the NTFS files and are stored in the same directory as the long filenames. The MFT record for a file with an autogenerated MS-DOS filename is shown in Figure 9-10.

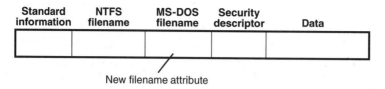

New filename attribute

Figure 9-10
MFT file record with an MS-DOS filename attribute

The NTFS name and the generated MS-DOS name are stored in the same file record and therefore refer to the same file. The MS-DOS name can be used to open, read from, write to, or copy the file. If a user renames the file using either the long filename or the short filename, the new name replaces both of the existing names. If the new name is not a valid MS-DOS name, NTFS generates another MS-DOS name for the file.

> **NOTE** POSIX hard links are implemented in a similar way. When a hard link to a POSIX file is created, NTFS adds another filename attribute to the file's MFT file record. The two situations differ in one regard, however. When a user deletes a POSIX file that has multiple names (hard links), the file record and the file remain in place. The file and its record are deleted only when the last filename (hard link) is deleted. If a file has both an NTFS name and an autogenerated MS-DOS name, however, a user can delete the file using either name.

Here's the algorithm NTFS currently uses to generate an MS-DOS name from a long filename:

1. Remove from the long name any characters that are illegal in MS-DOS names, including spaces and Unicode characters. Remove preceding and trailing periods. Remove all other embedded periods, except the last one.

2. Truncate the string before the period (if present) to six characters, and append the string "~1". Truncate the string after the period (if present) to three characters.

3. Put the result in uppercase letters. MS-DOS is case-insensitive, and this step guarantees that NTFS won't generate a new name that differs from the old only in case.

4. If the generated name duplicates an existing name in the directory, increment the "~1" string.

Table 9-2 shows the long Win32 filenames from Figure 9-9 and their NTFS-generated MS-DOS versions. The current algorithm and the examples in Figure 9-9 on page 413 should give you an idea of what NTFS-generated MS-DOS-style filenames look like. Application developers shouldn't depend on this algorithm, though, because it might change in the future.

Table 9-2   NTFS-Generated Filenames

Win32 Long Name	NTFS-Generated Short Name
LongFileName	LONGFI~1
UnicodeName.ΦΔΠΛ	UNICOD~1
File.Name.With.Dots	FILENA~1.DOT
File.Name2.With.Dots	FILENA~2.DOT
Name With Embedded Spaces	NAMEWI~1
.BeginningDot	BEGINN~1

Resident and Nonresident Attributes

If a file is small, all its attributes and their values (its data, for example) fit in the file record. When the value of an attribute is stored directly in the MFT, the attribute is called a *resident attribute*. (In Figure 9-8, for example, all attributes are resident.)

Each attribute begins with a standard header containing information about the attribute, information that NTFS uses to manage the attributes in a generic way. The header, which is always resident, records whether the attribute's value is resident or nonresident. For resident attributes, the header also contains the offset from the header to the attribute's value and the length of the attribute's value, as Figure 9-11 on the following page illustrates for the filename attribute.

When an attribute's value is stored directly in the MFT, the time it takes NTFS to access the value is greatly reduced. Instead of looking up a file in a table and then reading a succession of allocation units to find the file's data (as the FAT file system does, for example), NTFS accesses the disk once and retrieves the data immediately.

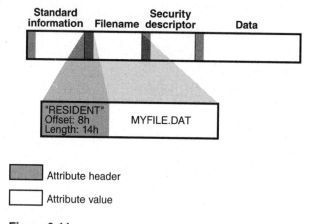

Figure 9-11
Resident attribute header and value

The attributes for a small directory, as well as for a small file, can be resident in the MFT, as Figure 9-12 shows. For a small directory, the index root attribute contains an index of file references for the files and the subdirectories in the directory.

Standard information	Filename	Security descriptor	Index root	
			Index of files	Empty
			file1, file2, file3, . . .	

Figure 9-12
MFT file record for a small directory

Of course, many files and directories can't be squeezed into the 1-KB fixed-size MFT record. If a particular attribute, such as a file's data attribute, is too large to be contained in the MFT file record, NTFS allocates a 2-KB area on the disk (4 KB for volumes with a 4 KB or larger cluster size), separate from the MFT. This area, called a *run* (or an *extent*), stores the value of the attribute (the file's data, for example). If the attribute's value later grows (if a user appends data to the file, for instance), NTFS allocates another run for the additional data. Attributes whose values are stored in runs rather than in the MFT are called *nonresident attributes*. The file system decides whether a particular attribute is resident or nonresident; the location of the data is transparent to the process accessing it.

When an attribute is nonresident, as the data attribute for a large file might be, its header contains the information NTFS needs to locate the attribute's value on the disk. Figure 9-13 shows a nonresident data attribute stored in two runs.

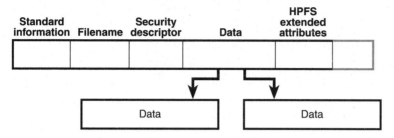

Figure 9-13
MFT file record for a large file with two data runs

Among the standard attributes, only those that can grow can be nonresident. For files, the attributes that can grow are the security descriptor, the data, and the attribute list (not shown in Figure 9-13). The standard information and filename attributes are always resident.

A large directory can also have nonresident attributes (or parts of attributes), as Figure 9-14 shows. In this example, the MFT file record doesn't have enough room to store the index of files that make up this large directory. A part of the index is stored in the index root attribute, and the rest of the index is stored in nonresident runs called *index buffers.* The index root, index allocation, and bitmap attributes are shown here in a simplified form. They are described in more detail in the next section. The standard information and filename attributes are always resident. The header and at least part of the value of the index root attribute are also resident for directories.

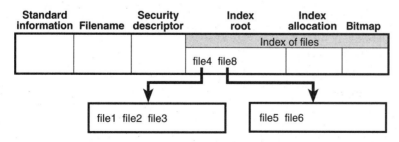

Figure 9-14
MFT file record for a large directory with a nonresident filename index

417

When a file's (or a directory's) attributes can't fit in an MFT file record and separate allocations are needed, NTFS keeps track of the runs by means of VCNs. LCNs represent the sequence of clusters on an entire volume from 0 through *n*. VCNs number the clusters belonging to a particular file from 0 through *m*. For example, the clusters in the runs of a nonresident data attribute are numbered as shown in Figure 9-15.

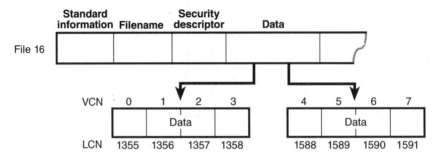

Figure 9-15
VCNs for a nonresident data attribute

If this file had more than two runs, the numbering of the third run would start with VCN 8. As Figure 9-16 shows, the data attribute header contains VCN-to-LCN mappings for the two runs here, which allows NTFS to easily find the allocations on the disk.

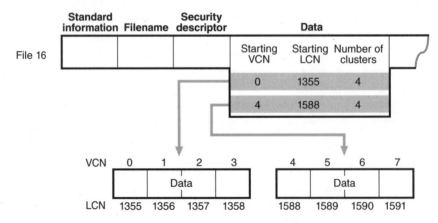

Figure 9-16
VCN-to-LCN mappings for a nonresident data attribute

Although Figure 9-16 shows just data runs, other attributes can be stored in runs if there isn't enough room in the MFT file record to contain them. And if a particular file has too many attributes to fit in the MFT record, a second MFT record is used to contain the additional attributes (or attribute headers for nonresident attributes). In this case, an attribute called the *attribute list* is added. The attribute list attribute contains the name and type code of each of the file's attributes and the file reference of the MFT record where the attribute is located. The attribute list attribute is provided for those cases in which a file grows so large or so fragmented that a single MFT record can't contain the multitude of VCN-to-LCN mappings needed to find all of its runs. NTFS needs this attribute so rarely that special dysfunctional programs had to be written to test the NTFS code that implements attribute lists.

 NOTE With Windows NT 5.0, NTFS will support efficient allocation of sparse files, that is, files that might contain large amounts of unused (either zero or undefined) space.

Filename Indexing

In NTFS, a file directory is simply an index of filenames—that is, a collection of filenames (along with their file references) organized in a particular way for quick access. To create a directory, NTFS indexes the filename attributes of the files in the directory. The MFT record for the root directory of a volume is shown in Figure 9-17.

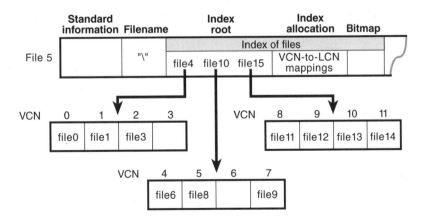

Figure 9-17
Filename index for a volume's root directory

Conceptually, an MFT entry for a directory contains in its index root attribute a sorted list of the files in the directory. For large directories, however, the filenames are actually stored in 4-KB fixed-size index buffers that contain and organize the filenames. Index buffers implement a *b+ tree* data structure, which minimizes the number of disk accesses needed to find a particular file, especially for large directories. The index root attribute contains the first level of the b+ tree (root subdirectories) and points to index buffers containing the next level (more subdirectories, perhaps, or files). The index allocation attribute maps the VCNs of the index buffer runs to the LCNs that indicate where the index buffers reside on the disk.

Figure 9-17 on the preceding page shows only filenames in the index root attribute and the index buffers (*file6*, for example), but each entry in an index also contains the file reference in the MFT where the file is described and time stamp and file size information for the file. NTFS duplicates the time stamp and file size information from the file's MFT record. This technique, which is used by FAT and NTFS, requires updated information to be written in two places. Even so, it's a significant speed optimization for directory browsing because it enables the file system to display each file's time stamps and size without opening every file in the directory.

The index allocation attribute contains the VCN-to-LCN mappings for the index buffers, and the bitmap attribute keeps track of which VCNs in the index buffers are in use and which are free. Figure 9-17 shows one file entry per VCN (that is, per cluster), but filename entries are actually packed into each cluster. Each 4-KB index buffer can contain about 20 to 30 filename entries.

The b+ tree data structure is a type of balanced tree that is ideal for organizing sorted data stored on a disk because it minimizes the number of disk accesses needed to find an entry. In the MFT, a directory's index root attribute contains several filenames that act as indexes into the second level of the b+ tree. Each filename in the index root attribute has an optional pointer associated with it that points to an index buffer. The index buffer it points to contains filenames with lexicographic values less than its own. In Figure 9-17, for example, *file4* is a first-level entry in the b+ tree. It points to an index buffer containing filenames that are (lexicographically) less than itself—the filenames *file0, file1,* and *file3*.

Storing the filenames in b+ trees provides several benefits. Directory lookups are fast because the filenames are stored in a sorted order. And when higher-level software enumerates the files in a directory, NTFS returns already-sorted names. Finally, because b+ trees tend to grow wide rather than deep, NTFS's fast lookup times don't degrade as directories get large.

NTFS currently indexes only the filename attribute, but as noted earlier, NTFS in Windows NT 5.0 will index other file attributes.

Data Compression

NTFS supports compression on a per-file, per-directory, or per-volume basis. (Currently, NTFS compression is performed only on user data, not file system metadata.) You can tell if a volume is compressed by using the Win32 *GetVolume-Information* function. To retrieve the actual compressed size of a file, use the Win32 *GetCompressedFileSize* function. Finally, to examine or change the compression setting for a file or directory, use the Win32 *DeviceIoControl* function. (See the FSCTL_GET_COMPRESSION and FSCTL_SET_COMPRESSION I/O function codes.) Keep in mind that although setting a file's compression state compresses (or decompresses) the file right away, setting a directory's compression state doesn't cause any immediate compression or decompression. Instead, setting a directory's compression state sets a default compression state that will be given to all newly created files and subdirectories.

The following section introduces NTFS compression by examining the simple case of compressing sparse files. The subsequent section extends the discussion to the compression of ordinary files.

Compressing a Sparse File

Sparse files are files, often large, that contain only a small amount of nonzero data relative to their size. A sparse matrix stored on disk is one example of a sparse file.

NOTE In this section, sparse files do not refer to the upcoming Windows NT 5.0 enhancement to eliminate allocation of unused or empty space in sparse files.

NTFS uses VCNs, from 0 through *m*, to enumerate the clusters of a file. Each VCN maps to a corresponding LCN, which identifies the disk location of the cluster. Figure 9-18 illustrates the runs (disk allocations) of a normal, noncompressed file, including its VCNs and the LCNs they map to.

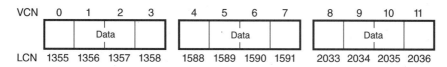

Figure 9-18
Runs of a noncompressed file

This file is stored in 3 runs, each of which is 4 clusters long, for a total of 12 clusters. Figure 9-19 shows the MFT record for this file. To save space, the MFT record's data attribute, which contains VCN-to-LCN mappings, records only one mapping for each run, rather than one for each cluster. Notice, however, that each VCN from 0 through 11 has a corresponding LCN associated with it. The first entry starts at VCN 0 and covers 4 clusters, the second entry starts at VCN 4 and covers 4 clusters, and so on. This entry format is typical for a noncompressed file.

Standard information	Filename	Security descriptor	Data		
			Starting VCN	Starting LCN	Number of clusters
			0	1355	4
			4	1588	4
			8	2033	4

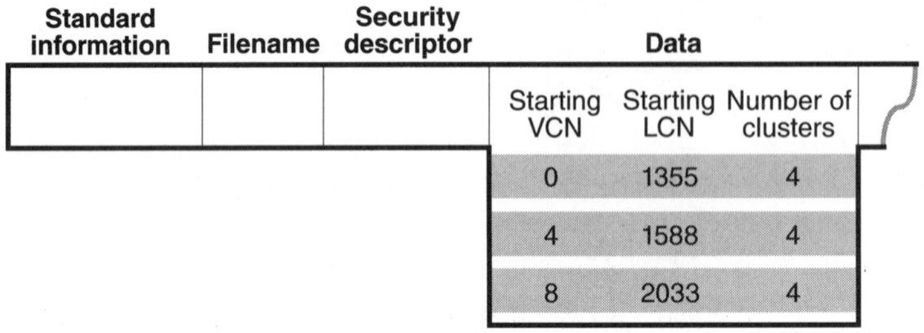

Figure 9-19
MFT record for a noncompressed file

When a user selects a file on an NTFS volume for compression, one NTFS compression technique is to remove long strings of zeros from the file. If the file is sparse, it typically shrinks to occupy a fraction of the disk space it would otherwise require. On subsequent writes to the file, NTFS allocates space only for runs that contain nonzero data.

Figure 9-20 depicts the runs of a compressed sparse file. Notice that certain ranges of the file's VCNs (16–31 and 64–127) have no disk allocations.

The MFT record for this sparse file omits blocks of VCNs that contain zeros and therefore have no physical storage allocated to them. The first data entry in Figure 9-21, for example, starts at VCN 0 and covers 16 clusters. The second entry jumps to VCN 32 and covers 16 clusters.

When a program reads data from a compressed file, NTFS checks the MFT record to determine whether a VCN-to-LCN mapping covers the location being read. If the program is reading from an unallocated "hole" in the file, it means that the data in that part of the file consists of zeros, so NTFS returns zeros without accessing the disk. If a program writes nonzero data to a "hole," NTFS quietly allocates disk space and then writes the data. This technique is very efficient for sparse files that contain a lot of zero data.

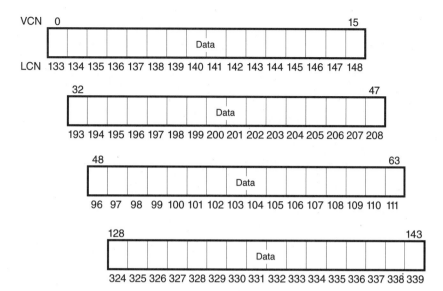

Figure 9-20
Runs of a compressed sparse file

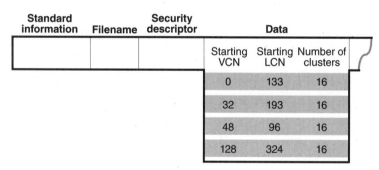

Figure 9-21
MFT record for a compressed sparse file

Compressing Nonsparse Data

The preceding example of compressing a sparse file is somewhat contrived. It describes "compression" for a case in which whole sections of a file were filled with zeros but the remaining data in the file wasn't affected by the compression. The data in most files is not sparse, but it can still be compressed by the application of a compression algorithm.

In NTFS, users can specify compression for individual files or for all the files in a directory. When it compresses a file, NTFS divides the file's unprocessed data into *compression units* 16 clusters long (equal to 8 KB for a 512-byte cluster). Certain sequences of data in a file might not compress much, if at all; so for each compression unit in the file, NTFS determines whether compressing the unit will save at least 1 cluster of storage. If compressing the unit won't free up at least 1 cluster, NTFS allocates a 16-cluster run and writes the data in that unit to disk without compressing it. If the data in a 16-cluster unit will compress to 15 or fewer clusters, NTFS allocates only the number of clusters needed to contain the compressed data and then writes it to disk. Figure 9-22 illustrates the compression of a file with four runs. The unshaded areas in this figure represent the actual storage locations that the file occupies after compression. The first, second, and fourth runs were compressed; the third run was not. Even with one noncompressed run, compressing this file saved 26 clusters of disk space, or 41 percent.

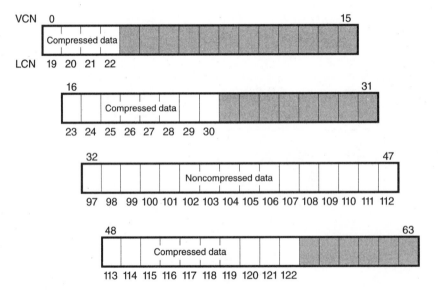

Figure 9-22
Data runs of a compressed file

NOTE Although the diagrams in this chapter show contiguous LCNs, a compression unit need not be stored in physically contiguous clusters. Runs that occupy noncontiguous clusters produce slightly more complicated MFT records than the one shown in Figure 9-23.

When it writes data to a compressed file, NTFS ensures that each run begins on a virtual 16-cluster boundary. Thus the starting VCN of each run is a multiple of 16, and the runs are no longer than 16 clusters. NTFS reads and writes at least one compression unit at a time when it accesses compressed files. When it writes compressed data, however, NTFS tries to store compression units in physically contiguous locations so that it can read them all in a single I/O operation. The 16-cluster size of the NTFS compression unit was chosen to reduce internal fragmentation: the larger the compression unit, the less the overall disk space needed to store the data. This 16-cluster compression unit size represents a trade-off between producing smaller compressed files and slowing read operations for programs that randomly access files. The equivalent of 16 clusters must be decompressed for each cache miss. (A cache miss is more likely to occur during random file access.) Figure 9-23 shows the MFT record for the compressed file shown in Figure 9-22.

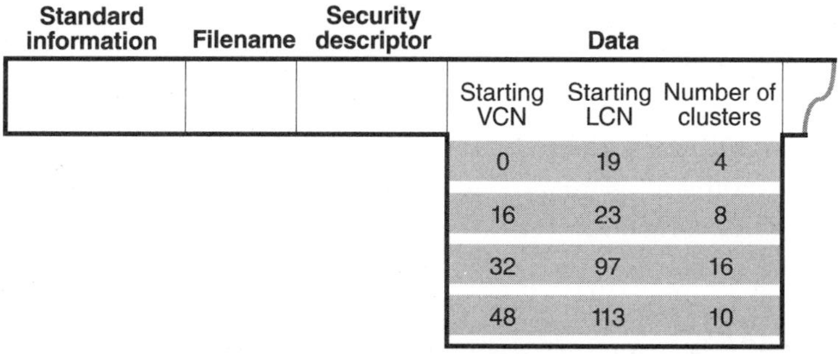

Standard information	Filename	Security descriptor	Data		
			Starting VCN	Starting LCN	Number of clusters
			0	19	4
			16	23	8
			32	97	16
			48	113	10

Figure 9-23
MFT record for a compressed file

One difference between this compressed file and the earlier example of a compressed sparse file is that three of the compressed runs in this file are less than 16 clusters long. Reading this information from a file's MFT file record enables NTFS to know whether data in the file is compressed. Any run shorter than 16 clusters contains compressed data that NTFS must decompress when it first reads the data into the cache. A run that is exactly 16 clusters long doesn't contain compressed data and therefore requires no decompression.

If the data in a run has been compressed, NTFS decompresses the data into a scratch buffer and then copies it to the caller's buffer. NTFS also loads the decompressed data into the cache, which makes subsequent reads from the same run as fast as any other cached read. NTFS writes any updates to the file in the cache, leaving the lazy writer to compress and write the modified data to disk asynchronously. This strategy ensures that writing to a compressed file produces no more significant delay than writing to a noncompressed file would.

NTFS keeps disk allocations for a compressed file contiguous whenever possible. As the LCNs indicate, the first two runs of the compressed file shown in Figure 9-22 on page 424 are physically contiguous, as are the last two. When two or more runs are contiguous, NTFS performs disk read-ahead, as it does with the data in other files. Because the reading and decompression of contiguous file data take place asynchronously before the program requests the data, subsequent read operations obtain the data directly from the cache, which greatly enhances read performance.

Recoverability Support

NTFS recovery support ensures that if a power failure or a catastrophic system failure occurs, no file system operations (transactions) will be left incomplete and the structure of the disk volume will remain intact without the need to run a disk repair utility. The NTFS Chkdsk utility is used to repair catastrophic disk corruption caused by I/O errors (bad disk sectors, electrical anomalies, or disk failures, for example) or software bugs. But with the NTFS recovery capabilities in place, Chkdsk is rarely needed.

NTFS uses a transaction-based logging scheme to implement recoverability. This strategy ensures a full disk recovery that is also extremely fast (on the order of seconds) for even the largest disks. NTFS limits its recovery procedures to file system data to ensure that at the very least the user will never lose a volume because of a corrupted file system; however, user data is not guaranteed to be fully updated if a crash occurs. Transaction-based protection of user data is available in most of the database products available for Windows NT, such as Microsoft SQL Server. The decision not to implement user data recovery in the file system represents a trade-off between a fully fault tolerant file system and one that provides optimum performance for all file operations.

The following sections describe the evolution of file system reliability as a context for an introduction to recoverable file systems, detail the transaction-logging scheme NTFS uses to record modifications to file system data structures, and explain how NTFS recovers a volume if the system fails.

Evolution of File System Design

The development of a recoverable file system is a step forward in the evolution of file system design. In the past, two techniques were common for constructing a file system's I/O and caching support: *careful write* and *lazy write*. The file systems developed for Digital Equipment Corporation's VAX/VMS and for some other proprietary operating systems employed a careful write algorithm, while OS/2 HPFS and most older UNIX file systems used a lazy write file system scheme.

The next two subsections briefly review these two types of file systems and their intrinsic trade-offs between safety and performance. The third subsection describes NTFS's recoverable approach and explains how it differs from the two other strategies.

Careful Write File Systems

When an operating system crashes or loses power, I/O operations in progress are immediately, and often prematurely, interrupted. Depending on what I/O operation or operations were in progress and how far along they were, such an abrupt halt can produce inconsistencies in a file system. An inconsistency in this context is a file system corruption—a filename appears in a directory listing, for example, but the file system doesn't know the file is there or can't access the file. The worst file system corruptions can leave an entire volume inaccessible.

A careful write file system doesn't try to prevent file system inconsistencies. Rather, it orders its write operations so that, at worst, a system crash will produce predictable, noncritical inconsistencies, which the file system can fix at its leisure.

When any kind of file system receives a request to update the disk, it must perform several suboperations before the update will be complete. In a file system that uses the careful write strategy, the suboperations are always written to disk serially. When allocating disk space for a file, for example, the file system first sets some bits in its bitmap and then allocates the space to the file. If the power fails immediately after the bits are set, the careful write file system loses access to some disk space—to the space represented by the set bits—but existing data is not corrupted.

Serializing write operations also means that I/O requests are filled in the order in which they are received. If one process allocates disk space and shortly thereafter another process creates a file, a careful write file system completes the disk allocation before it starts to create the file because interleaving the suboperations of the two I/O requests could result in an inconsistent state.

> **NOTE** The FAT file system uses a *write-through* algorithm that causes disk modifications to be immediately written to the disk. Unlike the careful write approach, the write-through technique doesn't require the file system to order its writes to prevent inconsistencies.

The main advantage of a careful write file system is that in the event of a failure the volume stays consistent and usable without the need to immediately run a slow volume repair utility. Such a utility is needed to correct the predictable, nondestructive disk inconsistencies that occur as the result of a system failure, but the utility can be run at a convenient time, typically when the system is rebooted.

Lazy Write File Systems

A careful write file system sacrifices speed for the safety it provides. A lazy write file system improves performance by using a *write-back* caching strategy; that is, it writes file modifications to the cache and flushes the contents of the cache to disk in an optimized way, usually as a background activity.

The performance improvements associated with the lazy write caching technique take several forms. First, the overall number of disk writes is reduced. Because serialized, immediate disk writes aren't required, the contents of a buffer can be modified several times before they are written to disk. Second, the speed of servicing application requests is greatly increased because the file system can return control to the caller without waiting for disk writes to be completed. Finally, the lazy write strategy ignores the inconsistent intermediate states on a file volume that can result when the suboperations of two or more I/O requests are interleaved. It is thus easier to make the file system multithreaded, allowing more than one I/O operation to be in progress at a time.

The disadvantage of the lazy write technique is that it creates intervals during which a volume is in too inconsistent a state to be corrected by the file system. Consequently, lazy write file systems must keep track of the volume's state at all times. In general, lazy write file systems gain a performance advantage over careful write systems—at the expense of greater risk and user inconvenience if the system fails.

Recoverable File Systems

A recoverable file system tries to exceed the safety of a careful write file system while achieving the performance of a lazy write file system. A recoverable file system ensures volume consistency by using logging techniques originally developed for transaction processing. If the operating system crashes, the recoverable file system restores consistency by executing a recovery procedure that accesses information that has been stored in a log file. Because the file system has logged its disk writes, the recovery procedure takes only seconds, regardless of the size of the volume.

The NTFS recovery procedure is exact, guaranteeing that the volume will be restored to a consistent state. None of the inadequate restorations associated with lazy write file systems can happen with NTFS.

A recoverable file system incurs some costs for the safety it provides. Every transaction that alters the volume structure requires that one record be written to the log file for each of the transaction's suboperations. This logging overhead is ameliorated by the file system's "batching" of log records—writing many records to the log file in a single I/O operation. In addition, the recoverable file system can employ the optimization techniques of a lazy write file system. It can even increase the length of the intervals between cache flushes because the file system can be recovered if the system crashes before the cache changes have been flushed to disk. This gain over the caching performance of lazy write file systems makes up for, and often exceeds, the overhead of the recoverable file system's logging activity.

Neither careful write nor lazy write file systems guarantee protection of user file data. If the system crashes while an application is writing a file, the file can be lost or corrupted. Worse, the crash can corrupt a lazy write file system, destroying existing files or even rendering an entire volume inaccessible.

NTFS implements several strategies that improve its reliability over that of the traditional file systems. First, NTFS recoverability guarantees that the volume structure won't be corrupted, so all files will remain accessible after a system failure.

Second, although NTFS doesn't currently guarantee protection of user data in the event of a system crash—some changes can be lost from the cache—applications can take advantage of the NTFS write-through and cache-flushing capabilities to ensure that file modifications are recorded on disk at appropriate intervals. Both *cache write-through*—forcing write operations to be immediately recorded on disk—and *cache flushing*—forcing cache contents to be written to disk—are efficient operations. NTFS doesn't have to do extra disk I/O to flush modifications to several different file system data structures because changes to the data structures are recorded—in a single write operation—in the log file; if a failure occurs and cache contents are lost, the file system modifications can be recovered from the log. Furthermore, unlike the FAT file system, NTFS guarantees that user data will be consistent and available immediately after a write-through operation or a cache flush, even if the system subsequently fails.

Finally, NTFS has all the underpinnings to support logging for user files in the future. In lieu of user data logging, users who require an added measure of data reliability can use FtDisk, the Windows NT fault tolerant disk driver, to set up and maintain redundant data storage. (See the section "Fault Tolerance Support" later in this chapter for more information about data redundancy.)

Logging

NTFS provides file system recoverability by means of a transaction-processing technique called *logging*. In NTFS logging, the suboperations of any transaction that alters important file system data structures are recorded in a log file before they are carried through on the disk. That way, if the system crashes, partially completed transactions can be redone or undone when the system comes back online. In transaction processing, this technique is known as *write-ahead logging*. In NTFS, transactions include writing to the disk or deleting a file and can be made up of several suboperations.

Log File Service (LFS)

LFS is a series of kernel-mode routines inside the NTFS driver that NTFS uses to access the log file. Although originally designed to provide logging and recovery services for more than one client, LFS is currently used only by NTFS. The caller—NTFS in this case—passes the LFS a pointer to an open file object, which specifies a log file to be accessed. The LFS either initializes a new log file or calls the Windows NT cache manager to access the existing log file through the cache, as shown in Figure 9-24.

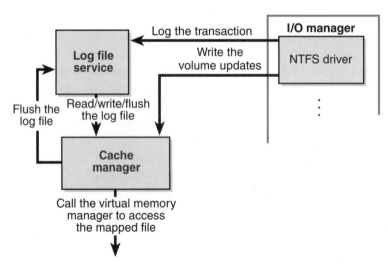

Figure 9-24.
Log file service (LFS)

The LFS divides the log file into two regions: a *restart area* and an "infinite" *logging area*, as shown in Figure 9-25.

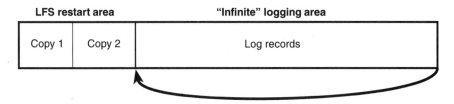

Figure 9-25
Log file regions

NTFS calls the LFS to read and write the restart area. NTFS uses the restart area to store context information such as the location in the logging area at which NTFS will begin to read during recovery after a system failure. The LFS maintains a second copy of the restart data in case the first becomes corrupted or otherwise inaccessible. The remainder of the log file is the logging area, which contains transaction records NTFS writes in order to recover a volume in the event of a system failure. The LFS makes the log file appear infinite by reusing it circularly (while guaranteeing that it doesn't overwrite information it needs). The LFS uses *logical sequence numbers* (LSNs) to identify records written to the log file. As the LFS cycles through the file, it increases the values of the LSNs. The number of possible LSNs is so large as to be virtually infinite.

NTFS never reads transactions from or writes transactions to the log file directly. The LFS provides services NTFS calls to open the log file, write log records, read log records in forward or backward order, flush log records up to a particular LSN, or set the beginning of the log file to a higher LSN. During recovery, NTFS calls the LFS to read forward through the log records in order to redo any transactions that were recorded in the log file but were not flushed to disk at the time of the system failure. NTFS calls the LFS to read backward through the log records in order to undo, or roll back, any transactions that weren't completely logged before the crash. NTFS calls the LFS to set the beginning of the log file to a record with a higher LSN when NTFS no longer needs the older transaction records in the log file.

Here's how the system guarantees that the volume can be recovered:

1. NTFS first calls the LFS to record in the (cached) log file any transactions that will modify the volume structure.

2. NTFS modifies the volume (also in the cache).

431

3. The cache manager calls the LFS to prompt the LFS to flush the log file to disk. (The LFS implements the flush by calling the cache manager back, telling it which pages of memory to flush. Refer back to the calling sequence shown in Figure 9-24 on page 430.)

4. After the cache manager flushes the log file to disk, it flushes the volume changes (the transactions themselves) to disk.

These steps ensure that if the file system modifications are ultimately unsuccessful, the corresponding transactions can be retrieved from the log file and can be either redone or undone as part of the file system recovery procedure.

File system recovery begins automatically the first time the volume is used after the system is rebooted. NTFS checks whether the transactions that were recorded in the log file before the crash were applied to the volume, and if they weren't, it redoes them. NTFS also guarantees that transactions not completely logged before the crash are undone so that they don't appear on the volume.

Log Record Types

The LFS allows its clients to write any kind of record to their log files. NTFS writes several types of records. Two types, *update records* and *checkpoint records,* are described here.

Update records   Update records are the most common type of record NTFS writes to the log file. Each update record contains two kinds of information:

- **Redo information**   How to reapply one suboperation of a fully logged ("committed") transaction to the volume if a system failure occurs before the transaction is flushed from the cache

- **Undo information**   How to reverse one suboperation of a transaction that was only partially logged ("not committed") at the time of a system failure

Figure 9-26 shows three update records in the log file. Each record represents one suboperation of a transaction, creating a new file. The redo entry in each update record tells NTFS how to reapply the suboperation to the volume, and the undo entry tells NTFS how to roll back (undo) the suboperation.

After logging a transaction (in this example, by calling the LFS to write the three update records to the log file), NTFS performs the suboperations on the volume itself, in the cache. When it has finished updating the cache, NTFS

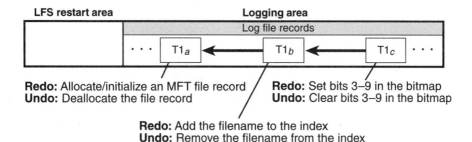

Figure 9-26
Update records in the log file

writes another record to the log file, recording the entire transaction as complete—a suboperation known as *committing a transaction*. Once a transaction is committed, NTFS guarantees that the entire transaction will appear on the volume, even if the operating system subsequently fails.

When recovering after a system failure, NTFS reads through the log file and redoes each committed transaction. Although NTFS completed the committed transactions before the system failure, it doesn't know whether the cache manager flushed the volume modifications to disk in time. The updates might have been lost from the cache when the system failed. Therefore, NTFS executes the committed transactions again just to be sure that the disk is up to date.

After redoing the committed transactions during a file system recovery, NTFS locates all the transactions in the log file that were not committed at failure and rolls back (undoes) each suboperation that had been logged. In Figure 9-26, NTFS would first undo the $T1_c$ suboperation and then follow the backward pointer to $T1_b$ and undo that suboperation. It would continue to follow the backward pointers, undoing suboperations, until it reached the first suboperation in the transaction. By following the pointers, NTFS knows how many and which update records it must undo to roll back a transaction.

Redo and undo information can be expressed either physically or logically. Physical descriptions specify volume updates in terms of particular byte ranges on the disk that are to be changed, moved, and so on. Logical descriptions express updates in terms of operations such as "delete file A.DAT." As the lowest layer of software maintaining the file system structure, NTFS writes update records with physical descriptions. Transaction-processing or other application-level software might benefit from writing update records in logical terms, however, because logically expressed updates are more compact than physically expressed ones. Logical descriptions necessarily depend on NTFS to understand what operations, such as deleting a file, involve.

NTFS writes update records (usually several) for each of the following transactions:

- Creating a file
- Deleting a file
- Extending a file
- Truncating a file
- Setting file information
- Renaming a file
- Changing the security applied to a file

The redo and undo information in an update record must be carefully designed because although NTFS undoes a transaction, recovers from a system failure, or even operates normally, it might try to redo a transaction that has already been done or, conversely, to undo a transaction that never occurred or that has already been undone. Similarly, NTFS might try to redo or undo a transaction consisting of several update records, only some of which are complete on disk. The format of the update records must ensure that executing redundant redo or undo operations is *idempotent,* that is, has a neutral effect. For example, setting a bit that is already set has no effect, but toggling a bit that has already been toggled does. The file system must also handle intermediate volume states correctly.

Checkpoint records   In addition to update records, NTFS periodically writes a checkpoint record to the log file, as illustrated in Figure 9-27.

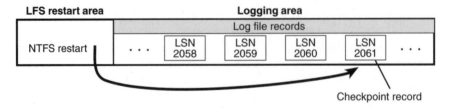

Figure 9-27
Checkpoint record in the log file

A checkpoint record helps NTFS determine what processing would be needed to recover a volume if a crash were to occur immediately. Using information stored in the checkpoint record, NTFS knows, for instance, how far back in the log file it must go to begin its recovery. After writing a checkpoint record, NTFS stores the LSN of the record in the restart area so that it can quickly find its most recently written checkpoint record when it begins file system recovery after a crash occurs.

Although the LFS presents the log file to NTFS as if it were infinitely large, it isn't. The generous size of the log file and the frequent writing of checkpoint records (an operation that usually frees up space in the log file) make the possibility of the log file's filling up a remote one. Nevertheless, the LFS accounts for this possibility by tracking several numbers:

- The available log space

- The amount of space needed to write an incoming log record and to undo the write, should that be necessary

- The amount of space needed to roll back all active (noncommitted) transactions, should that be necessary

If the log file doesn't contain enough available space to accommodate the total of the last two items, the LFS returns a "log file full" error and NTFS raises an exception. The NTFS exception handler rolls back the current transaction and places it in a queue to be restarted later.

To free up space in the log file, NTFS must momentarily prevent further transactions on files. To do so, NTFS blocks file creation and deletion and then requests exclusive access to all system files and shared access to all user files. Gradually, active transactions either are completed successfully or receive the "log file full" exception. NTFS rolls back and queues the transactions that receive the exception.

Once it has blocked transaction activity on files as described above, NTFS calls the cache manager to flush unwritten data to disk, including unwritten log file data. After everything is safely flushed to disk, NTFS no longer needs the data in the log file. It resets the beginning of the log file to the current position, making the log file "empty." Then it restarts the queued transactions. Beyond the short pause in I/O processing, the "log file full" error has no effect on executing programs.

This scenario is one example of how NTFS uses the log file not only for file system recovery but also for error recovery during normal operation. You'll find out more about error recovery in the following section.

Recovery

NTFS automatically performs a disk recovery the first time a program accesses an NTFS volume after the system has been booted. (If no recovery is needed, the process is trivial.) Recovery depends on two tables NTFS maintains in memory:

- The *transaction table* keeps track of transactions that have been started but are not yet committed. The suboperations of these active transactions must be removed from the disk during recovery.

- The *dirty page table* records which pages in the cache contain modifications to the file system structure that have not yet been written to disk. This data must be flushed to disk during recovery.

NTFS writes a checkpoint record to the log file once every 5 seconds. Just before it does, it calls the LFS to store a current copy of the transaction table and of the dirty page table in the log file. NTFS then records in the checkpoint record the LSNs of the log records containing the copied tables. When recovery begins after a system failure, NTFS calls the LFS to locate the log records containing the most recent checkpoint record and the most recent copies of the transaction and dirty page tables. It then copies the tables to memory.

The log file usually contains more update records following the last checkpoint record. These update records represent volume modifications that occurred after the last checkpoint record was written. NTFS must update the transaction and dirty page tables to include these operations. After updating the tables, NTFS uses the tables and the contents of the log file to update the volume itself.

To effect its volume recovery, NTFS scans the log file three times, loading the file into memory during the first pass to minimize disk I/O. Each pass has a particular purpose:

1. Analysis

2. Redoing transactions

3. Undoing transactions

Analysis Pass

During the *analysis pass,* as shown in Figure 9-28, NTFS scans forward in the log file from the beginning of the last checkpoint operation in order to find update records and use them to update the transaction and dirty page tables it copied to memory. Notice in the figure that the checkpoint operation stores

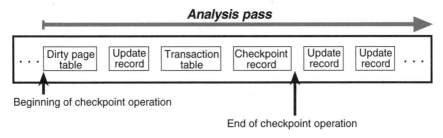

Figure 9-28
Analysis pass

three records in the log file and that update records might be interspersed among these records. NTFS therefore must start its scan at the beginning of the checkpoint operation.

Each update record that appears in the log file after the checkpoint operation begins represents a modification to either the transaction table or the dirty page table. If an update record is a "transaction committed" record, for example, the transaction the record represents must be removed from the transaction table. Similarly, if the update record is a "page update" record that modifies a file system data structure, the dirty page table must be updated to reflect that change.

Once the tables are up to date in memory, NTFS scans the tables to determine the LSN of the oldest update record that logs an operation that has not been carried out on disk. The transaction table contains the LSNs of the noncommitted (incomplete) transactions, and the dirty page table contains the LSNs of records in the cache that have not been flushed to disk. The LSN of the oldest record that NTFS finds in these two tables determines where the redo pass will begin. If the last checkpoint record is older, however, NTFS will start the redo pass there instead.

Redo Pass

During the *redo pass,* as shown in Figure 9-29 on the following page, NTFS scans forward in the log file from the LSN of the oldest record it has found in the analysis pass. It looks for "page update" records, which contain volume modifications that were written before the system failure but that might not have been flushed to disk. NTFS redoes these updates in the cache.

When NTFS reaches the end of the log file, it has updated the cache with the necessary volume modifications and the cache manager's lazy writer can begin writing cache contents to disk in the background.

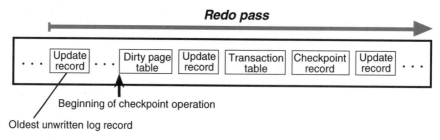

Figure 9-29
Redo pass

Undo Pass

After it completes the redo pass, NTFS begins its *undo pass*, in which it rolls back any transactions that weren't committed when the system failed. Figure 9-30 shows two transactions in the log file; transaction 1 was committed before the power failure, but transaction 2 was not. NTFS must undo transaction 2.

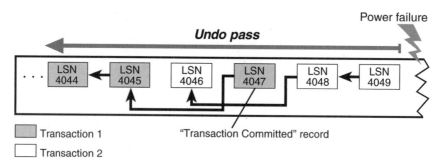

Figure 9-30
Undo pass

Suppose that transaction 2 created a file, an operation that comprises three suboperations, each with its own update record. The update records of a transaction are linked by backward pointers in the log file because they are usually not contiguous.

The NTFS transaction table lists the LSN of the last-logged update record for each noncommitted transaction. In this example, the transaction table identifies LSN 4049 as the last update record logged for transaction 2. As shown from right to left in Figure 9-31, NTFS rolls back transaction 2.

Each update record contains two kinds of information: how to redo a suboperation and how to undo it. After locating LSN 4049, NTFS finds the undo information and executes it, clearing bits 3 through 9 in its allocation bitmap. NTFS then follows the backward pointer to LSN 4048, which directs it

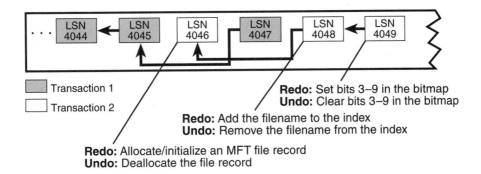

Figure 9-31
Undoing a transaction

to remove the new filename from the appropriate filename index. Finally, it follows the last backward pointer and deallocates the MFT file record reserved for the file, as the update record with the LSN 4046 specifies. Transaction 2 is now rolled back. If there are other noncommitted transactions to undo, NTFS follows the same procedure to roll them back. Because undoing transactions affects the volume's file system structure, NTFS must log the undo operations in the log file. After all, the power might fail again during the recovery, and NTFS would have to redo its undo operations!

When the undo pass of the recovery is complete, the volume has been restored to a consistent state. At this point, NTFS flushes the cache changes to disk to ensure that the volume is up to date. NTFS then writes an "empty" LFS restart area to indicate that the volume is consistent and that no recovery need be done if the system should fail again immediately. Recovery is complete.

NTFS guarantees that recovery will return the volume to some preexisting consistent state, but not necessarily to the state that existed just before the system crash. NTFS can't make that guarantee because, for performance, it uses a "lazy commit" algorithm, which means that the log file is not immediately flushed to disk each time a "transaction committed" record is written. Instead, numerous transaction committed records are batched and written together, either when the cache manager calls the LFS to flush the log file to disk or when the LFS writes a checkpoint record (once every 5 seconds) to the log file. Another reason the recovered volume might not be completely up to date is that several parallel transactions might be active when the system crashes and some of their transaction committed records might make it to disk whereas others might not. The consistent volume that recovery produces includes all the volume updates whose transaction committed records made it to disk and none of the updates whose transaction committed records didn't make it to disk.

NTFS uses the log file to recover a volume after the system fails, but it also takes advantage of an important "freebie" it gets from logging transactions. File systems necessarily contain a lot of code devoted to recovering from file system errors that occur during the course of normal file I/O. Because NTFS logs each transaction that modifies the volume structure, it can use the log file to recover when a file system error occurs and thus can greatly simplify its error handling code. The "log file full" error described earlier is one example of using the log file for error recovery.

Most I/O errors a program receives are not file system errors and therefore can't be resolved entirely by NTFS. When called to create a file, for example, NTFS might begin by creating a file record in the MFT and then enter the new file's name in a directory index. When it tries to allocate space for the file in its bitmap, however, it could discover that the disk is full and the create request can't be completed. In such a case, NTFS uses the information in the log file to undo the part of the operation it has already completed and to deallocate the data structures it reserved for the file. Then it returns a "disk full" error to the caller, which in turn must respond appropriately to the error.

Fault Tolerance Support

The capabilities of NTFS are enhanced by underlying support from a Windows NT driver called FtDisk.sys, the fault tolerant disk driver. FtDisk lies above hard disk drivers in the I/O system's layered driver scheme and provides volume management capabilities, redundant data storage, and dynamic data recovery from bad sectors on SCSI (small computer system interface) disks.

Although FtDisk works with all of the Windows NT–supported file systems, using it with NTFS provides the highest level of data integrity. Even without FtDisk, NTFS removes bad clusters from use and provides the equivalent of FtDisk's bad-sector recovery for non-SCSI hard disks. It also also monitors and detects corruption in file system data structures and uses FtDisk to recover its own data and to ensure its own reliability.

The following two sections describe the volume management and data redundancy capabilities of FtDisk. The third section describes the additional features of NTFS that improve data reliability and recovery.

Volume Management Features

Although FtDisk is called the fault tolerant driver, it also implements some volume management features unrelated to fault tolerance. Volume sets and stripe sets don't provide data redundancy, but they do aid in organizing volumes and increasing I/O efficiency, respectively.

Volume Sets

A *volume set* is a single logical volume composed of a maximum of 32 areas of free space on one or more disks. The Windows NT Disk Administrator utility combines the areas into the volume set, which can then be formatted for any of the Windows NT–supported file systems. Figure 9-32 shows a 100-MB volume set identified by drive letter D: that has been created from the last third of the first disk and the first third of the second.

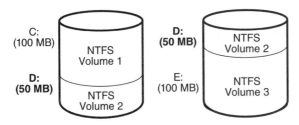

Figure 9-32
Volume set

A volume set is useful for consolidating small areas of free disk space to create a larger volume or for creating a single, large volume out of two or more small disks. If the volume set has been formatted for NTFS, it can be extended to include additional free areas or additional disks without affecting the data already stored on the volume. This is one of the biggest benefits of describing all data on an NTFS volume as a file. NTFS can dynamically increase the size of a logical volume because the bitmap that records the allocation status of the volume is just another file—the bitmap file. The bitmap file can be extended to include any space added to the volume. Dynamically extending a FAT volume, on the other hand, would require the FAT itself to be extended, which would dislocate everything else on the disk.

FtDisk hides the physical configuration of disks from the file systems installed on Windows NT. NTFS, for example, views D: in Figure 9-32 as an ordinary 100-MB volume. NTFS consults its bitmap to determine what space in the volume is free for allocation. It then calls FtDisk to read or write data beginning at a particular byte offset on the volume. FtDisk views the physical sectors in the volume set as numbered sequentially from the first free area on the first disk to the last free area on the last disk. It determines which physical sector on which disk corresponds to the supplied byte offset.

Stripe Sets

A *stripe set* is a series of partitions, one partition per disk, that the Disk Administrator utility combines into a single logical volume. Figure 9-33 shows a stripe

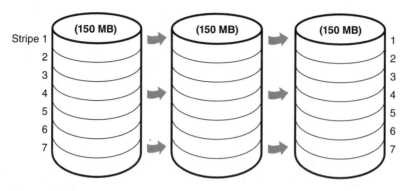

Figure 9-33
Stripe set

set consisting of three partitions, one on each of three disks. (A partition in a stripe set need not span an entire disk; the only restriction is that the partitions on each disk be the same size.)

To a file system, this stripe set appears to be a single 450-MB volume, but FtDisk optimizes data storage and retrieval times on the stripe set by distributing the volume's data among the physical disks. FtDisk accesses the physical sectors of the disks as if they were numbered sequentially in stripes across the disks, as illustrated in Figure 9-34.

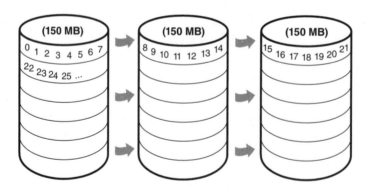

Figure 9-34
Logical numbering of physical sectors on a stripe set

Because each stripe is a relatively narrow 64 KB (a value chosen to prevent individual reads and writes from accessing two disks), the data tends to be distributed evenly among the disks. Stripes thus increase the probability that multiple pending read and write operations will be bound for different disks. And because data on all three disks can be accessed simultaneously, latency time for disk I/O is often reduced, particularly on heavily loaded systems.

Fault Tolerant Volumes

Volume sets make managing disk volumes more convenient, and stripe sets spread the I/O load over multiple disks. These two volume-management features don't provide the ability to recover data if a disk fails, however. For data recovery, FtDisk implements three redundant storage schemes: mirror sets, stripe sets with parity, and sector sparing. These features are created with the Windows NT Disk Administrator utility.

Mirror Sets

In a *mirror set,* the contents of a partition on one disk are duplicated in an equal-sized partition on another disk. A mirror set is shown in Figure 9-35.

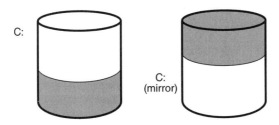

Figure 9-35
Mirror set

When a program writes to C:, FtDisk writes the same data to the same location on the mirror partition. If the first disk or any of the data on its C: partition becomes unreadable because of a hardware or software failure, FtDisk automatically accesses the data from the mirror partition. A mirror set can be formatted for any of the Windows NT–supported file systems. The file system drivers remain independent and are not affected by FtDisk's mirroring activity.

Mirror sets can aid in I/O throughput on heavily loaded systems. When I/O activity is high, FtDisk balances its read operations between the primary partition and the mirror partition (accounting for the number of unfinished I/O requests pending from each disk). Two read operations can proceed simultaneously and thus theoretically finish in half the time. When a file is modified, both partitions of the mirror set must be written, but disk writes are done asynchronously, so the performance of user-mode programs is generally not affected by the extra disk update.

Stripe Sets with Parity

A *stripe set with parity* is a fault tolerant variant of a regular stripe set. Fault tolerance is achieved by reserving the equivalent of one disk for storing parity for each stripe. Figure 9-36 is a visual representation of a stripe set with parity.

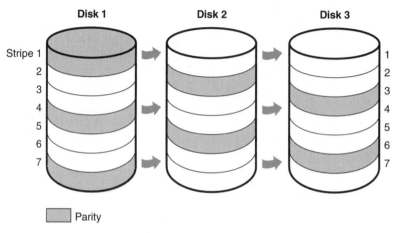

Figure 9-36
Stripe set with parity

In Figure 9-36, the parity for stripe 1 is stored on disk 1. It contains a byte-for-byte logical sum (XOR) of the first stripe on disks 2 and 3. The parity for stripe 2 is stored on disk 2, and the parity for stripe 3 is stored on disk 3. Rotating the parity across the disks in this way is an I/O optimization technique. Each time data is written to a disk, the parity bytes corresponding to the modified bytes must be recalculated and rewritten. If the parity were always written to the same disk, that disk would be busy continually and could become an I/O bottleneck.

Recovering a failed disk in a stripe set with parity relies on a simple arithmetic principle: in an equation with n variables, if you know the value of $n - 1$ of the variables, you can determine the value of the missing variable by subtraction. For example, in the equation $x + y = z$, where z represents the parity stripe, FtDisk computes $z - y$ to determine the contents of x; to find y, it computes $z - x$. FtDisk uses similar logic to recover lost data. If a disk in a stripe set with parity fails or if data on one disk becomes unreadable, FtDisk reconstructs the missing data by using the XOR operation (bitwise logical addition).

If disk 1 in Figure 9-36 fails, the contents of its stripes 2 and 5 are calculated by XOR-ing the corresponding stripes of disk 3 with the parity stripes on disk 2. The contents of stripes 3 and 6 are similarly determined by XOR-ing the corresponding stripes of disk 2 with the parity stripes on disk 3. At least three disks (or rather, three same-sized partitions on three disks) are required to create a stripe set with parity.

Sector Sparing

Redundant data storage is used not only for recovering data after a complete disk failure but also for recovering data from a single physical sector that goes bad. In a technique called *sector sparing*, FtDisk uses its redundant data storage to dynamically replace lost data when a disk sector becomes unreadable. The sector-sparing technique exploits a feature of some hard disks, which provide a set of physical sectors reserved as "spares." If FtDisk receives a data error from the hard disk, it obtains a spare sector from the disk driver to replace the bad sector that caused the data error. FtDisk recovers the data that was on the bad sector (by either reading the data from a disk mirror or recalculating the data from a stripe set with parity) and copies it to the spare sector. FtDisk performs sector sparing dynamically, without intervention from the file system or the user, and sector sparing works with any Windows NT–supported file system on SCSI-based hard disks.

If a bad-sector error occurs and the hard disk doesn't provide spares, runs out of them, or is a non-SCSI-based disk, FtDisk can still recover the data. It recalculates the unreadable data by accessing a stripe set with parity, or it reads a copy of the data from a disk mirror. It then passes the data to the file system along with a warning status that only one copy of the data remains in a disk mirror or that one stripe is inaccessible in a stripe set with parity and that data redundancy is therefore no longer in effect for that sector. It's up to the file system to respond to (or ignore) the warning. FtDisk will re-recover the data each time the file system tries to read from the bad sector.

NTFS Bad-Cluster Recovery

FtDisk can recover data from a bad sector on a fault tolerant volume, but if the hard disk doesn't use the SCSI protocol or runs out of spare sectors, FtDisk can't perform sector sparing to replace the bad sector. When the file system reads from the sector, FtDisk instead recovers the data and returns the warning to the file system that there is only one copy of the data.

The FAT file system doesn't respond to this FtDisk warning. Moreover, neither these file systems nor FtDisk keeps track of the bad sectors, so a user must run the Chkdsk or Format utility to prevent FtDisk from repeatedly recovering data for the file system. Both Chkdsk and Format are less than ideal for removing bad sectors from use. Chkdsk can take a long time to find and remove bad sectors, and Format wipes all the data off the partition it is formatting.

In the file system equivalent of FtDisk's sector sparing, NTFS dynamically replaces the cluster containing a bad sector and keeps track of the bad cluster so that it won't be reused. (As described earlier, NTFS maintains portability by addressing logical clusters rather than physical sectors.) NTFS performs these functions when FtDisk can't perform sector sparing or when FtDisk is not installed in the system. When FtDisk returns a bad-sector warning or when the hard disk driver returns a bad-sector error, NTFS allocates a new cluster to replace the one containing the bad sector. If FtDisk is present, NTFS copies the data that FtDisk has recovered into the new cluster to reestablish data redundancy.

Figure 9-37 shows an MFT record for a user file with a bad cluster in one of its data runs. When it receives a bad-sector error, NTFS reassigns the cluster containing the sector to its bad-cluster file. This prevents the bad cluster from being allocated to another file. NTFS then allocates a new cluster for the file and changes the file's VCN-to-LCN mappings to point to the new cluster. This bad-cluster remapping (introduced earlier in this chapter) is illustrated in Figure 9-38 on page 448. Cluster number 1357, which contains the bad sector, is replaced by a new cluster, number 1049 (as you'll see in Figure 9-38).

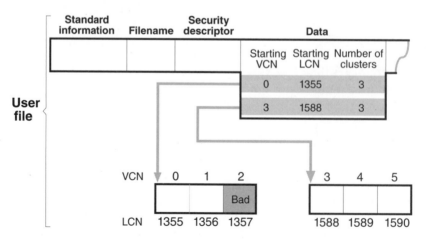

Figure 9-37
MFT record for a user file with a bad cluster

Bad-sector errors are undesirable, but when they do occur, the combination of NTFS and FtDisk provides the best possible solution. If the bad sector is on a redundant volume, FtDisk recovers the data and replaces the sector if it can. If it can't replace the sector, it returns a warning to NTFS and NTFS replaces the cluster containing the bad sector.

If FtDisk isn't loaded or if the volume isn't configured as a redundant volume, the data in the bad sector can't be recovered. When the volume is formatted as a FAT volume and FtDisk can't recover the data, reading from the bad sector yields indeterminate results. If some of the file system's control structures reside in the bad sector, an entire file or group of files (or potentially, the whole disk) can be lost. At best, some data in the affected file (often, all the data in the file beyond the bad sector) is lost. Moreover, the FAT file system is likely to reallocate the bad sector to the same or another file on the volume, causing the problem to resurface.

Like the other file systems, NTFS can't recover data from a bad sector without help from FtDisk. However, NTFS greatly contains the damage a bad sector can cause. If NTFS discovers the bad sector during a read operation, it remaps the cluster the sector is in, as shown in Figure 9-38 on the following page. If the volume is not configured as a redundant volume, NTFS returns a "data read" error to the calling program. Although the data that was in that cluster is lost, the rest of the file—and the file system—remains intact; the calling program can respond appropriately to the data loss; and the bad cluster won't be reused in future allocations. If NTFS discovers the bad cluster on a write operation rather than a read, NTFS remaps the cluster before writing and thus loses no data and generates no error.

The same recovery procedures are followed if file system data is stored in a sector that goes bad. If the bad sector is on a redundant volume, NTFS replaces the cluster dynamically, using the data recovered by FtDisk. If the volume isn't redundant, the data can't be recovered and NTFS sets a bit in the volume file that indicates corruption on the volume. The NTFS Chkdsk utility checks this bit when the system is next rebooted, and if the bit is set, Chkdsk executes, fixing the file system corruption by reconstructing the NTFS metadata.

In rare instances, file system corruption can occur even on a fault tolerant disk configuration. A double error can destroy both file system data and the means to reconstruct it. If the system crashes while NTFS is writing the mirror copy of an MFT file record, of a filename index, or of the log file, for example, the mirror copy of such file system data might not be fully updated. If the system were rebooted and a bad-sector error occurred on the primary disk at exactly the same location as the incomplete write on the disk mirror,

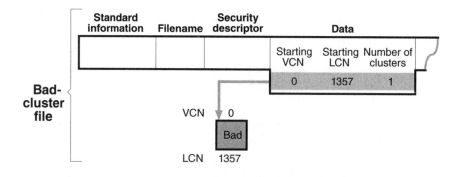

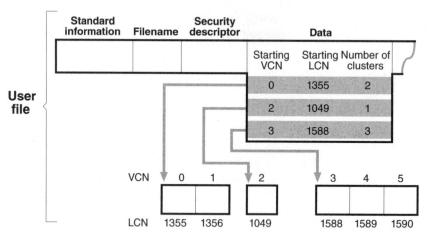

Figure 9-38
Bad-cluster remapping

NTFS would be unable to recover the correct data from the disk mirror. NTFS implements a special scheme for detecting such corruptions in file system data. If it ever finds an inconsistency, it sets the corruption bit in the volume file, which causes Chkdsk to reconstruct the NTFS metadata when the system is next rebooted. Because file system corruption is rare on a fault tolerant disk configuration, Chkdsk is seldom needed. It is supplied as a safety precaution rather than as a first-line data recovery strategy.

Use of Chkdsk on NTFS is vastly different from its use on the FAT file system. Before writing anything to disk, FAT sets the volume's "dirty bit" and then resets the bit after the modification is complete. If any I/O operation is in progress when the system crashes, the dirty bit is left set and Chkdsk runs when the system is rebooted. On NTFS, Chkdsk runs only when unexpected or unreadable file system data is found and NTFS can't recover the data from a redundant volume or from redundant file system structures on a single volume. (The system boot sector is duplicated, as are the parts of the MFT required for booting the system and running the NTFS recovery procedure. This redundancy ensures that NTFS will always be able to boot and recover itself.)

Table 9-3 summarizes what happens when a sector goes bad on a disk volume formatted for one of the Windows NT–supported file systems according to various conditions that have been described in this section.

Table 9-3 **Summary of FtDisk and NTFS Data Recovery Scenarios**

Scenario	FtDisk Installed... With a SCSI disk that has spare sectors	FtDisk Installed... With a non-SCSI disk or a disk with no spare sectors*	FtDisk Not Installed... With any kind of disk
Fault tolerant volume**	1. FtDisk recovers the data. 2. FtDisk performs *sector sparing* (replaces the bad sector). 3. File system remains unaware of the error.	1. FtDisk recovers the data. 2. FtDisk sends the data and a bad-sector error to the file system. 3. NTFS performs *cluster remapping*.	N/A
Non-fault-tolerant volume	1. FtDisk can't recover the data. 2. FtDisk sends a bad-sector error to the file system. 3. NTFS performs *cluster remapping.* Data is lost†.	1. FtDisk can't recover the data. 2. FtDisk sends a bad-sector error to the file system. 3. NTFS performs *cluster remapping.* Data is lost†.	1. Disk driver returns a error to the file system. 2. NTFS performs *cluster remapping.* Data is lost†.

* In neither of these cases can FtDisk perform sector sparing: (1) hard disks that don't use the SCSI protocol have no standard interface for providing sector sparing; (2) some hard disks don't provide hardware support for sector sparing, and SCSI hard disks that do provide sector sparing can eventually run out of spare sectors if a lot of sectors go bad.

** A fault tolerant volume is one of the following: a mirror set or a stripe set with parity.

† In a write operation, no data is lost: NTFS remaps the cluster before the write.

449

Note that if FtDisk is installed, if the volume on which the bad sector appears is a fault tolerant volume, and if the hard disk is one that supports sector sparing (and that hasn't run out of spare sectors), which file system you are using—FAT or NTFS—doesn't matter. FtDisk replaces the bad sector without the need for user or file system intervention.

If FtDisk is not installed or is installed on a hard disk that doesn't support sector sparing, the file system is responsible for replacing (remapping) the bad sector or—in the case of NTFS—the cluster in which the bad sector resides. The FAT file system does not provide sector or cluster remapping. The benefits of NTFS cluster remapping are that bad spots in a file can be fixed without harm to the file (or harm to the file system, as the case may be) and that the bad cluster won't be reallocated to the same or another file.

Conclusion

As you saw in the introduction to this chapter, the overriding goal for NTFS was to provide a file system that was not only reliable but also fast. The performance of Windows NT disk I/O is not due solely to the implementation of NTFS, however. It comes in large measure from synergy between NTFS and the Windows NT cache manager. Together, NTFS and the cache manager achieve respectable I/O performance while providing an unprecedented level of reliability and high-end data storage features for both workstation and server systems.

Windows NT 5.0 and Beyond

In this chapter, we'll take a look ahead at Microsoft Windows NT 5.0. Windows NT 5.0 is a massive release, with significant new operating system and network functionality being added to many areas of the system. It is not, however, a rewrite—many aspects of the kernel system architecture remain the same or are being extended. And like all releases of Windows NT, it will be upward compatible with existing applications and network installations.

The first part of this chapter is an overview of the new features in Windows NT 5.0. I won't describe the internal changes here (and I'll explain why in a bit) but rather the new external features. Although some of these features required extensions to the executive and the kernel (notably Plug and Play, power management, 64-bit large memory support, and the job object), most of them are additions to the existing code base and didn't involve major structural changes. In other words, the fundamental operating system architecture is *not* changing in Windows NT 5.0. This stability affirms that Windows NT has met one of its key design goals mentioned in Chapter 1—extensibility. The fact that the system has been able to evolve to the degree it has without rearchitecting fundamental mechanisms in the executive and the kernel is a testimony to the forward thinking of the original design team.

I'll also briefly describe the enhancements being made to Microsoft Cluster Server and Microsoft Windows NT Terminal Server. We'll then take a closer look at Plug and Play and power management, since the changes to these features are been more significant and involve the subsystems covered in this book. At the end of the chapter, you'll get a brief introduction to the plans for a true 64-bit version of Windows NT.

Overview of the New Features in Windows NT 5.0

In this section, I'll briefly summarize the major new features in Windows NT 5.0. This overview is based on information available in early 1998. Many of you will already be running Windows NT 5.0 (either in its beta form or possibly in its final release) and hence are already working with these new features.

When Microsoft released the Windows NT 5.0 beta 1, it made available a number of technical white papers that explain the key enhancements in Windows NT 5.0. You can find these white papers at *www.microsoft.com/ntserver* (just follow the links to Windows NT 5.0 white papers) and *www.microsoft.com/ntworkstation*. The new programming interfaces in the Microsoft Win32 application programming interface (API) are already showing up in the Platform Software Development Kit (SDK) documentation on MSDN. (Even the Win32 API header files in the Platform SDK contain the entry points for new Windows NT 5.0 functions.) The changes to the device driver model are also explained in the beta version of the Windows NT Device Driver Kit (DDK).

Now let's begin our tour of Windows NT 5.0.

Active Directory

The Active Directory is one of the most important new features in Windows NT 5.0. It will greatly simplify the tasks involved in administering and managing large Windows NT networks, and it will improve the user's interaction with networked resources.

The Active Directory stores information about all resources on the network and makes this information easy for developers, administrators, and users to find and use. It provides a single, consistent, open set of interfaces for performing common administrative tasks, such as adding new users, managing printers, and locating resources throughout the distributed computing environment. The Active Directory data model has many concepts similar to X.500. The directory holds objects that represent various resources, which are described by attributes. The universe of objects that can be stored in the directory is defined in the schema. For each object class, the schema defines what attributes an instance of the class must have, what additional attributes it can have, and what object class can be a parent of the current object class. This directory structure has the following key features:

- Flexible hierarchical structure
- Efficient multimaster replication
- Granular security delegation
- Extensible storage of new classes of objects and properties
- Standards-based interoperability through Lightweight Directory Access Protocol (LDAP) version 3 support
- Scalability to millions of objects per store

■ Integrated dynamic Domain Name System (DNS) server

■ Programmable class store

The Active Directory also makes it easier for users, administrators, and application code to find resources on the network. A user can search for resources from the In The Directory option on the Find utility or browse for resources from the Directory icon in Network Neighborhood. Application code can also search or browse for resources using a well-defined set of APIs from any programming language.

Programmability and extensibility are significant capabilities of the Active Directory. Developers and administrators deal with a single set of directory service interfaces, regardless of the installed directory service(s). The programming interface, called the Active Directory Service Interfaces (ADSI), is accessible by any language. Details on ADSI are on MSDN in the Platform SDK documentation. You can also access the directory using the LDAP API. The LDAP C API, defined in RFC 1823, is a lower-level interface available to C programmers.

The Active Directory is also the key underpinning that enables the improvements in distributed system security.

Distributed Security Extensions

Windows NT distributed security has many new features to simplify domain administration, improve performance, and integrate Internet security technology based on public-key cryptography. Here are some highlights of the Windows NT 5.0 Distributed Security Services:

■ The Active Directory provides the store for all domain security policy and account information. The Active Directory, which provides replication and availability of account information to multiple Domain Controllers (formerly known as Backup Domain Controllers), is available for remote administration. Multiple master replicas of the Active Directory at other Domain Controllers are updated and synchronized automatically.

■ The Active Directory supports a multilevel hierarchical tree namespace for user, group, and machine account information. Accounts can be grouped by organizational units rather than with the flat-domain account namespace provided by earlier versions of Windows NT. Management of trust relationships among domains is simplified through treewide transitive trust throughout the domain tree.

- Administrator rights to create and manage user or group accounts can be delegated to the level of organizational units. Access rights can be granted to individual properties on user objects to allow, for example, a specific individual or group to have the right to reset passwords but not to modify other account information.

- Windows NT security includes new authentication based on Internet standard security protocols, including Kerberos version 5 and transport layer security (TLS) for distributed security protocols, in addition to supporting Windows NT LAN Manager authentication protocols for compatibility.

- The implementation of secure channel security protocols supports strong client authentication by mapping user credentials in the form of public-key certificates to existing Windows NT accounts. Common administration tools are used to manage account information and access control, whether you are using shared secret authentication or public-key security.

- Windows NT supports the optional use of smart cards for interactive logon in addition to passwords. Smart cards support cryptography and secure storage for private keys and certificates, enabling strong authentication from the desktop to the Windows NT domain.

- Windows NT provides the Microsoft Certificate Server for organizations to issue X.509 version 3 certificates to their employees or business partners. Windows NT 5.0 introduces CryptoAPI certificate management APIs and modules to handle public-key certificates, including standard format certificates issued by either a commercial certificate authority, third-party certificate authority, or the Microsoft Certificate Server included in Windows NT. System administrators define which certificate authorities are trusted in their environment and, therefore, which certificates are accepted for client authentication and access to resources.

- External users who don't have Windows NT accounts can be authenticated using public-key certificates and mapped to an existing Windows NT account. Access rights defined for the Windows NT account determine the resources the external users can use on the system. Client authentication using public-key certificates allows Windows NT to authenticate external users based on certificates issued by trusted certificate authorities.

- Windows NT users have easy-to-use tools and common interface dialog boxes for managing the private-key/public-key pairs and the certificates they use to access Internet-based resources. Storage of personal security credentials, which uses secure disk-based storage, is easily transported with Microsoft's proposed industry-standard protocol, Personal Information Exchange. The operating system also has integrated support for smart-card devices.

Encryption

The encrypting file system (EFS) in Windows NT 5.0 allows the storing of encrypted files on NTFS volumes. The EFS particularly addresses security concerns raised by tools that allow users to access files from an NTFS volume without an access check (such as NtRecover from *www.winternals.com*). With the EFS, data in NTFS files is encrypted on disk. The encryption technology used is based on public keys and runs as an integrated system service, making it easy to manage, difficult to attack, and transparent to the user. If a user attempting to access an encrypted NTFS file has the private key to that file, he or she will be able to open the file and work with it as a normal document. A user without the private key to the file is simply denied access.

The EFS is tightly integrated with NTFS. Its device driver component runs in kernel mode and uses the nonpaged pool to store file-encryption keys, ensuring that they never make it to the paging file. The following key components comprise the EFS:

- ■ **Win32 APIs** These APIs provide programming interfaces for encrypting plaintext files, decrypting or recovering ciphertext files, and importing and exporting encrypted files (without decrypting them first).

- ■ **EFS driver** The EFS driver is layered on top of the NTFS. It communicates with the EFS service to request file-encryption keys, DDFs, DRFs, and other key management services. It passes this information to the EFS file system run-time library (FSRTL) to perform various file system operations (open, read, write, and append) transparently.

- ■ **FSRTL callouts** The FSRTL is a module within the EFS driver that implements NTFS callouts to handle various file system operations (such as reads, writes, and opens) on encrypted files and directories as well as operations to encrypt, decrypt, and recover file data when it is written to or read from disk. Even though the EFS driver and the FSRTL are implemented as a single component, they never communicate directly. They use the NTFS file control callout mechanism to pass messages to each other, which ensures that NTFS participates in all file operations. The operations implemented using the file control mechanisms include writing the EFS attribute data (data decryption field [DDF] and date recovery field [DRF]) as file attributes and communicating the file-encryption key computed in the EFS service to FSRTL such that it can be set up in the open file context. This file context is then used for transparent encryption and decryption on writes and reads of file data from disk.

■ **EFS service** The EFS service is part of the security subsystem. It uses the existing LPC communication port between the local security authority server and the kernel-mode security reference monitor (described in Chapter 6) to communicate with the EFS driver. In user mode, the EFS service interfaces with CryptoAPI to provide file-encryption keys and generate DDFs and DRFs.

These components are illustrated in Figure 10-1.

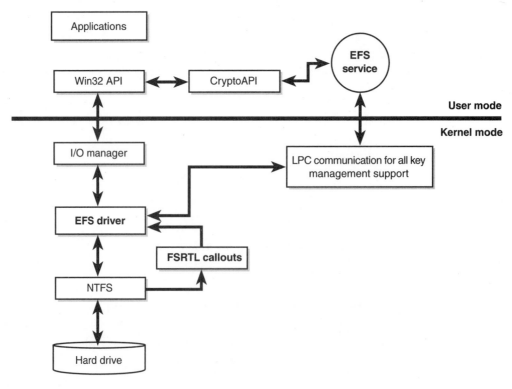

Figure 10-1
Encryption architecture

File encryption can use any symmetric encryption algorithm. The first release of the EFS will expose DES (Data Encryption Standard) as the encryption algorithm. Future releases will allow alternate encryption schemes.

Security Configuration Editor

Another key enhancement in the area of security is the new Security Configuration Editor. The primary goal of this editor is to provide a single point of administration for Windows NT–based system security. It will allow administrators to configure and analyze the system security policy, such as how and when users can log on to the system, password policy, overall system object security, audit settings, domain policy, and so forth. It can also be used to modify security settings on users, files, directories, services, and the registry.

To address the need for security analysis in Windows NT, the Security Configuration Editor will provide analysis at a micro level. It is designed to provide information about all system aspects related to security. Security administrators can view the information and perform security risk management for their entire information technology (IT) infrastructure.

The process of configuring security in a Windows NT–based network can be complex and detailed in terms of the system components involved and the level of change that might be required. The Security Configuration Editor allows the administrator to define a number of configuration settings and have them enacted in the background. With this tool, configuration tasks can be grouped and automated; they no longer require numerous, iterative key presses and repeat visits to a number of different applications to configure a group of machines.

What the Security Configuration Editor is not designed to do is replace system tools that address different aspects of system security—such as User Manager, Server Manager, Access Control List Editor, and so forth. Rather, its goal is to complement them by defining an engine that can interpret a standard configuration template and perform the required operations automatically in the background. Administrators can continue to use existing tools to change individual security settings whenever necessary.

Distributed File Services

Microsoft Distributed File System (DFS) for Windows NT Server is a network server component that makes it easier for users to find and manage data on the network. DFS makes it easy to create a single directory tree that includes multiple file servers and file shares in a group, division, or enterprise. In addition, DFS gives the user a single directory that can span a vast number of file servers and file shares, making it easy to "browse" the network to find the data and files needed. Browsing the DFS directory is easy because DFS subdirectories can be assigned logical, descriptive names no matter what name the file server or file share has.

DFS was shipped as a layered extension to Windows NT 4.0, but it had a number of limitations that are corrected with Windows NT 5.0 (such as a single location for the distributed directory information, which, if not accessible, limits access to DFS shares).

NTFS Extensions

Besides integration with encryption, NTFS in Windows NT 5.0 contains a number of extensions for server systems. These extensions require converting existing NTFS 4.0 partitions to a modified on-disk format called NTFS 5. Here are the main enhancements:

- Disk quotas can be specified on a per-user basis, thus providing the ability to limit the use of disk storage.

- Security descriptors (access control lists, or ACLs) can be stored once but referenced in multiple files, thus saving disk space.

- Native support for properties (such as found on OLE compound files), including general indexing support for these properties, is available. Properties are stored natively as NTFS streams, allowing fast querying.

- Reparse points, which allow the implementation of symbolic links, mount points for arbitrary file system volumes, and remote storage for Hierarchical Storage Management (HSM).

- Support for sparse files means that you can create files or extend them to a large size without allocating the disk space at the time of the file extend. Instead, disk allocation is deferred until specified in a write operation.

- Distributed link tracking through the use of unique IDs that can be assigned to files or directories is now possible. This capability will improve the current method of storing a reference to a file (for example, in OLE links or desktop shortcuts). Renaming the target file breaks the links to that file. Renaming a directory breaks all the links to files in that directory and all files and directories underneath it. NTFS 5.0 will support the creation and assignment of unique IDs to a file or directory and guarantee that it will retain that ID.

■ The ability to add disk space to an NTFS volume without rebooting has been added.

■ Decompressing and recompressing compressed file data when transmitted over a network can be avoided, reducing CPU overhead on the server.

Microsoft Management Console

The Microsoft Management Console (MMC) provides system administrators with a common console for viewing network functions and using administrative tools. The MMC displays consoles that host programs called *snap-ins*, which provide the functionality needed to administer the network. The MMC meets the following goals:

■ **Offers a single, integrated user interface for management tools** Instead of the variety of interfaces in today's management tools, MMC provides a common, consistent user interface to management functions.

■ **Provides a single host for all management tools** The MMC doesn't replace existing enterprise console and management applications; it allows them to be packaged as snap-ins so that they can be accessed from a single interface.

■ **Facilitates task delegation** Using the MMC, a system administrator can group subsets of administrative tasks into tools and forward those tools to other users for task completion.

■ **Lowers total cost of ownership for the desktop** Being able to delegate tasks, group tools and processes logically, and manage through a single interface allows systems administrators to better organize their tools and tasks and simplify remote administration.

In addition to providing integration and commonality of administrative tools, the MMC also enables total console customization so that administrators can create management consoles that include only the administrative tools they need. Customization helps make administration more task-based because the tools relate more closely to the tasks that need to be performed.

Besides the MMC, Windows NT 5.0 adds Web-Based Enterprise Management (WBEM), which provides the Common Information Model (CIM)–based system instrumentation required to build management applications. The Windows Management Interface (WMI) layer enables device drivers and system

459

components to surface instrumentation data and events to WBEM-based applications. Microsoft will use the MMC (not WBEM) for future management applications in Windows NT and the BackOffice family of applications. Also, the MMC is user extensible—the programming interfaces will be documented on MSDN.

Microsoft Software Installer

Automatic application installation allows an administrator to specify a set of applications that will always be available to a user or a group of users. If a required application isn't available when needed, it is automatically installed. By using Windows NT 5.0 installation services, IT managers will be able to deploy or update applications to any user or group of users with a few simple steps from a central location. Applications will be automatically loaded onto the machine of a user in the group either in part or entirely, depending on the need, the next time the user logs on.

The new Windows NT Server 5.0 transaction-based software installer plays a key role in the Zero Administration Windows initiative by providing several key features, including these:

- Integration with the Active Directory

- Standard package format and installation service, which handles installing, repairing, removing, and dependency tracking of components

- Resiliency, which means that products can be repaired, transactions can be rolled back, and redundant install points can be used to help maintain applications over time

- Just-in-time (JIT) installations in which applications can be designed to install components on demand

- Support for lockdown, which allows installation of advertised applications to be successfully completed even when logged-on users don't have enough rights to install these applications

The Microsoft Software Installer (MSI) allows "no touch" application and operating system maintenance. Windows NT Workstation 5.0 will virtually eliminate the need to "visit" desktops for any type of software-related issues. MSI is an enabling technology on which scalable software life-cycle management products can be built.

Storage Management

Windows NT 5.0 includes improved disk management capabilities that allow administrators to perform online tasks without shutting down the system or interrupting users (for example, to create, extend, or mirror a volume). The new Windows NT 5.0 Backup utility allows administrators to back up data to disk as well as to tape. Unlike previous versions of the Windows NT Backup utility, which required users to back up data to tape drives only, this version allows users to back up data to a wide variety of media, such as tape drives, external hard disk drives, Zip disks, and logical drives.

Management tasks such as mounting and dismounting media or drive functions are now done by a utility called the Windows NT Media Services (NTMS). This utility presents a common interface to robotic changers and media libraries, enables multiple applications to share local libraries and tape or disk drives, and controls removable media within a single-server system.

Other improvements include an enhanced version of the NTFS file system, which offers many performance enhancements and support for file encryption and per-user disk quotas to monitor and limit disk space use.

IntelliMirror

IntelliMirror is a set of management technologies that benefits users and IT managers by combining the power and flexibility of distributed computing with the reliability and security of a tightly managed environment. At its core, IntelliMirror works by "intelligently mirroring" a user's data, applications, system files, and administrative settings on Windows NT 5.0–based servers. The MIS is an enabler of IntelliMirror. This new technology enables the following improvements in administration, setup, and recovery of user environments:

- **Replaceable PCs**   If a user's PC breaks, because the user's environment is mirrored on the server, PCs will be easily and quickly replaced. When the user logs on, his or her complete environment, including data, applications, preferences, and administrative policies is automatically restored.

- **Policy-based administration**   Administrators will find it easy to apply policies, such as custom desktops, automatic application installation, and controlled access to applications, to any user or group of users. To support roaming users, these profiles follow the user while he or she is logging onto any Windows NT Workstation 5.0–based PC on the corporate network.

IntelliMirror offers the following user-oriented benefits:

■ **Automatic installation of operating system and applications**   If a user's PC stops working, the complete desktop environment—including data, applications, preferences, and administrative policies—will be restored quickly and easily the next time the user logs on to an existing or a new Windows NT Workstation 5.0–based PC.

■ **True roaming user support**   Users will be able to access their complete desktop environment while "roaming" to any Windows NT Workstation 5.0–based PC on a corporate network.

■ **Offline storage**   Users will be able to more easily take local and key network-based resources offline, such as on a laptop computer. Personal data will automatically synchronize when the user reconnects to the network.

Application Development

Windows NT 5.0 is the platform that enables the next generation of distributed Internet and intranet applications. Built-in services such as Active Directory, Microsoft Internet Information Server, Microsoft Message Queue Server, and Microsoft Transaction Server provide developers with the infrastructure to rapidly develop richer, more reliable enterprise applications. Application services such as dynamic HTML, multimedia, transactions, and server-side scripting enable rich clients and robust servers.

Extensions to Distributed COM (DCOM) will support communication among objects on different computers—on a local area network (LAN), on a wide area network (WAN), or even on the Internet—so that applications can be distributed at locations that make the most sense. DCOM makes it easy to write a distributed application that scales from the smallest single computer environment to the largest pool of server machines while using network bandwidth carefully and providing great response times for users. DCOM also takes advantage of existing custom and off-the-shelf components and provides a smooth migration path to sophisticated load-balancing and fault-tolerance features.

Job Object

Windows NT 5.0 contains an extension to the process model called a *job*. A job object is a namable, securable, sharable object that controls certain attributes of processes associated with the job. A job object's basic function is to allow groups of processes to be managed and manipulated as a unit. In some ways, the job object compensates for the lack of a structured process tree on Windows NT (yet in many ways is more powerful than a UNIX-style process tree). The job object also records basic accounting information for all processes associated with the job and for all processes that were associated with the job but have since terminated.

A job object can contain limits that are forced on each process associated with the job, limits such as these:

- **Default working set minimum and maximum** Defines the specified working set minimum and maximum for each process in the job. (This is not a jobwide working set—each process has its own working set with the same minimum and maximum values.)

- **Jobwide user-mode CPU time limit** Limits the maximum amount of user-mode CPU time that the processes in the job can consume (including processes that have run and exited). Once this limit is reached, all the processes in the job will be terminated with an error code and no new processes can be created in the job (unless the limit is reset). The job object is signaled, so any threads waiting on the job will be released.

- **Per-process user-mode CPU time limit** Allows each process in the job to accumulate only a fixed maximum amount of user-mode CPU time and then terminates it (with no chance to clean up).

- **Maximum number of active processes** Limits the number of concurrently executing processes in the job.

- **Job processor affinity** Sets the processor affinity mask for each process in the job. (Individual threads can alter their affinity to any subset of the job affinity, but processes can't alter their process affinity setting.)

- **Job process priority class** Sets the priority class for each process in the job. Threads can't increase their priority relative to the class (as they normally can). Attempts to increase thread priority are ignored. (No error is returned on calls to *SetThreadPriority*, but the increase doesn't occur.)

Jobs can also be set to queue an entry to an I/O completion port object, which other threads might be waiting on with the Win32 *GetQueuedCompletionStatus* function.

You can also place security limits on processes in a job. You can set a job such that each process runs under the same jobwide access token. You can then create a job to restrict processes from impersonating or creating processes that have access tokens that contain the local administrator's group. In addition, you can apply security filters such that when threads in processes contained in a job impersonate client threads, certain privileges and security IDs (SIDs) can be eliminated from the impersonation token.

Finally, you can also place user interface limits on processes in a job. Such limits include being able to restrict processes from opening handles to windows owned by threads outside the job, reading and/or writing to the clipboard, and changing the many user interface system parameters via the Win32 *SystemParametersInfo* function.

A process can be a member of only one job object, and once established, its association with the job can't be broken; all processes created by the process and its descendents are associated with the same job as well. Operations performed on the job object affect all processes associated with the job object.

As you can see in Table 10-1, several new Win32 functions are being added to create and manipulate jobs.

Table 10-1   New Win32 API Functions for Jobs

Function	Description
CreateJobObject	Creates a job object (with an optional name)
OpenJobObject	Opens an existing job object by name
AssignProcessToJobObject	Adds a process to a job
TerminateJobObject	Terminates all processes in a job
SetInformationJobObject	Sets limits
QueryInformationJobObject	Retrieves information about the job, such as CPU time, page fault count, number of processes, list of process IDs, quotas or limits, and security limits

Details on the job object will be included in a future edition of the Platform SDK.

Plug and Play and WDM

Windows NT 5.0 will include enhancements to simplify device driver development and device management. These enhancements include power management, Plug and Play, and support for the new Microsoft Win32 Driver Model (WDM).

Plug and Play makes it easy to install and troubleshoot new hardware. Plug and Play support in Windows NT 5.0 includes a new Hardware Wizard, the Device Manager, and improved support for laptop computers. The new Hardware Wizard consolidates the most commonly used hardware-related tools and functions into a single wizard, making device management easier and faster. Adding new hardware, changing device properties, unplugging or ejecting devices, and resolving hardware conflicts are just a few of the operations that the Hardware Wizard can perform.

Plug and Play is part of the WDM, which is a new, unified driver model for Windows NT 5.0 and Microsoft Windows 98. WDM will enable new devices to have a single driver for both operating systems. (Windows NT 5.0 will continue to support existing Windows NT 4.0 drivers.) WDM drivers are binary-compatible across Windows NT 5.0 *x86* and Windows 98 platforms and are source-portable to Windows NT 5.0 RISC-based platforms. The WDM interfaces are based on the Windows NT driver model but have significant extensions for Plug and Play and power management.

A WDM driver includes the DDK header file *wdm.h*. Exclusively Windows NT 5.0 kernel-mode drivers continue to include the same DDK header file as for previous releases, *ntddk.h*, or another system-supplied header specific to a type of device, such as *scsi.h*.

Windows NT 5.0 Plug and Play drivers aren't limited to using the WDM interfaces. Drivers can call other interfaces to support legacy Windows NT drivers, detection, or other Windows NT–specific capabilities that WDM doesn't provide. Keep in mind that if a driver uses features specific to Windows NT, it is no longer compatible with Windows 98. If a driver will be used under both Windows NT and Windows 98, only WDM interfaces can be used.

Plug and Play is described in more detail later in the chapter.

Very Large Memory on Alpha

Windows NT 5.0 adds support for accessing up to 28 GB of memory on Digital Alpha AXP systems. This extension is called *VLM*, for *Very Large Memory*. VLM won't be supported on the *x86* family of processors. As you'll see in the next section, Microsoft is building a true 64-bit version of Windows NT that will run on the Alpha AXP and the upcoming Intel IA64 architecture.

Windows NT 4.0 has always supported 64-bit offsets for file I/O operations but has limited each process to a private 2-GB (or on Windows NT Server, Enterprise Edition, a 3-GB) address space. VLM allows an application to use 64-bit pointers and therefore directly access an address space that is much larger than 2 GB. This extension is being implemented to meet the needs of data-intensive applications, such as database management systems, in which the application needs to keep a large amount of information in physical memory. Restricting that information to fit within the 2-GB (or even the 3-GB) address space isn't acceptable for such applications.

With VLM, applications on Alpha systems can address up to 28 GB of memory beyond their 2-GB private address space. Figure 10-2 shows the address space layout and where the VLM region exists.

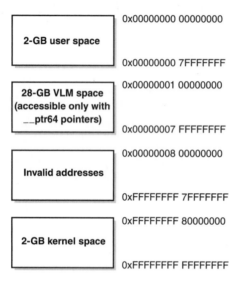

2-GB user space	0x00000000 00000000
	0x00000000 7FFFFFFF
28-GB VLM space (accessible only with __ptr64 pointers)	0x00000001 00000000
	0x00000007 FFFFFFFF
Invalid addresses	0x00000008 00000000
	0xFFFFFFFF 7FFFFFFF
2-GB kernel space	0xFFFFFFFF 80000000
	0xFFFFFFFF FFFFFFFF

Figure 10-2
Address space layout on Alpha

To provide access to the large memory area, a 64-bit pointer data type is required. (See __ptr64 added in Visual C++ 5.0 for Alpha.) A small set of new Win32 APIs is being added to operate on memory using 64-bit pointers. These functions provide the following basic services:

■ Allocate, free, protect, and query page-aligned blocks of memory addressable through 64-bit pointers (*VirtuaAllocVlm*, *VirtualFreeVlm*, *VirtualProtectVlm*, and *VirtualQueryVlm*).

■ Copy, move, zero, and fill memory using either 32-bit or 64-bit addresses (*MoveMemoryVlm*, *CopyMemoryVlm*, *FillMemoryVlm*, and *ZeroMemoryVlm*).

■ Map files into the large memory area (*MapViewOfFileVlm*, *UnMapViewOfFileVlm*).

■ Read data from a noncached file into memory using a 64-bit address. I/O can be done asynchronously only by using either an I/O completion port or an event object for notification (*ReadFileVlm*).

■ Write data from memory into a noncached file using a 64-bit pointer. I/O can be done asynchronously only by using either a completion-port-based completion or an event-object-based completion (*Write-FileVlm*).

■ Read and write the virtual memory of a specified process using 64-bit pointers to define the memory range in the other process to be addressed (*ReadProcessMemoryVlm*, *WriteProcessMemoryVlm*).

For interface details on these services, see MSDN.

VLM has an important restriction on the virtual addresses that can be addressed by 64-bit pointers, namely that such addresses must be backed by locked-down physical memory. In other words, all committed VLM memory must be backed by physical memory that must be available at the time the address space is committed. The virtual address space used to map this memory can be reserved, but the actual memory committed must be backed by physical memory. Page faults are never taken on VLM addresses unless these addresses are being used to map an actual data file; hence, paging files are never used for any of this memory. Page faults are taken only on mapped data files, and each page will be faulted only once (when first accessed) and then effectively locked into memory, never to be removed.

Despite these restrictions, VLM does meet the need for the class of applications described above that demand high-speed access to large portions of memory.

User Improvements

Windows NT 5.0 will include the same Web-integrated graphical user interface (GUI) as Windows 98, called the *Active Desktop*. This GUI is based on the evolution of Dynamic HTML rendering technology. The Active Desktop allows you to browse your computer in the same way you surf Web sites. You can also use Web pages as backgrounds in individual folder windows supported by the shell. The following are some of the other user interface improvements included in Windows NT 5.0:

■ Customizable taskbar with a user-defined toolbar

■ Personal FAX services (This capability was added after the release of Windows NT 4.0.)

- Content-indexing support in the file system, which allows searches based on the value of attributes of compound documents

- DirectX 5.0 support, which affords high-performance execution of graphics-intensive applications, such as games

- DVD support

- Multiple monitor support

Three other user improvements—Task Scheduler, Windows Scripting Host, and international extensions—warrant special attention.

Task Scheduler

Windows NT has a rudimentary scheduling facility called the Schedule service. Its basic user interface is the At command, not an especially user-friendly tool because it requires a fair amount of familiarity with the arcane world of the command prompt. (The Windows NT Resource Kit includes a GUI interface to the Schedule service.)

The new Task Scheduler in Windows NT 5.0 provides a user-friendly GUI that is the same on both Windows 98 and Windows NT, with the exception of added security features in Windows NT. The interface is fully integrated into the operating system and is accessible from the My Computer icon on the desktop. You can drag and drop programs right into Task Scheduler to quickly add a new task, or you can use the Create Scheduled Task wizard.

You can schedule any script, program, or document to be invoked at any time or any interval, every day to once a year, and on events such as system boot, user logon, or system idle. A task is saved as a file with a .JOB extension, which enhances the ability to move from computer to computer. Administrators can create scheduled maintenance task files and place them where needed. You can access the Task Folder remotely from the Network Neighborhood as well as send tasks in e-mail.

On Windows NT, scheduled tasks are created and executed based on standard Windows NT security permissions. Because Windows NT is a multiuser environment, when tasks are created, a username and password are required that will set the current security context in which the task will execute. This requirement allows multiple tasks to run on a single computer in the security context that was supplied. Multiple users can each have their own individual scheduled tasks.

The Task Scheduler also provides a fully programmable set of interfaces. The Task Scheduler is a COM-based object, which adds all the advantages of

COM, including language independence and platform independence (as well as remote capabilities provided by DCOM). All of the functionality in the Task Scheduler is completely accessible from these APIs.

Windows Scripting Host

Windows NT 5.0 supports direct script execution from the GUI or the command line. This support is provided through the Windows Scripting Host (WSH) and allows administrators or users to save time by automating many user interface actions, such as creating a shortcut, connecting to a network server, disconnecting from a network server, and so on.

Previously, the only native scripting language supported by the Windows operating system was based on the MS-DOS command language. Although this MS-DOS-based scripting language is fast and small, it has limited features compared to modern scripting languages. WSH supports a language-independent architecture called *ActiveX scripting,* which supports newer, more robust scripting languages such as Microsoft Visual Basic script and JavaScript but also allows other software companies to build Microsoft ActiveX scripting engines for languages such as Perl, TCL, REXX, and Python.

International Extensions

Since its initial design stages, Windows NT has incorporated international support through Unicode and resource files that store user interface elements in multiple languages. Windows NT 5.0 is the culmination of several years of progressive improvements in the operating system's international support.

In previous editions of Windows NT, Asian and Middle East editions were a superset of the core U.S. and European editions and contained additional APIs to handle more complex text input and layout requirements. In Windows NT 5.0, all APIs are contained in all language editions.

Windows NT 5.0 will support the input and display of languages used in many locales. Because all language editions of Windows NT 5.0 are based on the same core code—the same API set, the same character encoding, the same fonts and character tables—it will be much easier to maintain multilingual networks and machines using Windows NT 5.0 and to create applications that can easily support multilingual documents.

In addition, every language edition will ship with the components necessary to support the input, display, and formatting of text in all languages that Windows NT supports. For example, each CD will include at least one font to represent each script supported by the system.

System Extensions

Windows NT Server supports two integrated extensions to the operating system: Microsoft Cluster Server (bundled with Windows NT Server, Enterprise Edition) and Windows NT Terminal Server for Windows NT Server 4.0. Windows NT 5.0 is being enhanced to support the evolution of these products.

Clusters

The first release of clustering support for Windows NT shipped with Windows NT Server, Enterprise Edition 4.0. This initial version supported a two-server cluster. This feature improves data and application availability by allowing two servers to trade ownership of the same hard disks within a cluster. When a system in the cluster fails, the cluster software automatically recovers the resources and transfers the work from the failed system to the other server within the cluster. As a result, the failure of one system in the cluster doesn't affect the other systems, and in many cases, the client applications are completely unaware of the failure—meaning high server availability for users. In addition, this two-server cluster system can be used for manual load-balancing and for unloading servers for planned maintenance, without downtime.

With Windows NT 5.0, the same technology will roll forward with enhancements for setup and ease of management as the primary focus. Future releases will incorporate support for more than two nodes.

Microsoft Terminal Server

Microsoft Windows NT Terminal Server is an extension to Windows NT Server 4.0 that provides multiuser access support to the Windows operating system family product line. This allows access to 16-bit or 32-bit Windows-based applications from any of the following types of desktops:

- A new class of low-cost hardware, commonly referred to as Windows-based Terminals, that will be marketed by third-party hardware vendors

- Any existing 32-bit Windows desktop operating system, such as Microsoft Windows 95, Windows 98, or Windows NT Workstation (running the 32-bit Windows NT Terminal Server client as a window within the local desktop environment)

- Older 16-bit Windows-based desktops running the Windows 3.11 operating system (running the 16-bit Windows NT Terminal Server client as a window within the local desktop environment)

■ X-based Terminals, Apple Macintosh, MS-DOS, Network Computers, and UNIX-based desktops (via a third-party add-on product)

Components of Windows NT Terminal Server

Windows NT Terminal Server consists of three components—the Windows NT Server multiuser core, the "super-thin" Windows-based client software, and the Remote Desktop Protocol.

Windows NT Server multiuser core The multiuser server core provides the ability to host multiple, simultaneous client sessions on Windows NT Server. Windows NT Terminal Server is capable of directly hosting compatible multiuser client desktops running on a variety of Windows-based and non-Windows-based hardware. Standard Windows-based applications don't need to be modified to run on the Windows NT Terminal Server, and all standard Windows NT–based management infrastructure and technologies can be used to manage the client desktops.

Super-thin client The client software presents, or displays, the familiar 32-bit Windows user interface on a range of desktop hardware, from Windows-based Terminal devices to PCs running Windows 95, Windows 98, Windows NT Workstation, or Windows for Workgroups.

Remote Desktop Protocol This protocol allows a super-thin client to communicate with the Windows NT Terminal Server over the network. This protocol is based on the International Telecommunications Union (ITU) T.120 protocol, which is currently used in Microsoft NetMeeting. It is tuned for high-bandwidth enterprise environments and will also support encrypted sessions.

Operating System Support in Windows NT 5.0

Windows NT Terminal Server for Windows NT 4.0 replaced a number of key system components, such as the Win32 subsystem and NTOSKRNL.EXE. In Windows NT 5.0, all the changes necessary to support Windows NT Terminal Server are being integrated into the base product. (Details on packaging, pricing, and licensing of Windows NT Terminal Server in the Windows NT 5.0 time frame are yet to be decided.)

The main extension is the virtualization of sessions. A session consists of the processes and other system objects (such as the window station, desktops, and windows) that represent a single user's workstation logon session. Each process will now map to a session-specific copy of the kernel-mode portion of the Win32 subsystem (WIN32K.SYS). In addition, each session will have its own copy of the Win32 subsystem process (CSRSS.EXE) and logon process (WINLOGON.EXE). The session manager process (SMSS.EXE) is responsible for creating new session objects, which means loading a session-private copy of WIN32K.SYS and creating the session-specific instances of CSRSS and WINLOGON.

To accomplish the virtualization of sessions, all sessionwide data structures allocated by the Win32 subsystem are being moved from systemwide paged pool to a new session pool, mapped at system virtual address 0xA4000000. When the process is first created, the address range 0xA0000000 through 0xAFFFFFFF will be mapped to the session-specific copy of WIN32K.SYS and its associated memory pool that corresponds to the session that process belongs to. A *session working set* is also being added so that processes within a session will compete for physical memory among themselves, not against other sessions.

The system will still see a single pool of threads when it comes to scheduling decisions—the scheduling code isn't being changed to be aware of sessions. And no changes are being made to the context-switch code to recognize when switching from one thread in one session to another thread in another session, because the process page directory for the process that owns the thread will already have been initialized properly to point to the session-specific memory areas in system space.

Session objects are created only if Terminal Server is enabled—in other words, a typical Windows NT Workstation or Windows NT Server system won't have the additional session data structures added to support Terminal Server.

Plug and Play and Power Management

Plug and Play is a combination of hardware and software support that enables a computer system to recognize and adapt to hardware configuration changes with little or no user intervention. With Plug and Play, a user can add or remove devices dynamically, without manual configuration and without any intricate knowledge of computer hardware. For example, a user can dock a portable computer and use the docking station's Ethernet card to connect to the network without changing the configuration. Later, the user can undock that same computer and use a modem to connect to the network—again without making any manual configuration changes.

Plug and Play allows a user to change a computer's configuration with the assurance that all devices will work together and that the machine will boot correctly after the changes are made. Before I describe the changes being made to Windows NT to support Plug and Play and power management, let's review how the Plug and Play architecture has evolved.

The Evolution of Plug and Play

Support for Plug and Play was first provided in Windows 95; since that time, however, Plug and Play has evolved dramatically. This evolution is largely a result of the OnNow design initiative, which defines a comprehensive, systemwide approach to controlling system and device configuration and power management. One product of the OnNow initiative is the Advanced Configuration and Power Interface (ACPI) version 1.0 specification, which defines a new system board and BIOS interface that extends Plug and Play data to include power management and other new configuration capabilities, all under complete control of the operating system.

Unlike Plug and Play support in Windows 95, the Windows NT 5.0 Plug and Play implementation doesn't rely on an Advanced Power Management (APM) BIOS or a Plug and Play BIOS. These two BIOS implementations designed for Windows 95 were early attempts to support Plug and Play and power management. ACPI provides these services for both Windows NT 5.0 and Windows 98.

The ACPI methods defined are independent of the operating system or the CPU. ACPI specifies a register-level interface to core Plug and Play and power management functions and defines a descriptive interface for additional hardware features. This arrangement gives system designers the ability to implement a range of Plug and Play and power management features with different hardware designs while using the same operating system driver. ACPI also provides a generic system-event mechanism for Plug and Play and power management.

Windows NT 5.0 Implementation

The Windows NT 5.0 Plug and Play architecture is designed to meet the following two goals:

- Extend the existing Windows NT input/output infrastructure to support Plug and Play and power management while also supporting industry hardware standards for Plug and Play

- Achieve common device driver interfaces that support Plug and Play and power management for many device classes under Windows NT 5.0 and Windows 98

In Windows NT 5.0, Plug and Play support is optimized for laptop, workstation, and server computers that include ACPI system boards. In addition, Plug and Play device driver support for many device classes is provided by

WDM, which also supports power management and other new capabilities that the operating system can configure and control.

Windows NT 5.0 provides the following support for Plug and Play:

- **Automatic and dynamic recognition of installed hardware**   This support includes initial system installation, recognition of Plug and Play hardware changes that occur between system boots, and response to run-time hardware events such as dock/undock and device insertion/removal.

- **Hardware resource allocation (and reallocation)**   Drivers for Plug and Play devices do not assign their own resources. Instead, the required resources for a device are identified when the operating system enumerates the device. The Plug and Play Manager retrieves the requirements for each device during resource allocation. Based on the resource requests each device makes, the Plug and Play Manager assigns the appropriate hardware resources such as I/O ports, IRQs, DMA channels, and memory locations. The Plug and Play Manager reconfigures resource assignments when needed, such as when a device is added to the system and requests resources that are already in use.

- **Loading of appropriate drivers**   The Plug and Play Manager determines which drivers are required to support a particular device and loads those drivers.

- **An interface for driver interaction with the Plug and Play system**   The interface consists primarily of I/O routines, Plug and Play I/O request packets (IRPs), required driver entry points, and information in the registry.

- **Interaction with power management**   One of the key features of both Plug and Play and power management is dynamic handling of events. The addition or removal of a device is an example of such a dynamic event, as is the ability to awaken a device or put it to sleep. Plug and Play and power management both use WDM-based functions and have similar methods for responding to dynamic events.

- **Registration for device notification events**   Plug and Play enables user-mode code to register for and be notified of certain Plug and Play events. The *RegisterDeviceNotification* routine allows callers to filter exactly the class or device for which they want to receive notification. The method of notification can be specific, such as a file system handle, or general, such as a class of devices. Legacy Windows NT notification methods will continue to work as before.

Driver Changes

The native Windows NT 5.0 Plug and Play support results in the following changes for developers who previously created drivers under the Windows NT 4.0 device driver model:

■ **Bus drivers separate from the HAL** Bus drivers control an I/O bus, including per-slot functionality that is device-independent. In the new architecture, bus drivers have moved out of the hardware abstraction layer (HAL) to coordinate with changes and extensions made to existing kernel-mode components, such as the executive, device drivers, and the HAL. (Microsoft generally provides Bus drivers.)

■ **New methods and capabilities to support device installation and configuration** The new design includes changes and extensions to existing user-mode components, such as the Spooler, class installers, Control Panel applications, and Setup. In addition, new kernel-mode and user-mode Plug and Play–enabled components have been added.

■ **New Plug and Play APIs to read and write information from the registry** For the new design, changes and extensions were made to the registry structure. This structure supports Plug and Play and allows the registry to be enhanced in future versions of Windows NT, while also providing backward compatibility.

Windows NT 5.0 will support legacy Windows NT drivers, but since these don't support Plug and Play and power management, systems running these drivers will have reduced capabilities in these two areas. Manufacturers who want to support complete Plug and Play capabilities for their devices and who want the same drivers to function on both Windows NT and Windows 98 will need to develop new drivers that integrate the latest Plug and Play and power management functionality.

The Windows NT 5.0 DDK documents the driver modifications required to allow current drivers to work in a Windows NT 5.0 Plug and Play system.

Windows NT 5.0 Plug and Play Architecture

The components involved in Plug and Play are shown in Figure 10-3 and described in the following subsections.

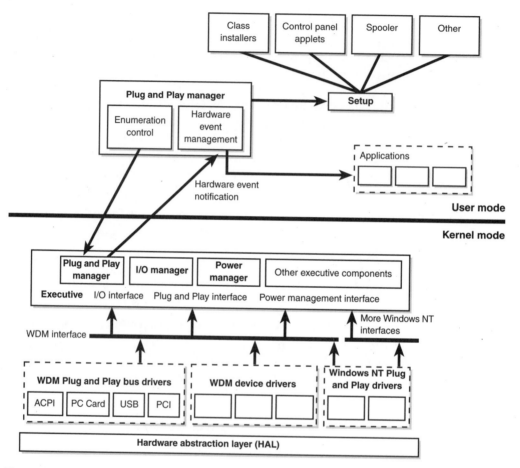

Figure 10-3
Windows NT 5.0 Plug and Play architecture

I/O Manager

The I/O manager, described in Chapter 7, provides core services for device drivers. It translates user-mode read and write commands into read or write IRPs. It manages all the other main operating system IRPs. These interfaces work as they did in Windows NT 4.0.

Kernel-Mode Plug and Play Manager

The kernel-mode Plug and Play Manager directs bus drivers to perform enumeration and configuration and device drivers to add devices, start devices, and so on. It also coordinates with the user-mode Plug and Play counterpart to pause or remove devices that are available for such actions.

The Plug and Play Manager maintains a device tree, viewable through Device Manager, which keeps track of the active devices in the system and information about those devices. The Plug and Play Manager updates the device tree as devices are added and removed or as resources are reallocated. The device tree is hierarchical, with devices on a bus represented as children of the bus adapter or controller. The registry is the central repository for static hardware information. Plug and Play system components and drivers build, maintain, and access new and existing subtrees in the registry.

Power Manager and Policy Manager

The Power Manager is the kernel-mode component that works in combination with the Policy Manager to handle power management APIs, coordinate power events, and generate power management IRPs. For example, when several devices need to be turned off, the Power Manager collects those requests, determines which requests must be serialized, and then generates appropriate power management IRPs.

The Policy Manager monitors activity in the system and integrates user status, application status, and device driver status into power policy. In specified circumstances or on request, the Policy Manager generates IRPs to change device power states.

WDM Interface for Plug and Play

The I/O system provides a layered architecture for drivers that includes WDM drivers, driver layers, and device objects.

Types of drivers   From the Plug and Play perspective, there are three kinds of drivers:

- A *bus driver* services a bus controller, adapter, bridge, or any device that has child devices. Bus drivers are required drivers, and Microsoft generally provides them; each type of bus on a system has one bus driver.

- A *function driver* is the main device driver and provides the operational interface for its device. It is a required driver unless the device is used raw (an implementation in which I/O is done by the bus driver and any bus filter drivers). The function driver for a device is typically implemented as a driver/minidriver pair. In such driver pairs, a *class driver* (usually written by Microsoft) provides the functionality required by all devices of that type, and a *minidriver* (usually written by the device vendor) provides device-specific functionality. The Plug and Play Manager loads one function driver for each device.

- A *filter driver* sorts I/O requests for a bus, a device, or a class of devices. Filter drivers are optional and can exist in any number, placed above or below a function driver and above a bus driver. Usually, filter drivers are supplied by system original equipment manufacturers (OEMs) or independent hardware vendors (IHVs).

In most cases, lower-level filter drivers modify the behavior of device hardware. For example, a lower-level class-filter driver for mouse devices could provide acceleration, performing a nonlinear conversion of mouse movement data.

Upper-level filter drivers usually provide added-value features for a device. For example, an upper-level device filter driver for a keyboard can enforce additional security checks.

Driver layers   Each device has two or more driver layers: a bus driver for the underlying I/O bus (or the Plug and Play Manager for root-enumerated devices) and a function driver for the device. Optionally, one or more filter drivers can be provided for the bus or device.

Device objects   A driver creates a device object for each device it controls; the device object represents the device to the driver. The three kinds of device objects that pertain to Plug and Play are physical device objects, functional device objects, and filter device objects. Physical device objects represent a device on a bus; every Plug and Play API that refers to a device refers to the physical device object. Functional device objects represent the functionality of a device to a function driver. Filter device objects represent a filter driver as a hook to add value. These three kinds of device objects are all of the type DEVICE_OBJECT, but they are used differently and can have different device extensions.

WDM Bus Drivers

Bus power management and Plug and Play are controlled by WDM bus drivers, which are standard WDM drivers that expose bus capabilities. In the Plug and Play context, any device from which other devices are enumerated is referred to as a *bus*. A bus driver responds to new Plug and Play and power management IRPs and can be extended using filter drivers.

The bus driver is primarily responsible for the following tasks:

- Enumerating the devices on its bus

- Reporting dynamic events on its bus to the operating system

- Responding to Plug and Play and power management IRPs

- Multiplexing access to the bus (for some buses)

- Generically administering the devices on its bus

During enumeration, a bus driver identifies the devices on its bus and creates device objects for them. The method a bus driver uses to identify connected devices depends on the particular bus.

A bus driver performs certain operations on behalf of the devices on its bus but usually doesn't handle reads and writes to the devices on its bus. (A device's function driver handles these.) A bus driver acts as a function driver for its controller, adapter, bridge, or other device.

Microsoft provides bus drivers for most common buses, including Peripheral Component Interconnect (PCI), Plug and Play Industry Standard Architecture (ISA), Small Computer System Interface (SCSI), and universal serial bus (USB). IHVs or OEMs can provide other bus drivers. A bus driver can be implemented as a driver/minidriver pair, the way a SCSI port/miniport pair drives a SCSI host adapter. In such driver pairs, one driver is linked to the second driver, and the second driver is a DLL.

The ACPI driver fulfills the role of both bus driver and function driver. ACPI allows the system to learn about devices that either don't have a standard way to enumerate themselves (that is, legacy devices) or are newly defined ACPI devices to be enumerated by ACPI. ACPI also installs upper-level filter drivers for devices that have functionality beyond the standard for their bus. For example, if a PCI bus driver installs a graphics controller with power controls that aren't supported by the PCI bus, the device can access its added functionality if the ACPI driver loads an upper-level filter driver for it.

WDM Device Drivers

WDM device drivers are usually the function driver/minidriver pair and filter drivers mentioned earlier. In addition to providing the operational interface for its device, function drivers play an important role in a power-managed system, contributing information (as the policy owner for the device) about power management capabilities and carrying out actions related to transitions between sleeping and fully-on power states.

User-Mode Plug and Play Components

The Windows NT 5.0 user-mode APIs for controlling and configuring devices in a Plug and Play environment are 32-bit extended versions of Windows 95–based Configuration Manager APIs. In Windows 95, the Configuration Manager is a virtual device driver (VxD) that exposes these routines as services to both ring 0 and ring 3 components. In Windows NT 5.0, these routines expose functionality from the user-mode Plug and Play Manager and are exclusively user-mode APIs. These APIs can be used by applications for customized hardware event management and to create new hardware events.

Plug and Play Certification

Although Plug and Play brings exciting new functionality to the Windows NT I/O system, its success will rely on the timely availability of certified Plug and Play device drivers when the operating system ships. Therefore, device driver writers need to incorporate Plug and Play and power management functionality into their drivers as soon as possible so that they can be submitted to the Microsoft Windows Hardware Quality Lab for testing and certification. (See *www.microsoft.com/hwdev* for more information.)

64-Bit Windows NT

In 1997, Microsoft announced plans to implement a fully 64-bit version of Windows NT. The target processor architectures are the existing 64-bit Alpha AXP platform and the upcoming Intel 64-bit (IA64) processors (the first implementation code-named Merced). A fully 64-bit Windows NT means that each 64-bit process will have a large, flat address space (initially at least 512 GB in size). The reason for supporting this platform is the same reason Microsoft moved from a 16-bit to a 32-bit address space—ever increasing requirements for storing and processing huge amounts of data in memory.

NOTE Although the VLM extensions in Windows NT 5.0 alleviate to some degree the address space limitations in 32-bit Windows NT, they present a variation of the process address space that requires special application support. Also, processes are limited to the storing of data in the large memory area. Finally, only the VLM-enabled Win32 API functions support 64-bit pointers—many other system functions don't. In 64-bit Windows NT, all APIs that accept pointers will accept 64-bit pointers.

In 64-bit Windows NT, the Win32 API will be extended to a true 64-bit programming interface called *Win64*. Various parameters that currently reference 32-bit memory addresses will be widened to 64-bit pointers. This new API will be designed to make porting from Win32 as straightforward as possible and will allow a vendor to maintain a single source that can be compiled to produce both a Win32 and Win64 binary. The 64-bit Windows NT will run existing 32-bit applications on both Alpha and Merced and new 64-bit applications in native 64-bit mode. However, mixing of the two within the same process won't be permitted.

This was just a brief preview of the strategy to provide 64-bit Windows NT. Developers should stay tuned for further information from Microsoft on plans for 64-bit Windows NT and how you can port your 32-bit source code to a Win32/Win64 common code base to prepare for 64-bit Windows NT.

Conclusion

In this chapter, you've gotten a glimpse of the changes in Windows NT 5.0. Again, for more complete information about the new or enhanced features in Windows NT 5.0, see the white papers and technical specifications available on Microsoft's Web site as well as on MSDN and TechNet.

GLOSSARY

access control list (ACL)   The part of a security descriptor that enumerates who has what access to an object. The owner of an object can change the object's ACL to allow or disallow others access to the object. An ACL is made up of an ACL header and zero or more access control entry (ACE) structures. An ACL with zero ACEs is called a null ACL and indicates that no user has access to the object.

access token   A data structure that contains the security identification of a process or a thread, which includes its security ID (SID), the list of groups that the user is a member of, and the list of privileges that are enabled and disabled. Each process has a primary access token that it inherits by default from its creating process.

affinity mask   A bitmask that specifies the processors on which the thread is allowed to run. The initial thread affinity mask is inherited from the process affinity mask.

APC queue   A queue in which asynchronous procedure calls (APCs) waiting to execute reside. The APC queues (one for user mode and one for kernel mode) are thread-specific—each thread has its own APC queues (unlike the DPC queue, which is systemwide).

asymmetric multiprocessing (ASMP)   A multiprocessing operation system that typically selects one processor to execute operating system code while other processors run only user code.

asynchronous I/O   An I/O model that allows an application to issue an I/O request and then continue executing while the device transfers the data. This type of I/O can improve an application's throughput because it allows the application to continue with other work while an I/O operation is in progress.

asynchronous procedure call (APC)   A function that provides a way for user programs and system code to execute code in the context of a particular user thread (and hence a particular process address space). An APC can be either kernel mode or user mode. (Kernel-mode APCs don't require "permission" from a target thread to run in that thread's context, as user-mode APCs do.)

attribute list   A special kind of file attribute in an NTFS file header that contains additional attributes. The attribute list is created if a particular file has too many attributes to fit in the MFT record. The attribute list attribute contains the name and type code of each of the file's attributes and the file reference of the MFT record where the attribute is located.

automatic working set trimming   A technique the memory manager uses when physical memory runs low to increase the amount of free memory available in the system.

bad-cluster file   A system file (filename $BadClus) that records any bad spots on the disk volume.

balance set manager   A system thread that wakes up once per second to check and possibly initiate various scheduling and memory management–related events.

bitmap file   A system file (filename $Bitmap) in which NTFS records the allocation state of the volume. The data attribute for the bitmap file contains a bitmap, each of whose bits represents a cluster on the volume, identifying whether the cluster is free or has been allocated to a file.

boot file   A system file (filename $Boot) that stores the Windows NT bootstrap code.

cache manager   The component of the Windows NT executive that provides systemwide caching services for NTFS and other file system drivers, including network file system drivers (servers and redirectors).

careful write   A technique for constructing a file system's I/O and caching support. *See also* write-through.

checked build   A special debug version of Windows NT Workstation that is available only as part of the MSDN Professional (or higher) subscription. (No checked build is available for Windows NT Server.) The checked build is created by compiling the Windows NT sources with the compile-time flag DEBUG set to TRUE.

checkpoint records   A checkpoint record that helps NTFS determine what processing would be needed to recover a volume if a crash were to occur immediately. This record also includes redo and undo information.

class drivers   A type of kernel-mode device driver that implements the I/O processing for a particular class of devices, such as disk, tape, or CD-ROM.

clock interrupt handler   A system routine that updates the system time and then decrements a counter that tracks how long the current thread has run.

cluster factor   The cluster size on a volume, which is established when a user formats the volume with either the Format command or the Disk Administrator utility.

clusters   Same-size allocation units into which a volume is divided. Each cluster must be uniquely numbered using 16 bits.

collided page fault   A fault that occurs when another thread or process faults a page that is currently being in-paged.

context switch   The procedure of saving the volatile machine state associated with a running thread, loading another thread's volatile state, and starting the new thread's execution.

control objects   A set of kernel objects that establishes semantics for controlling various operating system functions. This set includes the kernel process object, the asynchronous procedure call (APC) object, the deferred procedure call (DPC) object, and several objects used by the I/O system, such as the interrupt object.

deferred procedure call (DPC)   A routine that performs most of the work involved in handling a device interrupt after the interrupt service routine (ISR) executes. The DPC routine executes at an interrupt request level (IRQL) that is lower than that of the ISR to avoid blocking other interrupts unnecessarily. A DPC routine initiates I/O completion and starts the next queued I/O operation on a device.

device drivers   Loadable kernel-mode modules (typically ending in .SYS) that interface between the I/O system and the relevant hardware. Device drivers on Windows NT don't manipulate hardware directly, but rather they call parts of the HAL to interface with the hardware.

device objects   Data structures that represent a physical, logical, or virtual device on the system and describe its characteristics, such as the alignment it requires for buffers and the location of its device queue to hold incoming I/O request packets.

dirty page threshold   The number of pages that the system cache keeps in memory before waking up the cache manager's lazy writer system thread to write out pages back to the disk. This value is computed at system initialization time and depends on physical memory size and the value of the registry key HKLM\System...\Control\Session Manager\Memory Management\ LargeSystemCache.

dispatch code   Instructions of assembly language code stored in an interrupt object when it is initialized. When an interrupt occurs, this code is executed.

dispatch routines   The main functions that a device driver provides. Some examples of dispatch routines are open, close, read, and write, and any other capabilities the device, file system, or network supports. When called on to perform an I/O operation, the I/O manager generates an IRP and calls a driver through one of the driver's dispatch routines.

dispatcher database   A set of data structures the kernel maintains to make thread-scheduling decisions. The dispatcher database keeps track of which threads are waiting to execute and which processors are executing which threads. *See also* dispatcher ready queue.

dispatcher header   A data structure that contains the object type, signaled state, and a list of the threads waiting on that object.

dispatcher objects   A set of kernel objects that incorporates synchronization capabilities and alters or affects thread scheduling. The dispatcher objects include the kernel thread, mutex (called *mutant* internally), event, kernel event pair, semaphore, timer, and waitable timer.

dispatcher ready queue   The most important structure in the dispatcher database (located at *KiDispatcherReadyListHead*). The dispatcher ready queue is really a series of queues, one queue for each scheduling priority. The queues contain threads that are in the ready state, waiting to be scheduled for execution.

driver objects   Data structures that represent an individual driver in the system and record for the I/O manager the address of each of the driver's dispatch routines (entry points).

driver support routines   Routines called by device drivers to accomplish their I/O requests.

dynamic-link library (DLL)   A set of callable subroutines linked as a binary image that can be dynamically loaded by applications that use them.

environment subsystems   User processes that expose the native operating system services to user applications, thus providing an operating system environment, or personality. Windows NT ships with three environment subsystems: Win32, POSIX, and OS/2 1.2.

event   An object with a persistent state (signaled or not signaled) that can be used for synchronization.

exception   A synchronous condition that results from the execution of a particular instruction. Running the same program with the same data under the same conditions can reproduce exceptions.

exception dispatcher   A kernel module that services all exceptions, except those simple enough to be resolved by the trap handler. The exception dispatcher's job is to find an exception handler that can "dispose of" the exception.

executive   The upper layer of NTOSKRNL.EXE. (The kernel is the lower layer.) The executive contains the process and thread manager, the virtual memory manager, the memory manager, the security reference monitor, the I/O system, and the cache manager. *See also* kernel.

executive objects   Objects implemented by various components of the executive (such as the process manager, memory manager, I/O subsystem, and so on). The executive objects and object services are primitives that the environment subsystems use to construct their own versions of objects and other resources. Because executive objects are typically created either by an environment subsystem on behalf of a user application or by various components of the operating system as part of their normal operation, many of them contain (encapsulate) one or more kernel objects. *See also* kernel objects.

executive resources   Resources that provide both exclusive access (like a mutex) as well as shared read access (multiple readers sharing read-only access to a structure). Because executive resources are available only to kernel-mode code, they are not accessible from the Win32 API.

fast I/O   A means of reading or writing a cached file without going through the work of generating an I/O request packet (IRP).

fast LPC   A special interprocess communication facility used to send messages between threads.

file mapping objects   Win32 API underlying primitives in the memory manager that are used to implement shared memory (called *section objects* internally). *See also* section object.

file reference   A 64-bit value that identifies a file on an NTFS volume. The file reference consists of a file number and a sequence number. The file number corresponds to the position of the file's file record in the master file table minus 1 (or to the position of the base file record minus 1 if the file has more than one file record).

file system driver   A type of kernel-mode device driver that accepts I/O requests to files and satisfies the requests by issuing its own, more explicit, requests to physical device drivers.

file system filter driver   A type of kernel-mode device driver that intercepts I/O requests, performs additional processing, and passes them on to lower-level drivers.

filter drivers   *See* file system filter driver.

foreground application   The process that owns the thread that owns the window that is in focus.

free build   The version of the Windows NT system that can be purchased as a retail product. It is built with full compiler optimizations turned on and has internal symbol table information stripped out from the images. *See also* checked build.

GDI batching   A technique for accumulating graphics calls made by a Win32 application and then sending them as a "batch." GDI batching prevents unnecessary calls to the graphics subsystem, thus improving graphics performance.

hardware abstraction layer (HAL)   A loadable kernel-mode module (HAL.DLL) that provides the low-level interface to the hardware platform on which Windows NT is running. The HAL hides hardware-dependent details such as I/O interfaces, interrupt controllers, and multiprocessor communication mechanisms—any functions that are architecture-specific and machine-dependent.

heap   A region of one or more pages that can be subdivided and allocated in smaller chunks by a set of functions provided by the heap manager.

heap manager   A set of functions that allocate and deallocate variable amounts of memory (not on a page-size granularity). The heap manager functions exist in two places: NTDLL.DLL and NTOSKRNL.EXE. The subsystem APIs (such as the Win32 heap APIs) use the copy in NTDLL, and various executive components and device drivers use the copy in NTOSKRNL.

hyperspace   A special region used to map the process working set list and to temporarily map other physical pages for such operations as zeroing a page on the free list (when the zero list is empty and a zero page is needed), invalidating page table entries in other page tables (such as when a page is removed from the standby list), and on process creation to set up a new process's address space.

I/O request packet (IRP)   A data structure that controls how the I/O operation is processed at each stage. Most I/O requests are represented by an IRP, which travels from one I/O system component to another.

I/O subsystem API   The internal executive system services (such as *NtReadFile* and *NtWriteFile*) that subsystem DLLs call to implement a subsystem's documented I/O functions.

I/O system   The Windows NT executive component that accepts I/O requests (from both user-mode and kernel-mode callers) and delivers them, in a different form, to I/O devices.

ideal processor   The preferred processor that a particular thread should run on.

idle summary   A bitmask (*KiIdleSummary*) in which each set bit represents an idle processor.

impersonation   A capability that allows threads to have a different access token than that of the process.

initialization routine   A driver routine that the I/O manager executes when it loads the driver into the operating system. The initialization routine creates system objects that the I/O manager uses to recognize and access the driver.

in-paging I/O   A condition that occurs when a read operation must be issued to a file (paging or mapped) to satisfy a page fault. The in-page I/O operation is synchronous—the thread waits on an event until the I/O completes—and is not interruptible by asynchronous procedure call (APC) delivery.

intelligent file read-ahead   A technique that predicts what data the calling thread is likely to read next based on the data that it is currently reading.

interrupt   An asynchronous event (one that can occur at any time) that is unrelated to what the processor is executing. Interrupts are generated primarily by I/O devices, processor clocks, or timers, and they can be enabled (turned on) or disabled (turned off).

interrupt dispatch table (IDT)   A data structure that Windows NT uses to locate the routine that will handle a particular interrupt. The interrupt request level (IRQL) of the interrupting source serves as a table index, and table entries point to the interrupt-handling routines.

interrupt dispatcher   A submodule of the kernel's trap handler that responds to interrupts.

interrupt object   A kernel control object that allows device drivers to register interrupt service routines (ISRs) for their devices. An interrupt object contains all the information the kernel needs to associate a device ISR with a particular level of interrupt, including the address of the ISR, the interrupt request level (IRQL) at which the device interrupts, and the entry in the kernel's interrupt dispatch table with which the ISR should be associated.

interrupt request levels (IRQLs)   A ranking of interrupts by priority. A processor has an IRQL setting that threads can raise or lower. Interrupts that occur at or below the processor's IRQL setting are blocked, or masked, whereas interrupts that occur above the processor's IRQL setting are not masked.

interrupt service routine (ISR)   A device driver routine that the kernel's interrupt dispatcher transfers control to when a device issues an interrupt. In the Windows NT I/O model, ISRs run at a high device interrupt request level

(IRQL), so they perform as little work as possible to avoid blocking lower-level interrupts unnecessarily. An ISR queues a deferred procedure call (DPC), which runs at a lower IRQL, to execute the remainder of interrupt processing. Only drivers for interrupt-driven devices have ISRs; a file system, for example, doesn't have one.

job object   New namable, securable, sharable object in Windows NT 5.0 that controls certain attributes of processes associated with the job. A job object's basic function is to allow groups of processes to be managed and manipulated as a unit. The job object also records basic accounting information for all processes associated with the job and for all processes that were associated with the job but have since terminated.

kernel   The lowest layer in NTOSKRNL.EXE. The kernel, a component of the executive, determines how the operating system uses the processor or processors and ensures that they are used prudently. The kernel provides thread scheduling and dispatching, trap handling and exception dispatching, interrupt handling and dispatching, and multiprocessor synchronization. *See also* executive.

kernel mode   A privileged mode of code execution in a processor in which all memory is totally accessible and all CPU instructions can be issued. Operating system code (such as system services and device drivers) runs in kernel mode. *See also* user mode.

kernel objects   A primitive set of objects implemented by the Windows NT kernel. These objects are not visible to user-mode code but are created and used only within the executive. Kernel objects provide fundamental capabilities, such as synchronization, on which executive objects are built. *See also* executive objects.

kernel-mode device driver   The only type of driver that can directly control and access hardware devices.

kernel-mode graphics driver   A Win32 subsystem display or print device driver that translates device-independent graphics (GDI) requests into device-specific requests.

key   A mechanism to refer to data in the registry. Although keys appear in the object manager namespace, the registry manages them, in a way similar to how it manages file objects. Zero or more key values are associated with a key object; key values contain data about the key.

lazy writer A set of system threads that call the memory manager to flush cache contents to disk as a background activity (asynchronous disk writing). The cache manager optimizes disk I/O by using its lazy writer.

local procedure call (LPC) An interprocess communication facility for high-speed message passing (not available through the Win32 API but rather an internal mechanism available only to Windows NT operating system components). LPCs are typically used between a server process and one or more client processes of that server. An LPC connection can be established between two user-mode processes or between a kernel-mode component and a user-mode process.

local security authority (LSA) server A user-mode process running the image LSASS.EXE that is responsible for the local system security policy (such as which users are allowed to log on to the machine, password policies, the list of privileges granted to users and groups, and the system security auditing settings), user authentication, and sending security audit messages to the Event Log.

local security authority (LSA) server policy database A database (stored in the registry under HKEY_LOCAL_MACHINE\Security) that contains the system security policy settings. This database includes such information as what domains are trusted to authenticate logon attempts, who has permission to access the system and how (interactive, network, and service logons), who is assigned which privileges, and what kind of security auditing is to be performed.

log file A metadata file (filename $LogFile) NTFS uses to record all operations that affect the NTFS volume structure, including file creation or any commands, such as Copy, that alter the directory structure. The log file is used to recover an NTFS volume after a system failure.

logging A transaction-processing technique NTFS uses to maintain file system integrity in the case of system crashes or other failures. In NTFS logging, the suboperations of any transaction that alters important file system data structures are recorded in a log file before they are carried through on the disk so that if the system crashes, partially completed transactions can be redone or undone when the system comes back online.

logical cluster numbers (LCNs) The numbering of all clusters from the beginning of the volume to the end with which NTFS refers to physical locations on a disk. To convert an LCN to a physical disk address, NTFS multiplies the LCN by the cluster factor to get the physical byte offset on the volume, as the disk driver interface requires.

logical sequence numbers (LSNs)   The numbers that NTFS uses to identify records written to the log file.

logon process   A user-mode process running WINLOGON.EXE that is responsible for capturing the username and password, sending them to the local security authority server for verification, and creating the initial process in the user's session.

look-aside list   A fast memory allocation mechanism that contains only fixed-sized blocks. Look-aside lists can be either pagable or nonpagable, so they are allocated from paged or nonpaged pool.

mapped file I/O   The ability to view a file residing on disk as part of a process's virtual memory. A program can access the file as a large array without buffering data or performing disk I/O. The program accesses memory, and the memory manager uses its paging mechanism to load the correct page from the disk file. If the application writes to its virtual address space, the memory manager writes the changes back to the file as part of normal paging.

master file table (MFT)   The heart of the NTFS volume structure. The MFT is implemented as an array of file records. The size of each file record is fixed at 1 KB, regardless of cluster size.

memory manager   The Windows NT executive component that implements demand-paged virtual memory, giving each process the illusion that it has a 4-GB 32-bit address space (while mapping a subset of that address space to physical memory).

metadata   Data that describes the files on a disk; also called *volume structure data*.

metadata files   A set of files in each NTFS volume that contains the information used to implement the file system structure.

MFT mirror   An NTFS metadata file (filename $MFTMirr) located in the middle of the disk called that contains a copy of the first few rows of the master file table.

miniport drivers   A type of kernel-mode device driver that maps a generic I/O request to a type of port into a adapter type, such as a specific SCSI adapter.

mirror   A capability of the fault tolerant driver to duplicate data from one disk onto another disk so that a redundant copy can always be retrieved. This support is commonly called *RAID level 1*.

mirror set   A technique by which the contents of a partition on one disk are duplicated in an equal-size partition on another disk.

modified page writer   A thread in the virtual memory manager that is responsible for limiting the size of the modified page list by writing pages to their backing store locations when the list becomes too big. The modified page writer consists of two system threads: one to write out modified pages (*MiModifiedPageWriter*) to the paging file and a second one to write modified pages to mapped files (*MiMappedPageWriter*).

mount   A technique NTFS uses when it first accesses a volume; in this context, to mount means to prepare the volume for use. To mount the volume, NTFS looks in the boot file to find the physical disk address of the master file table.

MSDN   Microsoft Developer Network, Microsoft's support program for developers. MSDN offers four CD-ROM subscription programs: MSDN Library, Professional, Enterprise, and Universal

mutant   Internal name for a mutex.

mutex   A synchronization mechanism used to serialize access to a resource.

network logon service   A user-mode service inside the SERVICES.EXE process that responds to network logon requests. Authentication is handled as local logons are, by sending them to the LSASS process for verification.

network redirectors and servers   File system drivers that transmit remote I/O requests to a machine on the network and receive such requests, respectively.

nonpaged pool   Memory pool that consists of ranges of system virtual addresses that are guaranteed to be resident in physical memory at all times and thus can be accessed from any address space without incurring paging

I/O. Nonpaged pool is created at system initialization and is used by kernel-mode components to allocate system memory. There are two types of nonpaged pools: one for general use, and a small one (four pages) reserved for emergency use when nonpaged pool is full and the caller can't tolerate allocation failures.

NTDLL.DLL A special system-support library primarily for the use of subsystem DLLs that contains System service dispatch stubs to Windows NT executive system services and internal support functions used by subsystems, subsystem DLLs, and other native images.

NTKRNLMP.EXE The executive and kernel for multiprocessor systems.

NTOSKRNL.EXE The executive and kernel for uniprocessor systems.

object In the Windows NT executive, a single, run-time instance of a statically defined object type.

object attribute A field of data in an object that partially defines the object's state.

object directory A container object for other objects. The object directory is used to implement the hierarchical namespace within which other object types are stored.

object handle An index into a process-specific handle table, pointed to by the executive process (EPROCESS) block.

object manager The Windows NT executive component responsible for creating, deleting, protecting, and tracking objects. The object manager centralizes resource control operations that would otherwise be scattered throughout the operating system.

object type A system-defined data type, services that operate on instances of the data type, and a set of object attributes (sometimes called an *object class*).

page directory A page the memory manager creates to map the location of all page tables for that process. Each process has a single page directory.

page directory entries (PDEs) The page directory is composed of PDEs, each of which is currently 4 bytes long and describes the state and location of all the possible page tables for that process.

page fault   A reference to an invalid page. The kernel trap handler dispatches this kind of fault to the memory manager fault handler (*MmAccessFault*) to resolve.

page frame database   A database that describes the state of each page in physical memory. Pages are in one of eight states: active (also called valid), transition, standby, modified, modified no write, free, zeroed, or bad.

page table   A page of mapping information (made up of any array of page table entries) the operating system constructs that describes the location of the virtual pages in a process address space. Because Windows NT provides a private address space for each process, each process has its own set of process page tables to map that private address space, since the mappings will be different for each process. The page tables that describe system space are shared among all processes.

page table entry (PTE)   An entry in a process's page table that contains the address to which the virtual address is mapped. The page can be in physical memory or it can be on disk.

paged pool   A region of virtual memory in system space that can be paged in and out of the system process's working set. Paged pool is created at system initialization and is used by kernel-mode components to allocate system memory. Uniprocessor systems have two paged pools; multiprocessor systems have four. Having more than one paged pool reduces the frequency of system code blocking on simultaneous calls to pool routines.

PALcode   "Privileged Architecture Library," the Alpha operating system–specific support code that is similar to BIOS libraries.

port drivers   A type of kernel-mode device driver that implements the processing of an I/O request specific to a type of I/O port, such as SCSI.

private cache map   A structure that contains the location of the last two reads so that the cache manager can perform intelligent read-ahead.

process   The virtual address space and control information necessary for the execution of a set of thread objects.

process ID   A unique identifier for a process (internally called a *client ID*).

prototype page table entries (prototype PTEs)   A software structure the memory manager relies on to map potentially shared pages when a page can be shared between two processes. An array of prototype PTEs is created when a section object is first created.

quantum   The length of time a thread is allowed to run before Windows NT interrupts the thread to find out whether another thread at the same priority level is waiting to run or whether the thread's priority needs to be reduced.

queue   A method for threads to enqueue and dequeue notifications of the completion of I/O operations (called an *I/O completion port* in the Win32 API).

quota charges   In the Windows NT object manager, the record of how much the object manager subtracts from a process's allotted paged and/or non-paged pool quota when a thread in the process opens a handle to the object.

ready summary   A 32-bit mask (*KiReadySummary*) that Windows NT maintains to speed up the selection of which thread to run or preempt.

redo information   Information included in the NTFS checkpoint record that explains how to reapply one suboperation of a fully logged ("committed") transaction to the volume if a system failure occurs before the transaction is flushed from the cache.

reference count   The object manager's record of how many object pointers it has dispensed to operating system processes. The object manager increments a reference count for an object each time it gives out a pointer to the object; when kernel-mode components finish using the pointer, they call the object manager to decrement the object's reference count.

resident attribute   If a file is small, all its attributes and their values (its data, for example) fit in the file record. When the value of an attribute is stored directly in the master file table, the attribute is called a resident attribute.

SAM database   A database (stored in the registry under HKEY_LOCAL-_MACHINE\SAM) that contains the defined users and groups, along with their passwords and other attributes.

scatter/gather I/O   A kind of high-performance I/O Windows NT supports, available via the Win32 *ReadFileScatter* and *WriteFileScatter* functions. These functions allow an application to issue a single read or write from more than one buffer in virtual memory to a contiguous area of a file on disk. To use scatter/gather I/O, the file must be opened for noncached I/O, the user buffers being used have to be page-aligned, and the I/Os must be asynchronous (overlapped).

section   *See* section object.

section object   An object that represents a block of memory that two or more processes can share. A section object can be mapped to the paging file or to another file on disk. The executive uses section objects to load executable images into memory, and the cache manager uses them to access data in a cached file. In the Win32 subsystem, a section object is called a *file-mapping object.*

section object pointers   Structure for each open file (represented by a file object) that is the key to maintaining data consistency for all types of file access as well as to providing caching for files. The section object pointers structure points to one or two control areas. One control area is used to map the file when accessed as a data file, and one is used to map the file when it is run as an executable image.

secure attention sequence (SAS)   A keystroke combination that when entered notifies WINLOGON of a user logon request.

security accounts manager (SAM) server   A set of subroutines responsible for managing the database that contains the usernames and groups defined on the local machine or for a domain (if the system is a domain controller). The SAM runs in the context of the LSASS process.

security auditing   A way in which Windows NT detects and records important security-related events or any attempts to create, access, or delete system resources. Logon identifiers record the identities of all users, making it easier to trace anyone who performs an unauthorized action.

security descriptor   Information that controls who has what access to an object. A security descriptor consists of the owner's security ID; the security ID of the primary group for the object (used only by POSIX); the discretionary access control list (DACL), which specifies who has what access to the object; and the system access control list (SACL), which specifies which operations by which users should be logged in the security audit log.

security reference monitor (SRM)   A component in the Windows NT executive (NTOSKRNL.EXE) that is responsible for performing security access checks on objects, manipulating privileges (user rights), and generating any resulting security audit messages.

semaphore   A counter that provides a resource gate by allowing some maximum number of threads to access the resources protected by the semaphore.

server processes   User processes that are Windows NT services, such as the Event Log and Schedule services. Many add-on server applications, such as Microsoft SQL Server and Microsoft Exchange Server, also include components that run as Windows NT services.

shared cache map   A structure that describes the state of a cached file, including its size and (for security reasons) its valid data length.

shared memory   Memory visible to more than one process or that is present in more than one virtual address space.

signal state   The state of a synchronization object.

sparse files   Files, often large, that contain only a small amount of nonzero data relative to their size.

spinlock   The locking mechanism the kernel uses to achieve multiprocessor mutual exclusion. The spinlock gets its name from the fact that the kernel (and thus, the processor) is held in limbo, "spinning," until it gets the lock. Spinlocks, like the data structures they protect, reside in global memory.

stream   A sequence of bytes within a file.

stripe set with parity   A fault tolerant variant of a regular stripe set. Fault tolerance is achieved by reserving the equivalent of one disk for storing parity for each stripe.

structured exception handling   A type of exception handling that allows applications to gain control when exceptions occur. The application can then either fix the condition and return to the place the exception occurred, unwind the stack (thus terminating execution of the subroutine that raised the exception), or declare back to the system that the exception isn't recognized, and to continue searching for an exception handler that might process the exception.

subsystem dynamic-link libraries (DLLs)   DLLs that translate a documented function into the appropriate undocumented Windows NT system service calls. This translation might or might not involve sending a message to the environment subsystem process that is serving the user application.

symbolic link   A mechanism for referring to an object name indirectly.

symmetric multiprocessing (SMP)   A multiprocessing operating system in which there is no master processor—the operating system as well as user threads can be scheduled to run on any processor. All the processors share just one memory space.

synchronization   A thread's ability to synchronize its execution by waiting for an object to change from one state to another. A thread can synchronize with executive process, thread, file, event, semaphore, mutex, and timer objects. Section, port, access token, object directory, symbolic-link, profile, and key objects don't support synchronization

synchronous I/O   A model for I/O in which a device performs a data transfer and returns a status code when the I/O is complete. The program can then access the transferred data immediately. When used in their simplest form, the Win32 *ReadFile* and *WriteFile* functions are executed synchronously. They complete an I/O operation before returning control to the caller.

system cache   Pages used to map files open in the system cache.

system page table entries (PTEs)   Pool of system PTEs used to map system pages such as I/O space, kernel stacks, and memory descriptor lists.

system service dispatch table   Table in which each entry contains a pointer to a system service rather than to an interrupt handling routine.

system support processes   User processes, such as the logon process and the session manager, that are not Windows NT services (that is, not started by the service controller).

system thread   A kind of thread that runs only in kernel mode. System threads always reside in the System process (always process ID 2). These threads have all the attributes and contexts of regular user-mode threads (such as a hardware context, priority, and so on) but run only in kernel-mode executing code loaded in system-space code, whether that be in NTOSKRNL.EXE or in any other loaded device driver. System threads don't have a user process address space and hence must allocate any dynamic storage from operating system memory heaps, such as paged or nonpaged pool.

system working set   The physical memory being used by the system cache, paged pool, pagable code in NTOSKRNL.EXE, and pagable code in device drivers.

thread   An entity within a process that Windows NT schedules for execution. A thread includes the contents of a set of volatile registers representing the state of the processor; two stacks, one for the thread to use while executing in kernel mode and one for executing in user mode; a private storage area for use by subsystems, run-time libraries, and DLLs; a unique identifier called a *thread ID* (also internally called a *client ID*).

thread context   A thread's volatile registers, the stacks, and the private storage area.

timer   A mechanism that notifies a thread when a fixed period of time elapses.

transaction   An I/O operation that alters file system data or changes the volume's directory structure. The separate disk updates that make up the transaction must be executed atomically; that is, once the transaction begins to execute, all of its disk updates must be completed. If a system failure interrupts the transaction, the part that has been completed must be undone, or rolled back. The rollback operation returns the database to a previously known and consistent state, as if the transaction had never occurred.

transaction table   A table that keeps track of transactions that have been started but that are not yet committed. The suboperations of these active transactions must be removed from the disk during recovery.

transition   A kind of invalid page table entry (PTE) in which the desired page is in memory on either the standby, modified, or modified-no-write list. The page is removed from the list and added to the working set.

translation look-aside buffer   A CPU cache of recently translated virtual page numbers.

trap   A processor's mechanism for capturing an executing thread when an exception or an interrupt occurs, switching it from user mode into kernel mode, and transferring control to a fixed location in the operating system. In Windows NT, the processor transfers control to the kernel's trap handler.

trap frame   A data structure in which the execution state of the interrupted thread is stored. This information allows the kernel to resume execution of the thread after handling the interrupt or the exception. The trap frame is usually a subset of a thread's complete context.

trap handler   A module in the kernel that acts as a switchboard, fielding exceptions and interrupts detected by the processor and transferring control to code that handles the condition.

type object   An internal system object that contains information common to each instance of the object.

Unicode   An international character set standard that defines unique 16-bit values for most of the world's known character sets.

update records   The most common type of record NTFS writes to the log file. Each update record contains the information needed to redo an operation that updated the file system structure.

user mode   The nonprivileged processor mode that applications run in. A limited set of interfaces are available in this mode, and the access to system data is limited. *See also* kernel mode.

virtual address descriptors (VADs)   Data structures the memory manager maintains that keep track of which virtual addresses have been reserved in the process's address space. VADs are structured as a self-balancing binary tree to make lookups efficient.

virtual address space   A set of virtual memory addresses that the process can use.

virtual block caching   A method the Windows NT cache manager uses to keep track of which parts of which files are in the cache.

virtual cluster numbers (VCNs)   VCNs number the clusters belonging to a particular file from 0 through *m*. VCNs are not necessarily physically contiguous, but they can be mapped to any number of logical cluster numbers (LCNs) on a volume.

virtual device drivers (VDDs)   Drivers used to emulate 16-bit MS-DOS applications. They trap what an MS-DOS application thinks are references to

I/O ports and translate them into native Win32 I/O functions. Because Windows NT is a fully protected operating system, user-mode MS-DOS applications can't access hardware directly and thus must go through a real kernel-mode device driver.

volume   One or more logical disk partitions that are treated as a single unit.

volume file   A system file (filename $Volume) that contains the volume name, the version of NTFS for which the volume is formatted, and a bit that when set signifies that a disk corruption has occurred and must be repaired by the Chkdsk utility.

volume set   A single logical volume composed of a maximum of 32 areas of free space on one or more disks.

wait block   A data structure that represents a thread waiting on an object. Each thread that is in a wait state has a list of the wait blocks that represent the object(s) the thread is waiting on. Each dispatcher object has a list of the wait blocks that represent which threads are waiting on the object.

Win32 application programming interface (API)   The primary programming interface to the Microsoft Windows operating system family, including Windows NT, Microsoft Windows 9*x* (including both Windows 95 and Windows 98), and Microsoft Windows CE.

Windows NT internal routines   Subroutines inside the Windows NT executive, kernel, or hardware abstraction layer (HAL) callable only from kernel mode (such as from device drivers or other Windows NT operating system components).

Windows NT services   Processes started by the Windows NT service control manager. For example, the Schedule service is a user-mode process that supports the *at* command (which is equivalent to the UNIX command *cron*).

Windows NT system services   Undocumented functions callable from user mode (also called executive system services). For example, *NtCreateProcess* is the internal system service the Win32 *CreateProcess* function calls to create a new process.

working set   A subset of virtual pages resident in physical memory. There are two kinds of working sets—process working sets and the system working set.

write-back   A caching strategy the lazy write file system uses to improve performance. In write-back, the file system writes file modifications to the cache and flushes the contents of the cache to disk in an optimized way, usually as a background activity.

write-through   An algorithm the FAT file system uses that causes disk modifications to be immediately written to the disk. Unlike the careful-write approach, the write-through technique doesn't require the file system to order its writes to prevent inconsistencies. *See also* careful write.

INDEX

Note: Italicized page references indicate figures or tables.

Numbers

A

David Solomon

David Solomon, president of David Solomon Expert Seminars, Inc. (*www.solsem.com*), has been teaching seminars on Microsoft Windows NT internals and systems programming since 1992. His company delivers high-end developer training to the world's major software and hardware vendors.

Formerly a consulting software engineer at Digital Equipment Corporation (DEC), David worked for over nine years as a project leader and developer in the VMS operating system development group. He left DEC to focus on evangelizing Windows NT to the VMS customer base. His first book, *Windows NT for OpenVMS Professionals* (Digital Press/Butterworth Heinemann), was based on his initial classes, which explained Windows NT to VMS-knowledgeable programmers and system managers.

In addition to organizing and teaching seminars, David is a regular speaker at industry events such as Microsoft TechEd, WinDev, and Software Development. He has also served as technical chair for several Windows NT conferences. When he's not researching Windows NT, David enjoys sailing, reading, and *Star Trek*.

The manuscript for this book was prepared and submitted to Microsoft Press in electronic form. Text files were prepared using Microsoft Word 97. Pages were composed by Microsoft Press using Adobe PageMaker 6.5 for Windows, with text in New Baskerville and display type in Helvetica bold. Composed pages were delivered to the printer as electronic prepress files.

Cover Graphic Designer
Tim Girvin Design, Inc.

Cover Illustrator
Glenn Mitsui

Interior Graphic Artist
Joel Panchot

Principal Compositor
Jeffrey Brendecke

Principal Proofreader/Copy Editor
Devon Musgrave

Indexer
Hugh Maddocks

This is how *Microsoft* Windows NT

pros become incredibly resourceful.

This three-volume kit provides the valuable technical and performance information and the tools you need for handling rollout and support issues surrounding Microsoft® Windows NT® Server 4.0. You get a full 2500 pages—plus a CD-ROM—loaded with essential information not available anywhere else. For support professionals, MICROSOFT WINDOWS NT SERVER RESOURCE KIT is more than a guide. It's a natural resource.

U.S.A.	**$149.95**
U.K.	£140.99 [V.A.T. included]
Canada	$199.95
ISBN	1-57231-344-7

***Microsoft*®*Press**

The *ultimate* companion to

Microsoft® *Windows NT*® *Workstation*
version 4.0

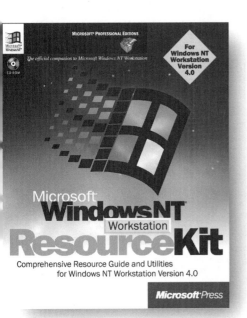

This exclusive Microsoft kit, written in cooperation with the Microsoft Windows NT Workstation development team, provides the complete technical information and tools you need to understand and get the most out of Microsoft Windows NT Workstation version 4.0. The comprehensive technical guide and a CD-ROM containing more than 100 useful tools help you take full advantage of the power of Microsoft Windows NT Workstation version 4.0. Administrators will especially like the section that describes strategies for deployment in large organizations and compatibility with other network and operating systems. Get the MICROSOFT WINDOWS NT WORKSTATION RESOURCE KIT—and get *the* essential reference for installing, configuring, and troubleshooting Microsoft Windows NT Workstation version 4.0.

U.S.A.	**$69.95**
U.K.	£64.99 [V.A.T. included]
Canada	$94.95
ISBN 1-57231-343-9	

Microsoft®*Press*

YOU'VE **read** THEIR BOOKS...
NOW **hear** THEM SPEAK
on-site IN PERSON!

Have the following authors and industry experts come to your company to deliver their personally developed courses.

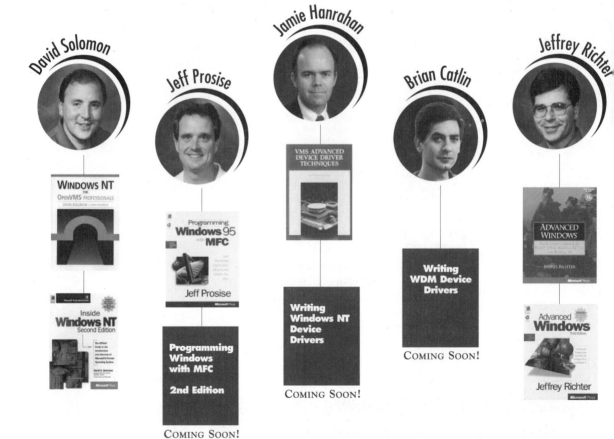

David Solomon

WINDOWS NT for OpenVMS Professionals

Inside Windows NT Second Edition

Jeff Prosise

Programming Windows 95 with MFC — Jeff Prosise

Programming Windows with MFC 2nd Edition

COMING SOON!

Jamie Hanrahan

VMS ADVANCED DEVICE DRIVER TECHNIQUES

Writing Windows NT Device Drivers

COMING SOON!

Brian Catlin

Writing WDM Device Drivers

COMING SOON!

Jeffrey Richter

ADVANCED WINDOWS — Jeffrey Richter

Advanced Windows Third Edition — Jeffrey Richter

David Solomon Expert Seminars

Offers These Leading Edge Developer Courses

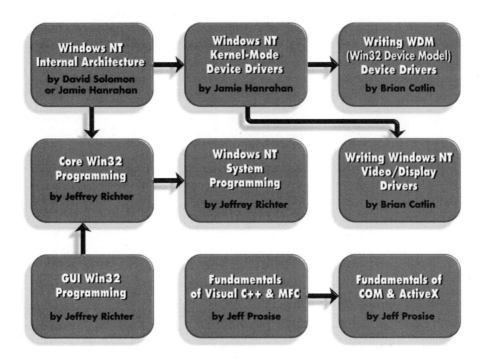

On-Site Seminars: These seminars are available for delivery on-site at companies worldwide. Classes are available in lecture format or with hands-on labs.

Public Seminars: We occasionally run public seminars. Please check our web site to see when and where our next seminars are scheduled.

Interest List: To receive notifications of new seminars and public offerings, join either our electronic mail or regular postal mailing list. Just fill out our on-line form on our web site, or send an email to seminars@solsem.com stating your preference. If you wish to receive printed mailings, please include your full mailing address.

For More Information: See our web site for the latest course map and…

- Detailed course descriptions, prerequisites, and durations for all our seminars.
- Biographies of each of our instructors with links to their books and articles.
- List of conferences at which we are speaking or exhibiting.
- Schedules for upcoming public seminars.
- Current pricing and terms.

www.solsem.com

Web: http://www.solsem.com
Email: seminars@solsem.com
Tel: 800-492-4898
outside USA: +1-860-355-9029
Fax: 860-355-9050

Learn to administer
this **hot new** operating system—

and prepare for the

Microsoft Certified Professional exam
at the same time.

U.S.A. $79.99
U.K. £74.99 [V.A.T. included]
Canada $107.99
ISBN 1-57231-439-7

If you're a system administrator or need to become one, you can teach yourself to manage today's hot operating system technology—Microsoft® Windows NT® Workstation 4.0 and Microsoft Windows NT Server 4.0. Work through this self-paced learning package and you'll be able to provide critical day-to-day administration in any environment—single user, single domain, or enterprise. And because this kit is based on Microsoft Official Curriculum, it also prepares you for the Microsoft Certified Professional exams. Get the hands-on training you want. Get MICROSOFT WINDOWS NT NETWORK ADMINISTRATION TRAINING.

Microsoft®Press

Register Today!

Return this
Inside Windows NT®, Second Edition,
registration card for
a Microsoft Press® catalog

U.S. and Canada addresses only. Fill in information below and mail postage-free. Please mail only the bottom half of this page.

1-57231-677-2

**INSIDE WINDOWS NT®,
SECOND EDITION**

Owner Registration Card

_____

NAME

_____

INSTITUTION OR COMPANY NAME

_____

ADDRESS

_____

_____

CITY   STATE   ZIP

Microsoft *Press*
Quality Computer Books

For a free catalog of
Microsoft Press® products, call
1-800-MSPRESS